# THE MEDAL OF HONOR

## A History of Service Above and Beyond

The Editors of Boston Publishing Company

Produced in cooperation with
the Congressional Medal of Honor Society
of the United States of America

ZENITH
PRESS

This edition published in 2014 by Zenith Press, an imprint of Quarto Publishing Group USA Inc., 400 First Avenue North, Suite 400, Minneapolis, MN 55401 USA. First edition published in 1985 as *Above and Beyond* by Boston Publishing Company, Inc.

This publication has been prepared in conjunction with the Congressional Medal of Honor Society of the United States of America.

We recognize, further, that some words, model names, and designations mentioned herein are the property of the trademark holder. We use them for identification purposes only. This is not an official publication.

Zenith Press titles are also available at discounts in bulk quantity for industrial or sales-promotional use. For details write to Special Sales Manager at Quarto Publishing Group USA 400 First Avenue North, Suite 400, Minneapolis, MN 55401 USA.

To find out more about our books, visit us online at www.zenithpress.com.

Library of Congress Cataloging-in-Publication Data

Above and beyond.
   The Medal of Honor : a history of service above and beyond / the editors of Boston Publishing Company. — [New edition]
      pages cm
   ISBN 978-0-7603-4624-2 (hardcover)
   1. Medal of Honor. 2. United States—Armed Forces—Biography. 3. United States—History, Military.   I. Boston Publishing Company. II. Title.

   UB433.A565 2014

   355.1'342—dc23

                              2014009136

**Zenith Press**
Editorial Director: Erik Gilg
Acquiring Editor: Elizabeth Demers
Project Manager: Madeleine Vasaly
Design Manager: James Kegley
Cover Designer: Andrew Brozyna
Layout Designer: Rebecca Pagel

**Boston Publishing Company**
Publisher: Robert George
Managing Editor: Carolyn Medeiros
Senior Writer and Photo Researcher: Douglas Hardy
Senior Editor: David Shapira
Research Assistant: Michele Tezduyar

Printed in China

10 9 8 7 6 5 4 3 2 1

*Frontispiece*: US soldiers patrol near Bastogne, Belgium, during World War II's Battle of the Bulge, in which twenty-two soldiers earned the Medal of Honor.

# CONTENTS

# FOREWORD

WHY UPDATE A HISTORY of the Medal of Honor? Since this book was first published in 1985, more than ninety more medals have been awarded—some for actions taken since 1985 and some given "retroactively" as new information about past actions became available (for example, awarding the Medal to African American and Asian-American servicemen of World Wars I and II whose heroism was not sufficiently honored at the time).

Another reason is that changing times gives new perspective on such human qualities as sacrifice, honor, and service. Our war, Vietnam, was controversial. By the end of that war, the military stood discredited in the eyes of some Americans. Since those days, American men and women, all volunteers, have built a military for a different age. Today it is by far the most trusted and respected national institution. Its highest honor deserves a complete history.

The objective of this book is not to glorify war but to recognize, and demonstrate, that for all its destructiveness and inhumanity, war often brings out the best in people. Probably if heroes did not appear, mankind would have had to invent them, because history, made up as it is of so much trumpery, treachery, and tyranny, needs deeds of valor, of sacrifice, and of heroism if it is to be palatable.

America's history is well stocked with heroes. The most elevated of them are the men—and one woman—who have been awarded the Medal of Honor for displaying courage and sacrifice above and beyond the call of duty. Beginning with the Civil War, when the medal was created to help raise morale in the Union forces, it has been the supreme accolade the United States bestows on its military for combat valor. More than one American president has said he would have preferred it to his high office.

When the first edition, titled *Above and Beyond,* was published in 1985, there were 254 living medal recipients; as of press time there are fewer than eighty. As Medal of Honor recipients, we strive to provide a continuing legacy that will be visible to Americans long after we're gone off the face of the earth. We want to remind Americans that the freedom we have is based on the sacrifice and service of many men and women in the past and in the present.

That is one more reason the book is so important. Even though we as Medal of Honor recipients were recognized for our valor on the battlefield, there were many others who in fact were doing deeds of valor equal to ours, but were not recognized because the deeds were not seen by others and recorded for history. Or they didn't survive. They are commemorated on memorials we see throughout the country—names of men and women who died in the service of this country. They died because they thought freedom was worth that price to protect.

May all who read this book honor their selflessness and sacrifice.

*Hal Fritz and Leo Thorsness are both Medal of Honor recipients.*

*Hal Fritz, President of the Congressional Medal of Honor Society*

*Leo Thorsness, Immediate Past President of the Congressional Medal of Honor Society*

# PREFACE

# A History Told in Deeds

*Robert George,*
*Publisher, Boston*
*Publishing Company*

THE WRITTEN HISTORIES OF AMERICAN WARS are too numerous to count, and many include the deeds of valor that have been recognized with the awarding of the Medal of Honor. But this is the only history of the medal itself—how it began as an inspiration for Union soldiers in the Civil War, how it changed over a century and a half, and why it was awarded. The Medal of Honor has been conferred on individuals in times of formal conflict; during undeclared, unconventional wars from the Indian Campaigns to Afghanistan; and even awarded (rarely) for peacetime accomplishments. The Medal of Honor's story is a unique perspective on American history and individual heroism.

Our interest in this book began in the early 1980s, when Boston Publishing Company produced the book series *The Vietnam Experience*, a history of America's involvement in the war in Vietnam. For all the ugliness, frustrations, and rancor it provoked, the Vietnam War brought forth its own high quota of nobility, of men inspired to brotherhood, to bravery, and to risk and give their lives in the service of their country. We considered a book that would tell the stories of the 249 Americans (now 256, as of press time) who received the Medal of Honor for actions in Vietnam.

And then we discovered that no history had been written about the Medal of Honor itself, from its inception in 1861 to the present day. Surely, then, there was a book to be written about the nearly four thousand Americans who had been awarded the medal and the exploits for which they earned it. We soon discovered that it is impossible in one volume to tell all the deeds, and so we have by necessity told stories that we believe are representative of many of those actions.

Time and again since the first edition was published in 1985, librarians, historians, and interested readers would contact us to inquire if additional copies could be purchased. We had to tell them that it had gone out of print, and the technology of publishing has changed so radically that bringing the original book back into print was not feasible.

Since the first edition, American acts of valor continued the story of the Medal of Honor in Somalia, Afghanistan, and Iraq. In the 1990s and 2000s, brave servicemen not recognized in their time have received the Medal of Honor long after their wars ended. The story of the medal continued—as did the inquiries—until we decided that the time had come for an updated and revised edition.

The authoritative list of Medal of Honor recipients is found at the Congressional Medal of Honor Society. Its excellent website (www.cmohs.org) has been an invaluable source for this updated edition. The Society's collaboration with our editors and writers has given this book its extra scope and authenticity. We are also grateful to have had the resources of the military services (www.army.mil, www.navy.mil, www.marines.mil, www.af.mil) and the National Archives—resources of historical insight and research available to all. Using these and other resources, we have updated the medal's history to the present.

We ask the reader of this volume to think of the award by its correct name. Over the years, it has come to be known as the "Congressional Medal of Honor" because the holder of the medal, though chosen for it by his peers and superior officers, is nominally given it by writ of Congress. Its real name, however, is simply the Medal of Honor. This is perhaps a bit confusing since there is an organization called the *Congressional Medal of Honor Society* (because it is chartered by the US Congress).

The accounts here are fitted into the context of the wars in which they happened, which interestingly also provides a unique overview of American history as seen through the eyes of those who have fought its wars. In each war, the nature of Medal of Honor deeds or the kinds of incidents that provoked them differed, as the nature of war itself changed with advances in weaponry and the development of capabilities of attack from greater distances. Through them all, however, from the Civil War to the wars in Afghanistan and Iraq, there are the constants of singular bravery and sacrifice.

# INTRODUCTION

# A Badge for Valor

**O**N THE BLOODIEST SINGLE DAY of the Civil War, a Union color bearer is struck by a Confederate bullet. His regiment's flag falls from his grasp onto the ground between the opposing lines. Rebel riflemen intensify their fire, preparing to seize the enemy's precious standard. Suddenly a lone Yankee soldier dashes out from among the ranks, crouched low to avoid the lead flying all around him. He picks up the flag and rushes back to the Union lines, to the cheers of his comrades.

Thirty-eight years later, outside the massive stone walls of Peking (now known as Beijing), American infantrymen and Marines seek an entrance into the city, where a Chinese faction surrounds hundreds of foreigners. The commanding officer asks for volunteers to scale the sheer side of the fortress under enemy fire. A twenty-one-year-old Army trumpeter from Iowa steps forward. "I'll try, sir!" he shouts, and works his way over the top of the fortification.

In World War II, a Japanese gunboat is rammed by an American submarine in the dark, chilly waters of the Pacific. The Japanese fire at the men standing on the bridge of the sub, wounding several, including the commander of the vessel, a Naval Academy graduate and seventeen-year veteran of the sea. The commander quickly realizes that the sub must dive if it is to escape. He sends the rest of the men below, then sees that the enemy guns will find their mark before he will be able to climb down. "Take her down!" he shouts. The men below close the hatch, and the vessel slides under the waves with the wounded commander still on the bridge.

In the humid jungle of South Vietnam, three Americans are left behind during the evacuation of a besieged base. To rescue them, an Air Force cargo plane lands on a debris-covered runway as guerrilla fire rains down from all around. The pilot, a Georgia farm boy who had first enlisted in the Army Air Corps during World War II, slows the aircraft, and the three men jump from their hiding place and climb aboard. Suddenly, an enemy rocket flies down the runway, straight at the plane. Miraculously, it skids to a halt several yards from the cockpit and fails to explode. The pilot lifts off, and the men on board breathe a sigh of relief.

In a remote outpost in the mountains of Afghanistan, Staff Sgt. Ty Michael Carter twice sprints across a hundred yards of open ground to aid comrades while enemy fire pours in from all sides. He retrieves the unit's working radio to call in air support. Ignoring his own shrapnel wounds, he kills several attackers and pulls a wounded comrade to cover.

Stretched over more than 140 years, these exploits comprise just a few of the millions of stories of Americans at war. But these particular men gained a greater distinction. For their actions in combat, they were singled out for gallantry and intrepidity above and beyond the call of duty. Each was awarded the Medal of Honor, America's highest military decoration.

Since it first was cast in the Civil War, the medal has gone to decorate privates and generals, common seamen and admirals, virtually every rank in the armed forces. Men from all walks of life—midwestern farmers, northeastern factory workers, southern teachers, poor immigrants—have been decorated for actions ranging from charging an enemy bunker or capturing an enemy's flag to saving a fellow sailor from drowning. In war and peace, for more than 120 years, nearly 3,500 men—and one woman—have been judged to have performed outstanding individual acts, feats of bravery that have set them apart from their comrades.

The symbol of their distinction is the medal and ribbon bestowed by the president "in the name of Congress." It marks admission into a circle into which few can pass. Many men who have received other accolades have coveted the Medal of Honor. President Theodore Roosevelt wanted it. General George S. Patton once declared, "I'd give my immortal soul for that decoration." And President Harry S. Truman often told the men to whom he presented the medal, "I would rather have that medal than be president of the United States."

But the Medal of Honor is earned in action, at the risk of a soldier's life. Once decorated, many Medal of Honor recipients have been singled out for lifetimes of public exposure, even adulation. Alvin York, Eddie Rickenbacker, Audie Murphy, Jimmy Doolittle, and many others have had their stories told in books, articles, and motion pictures. Others have been feted at dedications, testimonials, and patriotic exercises. To their peers, and to millions of Americans, Medal of Honor recipients are the nation's heroes, "the bravest of the brave," as one general called them. The medal, says one who wears it, is "America's form of knighthood."

Many of the "knights" of America have stayed in the service and risen to its upper echelons. Others have left the armed forces and attained success in various occupations: law, medicine, politics, business, and many others. For many, the medal has afforded greater visibility and helped them advance.

A substantial number of recipients have simply returned to civilian life, their neighbors and associates never learning from the recipients themselves that they had been so highly honored. But usually the Medal of Honor brings with it the prospect of continuous public recognition. It has condemned some recipients to years of unwanted attention and even notoriety. They find themselves exploited by others seeking to turn the medal into profit. The spotlight of the medal can also expose the human shortcomings of ordinary men when they are thrust suddenly into the extraordinary role of war hero and public figure. Some have broken under the public pressures, the demands, and the intrusions that fame can bring. The Medal of Honor can be, in the words of one recipient, "a lot harder to wear than it is to earn."

For all the acclaim accorded it and the importance attached to it today, the Medal of Honor had a rather inauspicious beginning.

Wary of the trappings of European titles and nobility since colonial days, the first Americans were reluctant to bestow titles or lavish honors on their own. The Founding Fathers shared a vehement distaste for royalty and its privilege: the Constitution specifically prohibited the granting of any "title of nobility."

Wary of the trappings of European titles and nobility since colonial days, the first Americans were reluctant to bestow titles or lavish honors on their own.

11

Fittingly,
the Continental
Congress
awarded the first
American medal
to Gen. George
Washington for
his role in driving
British forces
from Boston in
March 1776.

When it comes to military honors, however, the nation has been more indulgent. While dukedoms and earldoms may not fit into the American psyche, the actions of warriors do. A successful soldier was seen as a common man who rose to fame not through birthright but through strength and resourcefulness, and it quickly became the practice to reward such attainment with a medal. Fittingly, the Continental Congress awarded the first American medal to Gen. George Washington for his role in driving British forces from Boston in March 1776. (There was no US Mint at the time, so the medal was crafted in Paris.) Medals also went to several other commanders, most notably Gen. Horatio Gates for his victory at Saratoga in 1777 and Adm. John Paul Jones for his battle with the *Serapis* in 1779. Yet with only a few exceptions, there was no recognition for individual acts by common soldiers.

On September 23, 1780, three New York militiamen intercepted Maj. John André, a British spy, on his way to meet with a co-conspirator, Benedict Arnold. André's capture foiled a British plot to take the American fort at West Point. On November 3, the Continental Congress, declaring that the actions of the three Americans had saved the country from "impending danger," ordered a silver medal struck and awarded to each man. The André medals were the first American instance of medals awarded to soldiers for individual actions, although the capture itself was not so much valorous as fortuitous.

Almost two years later, General Washington established the first formal system of rewarding individual gallantry. A directive designed to recognize "instances of unusual gallantry," signed August 7, 1782, read:

> The General, ever desirous to cherish a virtuous ambition in his soldiers, as well as to foster and encourage every species of Military merit, directs that whenever any singularly meritorious action is performed, the author of it shall be permitted to wear on his facings, over his left breast, the figure of a heart in purple cloth, or silk, edged with narrow lace or binding.

Washington declared, "[T]he road to glory in a citizen's army is thus open to all"; however, the records show that only three men received the Purple Heart. The award then fell into oblivion until 1932, when it was revived as an honor for those killed or wounded in combat.

The idea of a decoration for individual gallantry remained in the minds of many commanders in the early years of the nation. The outbreak of war with Mexico in 1846 led to the establishment of the first long-standing award for bravery. In March 1847, Congress approved a measure granting to any soldier who distinguished himself in action a "certificate of merit" signed by the president and additional pay of two dollars per month, on the recommendation of his regimental commander.

Five hundred and thirty-nine men received Certificates of Merit during the Mexican War. At the time there was no medal to mark this honor, and thus it received minimal public attention. In the words of one military historian, "New recruits might learn that the old sergeant in the next troop had received a Certificate . . . but there was no way this achievement might be perceived from inspection of his uniform."

The military establishment interpreted the law to mean that the Certificate of Merit was established only for the conflict at hand, so the end of the Mexican War left the country without a standing award for gallantry, or any military award at all. It was not until civil war split the nation in 1861 that the government again considered recognizing notable gallantry. Even then, the medal established was intended not so much to glorify warriors as to boost morale in a demoralized Army and Navy.

The summer of 1861 was a dark time for Union forces. Chased off the battlefield by the Confederates at Bull Run, Northern regiments were drained by wholesale desertions and enlistments of only nine months. The greatest battles, and the ultimate victory, of the Yankee forces were yet to come; for the time being, the likelihood of a long and exhausting conflict sapped Union spirits and resilience. The demands placed on the military necessitated the development of a tangible reward for meritorious action and service in the days ahead.

No one was more cognizant of this need than Lt. Col. Edward D. Townsend, assistant adjutant general of the Army. Townsend knew of the abuses and corruption of the system of brevet promotions of officers, which usually had little to do with valor, and that these rewards did not extend to enlisted men. In early 1861, he proposed to his superiors—General-in-Chief of the Army Winfield Scott, Secretary of War Simon Cameron, and the chairman of the Senate Committee on Military Affairs, Henry Wilson of Massachusetts—the creation of a medal for individual valor. But General Scott felt that medals and decorations smacked of European privilege and affectation and quashed any further discussion of the matter at the War Department.

Across the street at the Navy Department, however, the idea of a medal found support. Secretary Gideon Welles was exasperated with what he considered to be the poor quality and spirit of some naval personnel and believed that the conspicuous recognition of courage in the strife to come would infuse the Navy with a sense of strength and determination.

At least one powerful man on Capitol Hill shared this sentiment. On December 9, 1861, Senator James W. Grimes of Iowa, chairman of the Committee on Naval Affairs, rose to propose Public Resolution Number 82, "An Act to further promote the efficiency of the Navy." Buried on the second page of the measure, after provisions dealing with retired officers and promotions, was Section 7, which read:

> And be it further enacted, that the Secretary of the Navy be, and he is hereby authorized to cause two hundred "medals of honor" to be prepared, with suitable emblematic devices, which shall be bestowed upon such petty officers, seamen, landsmen, and marines as shall most distinguish themselves by their gallantry in action and other seamanlike qualities during the present war, and that the sum of one thousand dollars be, and the same is hereby appropriated out of any money in the treasury, for the purpose of carrying this section into effect.

After approval by Grimes's committee, the measure was approved by the Senate, and then by the House of Representatives. On December 21, President Abraham Lincoln signed Public Resolution 82 into law.

The approval of a medal of honor was a first step. Next came the choice of a design, with "suitable emblematic devices." Ten days after President Lincoln signed the Navy bill, Gideon Welles contacted James Pollock, then director of the US Mint in Philadelphia, and asked if the mint could prepare "an appropriate design for the medals." Pollock was eager to assume the task and promised to have a possible design ready within a week.

The Navy Department and the mint had no American precedent to guide them on their search for a medal design. Welles proposed a cross, similar to the Victoria Cross, which Great

The Navy Department and the mint had no American precedent to guide them on their search for a medal design.

Secretary of War Edwin Stanton played a key role in the creation of the Army Medal of Honor.

Britain had established seven years earlier during the Crimean War. The American cross would be attached to "three ribbons—the red, white and blue." The mint's experience with making coins suggested the use of a figure of Liberty or some other symbol of the "Indivisible Union." Over the next three months Pollock forwarded at least five different models, but Welles rejected all of them.

Finally, in May 1862, Pollock suggested an inverted five-pointed star, two inches long, suspended from an anchor and attached to a red, white, and blue ribbon. Pollock explained the two figures at the center of the star on the obverse:

> The foul spirit of secession and rebellion is represented by a male figure in a crouching attitude holding in his hands serpents, which with forked tongues are striking at a large female figure representing the Union or Genius of our Country, who holds in her right hand a shield and in her left the fasces. Around these figures are thirty-four stars, the number of states in the Union.

The female figure representing America and wearing a helmet bearing an eagle was Minerva, the Roman goddess of wisdom and the arts. In later years, this engraving came to be known as "Minerva Repulsing Discord."

Welles approved the design, and on May 15, the Navy Department ordered 175 medals from the mint. It further directed that the back of each medal be left blank except for the words "Personal Valor," under which the name of each recipient could later be engraved. The medals were made of copper and coated with bronze, which gave them a reddish tint. After preparation of the dies, the initial cost of what became America's premier military decoration was $1.85 apiece.

In the meantime, the Army, no doubt prompted at least in part by the passage of the Navy legislation, had come to favor the idea of a medal of its own. General Scott had retired, and Simon Cameron's successor as secretary of war, Edwin Stanton, was apparently more amenable to the concept of an award for valor.

On February 17, 1862, Henry Wilson, chairman of the Senate Committee on Military Affairs, introduced a resolution almost identical in language to its Navy counterpart of two months earlier. Signed into law July 12, the measure provided for the awarding of a medal of honor "to such noncommissioned officers and privates as shall most distinguish themselves by their gallantry in action, and other soldier-like qualities, during the present insurrection." As under the Navy legislation, commissioned officers were ineligible for the medal, the assumption being that they would be better rewarded or more honored by promotion. (A year later, Congress made Army officers eligible for the medal; a similar measure for the Navy was not passed until 1915.)

Like Secretary Welles, Edwin Stanton was unimpressed by the mint's early attempts at an Army medal. Pollock had suggested a slightly altered version of the Navy design, stating, "The devices do not pertain to either arm of the service, but are emblematic of the struggle in which the nation is now engaged." But Stanton wanted a distinctive design for the Army.

In October 1862, William Wilson & Son, Philadelphia silversmiths who, with the mint, had been responsible for the Navy design, forwarded to Stanton a sketch of another proposed medal. It included the inverse star and "Minerva Repulsing Discord" design of the Navy medal, but the anchor had been replaced by the figure of a spread-winged eagle standing on crossed cannons and cannonballs. At each wing the eagle was attached to the ribbon, which, like its naval counterpart, featured the national colors.

Stanton was finally satisfied. By mid-November, the War Department had contracted with Wilson & Son for the preparation of two thousand medals to be cast at the mint; the cost was two dollars each. After months of delay, the Army had its own medal of honor.

As the war dragged on and the prestige of its new award grew, the government realized that while it was created for the conflict at hand, the Medal of Honor—and the rewarding of bravery—would be applicable to any future conflicts. In 1863, Congress made the Medal of Honor a permanent decoration.

Over the years, the Medal of Honor has grown in stature, as evidenced by the many individuals who have received their country's highest award for gallantry. Throughout all of the nation's conflicts, they have been cited for singular acts of bravery that have impressed and roused others in the face of danger. The story of the medal is necessarily an assemblage of the tales of those who have earned it and of the inner strength and courage that made them perform, for at least one brief moment, "above and beyond the call of duty."

MEDAL OF HONOR MEN.

ARMY.     NAVY.

Have received Medals of Honor in
United States Army and Navy.
See official records following.

Portraits of fifteen African American soldiers and sailors who received Medals of Honor in the early days of the medal's existence for service in the Civil War, Indian Campaigns, and Spanish-American War: Sgt. John Denny, Co. B, 9th US Cavalry Regiment; Pvt. James Gardiner, Co. I, 36th US Colored Troops Infantry Regiment; Sgt. Maj. Milton M. Holland, Co. C, 5th US Colored Troops Infantry Regiment; Pvt. Dennis Bell, Troop H, 10th US Cavalry Regiment; Sgt. Brent Woods, Co. B, 9th US Cavalry Regiment; Sgt. Thomas Hawkins, Co. C, 6th US Colored Troops Infantry Regiment; Cpl. Isaiah Mays, Co. B, 24th US Infantry Regiment; Sgt. Robert A. Pinn, Co. I, 5th US Colored Troops Infantry Regiment; Lds. John Lawson, US Navy; Sgt. William H. Carney, Co. C, 54th Massachusetts Infantry Regiment; Sgt. Powhatan Beaty, Co. G, 5th US Colored Troops Infantry Regiment; Sgt. James H. Harris, Co. B, 38th US Colored Troops Infantry Regiment; Sgt. Thomas Shaw, Co. K, 9th US Cavalry Regiment; Sgt. Alexander Kelly, Co. F, 6th US Colored Troops Infantry Regiment; and Sgt. Maj. Christian Fleetwood, Co. G, 4th US Colored Troops Infantry Regiment.

# CHAPTER ONE

# The Civil War

## 1861-1865

# The War Between the States

**A**LL WARS ARE BORN in failure, the inability of men and nations to resolve their differences outside of conflict. Perhaps that, in part, explains the age-old penchant for honoring the heroics of the individual. Rulers, whether kings or legislatures, attempt to atone for their own failure to avert war by paying homage to the valorous deeds of those who fight their wars. Certainly it was no different in the 1860s, when America went mad and went to war with itself.

"We have pulled a temple down," exulted the men of Charleston, South Carolina, when they seceded from the Union in December 1860. Others spoke less reverently. "We are divorced," wrote diarist Mary Boykin Chesnut, "because we have hated each other so."

No single cause severed the Union in 1860. The split came, rather, from generations of low-grade aggravations and petty resentments, from jealousies personal and national, from fears that were deeply and sincerely felt, however groundless, and from a few elemental issues for which there simply were no universally satisfactory solutions. Typical of the people and the times that brought on that war, the two sides could not agree afterward on what started the conflict, or even on what to call it.

They were regions whose values stood in marked contrast. Americans North and South had followed different paths for two centuries at a separate pace. Divergent political, economic, and social views made the first half of the nineteenth century an era of almost continual crisis. By 1860, the differences between the two sections were being exaggerated aggressively on both sides.

The South had been comfortable in the Union at first, and so long as its interests dominated national affairs, the region and its leaders stood strongly for the nation. But by 1850, things had changed. The North outstripped the South in population and economic growth. Now its political power was ascendant, and it argued for the national view in public affairs. Southerners argued instead for sectional rights.

"States' rights" and their natural offspring, secession, were not distinctly Southern phenomena. The "will of the majority" is a democratic ideal with little appeal to those outside the majority. Finding itself now a minority, the South sensed a threat to its interests and values and sought guarantees, constitutional dispensations exempting it from the will, even the tyranny, of the majority. The consequences of such a course would have been democratic chaos, with the national government in constant danger of being paralyzed by parochial interest. But failing such guarantees, the South threatened to leave the Union.

*Previous pages*
The Siege of Vicksburg.

Everything seemed to set the sections against each other. Economically and socially, the land divided them early on. Southerners grew cash crops, such as tobacco and cotton, that exhausted the land and required vast acreage and massive cheap labor. The South had, thus, turned to slavery early on to keep pace with European demand for its commodities. The North, with abundant raw materials, turned to manufacturing and commerce.

In time, North and South found convenient justifications for their separate societies and cultures. Planters who relied on slavery pointed out the benevolent aspects of an institution that cared for otherwise presumably helpless blacks. The North called slavery a disgrace. To the Yankee, the planter was a lazy, conceited, debauched creature of contempt. To the Southerner, Northerners were money-grasping, humorless drones. As tempers rose in the decades before 1860, these false stereotypes became increasingly powerful.

Always the issue came down in the end to slavery. As the nation grew and more states came into the Union, an increasing number of them decided to join as "free" states, not countenancing bondage within their borders. Having more free states than slaves states in the Union threatened the South with the possibility that an anti-slavery majority in Washington might attempt to eradicate slavery where it already existed. Pro-slavery advocates believed that ending slavery would ruin the South economically and create social havoc when several million blacks were suddenly freed with no jobs, no homes, and no education.

Compromise had averted crisis in 1820, again in 1850, and once more in 1854 as the North gave in to Southern fears. But then came 1860, an election year in which a powerful new anti-slavery Republican Party became likely to capture the White House. Despite the assurances of its candidate, Abraham Lincoln, that his party would not interfere with slavery where it already existed, the Southern leadership foresaw their own doom in his election. By this time, sectional differences had become so divisive that neither North nor South could compromise without yielding its basic values.

Lincoln won election in November 1860 in the most purely sectional vote in history. Every Southern and slave state went against him; the Southern rights candidate, John C. Breckinridge, did not carry a single free state. Even though he got barely 40 percent of the popular vote, Lincoln carried all of the major states with their greater populations and electoral votes and won the presidency.

It was a bitter victory. At once, the call went out for a state convention in South Carolina. On December 20, that convention voted to secede from the Union, and within weeks, other

*Below*
An advertisement offering money for slaves. At the onset of war a single slave could fetch as much as $1,800.

*Bottom*
Factories such as this Paterson, New Jersey, ironworks spurred the growth of the North before the Civil War.

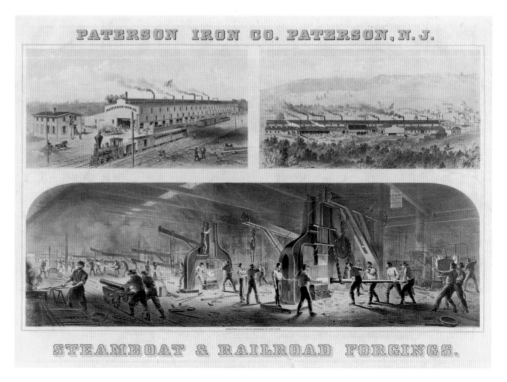

Lincoln's election only exacerbated the North-South rift and hastened secession.

states followed. Eventually eleven of them seceded, and in February 1861, in Montgomery, Alabama, the Confederate States of America was born.

Yet no one wanted war. As the newly elected Confederate president, Jefferson Davis, proclaimed, the South wanted merely "to be left alone." Confederates bloodlessly seized Federal military and naval installations and arsenals within their new borders and demanded that the Yankees turn over the rest. After all, places like Fort Sumter in Charleston Harbor were now on Confederate soil, and the Northerners had no business being there. Should they persist in remaining, it would be perceived as an act of aggression.

However, Lincoln saw himself as president of *all* the states, not just the Northern ones, and did not recognize the legality of secession. Thus, it was his constitutional duty to hold on to all Federal property, wherever located. He would not give up Fort Sumter, and that was all the hotbloods in Charleston needed. After delivering an unsuccessful ultimatum, Confederates stationed at the batteries ringing the harbor opened fire on the fort in the pre-dawn hours of April 12, 1861. The next day, the garrison surrendered. The Confederacy was jubilant; the Union called for seventy-five thousand volunteers to put down the rebellion. War had come.

No nation is ever ready for a civil war, and America in 1860 proved no exception. The United States Army consisted of barely sixteen thousand men and officers, most of them stationed in the West as a buffer against Indians. The enlisted men remained loyal to the Union almost to a man, but of the 1,080 officers on active duty, 313 abandoned their commissions to join the new Confederacy. Worse, the weapons and equipment of the Army were out of date, and only one of its four generals was under seventy. General-in-Chief Winfield Scott was seventy-five, still active in mind but too infirm to ride a horse. The situation in the US Navy was just as bad.

Since the Confederacy was too new to have raised a substantial standing army of its own, both sides were immediately led to the only expedient capable of quickly building large armies—volunteers. Davis had already been accepting volunteer regiments into the Confederate service for months, and now Lincoln issued the first of what would be many calls for regiments of his own.

North and South, these regiments would be infinite in their variety. The first regiments, enlisted in the expectation of a quick and speedy end to the fighting, were to serve only for ninety days. Later, some of them extended their service for an additional year. By 1862, when it was evident that this would be no summer's lark, both governments accepted regiments only for three years or the term of the war, whichever lasted longer.

At first, the most readily available units were the various state militia and home guard units. North and South rushed to their respective standards, bringing their own arms—anything from antique flintlock muskets to the latest breechloaders—and attired in a dazzling array of uniforms. Ironically, reversing what was to become the standard, many of the Southern militia regiments wore blue; scores of Yankee units were dressed in gray.

A Southern flag flies over Fort Sumter, April 15, 1861.

In time, some general standards evolved. The full-strength regiment on both sides numbered roughly one thousand men, led by officers chosen or elected by the men themselves. The men came to carry deadly powerful, muzzle-loading .58-caliber rifles that could be fired several times a minute. The rifles proved accurate at greater ranges than any military weapons before them. The men carrying those rifles were for the most part farm boys, men unaccustomed to drill and regimentation but very familiar indeed with guns. The volunteers were there from deeply felt conviction in their causes, for glory and adventure, for the fun of it, or just to escape the boredom of home. Whatever their motivations, they felt fierce loyalties to their states, their comrades, and their regiments.

The combination of these men—perhaps the finest citizen-soldiers in history—their powerful modern weapons, the natural animosities to be found in any civil conflict, and the dated tactics by which the war was fought, was destined to be lethal. The Union officer corps grew rapidly, and newer and younger generals rose to take command. Still, their military schooling at the US Military Academy at West Point and the manuals of warfare that the volunteer officers studied all harked back to the kinds of war fought generations before. These had been wars of limited range, fought with inaccurate muskets. Individual accuracy had mattered far less than massed firepower, and the bayonet at the end of the gun had been regarded as a more deadly instrument than the bullet within it. Battles were still expected to be fought much as in the days of Napoleon, with the regiments standing erect, two or more lines deep, without the benefit of earthworks or defenses. They were to be won with a few volleys and then a spirited bayonet charge. And all of it, of course, was expected to be glorious.

Loaded with canister (a tin can filled with lead balls) or case shot (an iron shell filled with iron balls), a cannon could virtually become a shotgun.

*Opposite*
The battlefields of the Civil War ranged from the Atlantic coast to the Midwest. Many of the key battles were fought in Virginia, largely because the Confederacy needed to defend its capital of Richmond against the Union Army.

Experience after Fort Sumter revealed just how fatally obsolete these old notions were. Instead of running into one, perhaps two, ineffectual volleys from the feeble muskets of their opponents, a regiment in the Civil War that dared to charge would face half a dozen or more powerful and accurate salvos, and anything more than a scratch from a massive .58 bullet was potentially fatal. Most wounds to the legs and arms resulted in amputation, and almost any bullet in the torso would kill a man. Thanks to the state of the medical arts at the time, those who survived the battle risked equal dangers, even if their wounds were slight.

This was bad enough. Compounding it was the stage on which the Civil War played. It occupied virtually a whole continent in warfare on a scale never before known. Regiments joined together to make brigades, brigades melded to make divisions, divisions gathered into corps, and corps united to become armies. A single division could be greater than the field army that Scott had led into Mexico in 1847, and an army now could number half a dozen such divisions or more. Between North and South, some three million men would take up arms during the four years of the conflict, serving in more than half a dozen major armies that contested possession of a land area of roughly three-quarters of a million square miles. More than ten thousand military actions were recorded, ranging from skirmishes to pitched battles.

The infantry regiments were not the only ones to fight this mammoth war. The Civil War also brought opposing cavalrymen face to face. Their regiments were smaller than the infantry, their role in campaigns was primarily reconnaissance, and their participation in major battles was relatively rare. Yet when cavalry fought cavalry, the combat was fierce, and the weapons were just as deadly. Worse, particularly west of the Mississippi, mounted men tended more to the nature of the partisan and guerrilla. Many cavalry and partisan outfits, North and South, were little more than uniformed brigands who would kill cold-bloodedly for the fun of it, whether the enemy was armed or not.

Far more conventional, and just as deadly, was the artillery. The field cannon was perhaps not quite as advanced as the shoulder rifle by 1861, but it was hellishly effective in certain circumstances just the same. Some cannon could fire their exploding projectiles five miles or more. Such firing was generally of little effect, since there were few engagements in which an artilleryman could even see five miles in any direction, but at close range, the field piece—and particularly the workhorse twelve-pound smoothbore—could visit wholesale slaughter. Loaded with canister (a tin can filled with lead balls) or case shot (an iron shell filled with iron balls), a cannon could virtually become a shotgun. Relatively light and quickly mobile, such guns could move to a threatened point in a defensive line in time to devastate attacking columns. Working in combination with well-disciplined infantrymen, six-gun cannon batteries could produce awful results. At Gettysburg on July 3, 1863, several batteries supporting the Federal infantry repulsed Pickett's Charge. As many as fifteen thousand Confederates took part in that frontal assault. Only a handful actually penetrated the Yankee line. More than half were killed or wounded.

It was all assurance that the American Civil War—or the War Between the States—would be among the most bloody and fiercely contested in history. The goal of Davis and the Confederacy was simply to hold on to every inch of Southern soil possible. Lincoln and the Union had to retake and occupy every one of those inches. So mutually exclusive were those two goals that no strictly military conclusion to the war was possible except absolute victory and absolute defeat.

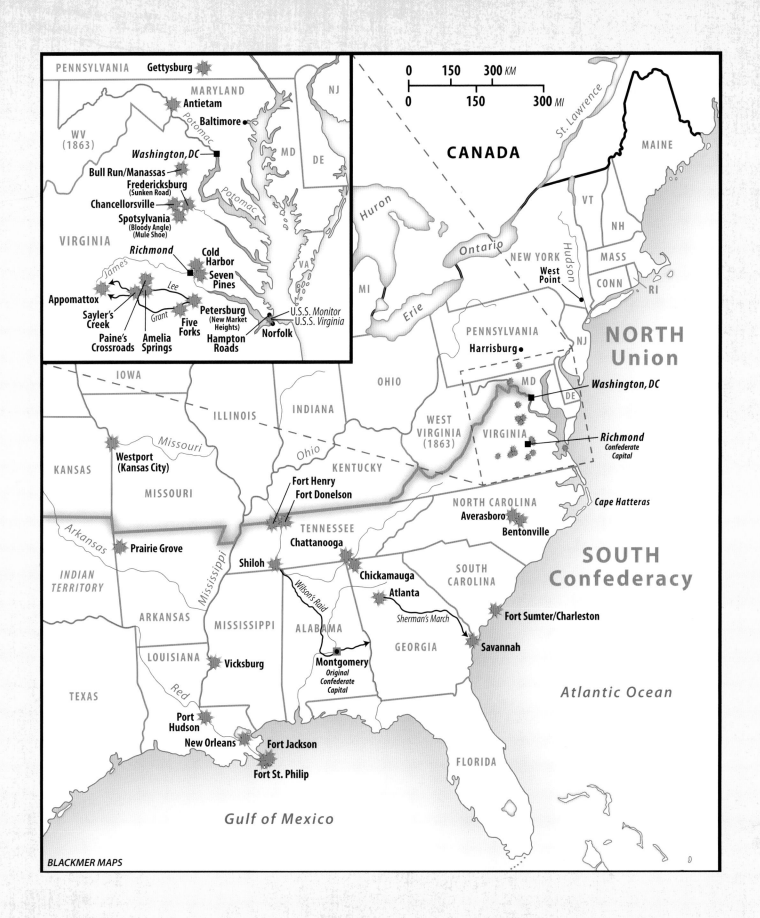

**PENNSYLVANIA**
Gettysburg

**MARYLAND**
Antietam
Baltimore

**WV (1863)**
Potomac

Washington, DC

Bull Run/Manassas
Fredericksburg
(Sunken Road)
Chancellorsville
Spotsylvania
(Bloody Angle)
(Mule Shoe)

**VIRGINIA**

Richmond
Cold Harbor
Seven Pines

James

Appomattox
Sayler's Creek
Paine's Crossroads
Amelia Springs
Five Forks
Petersburg
(New Market Heights)
Hampton Roads
Norfolk

Lee
Grant

U.S.S. Monitor
U.S.S. Virginia

VA

DE

MD

NJ

Potomac

**CANADA**

0  150  300 KM
0  150  300 MI

St. Lawrence

MAINE

Huron

Ontario

Erie

MI

NEW YORK
West Point

VT
NH
MASS
CONN
RI

**NORTH Union**

PENNSYLVANIA
Harrisburg

MD
DE
Washington, DC

OHIO

WEST VIRGINIA (1863)
VIRGINIA
Richmond
Confederate Capital

IOWA

ILLINOIS
INDIANA

Missouri

Ohio

KENTUCKY

KANSAS
Westport
(Kansas City)

MISSOURI

Arkansas

Prairie Grove

INDIAN TERRITORY

ARKANSAS

Mississippi

TENNESSEE

Fort Henry
Fort Donelson

Chattanooga

Shiloh

Chickamauga

Wilson's Raid

Atlanta

NORTH CAROLINA
Averasboro
Bentonville

Cape Hatteras

SOUTH CAROLINA

**SOUTH Confederacy**

Fort Sumter/Charleston

Sherman's March

Savannah

MISSISSIPPI

ALABAMA

GEORGIA

LOUISIANA

Vicksburg

Red

TEXAS

Montgomery
Original Confederate Capital

FLORIDA

*Atlantic Ocean*

Port Hudson
New Orleans
Fort Jackson
Fort St. Philip

*Gulf of Mexico*

BLACKMER MAPS

> Lincoln's army scampered back to the safety of Washington, leaving the battlefield to a victor that was almost as badly disorganized as the vanquished.

On land it was three wars, really, and there was much irony in the relative scope of their operations, their overall military importance, and the public's perceptions of them. Then, as now, the greatest attention and effort went into the campaigns in the East, primarily Virginia, and the meager hundred miles or so that separated the two warring capitals, Washington and Richmond.

Here the green volunteers fought the first major land battle of the war on July 21, 1861. Along the banks of Bull Run, in northern Virginia, the hastily raised and hastily trained armies collided in what, by 1864 standards, would be only a small engagement. But then it was a major battle, and the North, already wounded by the loss of Fort Sumter, suffered another defeat. Lincoln's army scampered back to the safety of Washington, leaving the battlefield to a victor that was almost as badly disorganized as the vanquished.

Lincoln tried to take Richmond in 1862 with a series of campaigns, all of them failures. In the spring, an army landed below Richmond and marched on the city, only to be stopped. Another Yankee army in northern Virginia was beaten near Bull Run again by a Confederate army now led by Gen. Robert E. Lee. On September 17, the Northern Gen. George B. McClellan won a battle at Antietam, Maryland, and stopped Lee's invasion of the North, but frittered away a chance to destroy Lee in the process. McClellan's replacement, Rhode Island Gen. Ambrose Burnside, did even worse when he almost lost his Army of the Potomac in terribly costly frontal assaults in December at Fredericksburg, Virginia.

The story was the same when next the armies met at Chancellorsville, Virginia, in May 1863. But then came Gettysburg. When Lee advanced once more into the North, Maj. Gen. George G. Meade, now commander of the Army of the Potomac, stopped him in Pennsylvania in the biggest battle of the war. Yet when it was done, little had changed from the way things had been two years before; Lee still held most of Virginia and Richmond was secure.

Lincoln changed that when he found Gen. Ulysses S. Grant out west and brought him to command all of the Union's armies early in 1864. Grant and Lincoln thought alike: press the enemy hard, everywhere, and simultaneously. When Grant ordered Meade and his army to start campaigning again in May 1864, they never stopped. The battles fought are legendary—the Wilderness, Spotsylvania, Cold Harbor, the Siege of Petersburg, and finally the pursuit of Lee to Appomattox.

While most of the warring nation—as well as the world—focused its attention on this struggle for Virginia, a huge war was being fought elsewhere. Grant and Lee contested a few hundred square miles of Virginia soil. West of the Mississippi, much smaller armies conducted unheralded campaigns and battles that decided the fate of two-thirds of the country, from the great river to the Pacific. The single, small battle of Prairie Grove in December 1862 saved Arkansas for the Union for more than a year. The greatest cavalry operation of the entire war came late in 1864 when an army of Rebel horsemen invaded Missouri, riding all the way to present-day Kansas City before they were stopped at Westport, where the biggest battle west of the Mississippi took place. And even out here, Grant made himself felt. When he marched against Lee in the spring of 1864, he ordered his armies in the West to move as well, up the Red River to try to cut in two the so-called Trans-Mississippi of the Confederacy. It was in this forgotten region that the final surrenders took place in 1865, themselves almost as much overlooked as the bitter warfare here that they ended.

# MR. LINCOLN'S ARMY

Far from the glory many enlistees anticipated, life in the Union Army was a combination of bad food, endless drills, disease, and hardship. *Right*: Veterans of Grant's 1864–1865 campaign through Virginia await the call to battle. *Clockwise from main, below*: The Ringgold Battery practices artillery formation and tactics; a camp scene, showing a company kitchen, circa 1860–1865; soldiers of the 96th Pennsylvania Infantry drill at Camp Northumberland, near Washington.

Having cut the South in two, Grant next went to work to cut it into three.

The third war was fought between the other two wars, between the Appalachians and the Mississippi, and a different sort of war it was. Here in Tennessee and Mississippi and Georgia, the Union truly won the war. There was seldom a day in which the North did not gain ground. When Grant, then an unknown, took Forts Henry and Donelson, Tennessee, in February 1862, all of Kentucky became untenable for the Confederates. At Shiloh in April, though badly surprised, Grant held out and held on to his gains. Grant's greatest triumph there was at Vicksburg. For more than a year he planned on taking the Mississippi River city. When it and its batteries fell, the Union would be able to navigate freely as far south as Port Hudson, Louisiana. New Orleans had already fallen to the Navy in April 1862, thus securing the lower Mississippi. On July 4, 1863, after forty-seven days of siege, Vicksburg fell, too. Port Hudson surrendered four days later, leaving the Union in control of the entire river and splitting off the entire Trans-Mississippi from the rest of the Confederacy.

Having cut the South in two, Grant next went to work to cut it into three. After the Union Army of the Cumberland suffered a disastrous defeat at Chickamauga, Georgia, in September 1863, Grant took command of its besieged remnant at Chattanooga, broke the siege, and routed the Confederate army facing him. And then in the spring of 1864, as part of his overall strategy of pressing the enemy at all points, he ordered his trusted lieutenant Gen. William Tecumseh Sherman to take this army and two others and march into Georgia. Atlanta fell to Sherman that summer, and by Christmas, Sherman had marched to the sea, taking Savannah, Georgia, and splitting the Confederacy yet again. Barely more than two weeks after Lee surrendered to Grant on April 9, 1865, the Confederate Army of Tennessee capitulated to Sherman, and the war east of the Mississippi was all but over.

In a war of such mammoth scope, with all the elements in it conspiring to raise the level of combat to heights previously unknown, it is no wonder that the cost proved so terrible. Roughly 623,000 men perished, a third of them killed or mortally wounded in battle. The rest died of disease and other causes, and nearly a half million more were wounded. One soldier in three was hit by a bullet in this war; one in five died. As a result, soldiers' attitudes toward the nature of war changed dramatically. In 1861, it was a lark, a posturing, swaggering exercise in Victorian heroics complete with florid expressions of love of flag and country. But by 1864, the cavalier boys who feared the war would end before they got a taste of it had become sober men who saw war for the grim, deadly business that it is.

Yet, however their attitudes toward war might have changed, the devotion and occasional heroism they showed remained constant. It took brave men to fight a conflict of this kind, to march into the face of enemy guns without flinching, to fight hand to hand and risk their lives for their cause, for their comrades, even for their regimental banners.

Both sides tried to honor their heroes. The Confederates created a Roll of Honor and intended to issue medals but never did. With the new Medal of Honor, the Union took a giant stride toward rewarding its heroes. Some 1,500 would be awarded, and the standards for receiving the honor varied from extreme heroism to simple political expedience. Most, however, went to men of a stripe, men who took risks, who rushed faster or farther for their cause, who explored new limits of human daring. So it is today, and so it was at the Medal of Honor's very beginning.

# FURY AT ANTIETAM CREEK
*First Awards for Battle*

With the war going badly for the Union in the first two years, there was an extra need to recognize personal valor. The first cadre of recipients consisted of men who had helped save the soil of the North from an enemy invasion. They were, as well, the first to earn the award for deeds done in actual combat.

And what a combat it was! On September 17, 1862, along the banks of Antietam Creek near Sharpsburg, Maryland, the bloodiest single day of the Civil War ravaged two armies. Robert E. Lee, already the preeminent general of the Confederacy, had led his thus-far invincible Army of Northern Virginia across the Potomac and into Maryland. Invading the North was a bold gamble, but Lee hoped to arouse Southern sympathy in Maryland, relieve the pressure on Virginia for a time, and perhaps follow up his August 30 victory at the Second Battle of Bull Run with yet another win on Northern soil. Such a victory might attract foreign aid for the Confederacy and force the Union into negotiations for peace.

But, on September 17, Gen. George B. McClellan and the Army of the Potomac met and stopped Lee. The cost was horrible: 4,700 men died and over 18,000 were wounded. The battle began on the Federal right, contesting some woods, cornfields, and the ground around a Dunker (a German-American sect) church. Soon the fighting spread to the center, where McClellan repeatedly attacked the Confederates posted in a sunken road that became immortalized as Bloody Lane. By the end of the day, when the fighting had ravaged the Yankee left as well, Lee was beaten, though still defiant. The Maryland fields were covered with the dead and wounded, and a few special men had covered themselves with glory.

One of them was Pvt. William P. Hogarty of the 23rd New York Infantry, although he did not fight with his own outfit this day. A call had gone out from the understrength 4th United States Artillery for volunteers from other units to man its guns, and Hogarty had stepped forward. Thus, trained as an infantryman, the twenty-two-year-old went into the opening of the battle that day manning a twelve-pounder instead.

Their orders sent them toward the Dunker church, where first two guns of the battery and then the remaining four did their part in repulsing withering attacks from Confederates under the command of Gen. Thomas J. "Stonewall" Jackson. For perhaps twenty minutes, Hogarty and his battery were in the thick of it, firing cannon that were double- and even triple-loaded with canister at the attacking Rebels, while themselves coming under a devastating fire from the enemy infantry and its supporting artillery.

As the fight raged, Hogarty looked to his right and saw that one of the battery's guns had lost every man, killed or wounded. There it sat, abandoned, some distance in front of the battle line, on a small rise of ground. It pointed at the enemy. On his own initiative, Hogarty grabbed a shell and ran through the storm of lead to the silent gun. He trimmed the shell's fuse to time it to explode just fractions of a second after firing, then single-handedly rammed it home, primed the gun, and fired the deadly missile into the ranks of Jackson's men not far in the distance.

This act of bravery alone might have earned him a medal, but later that morning Hogarty did more. When the badly mauled battery was withdrawn from active combat and sat resting

Private William P. Hogarty, an infantryman who served with the 4th US Artillery at Antietam, later lost an arm at Fredericksburg.

Federal forces advance near the Dunker Church at dawn on September 17, 1862. Beaten back, they nevertheless took a terrible toll of Southern lives.

and awaiting orders, Hogarty saw a dead infantryman's Springfield rifle lying on the ground. Apparently the New Yorker simply could not bear the sight of a gun going unused. Grasping the rifle, he calmly said to a comrade, "Bob, the supply of ammunition is running mighty low today. I think I will take this gun up to the firing line and help." And so he did.

Four months later, at Fredericksburg, the daring Hogarty would have his own left arm ripped off by an enemy cannon ball, yet he survived and continued his service, rising to the rank of captain. And to help his balance on that lighter left side, he could wear the Medal of Honor, thanks to his valor at Antietam.

When the fighting spread to the center of the line, other men were ready, among them Pvt. Samuel C. Wright of the 29th Massachusetts. In the early part of that morning, he and his regiment simply lay with their arms behind a wood, awaiting orders and listening to the sound of the battle being fought by Hogarty and thousands more off to the right. After an eternity of waiting, an officer ordered them forward across Antietam Creek and toward the Sunken Road.

What Wright and the others saw ahead of them was daunting, to say the least. Jackson's sharpshooters filled the road itself, firing from the cover of its banks, while the main Rebel line was just behind them. The men of Brig. Gen. Israel Richardson's Yankee division were ordered to drive the enemy out and take the road, but there was a high rail fence some two hundred yards in front of their line. Regiments that attempted to advance to the fence and scale it were almost destroyed by the Confederate fire. Wright could see that "they were actually torn in shreds and wedged into the fence." Those not killed were hugging the ground, unable to retreat, "for to stand was to be instantly killed by the sharpshooters."

The only way for Richardson's attack to proceed was for that fence to come down. Officers called for volunteers to risk almost-certain death, and seventy-six men stepped forward. Samuel Wright stood among them.

"We ran straight for the fence amid a hail of iron and lead," he recalled years later, "the dead falling all about us, but to reach the fence was our only thought." Part of the party actually reached the fence and began tearing it down. "As one would grasp a rail it would be sent flying out of his hands by rifle-shots," said Wright. Incredibly, they managed to level the obstruction and then faced the equally hazardous withdrawal under fire. "Few escaped death or wounds," Wright wrote, and he was no exception. Just before regaining his own lines, he was hit—one of five wounds he would receive in the war, including the loss of an eye. He would wear an eye patch as a badge of honor for the rest of his life, just as he would wear the medal he received for his daring at the Sunken Road.

There were more ways than combat to achieve distinction, and one of them was in caring for all the wounded who, like Wright, fell in their acts of daring. Richard Curran was assistant surgeon of the 33rd New York, and when his regiment went into the fight, he went with it. Superiors gave him no orders as to where his field hospital should be located, so he simply started treating the wounded immediately behind the battle line, where he was himself exposed to almost constant fire. Officers told him again and again to get back to safety, "but here were the wounded and suffering of my command," he declared, "and here I believed was my place of duty, even if it cost my life."

Even when he finally was able to move most of the wounded a few hundred feet back to the vicinity of some haystacks, he continued to work "exposed to the overhead firing of shot and shell." Always there was the danger of the hay catching fire, and even here the wounded were hit again. Curran was tending the leg of one soldier when he turned aside for more dressings. When he turned back, he found the soldier's leg shot away by a cannonball. Yet on he worked, well into the night. "He attended faithfully to his severe duties, and I beg to mention this officer with particular commendation," wrote Col. W. H. Irwin, who commanded Curran's brigade. "His example is most unfortunately but too rare."

There were many kinds of examples being set at Antietam. One that would be repeated over and over again in this war was the struggle for the colors, either to defend one's own or to capture the enemy's. When Gen. William H. French's division advanced against the Sunken Road and a nearby cornfield that day, one of its units, the 1st Delaware Infantry, lost 286 men in the charge and was forced back. One of the fallen was the flag bearer. He and eight others fell while trying to plant it atop the Sunken Road. Second Lieutenant Charles Tanner and those about him looked out with despair at their banner lying barely twenty yards from the line of enemy rifles blazing away from the road.

"We had become desperately enraged," he remembered, "thinking, not of life, but how to regain the broad stripes of bunting under which we had marched." To a Civil War regiment, loss of its colors was a disgrace. Men would vie with each other for the chance to die carrying them in victory or to save them in defeat.

Corporal Samuel Wright earned his Medal of Honor when he tore down a fence to aid the advance at the Sunken Road.

Dr. Richard Curran earned a Medal of Honor for treating Union wounded at Antietam.

Second Lieutenant Charles Tanner charged out to retrieve the fallen colors of the 1st Delaware Infantry at the Sunken Road and was wounded three times.

After a furious battle, the 7th Maine advances over the Confederate dead in the Sunken Road, known ever after as the Bloody Lane.

The best the 1st Delaware could do now was to send a withering fire at every Confederate attempt to advance and capture the grounded banner. Other regiments helped them, and then a party of thirty volunteers rushed forward to try to regain the flag. Less than ten returned, and without the prize. "Maddened, and more desperate than ever, I called for the men to make another effort," said Tanner. That, too, failed. Then, when Maj. Thomas Smyth proposed that twenty-five picked marksmen should lay down a covering fire directly over the colors, Tanner exclaimed, "Do it, and I will get there!" Twenty other men joined him.

"It seemed as if a million bees were singing in the air," Tanner later remembered. Men on both sides were shouting as well as firing. Somehow Tanner got to the banner and had just picked up the tattered flag when a bullet shattered his arm. Refusing to release the colors from his grasp, he found that his legs worked just fine. "I made the best eighty-yard time on record," he joked, and took two more wounds while running.

His pains earned him the regard of his men, a battlefield promotion, and the Medal of Honor. He had much in common with the other medal recipients of Antietam. Heroism and devotion tended to be repetitive. A year after Antietam, Tanner was disabled by another wound and discharged. After only three months, however, he enlisted once more and served almost until the end of the war.

# WAR IN THE NORTH
## *The Battle of Gettysburg*

There would be more heroes, more medals awarded, in the days after Antietam, but the Army of the Potomac was to wait another ten months, suffer disastrous defeats at Fredericksburg and Chancellorsville, and see the rise and fall of two more commanders before victory again crowned its banners. And, as before, it came at the climax of another Confederate invasion. In June 1863, his army flush from its triumph at Chancellorsville, Lee crossed the Potomac once more. This time he penetrated even deeper into the North, driving into Pennsylvania almost to the capital at Harrisburg before he turned back to meet his foe.

No one had planned to fight a battle at Gettysburg, yet all roads seemed to lead there. Isolated elements of the two armies clashed first and then reinforcements rushed rapidly to the scene until, by July 1, two entire armies were either there or on the way. It was a make-or-break battle for both Lee and his antagonist, Meade. Lee had to win or else withdraw into Virginia with nothing to show for his invasion; Meade had to win or else risk an attack on Washington or Baltimore. With the stakes so high, both had to fight, and fight hard. So they did. For three days the quiet Pennsylvania community thundered in the greatest and bloodiest battle of the war.

The first day had gone against the Yankees, as they lost the town to the enemy and were forced back onto heights to the south. The next day, with heavy reinforcements arriving, Meade was still on the defensive, but real fighting did not begin until well into the afternoon. The left center of his line was held by Gen. Daniel Sickles's III Corps. Without orders, Sickles moved his corps far in advance of the rest of the line, inviting attack that was not long in coming. The result, in a maelstrom of battle at places ever after called the Peach Orchard, Wheat Field, and Devil's Den, was the near-destruction of the corps.

# DEEDS OF VALOR

Many images of the Civil War heroes used here were published in *Deeds of Valor*, a collection of Medal of Honor stories published in 1906 by the Perrien-Keydel Company, which was a valuable source for this chapter. The book contains graphic treatments of Medal of Honor feats along with accounts drawn from "records in the archives of the United States government" and "personal reminiscences and records of officers and enlisted men who were rewarded by Congress for most conspicuous acts of bravery."

Second Lieutenant Edward M. Knox, 15th New York Light Artillery, rushed his cannon ahead of Union lines during the Battle of Gettysburg, July 2, 1863.

*Opposite*
A Southern casualty of the fight on July 2 for the Devil's Den.

The 15th New York Light Artillery was ordered into the line to the left of the Peach Orchard as the fighting was about to begin. The commanding captain took direction of the four guns on the left of the battery and told 2nd Lt. Edward M. Knox to command the two cannon on the right. They began firing against a Confederate battery that was supporting Lee's attacks on Sickles.

In fact, in his enthusiasm to rush his section into the fray, Knox led his guns too far forward. "My speed had carried me fully 100 yards ahead of the artillery line on the left." Seeing Knox's exposed cannon, the enemy rushed forward against him. He had to think fast, with only a handful of men facing hundreds. "I let go both pieces with double canister," he recalled, and then yelled at his men to lie down and feign being killed or wounded. As a result, when the Confederate charge swept over the battery and passed beyond, Knox and his men were left unmolested. Just then a Yankee countercharge struck the Rebels and drove them back through the cannon fire again. Once they were past, Knox and his men arose from the dead and hauled their guns back to safety. Even then he was himself wounded, though that did not prevent him from fighting again the next day and being disabled when a bullet passed through both his hips.

Knox would earn the Medal of Honor for his individual bravery. Others would earn it in a group, including four men of the 6th Pennsylvania. Sickles's extreme left was positioned near a rock outcropping called Devil's Den and was taking a beating from enemy sharpshooters inside a nearby log house. The colonel of the 6th Pennsylvania offered to rid Sickles of the nuisance and then asked his regiment, "Are any of you men willing to drive those Rebels out of that place there?"

Six men volunteered, among them Sgts. John Hart and George Mears and Cpls. James L. Roush and Chester Furman. They tried at first to approach the house by stealth but were soon discovered. That left them no choice but to jump up and rush it, all the while under a deadly fire from the Rebels inside. Miraculously they all reached the house unhurt, battered in the door with their rifle butts, and leaped inside screaming for the sharpshooters to surrender. With no choice but to give up or die, the Confederates capitulated, and the two sergeants and two corporals would earn the medal for their valor. (Why medals did not go to the other two is unknown, though very probably they did not survive the battle. It was not the custom at the time to bestow the Medal of Honor posthumously.)

There were other cases of Federals storming buildings full of the enemy that day. Captain John Lonergan of the 13th Vermont had already led his Company A in a charge that recaptured a battery the Confederates had taken from Sickles. No sooner was he moving the guns to safety than he noticed a severe fire was hitting his men from the house of the Codori family in front of him. At once he led his company to the house, surrounded it, and strode up to the door and knocked it in. "Surrender!" he shouted. "Fall out here, every damned one of you!"

At once the Rebels did as ordered, and soon Lonergan had eighty-three prisoners, more men than he had led to capture them. Lonergan's colonel ungenerously failed to mention the captain's heroic deed in his report of the battle, but others had seen what he did, and the Medal of Honor would be his.

An officer whose commander was unsparing in praise of him was Capt. James Parke Postles of the 1st Delaware. This same afternoon, Gen. Alexander Hays, commanding a

From top: Sergeant John Hart, Cpl. James Roush, Sgt. George Mears, and Cpl. Chester Furman, who captured Confederates near the Devil's Den.

division in the center of the Federal line, was infuriated at the fire hitting his men from a white house on the Bliss farm, several hundred yards in their front. His men did not take the house but did capture the barn about sixty-five yards away. There they sat when Hays ordered that the men in the barn be directed to attack and take the house.

Postles had felt ill all that day. At the moment he sat astride his mount, holding the reins on his arm and his head in his hands, barely able to stay on duty. But when no one else volunteered to take the assault order out to the men in the barn, he raised his head and said, "I will take it, sir."

He set out at once and almost immediately came under fire from the Confederates in the Bliss house. Though the fire grew increasingly hotter, not a bullet touched him, and Postles concluded that the reason was that he was in constant motion. No one could draw a true bead on him. That meant he would be safe enough until he finished his ride, but what about when he had to stop at the barn to deliver his message?

His solution was novel enough, though hard on his horse. When he reached the barn, he did not stop. Instead, he put all his weight into savagely yanking back on the reins, while at the same time sinking his spurs deeply into the animal's flanks. In pain and terror the horse reared and bucked "so that I was as bad a mark as though in full gallop." While thus pitching about he shouted his orders to the men in the barn and then galloped off again in a hail of Confederate lead. He reached safety untouched and soon saw the Confederates from the Bliss house brought in as prisoners. One of them confessed to having fired three times at him, all misses. "Well sir," said Johnny Reb, "I guess your time hain't come yet."

It was over the same ground where Postles earned his medal that the climactic act of the Battle of Gettysburg was fought, the so-called Pickett's Charge on July 3. Fifteen thousand of Lee's best troops marched across open fields in an attempt to destroy the Union center in a single blow. When the 19th Massachusetts was rushed into the Federal line to help defend against the mammoth enemy attack, Cpl. Joseph DeCastro went forward with the colors. Unarmed, he stood with the banner above him as a rallying place for his comrades. The contending lines mixed in a confusion of hand-to-hand fighting. DeCastro got separated from his regiment and came face to face with the color sergeant of the 14th Virginia. "I had the good fortune to get in the first blow," DeCastro recalled. In fact, he struck the Rebel with his own color staff, then grabbed the Confederate's colors from him and ran toward his own lines. Finding his colonel, he handed him the Southern banner, said not a word, and then ran back to his post. That was the kind of selfless heroism that turned back the attack and won the battle of Gettysburg for the North.

# SPLITTING THE SOUTH

## The Siege of Vicksburg

The fortunes of the Union appeared to turn everywhere in that July of 1863. Just the day after Meade's victory at Gettysburg, Grant finally received the surrender of Vicksburg, Mississippi, hundreds of miles to the west. The twin defeats broke the back of the Confederacy, leaving it on the defensive for the rest of the war.

Vicksburg had been a very different sort of operation from Gettysburg. Its fall came after forty-seven days of siege. Yet even then, interspersed among the tedious days of siege,

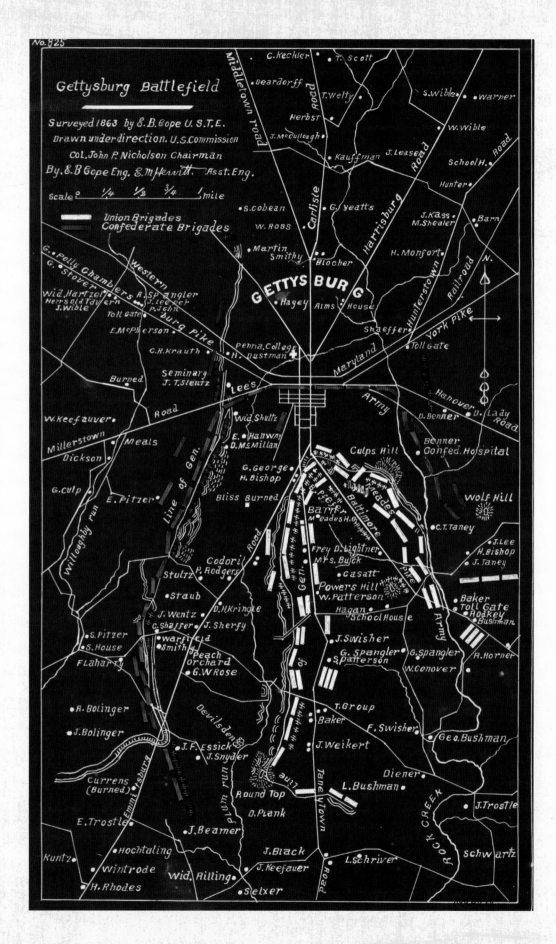

Badly surprised by the enemy on July 1, 1863, Federal troops held the high ground south of Gettysburg for two days while furious Southern assaults attempted to dislodge them. The climax came on July 3, when Lee sent fifteen thousand men against the Federals in the doomed Pickett's Charge.

The final Rebel assault,
Pickett's Charge.

there were fights between blue and gray. On May 19, the day after the siege commenced, Grant launched an attack, hoping to penetrate Gen. John C. Pemberton's fortifications. It failed, but three days later Grant tried again, sending almost forty-five thousand men against the enemy works on a three-mile front. The fighting everywhere was desperate, and here and there the Yankees topped the walls or made a brief breakthrough. But Pemberton held out, inflicting over three thousand casualties. Repulsed a second time, Grant would not attack again and, instead, slowly starved Vicksburg into submission.

May 22, 1863, produced many heroes and, as was often the case, their commanders and government seemed more anxious to honor them than when there had been a failed battle. Frequently they were honored for group endeavors, like the exploits of the Chicago Mercantile Battery. Captain Patrick M. White, who was to earn a Medal of Honor that day, was ordered to take two guns into a ravine to help batter down an enemy earthwork. Assisted by some infantrymen, he and his men dragged a cannon up to within a few feet of the Confederate fort, all the while under fire. Others carried ammunition by hand, and once he had the gun in place, White oversaw cutting the fuses so they would explode almost as soon as they left the gun's muzzle.

His first shot struck a Confederate twenty-four-pounder in the fort. After that, White and his men loaded and fired as fast as they could. "I never saw a gun loaded and fired so fast," he declared. "Every man was at his best." So quickly did they work that once or twice someone failed to swab carefully the remaining sparks out of the gun tube before the next charge was rammed home, and it discharged prematurely.

Soon they completely disabled the Confederate gun, and then their shells set ablaze the cotton bales that formed part of the Southern parapet. For twenty minutes the Confederates abandoned the fort, then came back with water to douse the fire, only to have White's gun blast the cotton to pieces. That lone gun continued to fire throughout the rest of the attack, and when it was brought back later that day "it was as hot as a live coal." Five other members of the Chicago Mercantile Battery manning the gun would earn the Medal of Honor along with White for their daring exploit.

Even more men earned that distinction elsewhere on the battle line around Vicksburg in what some of them ever after referred to as the "forlorn hope." In front of the XV Corps there stood an enemy fort, behind a ditch twelve feet wide and six feet deep. For Grant's attack to succeed, this fort had to fall. Late on May 21, every regimental colonel in the 2nd Division

# THE CASE OF THE 27TH MAINE

During the time that the Medal of Honor was America's only military decoration, wholesale distributions to units and groups of men occasionally threatened to demean its value as a combat award. Nothing illustrates this better than the peculiar case of the 27th Maine.

The 27th Maine was a nine months' regiment organized at Portland on September 30, 1862. Thereafter, with only brief exceptions, the regiment spent its entire term of service in the defenses of Washington performing routine garrison duty. The men saw no action and probably never even heard a hostile shot fired. On June 26, 1863, with just four days of their enlistments left, the men in the regiment were ordered to leave their position and prepare to be mustered out.

The timing could not have been worse, for just then Lee and the Army of Northern Virginia were invading the North, and the decisive battle of Gettysburg lay just five days hence. With every veteran regiment that could be spared going to Major General Meade to reinforce the Army of the Potomac, Washington's defenses were fairly stripped, and that left Lincoln and Secretary of War Stanton uneasy. Stanton appealed to the 27th Maine and another Down East regiment, the 25th, to extend their periods of service to see the capital through the emergency. The 25th Maine refused to a man, but when Col. Mark Wentworth spoke to the men of his 27th and explained the situation, about three hundred stepped forward and volunteered to remain on duty. Stanton was overjoyed, and on June 29 he directed the adjutant general to provide a Medal of Honor for every one of the men who volunteered.

In the end, those of the 27th Maine who volunteered were only kept in service an extra four days and played no role at all in the Gettysburg campaign. But it was too late. Stanton's order had opened the door to the virtual destruction of any meaning at all for the Medal of Honor.

There had been little heroism or self-sacrifice involved in a few hundred men remaining on duty a few extra days, which was bad enough. Worse, Stanton had not specified that only men of the 27th Maine receive it. The wording of his order allowed the presentation of the medal to any troops who volunteered to stay in the capital after their service expired. Furthermore, it granted the medal to volunteers who offered to serve temporarily in Pennsylvania and Maryland during the emergency. One estimate indicates that the total number of such men might have reached fifty thousand! Additionally, Stanton's order did not specify that these men should receive *the* Medal of Honor, only that "an appropriate Medal of Honor" be given them. The echoes of Stanton's promise would be heard in Maine

and Washington for the next fifty years.

Almost immediately there was a problem in getting an accurate listing of those who had stepped forward. There never would be agreement on the exact number. More than a year later, bureaucratic mix-ups resulted in an order that medals should be presented to all 864 of the men in the regiment, including those who refused to volunteer. No one in the chain of command caught the oversight.

*Colonel Mark Wentworth.*

The medals reached the governor of Maine in January 1865, and he immediately notified Colonel Wentworth and asked what should be done with them. Wentworth, meanwhile, had served in Grant's overland campaign of 1864 with the 32nd Maine. The regiment saw much battle and gave many examples of heroism, yet not a man in the 32nd was awarded the Medal of Honor for his deeds. To Wentworth, the idea of giving over five hundred of the medals to men who did nothing at all was intolerable.

Wentworth decided to give the medals only to men who had actually volunteered to help defend the capital. The roughly 560 that remained he simply stored in his barn.

But the case of the 27th Maine could not be forgotten. In 1892 the Record and Pension Office of the War Department undertook to compile a list of men in the regiment who had actually stayed in Washington and were thus deserving of a medal. Meanwhile, some of the veterans of the 27th who had not remained found out about the medals with their names on them in Wentworth's barn, and broke in and took them. Later that decade, after Wentworth's death, the remaining medals disappeared entirely.

Over the next several years, the Army continued to clarify the qualifications for the Medal of Honor and to gather a complete list of all of its recipients. In 1917, a review board considered all past Medals of Honor. It concluded that the 555 Maine men who had not volunteered (a total drawn from a regimental history published in 1895) were definitely not worthy of the award. Then, looking at the list of 309 who had stepped forward that June day in 1863, the board waffled, but the Judge Advocate General of the Army did not. These men had done nothing in any way heroic. Their medals should be rescinded along with all the others. And so, half a century after the emergency of 1863, the final coda was written to the strangest tale in all the varied history of America's highest military honor—which had very nearly become the cheapest.

A soldier of the "forlorn hope" throws a Southern bomb back at Confederate lines during the Siege of Vicksburg on the morning of May 22, 1863.

of the corps asked for volunteers. Those who stepped forward would lead the attack. Their mission was to build a bridge over the ditch for the attackers to cross and then erect scaling ladders against the side of the fort for them to climb. All of this would be done in plain view of the defenders and under a withering fire. Only unmarried men were to be accepted as volunteers, for it seemed tacitly agreed that few, if any, would survive.

More than enough answered the call in spite of the dangers, and the next morning they assembled at the staging area for their exploit. They found a pile of logs. Two men each were to run with a log toward the ditch and throw it across. As soon as two or more logs were successfully planted, more men were to rush forward with planks to throw across them to make the roadway for the attackers to follow. Then a final group of volunteers would rush across the bridge and throw up the scaling ladders.

There lay nearly a quarter mile of open ground for them to cover before they reached that ditch. As soon as the Yankees emerged in the open, their foes opened fire. Perhaps half of them survived to reach the ditch, but so many men had fallen that not enough of the long logs came up for them to start their work. Still under a deadly fire, they could not run back through that gauntlet and had no choice but to jump into the ditch and take what shelter they could find. Private Howell Trogden of the 8th Missouri Infantry had carried a flag along with the party, and here he climbed up part of the Confederate parapet and planted the banner before taking cover. Those Federals with guns kept up a steady fire on any Rebels who tried to reach out to take the colors.

The attackers who came behind the "forlorn hope" fared no better, and barely thirty men of the 11th Missouri reached the ditch to join their comrades. The enemy above could not lean far enough over the parapet to fire on them, nor could they depress their cannon sufficiently to send shot and shell into the ditch. And so, suiting necessity to the task, they took twelve-pounder shells and lit their fuses by hand, then dropped them down into the ditch like grenades. Only the fact that the fuses were cut too long saved the Federals, for while the shells still sputtered, there was time for them to get out of the way. A few even picked up the shells and threw them back up the parapet at the Rebels.

The "forlorn hope" remained in that ditch all day, from ten in the morning until nightfall ended the fighting. When the men finally pulled out in the dark, some 85 percent had been killed or wounded, all for an attack that failed. But fifty-three of the survivors, including Private Trogden, were awarded the Medal of Honor for their unexampled bravery, the largest number of medals given to a single group of men for a single action during the war.

There was heroism everywhere in Grant's attacking line on May 22, and even his foes did not fail to honor it. Private Thomas J. Higgins, a burly Irishman in the 99th Illinois, volunteered to carry the regimental colors when the regular color bearer could not do duty that day. His captain gave him orders for the attack that were simple enough: not to stop until he had that flag planted inside the Confederate works. Higgins obeyed to the letter.

For two hours a cannonade sounded the prelude to attack. Then the advancing column came in sight of the portion of the works held by the 2nd Texas Infantry. As soon as the Yankees were within range, the Texans' guns opened a devastating fire. "The blue lines vanished amid fearful slaughter," recalled Confederate Charles Evans of the 2nd Texas. The firing stopped.

Nothing seemed to move on the smoke-shrouded field. Then the defenders made out a single Union flag fluttering and moving forward. Thomas Higgins was still obeying his orders. In disbelief, the Confederates saw the lone Yank moving on toward their works. Even when several score rifles began to open fire on him, Higgins did not falter but kept coming on, tripping over the bodies of his dead comrades. "Suddenly," wrote Evans, "as if with one impulse, every Confederate soldier within sight of the Union color bearer seemed to be seized with the idea that the man ought not to be shot." Cries of "Don't shoot at that man again" ran up and down the line. Seconds later they were actually cheering Higgins on, throwing their hats in the air, and reaching out to pull him over the breastworks when he reached the parapet. Miraculously, he was untouched by the storm of fire through which he had passed.

General Ulysses S. Grant at City Point, Virginia, during the fighting at Petersburg.

General Pemberton himself interviewed Higgins before sending him to await prison, but with the fall of Vicksburg, the plucky Irishman was freed and returned to his regiment to serve out the war. Years later, at the instigation of the very Confederates who captured him that day, Congress awarded him the medal for his single-minded persistence in carrying out a soldier's orders.

# THE UNION JUGGERNAUT
## *Grant's Overland Campaign*

The ten months that followed the twin victories at Gettysburg and Vicksburg saw even more ground lost by the South out west in Tennessee and in north Georgia. But back in Virginia, where all eyes seemed always to turn, the Yankees stood no closer to Richmond than they had more than a year before. Always Lee stymied their efforts to penetrate his beloved state's interior. The coming of a new Yankee general, however, was to change the fortunes of war in Virginia.

Ulysses S. Grant came from his victories in the West to become general-in-chief of all Union armies in late 1863. He had directed major offensives in every other theater of the war and himself went to Virginia to be with the brave but troubled Army of the Potomac. The capable Meade remained in direct command of the army, but it was Grant who set the strategy, and on May 4, 1864, they all set out across the Rapidan River near Fredericksburg, Virginia—their objective, Lee's army.

# THE ONLY WOMAN

Mary Walker always stood out in a crowd. When she graduated from Syracuse Medical College in 1855, she became one of the first woman physicians in the country. She preferred pants as more functional than dresses or skirts and even wore a pair at her own wedding. An ardent advocate of women's rights, she often delivered lectures on the subject. Mary Edwards Walker is also the only woman in US history to have received the Medal of Honor.

At the outbreak of war in 1861, Dr. Walker, then twenty-nine, applied for a commission as an Army surgeon but was turned down because of her gender. Undaunted, she worked as a volunteer at a Washington hospital for several months. In November 1862, Walker presented herself at the Virginia headquarters of Maj. Gen. Ambrose Burnside and was taken on as a field surgeon, although still on a volunteer basis.

For much of the next two years, Dr. Walker could be found near the Union front lines, clad in the gold-striped trousers of an Army officer and a green surgeon's sash, topped off by an unorthodox straw hat with an ostrich feather. She treated the wounded at Fredericksburg in December 1862; almost a year later she was in Chattanooga tending the casualties of the battle of Chickamauga.

After the battle she again requested a commission as an Army doctor. But after an Army medical board in Chattanooga pronounced her "utterly unqualified for the position of medical officer," she could only continue as a volunteer. Finally, Maj. Gen. George H. Thomas appointed her to replace the assistant surgeon of the 52nd Ohio Infantry after the previous doctor's death.

Mary Walker tended soldiers and civilians and may also have been a spy for the Union at this time. One Army communication mentions her "secret services" for the North; another states that information she gleaned behind enemy lines saved Maj. Gen. William T. Sherman's forces from "a serious reverse."

Only a month after joining the 52nd Ohio, Walker was captured by the Rebels and sent to a Richmond prison. After four months she was traded for a Confederate officer; years later she took great pride in this "man for man" exchange.

Upon her release, Walker was granted a contract as an acting assistant surgeon at $100 a month and given back pay for her service with the 52nd Ohio (but not her desired commission as an officer). The Army denied her request for battlefield duty, and she spent the rest of the war practicing at a Louisville female prison (where she offended both inmates and staff with her abrupt manner) and a Tennessee orphans' asylum.

Though paid in full and released from government contract at the end of the war, Walker lobbied for a brevet promotion to major for her services. Secretary of War Stanton would not grant the request; it was impossible to give Walker a higher rank, the Judge Advocate General of the Army advised, because she was never an officer in the first place. After several angry letters from Walker, President Andrew Johnson asked Stanton if there was some other way to recognize her service. Stanton ordered that a Medal of Honor be prepared for Walker. It was presented to her in January 1866; she would wear it every day for the rest of her life.

After the war, Walker devoted herself to many unpopular causes, including women's rights, the wearing of pants, and opposition to smoking. Her taste in clothes caused frequent arrests on such charges as "impersonating a man." At one trial she asserted her right "to dress as I please in free America on whose tented fields I have served for four years in the cause of human freedom." The judge dismissed the case and ordered the police never to arrest Walker on the charge again. She left the courtroom to hearty applause.

Her private practice was never successful, however, and by the mid-1880s Mary Walker, now living on a government pension, was reduced to a sideshow existence. Amid various novelty acts, she spoke on women's rights and the advantages of pants, all the while wearing the Medal of Honor on her lapel. Some observers were indignant: In March 1893 an Ohio newspaper huffed, "There was a time when this remarkable woman stood upon the same platform with Presidents and the world's greatest women. There is something grotesque about her appearance on a stage built for freaks."

Age did not diminish her eccentricity. In 1901, Walker outraged her Oswego, New York, neighbors—and nearly lost her pension—by circulating a petition asking for clemency for the anarchist who had assassinated President McKinley.

But Mary Walker's greatest ignominy was yet to come. In 1916, Congress revised the Medal of Honor standards to include only "actual combat with an enemy." Several months later an Army board rescinded Walker's medal, citing her ambiguous military status and the fact that her "service does not appear to have been distinguished in action or otherwise." Advised that it was now a crime to wear her medal, she vowed to continue to wear it, every day if she pleased.

Over the next two years, Walker appealed to congressmen and War Department officials, but to no avail. On one of these visits she suffered a bad fall on the Capitol steps. She never fully recovered and died on February 21, 1919, at the age of eighty-six.

But like many of the actions of the Army review board of 1916–1917, the case of Mary Walker was not forgotten. Nearly sixty years after her death, at the urging of a descendant, the Army restored Walker's Medal of Honor. Some medal historians and recipients objected, citing her civilian status and allegations of incompetence. Nevertheless, Mary Walker remains on record as the sole female recipient of the Medal of Honor.

*Dr. Walker, in men's attire, with the new Army Medal of Honor, 1912.*

Private William Noyes, driven by revenge, was awarded the medal for his acts of valor on the battlefield at the Bloody Angle.

Corporal Orlando Boss dug a shallow ditch with just a spoon to help drag a critically wounded officer to safety in the heat of fierce rifle fire.

Battle was joined the next day in a tangled region known to local Virginians as the Wilderness. For two days they fought, then moved on toward Spotsylvania to renew the battle. The Confederates entrenched and the Yankees attacked again and again, especially at a bulge in the Rebel line called the Mule Shoe, and later at a place to be called Bloody Angle. Lee was the loser in the end, for after several days Grant began to move around his right flank, and Lee had no choice but to pull back.

The hardest fighting came on May 12, 1864. The Yankees awakened early that morning, among them Pvt. John Weeks of the 152nd New York. He was barely past his nineteenth birthday, but already a veteran, and when the order came to advance, he moved smartly.

"Soon the rebel skirmishers commenced firing," he recalled, "and then for the first time I began to realize that we had work before us." He and his comrades advanced across an open field and into felled trees, strung wire, and other obstructions placed by the enemy. Soon they reached the Rebel works, a ditch several feet deep with an earthen parapet behind it. And all the way in the advance the Federals received a murderous artillery and rifle fire. Still they charged, scaled the parapet, and poured into the Confederate line.

Confusion reigned for a time as the disorganized Yankees tried to consolidate their breakthrough while their foes sought to withdraw. Weeks looked to his right to see another part of the enemy line pull out. He saw a Rebel color company with its flag trying desperately to escape; they fired a volley, then made a run for it. "I made up my mind," wrote Weeks, "that I must have those colors."

Even though his own rifle was unloaded, Weeks ran out in front of the retreating enemy, confronted the Rebel color sergeant, and grabbed the colors from him. Throwing the banner to the ground, Weeks put his foot on it, cocked the hammer of his empty gun, leveled it at the sergeant, and demanded the surrender of the entire company. Bluffed completely, a half-dozen Confederates lay down their guns and became his prisoners. While taking them to the rear, Weeks met Gen. Winfield S. Hancock, his corps commander, who smiled incredulously at the boy's brave deed. But he believed it just the same. Several months later Weeks was in a hospital recovering from a wound when he received a package. "Upon opening it," he said, "I found it to be the Medal of Honor."

Dozens of heroes were born in that hell of fire at the Mule Shoe and the Bloody Angle, often because seeing their comrades fall erased all caution in the urge for revenge. Private William Noyes of the 2nd Vermont charged the Angle with his regiment and halted just at the pile of logs the enemy used for defenses. Apparently as a subterfuge, a Rebel raised his rifle with a white rag tied to the barrel, and one Vermont boy took it to mean surrender and raised his head above the parapet. He was shot dead instantly.

"Infuriated beyond control by such treachery," said Noyes, "and determined upon revenge, I called on the men near me to load their pieces as rapidly as possible and hand them up to me." He leaped atop the parapet, fired his rifle into the nearest Confederate, and then proceeded to take rifles from his comrades and fire them one after another into the startled enemy. Fifteen times he aimed and fired before the bullets whizzing past him forced him back to cover. How many Noyes hit is unknown, but the Medal of Honor would be his for this deed.

Concern for the living could be just as powerful a catalyst to bravery as anger over the dead. Six weeks later, at Cold Harbor, Grant again attacked Confederates placed behind well-built defenses. The result was a disastrous and bloody succession of assaults. In the confusion, the 25th Massachusetts, just 270 strong, advanced unsupported against the enemy breastworks, only to be repulsed with heavy losses. Corporal Orlando Boss and two privates were left on the field, pinned down in a rifle pit midway between the two contending armies. Nearby lay Lt. William Daly of the same regiment, mortally wounded.

Boss could hear Daly's agonized cries for water and risked his own life by crawling out of the pit to take his canteen to the officer. When he got back to the rifle pit, Boss found one of the privates wounded and the area too hot with Rebel fire to remain. He put the private on his back and staggered through a virtual gauntlet of Confederate fire to reach the safety of his own breastworks.

That was not enough for the plucky nineteen-year-old. He now asked permission to go back out to bring back Lieutenant Daly. Accompanied by another man, Boss rushed out to the original rifle pit. From here, using their mess spoons, they scraped their way toward Daly, digging a shallow ditch some fifteen yards long to reach him. Through that ditch they dragged him back to the rifle pit, after four hours of arduous digging under constant fire. More hours of furrowing followed until the two men and their dying officer returned safely to their own lines. It was an incredible feat made no less heroic by Daly's later death and one richly deserving of the Medal of Honor received by Boss.

During Grant's long campaign to conquer Lee there were other heroes who were out of the ordinary. For the medal was not restricted by station, or race. Nearly 179,000 African Americans served in the Union forces, and twenty-three of them would earn the Medal of Honor. The first had gone to William H. Carney back in 1863 for his part in attacking Battery Wagner outside Charleston, South Carolina (see sidebar, page 52). Another, Decatur Dorsey, earned it for his bravery in the so-called Battle of the Crater, when Grant had Lee besieged in Petersburg and used several African American regiments in an abortive assault made just after tunnelers had exploded a huge mine under the Rebel works.

The largest number of medals awarded to African Americans for any single action resulted from fighting at New Market Heights, Virginia, on September 29, 1864. In a bloody charge that failed, the 4th and 6th United States Colored Troops lost perhaps half their numbers. Sergeant Major Christian Fleetwood was in charge of the left half of the 4th's line, there being no field officers available. He led it forward in the charge, only to see the regiment cut to pieces. Of the color guard of twelve men, just one survived. When a second color bearer fell, Cpl. Charles Veal grabbed the regimental flag and Fleetwood himself took the national colors. On they went, struggling through successive lines of enemy defenses and obstructions, all the while under fire. "It was sheer madness," recalled Fleetwood, "and those of us who were able had to get out as best we could."

Once back in their own lines, Fleetwood rallied the remnant of the regiment around his flag. "I have never been able to understand how Veal and I lived under such

Sergeant Major Christian Fleetwood, Medal of Honor recipient in the Civil War for having "saved the regimental colors after eleven of the twelve color guards had been shot down around it." Sergeant Major was the top rank allowed to a colored soldier at the time.

Grant used African American troops in some of the worst fighting of his Virginia campaign.

a hail of bullets," Fleetwood said afterward. He was small, and that helped, but even then his luck was phenomenal. One bullet actually passed inside his running legs, cutting through his boot, trousers, and stocking without giving him a scratch. Fleetwood, Veal, another wounded color bearer, and an African American sergeant from the 6th Colored who also saved his banner would all receive the Medal of Honor for their courage in the service of the Union.

# HEROISM AT SEA
## *The Naval War*

Civil War battles at sea and on rivers are less well known today than those on land. The Union navy began the conflict woefully unprepared, consisting of about thirty-five modern service-able warships and just 7,600 seamen. The Confederates had no navy at all in the beginning. Thus both sides were forced to commence a crash program of building ships while at the same time developing their naval strategies.

The naval strategy of the South in the Civil War was simple enough: to defend its ports and try to keep them open for vital trade in war materiel from abroad; to hold its rivers to prevent the enemy from using them as avenues of invasion; and to interrupt Federal shipping on the high seas, thus drawing Yankee warships away from the coast to pursue Southern privateers. The Union's goals were directly related. Lincoln's ships must blockade the Confederate coastline, stop traffic into its harbors, control its rivers, and stop its commerce raiders on the ocean.

The building programs of both sides saw many innovations, not the least of them being the advent of practical ironclad worships. Almost simultaneously, the Confederates were converting a captured Yankee warship into the powerful CSS *Virginia*, while in the North a whole new sort of vessel was being created in the USS *Monitor*. In a case of timing unparalleled, both ships were ready at the same time and place for their first combat.

On March 8, 1862, the *Virginia*—still often called the *Merrimack* because of the ship from which it was made—steamed from its berth at Norfolk, down the Elizabeth River, and into Hampton Roads, Virginia. Its objective was the Yankee blockading fleet, and in a day's action it almost destroyed it, sinking or burning two warships, damaging another, and running others aground. The crew expected to return to the scene the next day to complete its work, but on the morning of March 9, the seamen came upon the unlikely looking *Monitor*. Miraculously, the single-turreted ironclad had arrived during the night after a harrowing passage from the North.

When the two ships met in battle that day, neither could gain the upper hand. For several hours they hammered at each other indecisively. Only late in the day did a well-aimed shot from the *Virginia* strike the *Monitor*'s pilothouse. It tore away part of the house's iron roof and sent sparks and iron fragments through the viewing slits, temporarily blinding Lt. John Worden, commander of the vessel.

The wheelman standing beside him, Peter Williams, was uninjured and, though dangerously exposed in the damaged pilothouse, remained at his post and skillfully steered the ship away from its antagonist until another officer could take over to renew the fight. Once the battle reached its end—a draw—Williams was rewarded for his coolness and bravery with the only Medal of Honor awarded for the battle.

The Union navy began the conflict woefully unprepared . . . The Confederates had no navy at all in the beginning.

There were to be more medals associated with the *Monitor*, though not for combat. Seven months later, on December 30, while being towed south along the coast of North Carolina just off Cape Hatteras, she ran into a heavy storm. As the weather worsened, the ironclad began taking in water faster than her pumps could eject it. In time the engines could no longer function, the water level continued to rise, and the order was given to abandon ship.

The USS *Rhode Island*, the towing ship, sent three boats across the water to rescue the sinking vessel's seamen, and one of them, a ship's cutter, made three perilous passages through the raging seas. Twice she brought back men to the *Rhode Island*, but when she returned a third time for the last of the seamen, they were nowhere to be seen. The *Monitor* had gone to the bottom. The seven men who rowed that cutter back and forth at peril to their own lives all received the medal for their valor.

Indeed, naval actions seemed to earn the medal in numbers. No fewer than twenty seamen earned it for their daring in Adm. David G. Farragut's April 24, 1862, attack on Forts Jackson and St. Philip, both of which guarded New Orleans. When they fell, and the city with them, the lower Mississippi was open to Union navigation, and a wedge was driven into the Confederacy.

Individual acts of bravery during the attack are too many to enumerate, yet a few stand out. Aboard the USS *Pensacola*, Seaman Thomas Lyons lashed himself off the port bow

Combat between the *Monitor*, two guns, and *Merrimack* (also known as the *Virginia*), ten guns. This confrontation—fought in Hampton Roads on March 9, 1862—was the first between ironclad ships of war.

The *Monitor's* turret house shows the damage incurred during its clash with the *Virginia*.

with a rope line in hand to take depth soundings as the ship passed the enemy batteries, all the while exposed to everything the Rebels could throw at him. Aboard the USS *Brooklyn*, Quartermaster James Buck stood at his wheel for seven hours, refusing to go below to safety even though a flying splinter—a deadly threat in the days of oak-hulled ships—had dangerously wounded him.

Perhaps most daring of all was the quick-thinking action of Gunner's Mate J. B. Frisbee on the USS *Pinola*. His ship took fire during the battle on April 24, and he watched as the flames advanced dangerously close to the ship's powder magazine. At once he left his post and ran around the flames and into the magazine itself. Then, drawing shut its heavy iron door behind him, he remained inside, ready to catch and extinguish any sparks that might penetrate while other crewmen fought to put out the fire.

Most of the naval combat of the war took place on the Mississippi after Farragut opened it up. More Yankee ships and seamen perished there than anywhere else, frequently not

# FIGHTING FOR THE COLORS

One of the many ironies of the Civil War is the fact that the one deed best calculated to earn any soldier the Medal of Honor was an act that—admittedly very dangerous—possessed almost no military significance whatever: capturing a flag. Men on both sides of the conflicts considered their regimental standards worth fighting and dying for. No statute or act of Congress specifically stated that taking an enemy banner was justification for the award, yet more were given for flag captures than for any other kind of heroic endeavor.

One of the very first Medals of Honor to be given for a battle action came as a result of a captured flag. Corporal Jacob Orth of the 28th Pennsylvania fought with his regiment at Antietam early on the morning of September 17 as they attacked Rebels placed in an apple orchard. In the melee, Orth took a bullet in his shoulder when he fought hand-to-hand with the color bearer of the 7th South Carolina. "The final result of our short but sharp conflict," said Orth, "was that the Carolinian was minus his flag, and I had secured the trophy."

A "trophy" is just what it was, but one terribly important to nineteenth-century soldiers, and they would risk their lives for it. At Gettysburg, during the Confederate assault of July 3, Sgt. Maj. William Hincks of the 14th Connecticut saw an enemy regiment advance to within 150 yards of his line before Yankee fire stopped it. Undaunted, the Rebel color bearer ran forward a few paces and stuck his flagstaff in the ground, then lay down beside it with other members of the color guard to avoid the hot fire.

Unaccountably, Hincks jumped over the low stone wall, his regiment knelt behind, and started running toward the Rebel banner. Two or three others from his outfit had the same idea at the same time, and a virtual footrace ensued to see who, if any of them, would reach the flag first. One fell to a bullet almost immediately. Hincks covered the hundred yards so quickly he beat his comrades to the flag and grabbed it and ran for his own line before the Confederate color guard came to its senses and started to fire at him. Hincks made it back to safety amid a storm of bullets and proudly waved the banner of the 14th Tennessee overhead.

In time, the men who took flags in battle would be honored wholesale. At the Battle of Sayler's Creek on April 6, 1865, as Lee retreated from a fallen Petersburg and Richmond seeking to escape to North Carolina, one Yankee division alone captured thirty-seven battle flags. It was the cavalry division of Gen. George A. Custer, and all thirty-six of the men who made the captures were sent to Washington to receive the thanks of their government and their Medals of Honor.

They rode down the capital's avenues in a horse-drawn streetcar, their captured banners fluttering from the windows. Secretary of War Edwin M. Stanton received them. Each presented his flag, told his story, and was promised his medal. Most of their tales were of a kind, yet one of these bold cavalrymen stood above the others, not the least because he was General Custer's brother. Second Lieutenant Thomas Custer of the 6th Michigan Cavalry had captured two of those flags personally.

The first one he took in a fight at Namozine Church on April 2, as Grant's cavalry tried to break up Lee's horsemen protecting his flanks. Exhilarated by his capture, Tom Custer apparently decided to try for another whenever an opportunity might appear. It came four days later at Sayler's Creek, where portions of Grant's army, mainly two infantry corps and Gen. Philip H. Sheridan's cavalry, cut off and captured one-third of Lee's dwindling army. Though the fighting was hot, Sayler's Creek was almost a walkover for many of the Yankees.

The brigade in which Tom Custer served was just charging an enemy battle line when Custer spied a Confederate flag fluttering above its color bearer. He spurred his horse and rode straight toward the prize. The Confederate carrying the flag raised his pistol and fired a shot that hit the advancing Custer in the face, the bullet entering his cheek and exiting behind his ear. The impact knocked him back on his horse, but he stayed in the saddle and kept on coming. Drawing his own revolver, Custer fired it into the Rebel with one hand and grabbed the flagstaff with the other. General Henry Capehart, who would himself be awarded the Medal of Honor thirty years later for his war services, saw 2nd Lt. Custer's act and later described that "for intrepidity I never saw this incident surpassed."

Men of his brigade saw an elated Tom Custer riding back into their lines, blood running down his face, the captured banner streaming behind him. His first thought was to ride to his brother and proudly show his trophy. General Custer was appalled when he first saw the lieutenant, expecting to see him fall dead from the saddle, though the wound proved to be less fearful than it looked. "The damned rebels have shot me," yelled a jubilant Tom Custer, "but I've got my flag." Only direct orders from the general prevented the boy from riding back into the fight again, perhaps hoping to garner yet another trophy.

Yet for the two flags that he captured, Tom Custer had already achieved a measure of extraordinary distinction. The War Department decided to honor him with two Medals of Honor, one for each of his banners. Though he got them for storybook heroics that had little to do with the outcome of the battles he had fought, there is little doubt that Tom Custer was a hero. His considerable courage, though, could not save him eleven years later, when he died beside his brother as they faced the Sioux at the Little Bighorn.

in major battles but during engagements with the enemy on the banks. On May 28, 1863, the thirteen-gun ironclad USS *Cincinnati* helped silence a Rebel battery that was impeding Grant's encirclement of Vicksburg. Due to confusion in communications and careful concealment of some of the cannon, the Confederate battery proved much more powerful than expected.

No sooner did the *Cincinnati* let loose her first broadside at the battery on a bluff than it returned fire. Its first shot penetrated the ship's magazine and went on to pierce her bottom. Another shot ruined her steering. Under constant fire the vessel tried to escape upstream again, then finally had to run ashore so the crew could abandon ship. The *Cincinnati* slipped back into the channel and sank in twenty feet of water.

In a circumstance not at all unusual in the Navy, many of the seamen could not swim. Fifteen men drowned trying to reach the shore while others were killed by Rebel fire. Those who could swim saved themselves, but four brave seamen, Thomas Corcoran, Henry Dow, Thomas Jenkins, and Martin McHugh, made repeated trips back and forth to the ship to save those who could not swim. Then they found a small boat that had not been blasted by the enemy fire and loaded it with half a dozen of the wounded from the *Cincinnati*'s upper deck. Among the boat's passengers was Lt. George N. Bache, commander of the sunken ship. Corcoran, a twenty-three-year-old Irishman, would earn the Medal of Honor for leading the rescue. Dow, Jenkins, and McHugh were similarly awarded.

Actual combat out on the high seas was very rare in this war, but when it happened, the world watched. No engagement captured more attention than the duel between the USS

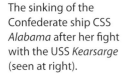

The sinking of the Confederate ship CSS *Alabama* after her fight with the USS *Kearsarge* (seen at right).

*Kearsarge* and the legendary Confederate commerce raider *Alabama*. The scourge of Yankee shipping, the *Alabama* and her commander, Adm. Raphael Semmes, were the object of a massive sea hunt that finally cornered the quarry at Cherbourg, France. On June 19, 1864, Semmes steamed out to meet his foe. Outgunned in a fight of only an hour, the *Alabama* went down to the bottom.

The *Kearsarge* fought like a fine watch, smoothly, efficiently, without missing a tick. She steamed circles around her opponent, thanks to the efficiency of her engine room crew, and her gunnery was markedly superior to Semmes's. Very few of the Confederate shots even struck the Yankee ship, and only three of its seamen were injured, one mortally. Indeed, it had been a one-sided battle from the start, but so delighted was the Union to be rid of the dreaded *Alabama* that Congress was more than happy to award seventeen Medals of Honor to crewmen of the *Kearsarge* for their "marked coolness and good conduct." Of heroism there was little, there being little need for it, but then, during the Civil War, the standard for awarding the medal was generally lower than in later years. Yet all of the recipients had done their duty, and their government was grateful.

# THE UNION RESTORED
## *Final Awards*

When the Medal of Honor was created, the only standard for awarding it was the legislative injunction that it be bestowed for "gallantry in action" and other "seamanlike" (or soldierly) qualities. This broad definition caused some actions to be recognized while

Elsewhere, generals found the medal and the standards for its award so unspecific that they simply failed to recommend worthy soldiers.

others, just as gallant, went unrewarded. As the Civil War drew to a close, the whims of commanders who recommended men for medals was often as important as the actions of the men themselves.

Examples of varied standards for the Medal of Honor occurred throughout the Civil War. In South Carolina in October 1863, Gen. Quincy Gillmore decreed that Medals of Honor were to be given out to those who distinguished themselves in his attempt to take Charleston, but that no more than 3 percent of the men in each regiment were to receive them. It is perhaps fortunate that Gillmore's plan never went into full effect, for the 3 percent of his command would have accounted for several hundred medals all by themselves.

Elsewhere, generals found the medal and the standards for its award so unspecific that they simply failed to recommend worthy soldiers. This accounts for the incredible disparity in the numbers given for different campaigns. In Sherman's campaign through the Carolinas in the early months of 1865, including major battles at Averasboro and Bentonville, North Carolina, only three Medals of Honor were awarded. In Gen. James H. Wilson's celebrated raid through Alabama, his three divisions of cavalry took five fortified cities, twenty-three colors, 288 cannon, and almost seven thousand prisoners, one of them Confederate President Jefferson Davis. Yet only twelve medals went to Wilson's troopers, all for flag captures.

By contrast, the number of awards that went to men of the Army of the Potomac just for its final week of the war in pursuit of Lee's retreating army to Appomattox was almost embarrassing. On April 1, 1865, when the Battle of Five Forks cut off Lee's right flank and forced him to give up Petersburg and Richmond, sixteen Yankees earned the award. The next day, another seventeen were earned as Grant and Meade pressed into the Petersburg fortifications. Only one was earned on April 3 and another on April 4, but then on the 5th, eight more medals were bestowed for skirmishes at Paine's Crossroads and Amelia Springs as Grant pursued Lee.

Then came April 6 and the Battle of Sayler's Creek. Fully fifty Medals of Honor were awarded just for flag captures alone, among them Tom Custer's. In all, 103 medals went to men of this army just for flag captures in those nine days, while other acts of daring and bravery raised the total number awarded to 155. In short, 13 percent of all the Medals of Honor given in the Civil War went to men in just one army, for barely more than a week's campaign against a retreating foe.

This is not to say that the men who earned them were not just as entitled as other recipients. It merely reflects the somewhat haphazard way in which the medal was given in its early years, as well as the constant preoccupation of Washington with its army in Virginia. And commanders with Grant, knowing that this must surely be their last campaign, may have been overzealous in trying to garner recognition for their men before they all returned to civilian life.

Indeed, the preoccupation with the Medal of Honor did not end with the war. Already men recognized it as a special badge of gallantry, prized by those who earned it, coveted by those who had not. If General Custer's often imaginative widow could be believed, a general officer of their acquaintance, upon seeing Tom Custer's *two* medals, declared that he would rather have earned one of those for capturing a flag than all the promotions the War Department had given him.

The story of the Medal of Honor for Civil War exploits did not end when the war itself came to a close. For one thing, there were men who had been granted the award who had not

Thomas Custer, the only soldier to receive two Medals of Honor in the Civil War.

# THE ROLL OF HONOR:
## AN AWARD FROM THE CONFEDERACY

Many Americans distinguished themselves in Civil War battles but were not eligible for the Medal of Honor. These men fought for the Confederacy. But, while Rebel soldiers could not receive the medal, they were cited for the highest award of the Confederate States of America and listed on its Roll of Honor, the closest the South ever came to its own Medal of Honor.

Like their counterparts in Washington, Confederate representatives and senators in Richmond favored the creation of an award for individual valor. In the fall of 1862, such a measure passed both chambers and was sent to President Jefferson Davis, who signed it into law on October 13. In language similar to the Union resolutions of the past year, the Confederate bill directed:

> That the President be, and he is hereby authorized to bestow medals, with proper devices, upon such officers of the armies of the Confederate States as shall be conspicuous for courage and good conduct on the field of battle, and also to confer a badge of distinction upon one private or non-commissioned officer of each company after every signal victory it shall have assisted to achieve.

The law made no provision for a medal for the Confederate navy.

In a radical departure from the tradition exemplified by the Union awards, the act mandated that enlisted men would be selected for the medals by majority vote of the men themselves. Such a democratic method of bestowing decorations was virtually unheard of. This was more than a typical campaign medal; only a select few from each battle would be recognized by their peers.

Delays in the creation of the medal, however, threatened to dilute the Confederate award's impact on the ranks of Southern soldiers. In October 1863, almost one full year after the original act, the Adjutant and Inspector General's Office of the Confederacy published an order

acknowledging "difficulties in procuring the medals and badges of distinction" promised earlier. "To avoid postponing the grateful recognition of [the men's] valor until it can be made in the enduring form provided by the act," the order established a "Roll of Honor," with the name of each man cited, to be read before every regiment and published in at least one newspaper in every Confederate state.

Two Rolls of Honor distributed in 1864 listed a man from each company from several battles. In the engagement at Seven Pines, Virginia, in June 1862, for example, nine men from the 8th Infantry Regiment were cited, although no mention was made of their particular actions. The details of elections to the roll are sparse, but the diary of a Confederate captain provides an example of a company election for the roll. Robert Emory Park of the 12th Alabama Regiment wrote the following entry for May 19 and 20, 1863, when his regiment was encamped at Macon, Georgia:

> The election held to decide who of the company should wear the "Badge of Honor" for gallantry at Chancellorsville resulted in twelve votes each for Sergeant Wright and Private Chappell. In drawing [as for lots or straws], the latter won, and his name was sent to General Lee.

The Confederate medals were never struck. Nor do any proposed designs survive. In May 1864, a Tennessee representative stood in the Confederate House chamber to ask what progress was being made on the medals and if any further legislation was needed to hasten their creation. There, any mention of the awards in the official records ends. The tide of the conflict had turned against the South, and within a year the Confederacy would be crushed, its medals forgotten, and its heroes never to be recognized by a badge of honor.

# SERGEANT CARNEY'S FLAG

The call for African American Union soldiers in late 1862 convinced William H. Carney to forgo his plans for the ministry. "I felt I could best serve my God by serving my country and my oppressed brothers," he later remembered. Enlisting in the 54th Massachusetts Colored Infantry in February 1863, the twenty-three-year-old former slave was soon in the thick of the fighting.

In the early afternoon of July 18, 1863, Sergeant Carney and the six hundred men of the 54th charged along a narrow stretch of sand outside the Confederate stronghold at Fort Wagner, South Carolina. Artillery shells of both sides whistled all around as they pushed forward.

Suddenly, the color bearer was hit by an enemy bullet. Carney threw aside his rifle and seized the flag before it fell. Rebel fire pierced his leg, but Carney made it to the shadow of the fort and planted the colors.

After thirty minutes, the Yankees fell back with heavy losses. When Confederate soldiers charged his position, Carney wrapped the flag around the staff and ran back to the Union lines, stumbling through a ditch filled waist-deep with water. Enemy bullets struck his chest, right arm, and right leg, but he kept crawling to the rear. Carney was grazed in the head but refused to let a New York soldier take the flag, saying, "No one but a member of the 54th should carry the colors."

Back at the Union camp, Carney was cheered by the men of his regiment as he proudly proclaimed, "Boys, I only did my duty. The flag never touched the ground."

Several months later, propped on a cane from his injuries, Carney posed with the standard for which he had risked his life. Though he did not receive his medal until 1900, his was the first Civil War exploit by an African American man to merit the Medal of Honor.

*Sergeant William Carney saved this Union flag at Fort Wagner, South Carolina.*

yet received it. Some survivors of battle never knew they had been honored with the award. Sergeant Llewellyn Norton of the 10th New York Cavalry had jumped his horse over the enemy works at Sayler's Creek and ridden straight for the six Confederates manning a field piece. He demanded their surrender, knocked aside the rifles of two with his saber, and finally captured them all with the assistance of another soldier. Both were awarded the medal on July 5, 1865, but Norton's regiment had already mustered out of service, and no one could find him. It was twenty-three years later that Norton, reading through a volume of Appleton's *Cyclopedia*, found his own name in a list of medal recipients and got in touch with the War Department.

In the years that followed the war, there was time to reflect on the way in which the medal had been given and who had received it. More than that, the War Department began looking into the matter of those deserving soldiers who had not received it. No doubt this was spurred in large part by the increasingly powerful veterans' lobby in the 1880s and 1890s, and especially by the enormously influential Grand Army of the Republic (G.A.R.). It may have been no accident that the veterans' organization chose an adaptation of the five-pointed medal as its own emblem.

As a result, in the 1890s especially, scores of medals were sent out to men who were recommended, and others were awarded even into the twentieth century. Beyond this, and often with the backing of the G.A.R. or influential officers or politicians, some men actually took it on themselves to apply to the War Department for the medal, submitting affidavits from wartime comrades as to their heroic service. Of course, there was always a danger in this, since now and then the affidavits were not all that complimentary. In May 1864 in the Shenandoah, at the Battle of New Market, Lt. Charles Hausmann's inefficiency helped lead to the loss of a cannon during that Federal defeat. In 1891 he, nevertheless, applied to the War Department for the medal in recognition of his services in the valley. One of his comrades who had seen Hausmann's folly attested, instead, that the government should give "such a gallant Nature a Medal of good Lasting Shoeleather." Hausmann never got his award.

And in time, mature thought led to the conclusion that in some cases the medal had been bestowed too readily, that the acts of some recipients simply did not stand up to the increasingly higher standards being set with the passing years. Consequently, many of the medals awarded during the Civil War came under review, and 911 were actually revoked, most of them from the 27th Maine (see page 37). It was one of the growing pains of a distinction created in the confusion and pain of war, with too little advance thought given to its intent and requirements. For all that having their medals taken away outraged those few who lost them, it was a step in the direction of making the medal more meaningful for those who would wear it in the future.

Born in chaos, administered haphazardly, sometimes misused for political purposes or military expedient, still the Medal of Honor stood at the pinnacle of soldierly aspirations by 1865. It had honored the bravery of hundreds and inspired the heroism of hundreds more. Most of all, it had begun a tradition of daring, of men reaching beyond themselves, whether to smite their foe or save a comrade or simply to take from the enemy that which he prized most, his battle flags. It captured, in its way, the spirit of the times.

In the years that followed the war, there was time to reflect on the way in which the medal had been given and who had received it.

CHAPTER TWO

# The Indian Campaigns

## 1861–1898

# Wars for the American Frontier

**B**RAVE MEN WHO WENT WEST with the Army after the Civil War discovered that more than bravery was needed to wrest control of the frontier lands from the many Native American tribes and nations collectively known as Indians. The soldiers and officers of the Civil War had known combat on a grand scale: artillery battles and massed troops, cavalry and infantry charges taking their toll by the thousands. On the frontier, small groups of soldiers confronted a foe adept in the tactics of guerrilla warfare. The Army regulars who fought in the West endured days of frustration and toil on endless marches, followed by moments of terror in sudden, running battles against an elusive enemy.

The same brutal strategy that had speeded the capitulation of the South in the Civil War eventually worked with equal success against the Indians. General William Tecumseh Sherman, who had burned a swath of destruction across the green fields of Georgia, fought the Indians with the same sort of ferocity. Sherman and his successor as western commander, Gen. Phil H. Sheridan, were extraordinarily effective. In 1865, over 270,000 Indians lived west of the Mississippi. Within thirty years, the Army had forced this huge population into the reservation system and brought an end to the conflict.

Many white Americans considered it their "Manifest Destiny" to expand westward, and most believed in the white prerogative to remove the Indians who stood in the way. Unwilling to be assimilated into white civilization, Indians tried to use war or treaties to preserve their land. The constant flow of white immigrants, however, demanded more land, and the treaties became unenforceable as white settlers, supported by the government, continued to march west.

White easterners at first believed that the Great Plains were a wasteland, and while that belief endured, the Plains Indians were undisturbed. In the 1840s, the southern plains of Kansas, Oklahoma, and the Texas panhandle were inhabited by the Cheyennes, the Kiowas, and the Comanches. Farther southwest, near the Arizona and New Mexico border with Mexico, the Apaches dominated. In the north, the Sioux, allied with the Northern Cheyennes, routed weaker tribes such as the Crows and Shoshones. The powerful Sioux held sway over land stretching from the Mississippi River in Minnesota to the Big Horn Mountains of Wyoming in the north, and as far south as the Platte and Republican rivers of Nebraska and Kansas.

The discovery of gold in California and in the Rockies brought thousands of whites westward and radically disrupted Indian life. The Homestead Act of 1862 opened vast areas

*Previous pages*
US scouts under Maj. George Forsyth (center, with rifle and pistol) hold out against Cheyenne warriors at Beecher's Island, Colorado, in September 1868.

of farmland to any white pioneer hardy enough to claim it. The railroads sliced through the Indians' hunting lands and brought more settlements along their routes. During the Civil War, state militia and volunteers of the wartime US Army patrolled the frontier. These men had to face an often-explosive situation created by the burgeoning movement of the settlers and miners to the west.

A major episode during the Civil War stands out. Elements of the Cheyenne, Kiowa, Comanche, and Arapahoe tribes had left their Colorado territory reservations to raid the surrounding countryside. On November 29, 1864, Col. John Chivington and his seven hundred volunteers rode into the camp of Black Kettle, a Cheyenne chief who had actually sought peace, at Sand Creek in Colorado. The volunteers went on a rampage of killing and mutilation, leaving 133 dead, 105 of them women and children. The memory of Sand Creek hardened the Indians' attitude toward all of the soldiers who wore the blue uniform. The soldiers who followed Chivington's volunteers west were to pay for the atrocity.

Sherman's regular army troops replaced the volunteer forces after the Civil War. The men who came west were a varied lot, and they had enlisted for reasons that were as diverse as their backgrounds. George A. Forsyth, a major during the Indian Wars, recalled a wagon escort that included "a bookkeeper, a farm boy, a dentist, and a blacksmith, a young man of position trying to gain a commission and a salesman ruined by drink, an ivory carver and a Bowery tough." Nearly half were recent immigrants, mainly from Ireland, Germany, and England. Many were illiterate, although a few formed library clubs and literary societies.

They went to an unforgiving country, wild and desolate. Their posts were islands in the ocean of plains, sometimes hundreds of miles away from what they would deem to be civilization. If a soldier was lucky, he lived in a wooden barracks and slept on a straw-filled mattress on a wooden-slatted bunk. He kept his possessions in a wooden footlocker or on a single wooden shelf that ran along the length of the barracks wall. Heat came from a cast-iron stove, light from kerosene lamps or candles. Most posts were not so sumptuous. One soldier described his accommodations at Fort Selden, New Mexico, as "huts of logs and round stones, with flat dirt roofs that in summer leaked and brought down rivulets of liquid mud . . . in the winter the hiding place of the tarantula and centipede."

In all cases, the food was abominable. Regular fare included salt pork, fried corn mush, beans, coffee, and hardtack or bread, with little variation. The salt pork sometimes arrived full of worms, or "yellow with age and bitter as quinine," or so rancid that the meat was sloughing off the fat. The flour often was speckled with weevils. The meals were almost always ill-prepared because the men took turns on cooking detail.

Far from the anticipated glory of the call to arms, a trooper found that his every waking moment was monitored, controlled by bugle calls. Bugles called him to a round of unending toil from reveille at 6:00 a.m., through fatigue duty, drills, and guard duty, to taps at 9:30 at night. He was a captive laborer on faraway posts, employed to construct and maintain telegraph lines and roads, to build and add to his fort, to serve as a logger and water carrier, and to work kitchen and stable details. For these duties, in addition to his main job of policing the West, the private was paid sixteen dollars a month until 1870, when Congress lowered his pay to thirteen dollars.

The job these troops did was to fight the "hardest kind of war" against a skillful opponent.

Their posts were islands in the ocean of plains, sometimes hundreds of miles away from what they would deem to be civilization.

It was fighting marked by long, often fruitless, marches of fifteen miles or more a day through all kinds of terrain and weather. They frequently spent weeks in the field without contact with Indians. When a fight came, it came quickly and brutally. In such a battle there was no calling for help. The soldiers were cut off, dependent on the reserves they had brought in with them. The Medal of Honor was often earned in such circumstances, especially when small groups fought with little hope of rescue. The bluecoat knew that if he allowed himself to be captured, he would surely face a painful death, often slowly, by torture. A maxim of the soldiers was, "Save the last bullet for yourself."

Culpability for the Indian Wars could often be traced to the actions of the government or of white civilians: Miners moved into Indian territory regardless of treaties; settlers squatted on Indian land; white hunters killed the precious buffalo until there were no more to kill. The agents of the Indian Bureau were often corrupt, cheating the Indians of their rightful due under treaty provisions. The government vacillated, changing policy and abrogating treaties, adapting its actions to political expediency.

A maximum of twenty-five thousand soldiers fought the wars that others had provoked over two million square miles of frontier. The Indian Wars, which included actions such as Sand Creek and Wounded Knee, represent the darker side of American history, and the soldiers on the western frontier have been stigmatized by the uglier aspects of the job they were sent to do. Brave men often fought in dishonorable circumstances, but that did not diminish the fact of their courage.

By 1890, the Census Bureau declared there was no longer a line of frontier anywhere in the United States. The agent of this change in the West had been the regular US Army. In the quarter-century after the Civil War, the Army fought more than a thousand combat actions in twenty-four operations officially designated as wars, campaigns, or expeditions. Nearly all of the Medals of Honor awarded for the Indian Wars were for actions of valor during these western campaigns.

## CLASH ON THE SOUTHERN PLAINS
*The Red River*

By 1874, the southern Plains Indians—the Kiowas, Cheyennes, and Comanches—had grown increasingly restive on their Oklahoma reservations. Opportunistic traders cheated them. Moreover, white buffalo hunters killed so many animals that the American bison, mainstay of the Plains Indians life, began to disappear.

On June 27, 1874, a group of Comanche, Kiowa, and Cheyenne raiders led by Lone Wolf, the Kiowa chief, attacked a settlement of twenty-eight buffalo hunters at Adobe Walls, Texas. The hunters, with their powerful rifles, beat the Indians badly. In revenge, the Indian survivors of the attack went on a rampage of raiding and killing from Texas to Kansas.

When the Army moved onto the reservation to separate hostile Indians from peaceful, most of the hostiles left and headed west, to their hunting grounds near the Red River in the Texas panhandle. General Sheridan responded by flooding the area with soldiers.

Colonel Nelson Miles's column of 744 troops fought a decisive battle on August 30 at the Staked Plains, deep in the panhandle of Texas. During the course of the fight, Miles chased the

*The Indian Wars, which included actions such as Sand Creek and Wounded Knee, represent the darker side of American history . . .*

raiders over a long stretch of the panhandle and far outstripped his supplies. Miles ordered Capt. Wyllys Lyman to take a detachment of 6th Cavalry and a company of 5th Infantry and ride north to escort a wagon train that was coming from Camp Supply in northern Oklahoma territory.

After several days without word from Lyman, Colonel Miles ordered dispatches carried to Camp Supply, presumably to discover the fate of Lyman and the supply train. In the group were four cavalrymen, Sgt. Zachariah Woodall and Pvts. John Harrington, George Smith, and Peter Roth. They were accompanied by two civilian scouts, Amos Chapman and Billy Dixon. Each man carried a rifle, a Colt revolver, and 200 rounds of ammunition. They would need it all.

On September 11, the first day of the journey, they traveled nearly fifty miles without incident, but at mid-morning on the twelfth, Chapman caught sight of a large number of horsemen in the distance and assumed that they were a party from Camp Supply. Too late they realized that the riders were Indians. On the treeless, rolling prairie there was no cover, so the six men made for a ravine, reaching it just before the Indians could mount a charge. They leaped from their horses to form a skirmish line. Smith took charge of the animals but was shot in the chest almost immediately. The horses stampeded away as he fell. The Indians dismounted and formed a circle around the men. Each time they drew near, the five other men charged madly, firing at the Indians in front of them, while the Indians in the rear held their fire for fear of hitting their own. The men broke through the circle several times, requiring the Indians to re-form. All the while the white men moved toward a nearby hill where there was a shallow buffalo wallow about ten feet across.

The Indians now mounted their horses and attacked with astounding displays of horsemanship. Some rode standing high in the stirrups while firing, then dropped suddenly as if hit and fired again from below their horses' bellies. Others fell to the ground as if they had been shot, then leaped up from behind some tall grass to open fire. Four of the whites were wounded: Woodall was hit in the groin and Harrington in the hip, but both reached the wallow, as did Dixon, who was grazed in the calf, and Roth, who was uninjured. Smith and Chapman lay outside the wallow. The others thought Smith was dead; Chapman's ankle was so badly shot the bone stuck out and his foot dragged uselessly behind him as he crawled toward the others.

Colonel Nelson Miles, a Civil War Medal of Honor recipient and Army commander in the West.

*Twenty-Five to One*, by Frederic Remington, depicts the ambush of Miles's couriers.

# WINNING THE WEST

The army that carried out US policy in the West traveled and fought over great distances. Quartered in spartan forts and often short of supplies, troopers used horses for transportation to outlying areas.

*Lieutenant William H. Carter, who earned the Medal of Honor at Cibecue Creek, Arizona, in 1881.*

*A young gallant astride his mount at Camp Cheyenne, circa 1890.*

*Soldiers on horseback plod through the snow in the return of Army Lt. Edward Casey's Cheyenne scouts from the fight at Wounded Knee, 1890.*

*Near Fort Bayard, New Mexico, men of the 6th US Cavalry train their horses to lie down to provide cover under fire.*

*View of a cavalry camp, 1891.*

Dixon saw Chapman pulling himself inch by inch along the ground. He broke from cover, ran out, and carried him in.

A thunderstorm arose from the southwest and gathered force, the sky growing blacker every moment. During the storm the Indians withdrew a short distance and tied up their horses. Roth used the respite to retrieve Smith's much-needed ammunition belt and was astounded to see the wounded man twitch. He returned to the wallow, and then set out a second time with Dixon to rescue Smith. They carried him back, but the valiant effort was in vain. Smith, shot through the lung and begging to be put out of his misery, died during the night. The others propped up his body to make the Indians think that he was still alive.

They decided to divide the ammunition and send the relatively able-bodied Roth and Dixon for help. Roth set out first, in the middle of the night, but was unable to find a trail. When he returned, Dixon waited until dawn and left with only four cartridges in his gun. He had traveled just a mile when he came upon Major Price's 8th Cavalry, who returned with him to rescue his comrades.

The Army awarded all six of the men the Medal of Honor, but later revoked the awards to the two civilian scouts because by law they were not eligible to receive it. Smith's medal was rare because it was not a common practice to give the medal posthumously during the Indian wars: Only eight such medals were awarded.

# CUSTER'S LAST STAND
## *The Little Bighorn*

The 1868 Laramie Treaty guaranteed the Black Hills of Dakota Territory to the Sioux as part of their reservation. But when gold was discovered on the land in 1874, white miners entered the reservation illegally. The government attempted to buy the Black Hills, but the Sioux refused to sell land they considered sacred. Many of the Indians left the reservation for Wyoming and Montana, where they joined Indians who had never come into the reservation. In December of 1875, the government delivered an ultimatum to the group's ostensible leader, Sitting Bull: Come into the agency by January 31, 1876, or face war. The Indian ignored the demand and war began.

The war that was to culminate at a small river called Little Bighorn began when General Sheridan determined to strike quickly and bring the Sioux into the reservation. But a winter campaign in the North proved considerably more difficult than one in the South. General George Crook and his men battled snow and cold for three weeks in the field before returning empty-handed and exhausted.

When spring came in 1876, the Army pressed on. Three large and mobile columns of troops marched toward eastern Montana to encircle and trap the Indians. In May, General Crook pushed north from Fort Fetterman, Wyoming, with more than a thousand soldiers, and Col. John Gibbon marched his 5th Infantry east from Fort Ellis, Montana. On May 17, the "Dakota Command" of Gen. Alfred H. Terry left Fort Abraham Lincoln, Dakota Territory, with over 925 men, 700 of whom were troops of the 7th Cavalry under the command of Lt. Col. George Armstrong Custer.

Custer had been the boy wonder of the Civil War. At the age of twenty-five he had been brevetted to Major General. Following the war he took a commission as a lieutenant colonel

Lieutenant Colonel George A. Custer, whose impetuosity brought disaster down on him and his men at the Little Bighorn.

in the Army and went west, where his long and flowing yellow hair, his buckskin clothing, and his flair for the dramatic caught the attention of the nation's press.

His flamboyance embroiled him in numerous controversies in his ten years in the West, but his penchant for attack and his aggressiveness put him at the heart of the Indian Wars. In the winter of 1868–1869 he attacked the village of the unfortunate Black Kettle, victim of the earlier attack at Sand Creek by Colonel Chivington. Custer's rakehell charge left 101 Cheyenne men, women, and children dead (including Black Kettle and his wife) and was hailed as a victory for Sheridan's policy of a winter war of attrition. Custer thereafter remained one of Sheridan's favorites.

In 1874, Custer led an expedition of four hundred civilians and one thousand soldiers into the Black Hills. Among his reports, Custer sent back word that there was "gold among the roots of the grass." This news brought an influx of miners to the Black Hills, which in turn ignited war.

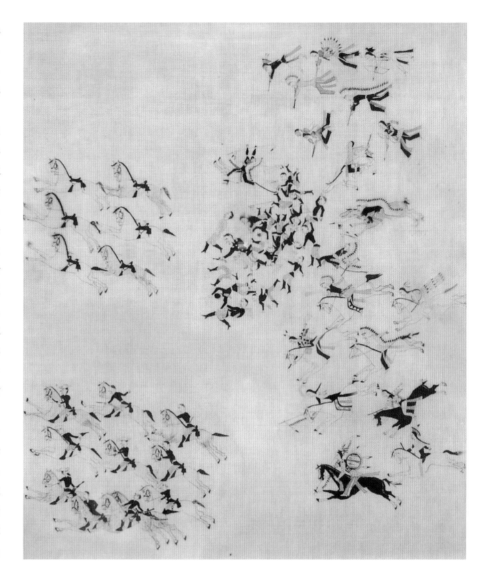

Using pigment on muslin, the Indian White Bird painted this view of Custer's last fight, 1894–1895.

Crook was the first to encounter the Indians in 1876. On June 17, his column fought a heated battle at Rosebud Creek against a much larger force than he had expected to find. (Later reports of Sioux and Cheyenne strength in the region ranged from 2,500 to 4,500 warriors.) After six hours of heavy fighting, the Indians withdrew. Crook claimed victory, but his losses of twenty-eight killed and fifty-six wounded were significant. He withdrew to his supply base at Goose Creek, eighty miles away, to await reinforcements.

That same day, Gen. Alfred Terry's column was closing in on the Indians from the east. On the twenty-first, Terry met with Gibbon and Custer to map a strategy for the campaign. The attack would target the Little Bighorn River, where scouts had seen fires from a large Indian village.

The plan called for Gibbon's 5th Infantry and Custer's 7th Cavalry to rendezvous, then attack on June 26. The night of the twenty-fourth, Custer led his men to within twenty miles of the Indian encampment and sent out scouts. When they returned to say they had seen dust from the Indian camp, Custer feared the Sioux were escaping.

Rather than wait for the arrival of the slower-moving infantry force, he decided to go ahead alone on the morning of Sunday, June 25, a day earlier than planned. He sent

Sergeant Benjamin Criswell, who recovered the body of Lieutenant Hodgson from the banks of the Little Bighorn.

Maj. Marcus Reno out with 112 men to attack from the south. Captain Frederick Benteen took 125 men in a wide arc farther west to enter from that direction, while Custer himself attacked from the northeast.

Reno surprised the Sioux, but they rallied quickly. The 1,200-lodge village proved to contain three times as many Indians as expected. Reno ordered his men to form a skirmish line, but resistance proved too fierce. He was forced to withdraw to a cottonwood grove near the banks of the river, where the battle raged. When the Indians pressed their attack, the major gave the order to cross to the bluffs on the other side of the Little Bighorn.

The men crossed the river in a mad, disorganized retreat, stranding several cavalrymen on the opposite bank in the noisy chaos. Of 112 men in Major Reno's initial force, three officers and twenty-nine regulars and scouts had been killed, and one officer and fifteen men were missing.

One officer, Lt. Benjamin Hodgson, had his leg broken by a bullet that also brought down his horse. Sergeant Benjamin Criswell rode to the rescue, waited while the wounded man grabbed hold of his stirrup, then dragged the wounded man across the river onto the opposite side. As they reached the bank, though, Hodgson was shot and fell lifeless.

Criswell dismounted under fire, threw the lieutenant's body over his horse, then moved along the riverbank picking up saddlebags full of ammunition. The Medal of Honor was his reward for performing so coolly under pressure and for the selfless attempt to bring his lieutenant to safety.

Reno and his remaining men turned back to the bluff where they had dug in earlier in the afternoon. During the retreat, one of the pack mules, laden with ammunition, became frightened at the firing, broke away from its handler, and started running in the direction of the advancing Indians.

Sergeant Richard Hanley grabbed his horse and rode to head the mule off. The mule eluded him, running first one way along the line and then the other. His officers shouted for him to give up the effort, but he remained in the open for twenty minutes under a rain of fire until he captured the mule. He brought it and its precious cargo back, to loud cheers from his lines. A Medal of Honor later punctuated those cheers for his gallantry.

Benteen's men joined Reno on the bluff. Impassable ravines had blocked the westward attack route. The men dodged Indian sniper fire until 5:00 p.m. when they attempted to move northward to join Custer's group. By the time the detachment crossed a ridge where they could see the Custer battlefield, Indians were galloping in their direction. All firing had ceased.

According to Indian witnesses of the battle, Custer was shot in the chest as he led his men across the Little Bighorn. The attack disintegrated, and the troopers retreated to a ridge on the east side of the river, their leader propped up in his saddle for the ride.

All 215 of Custer's men were killed in the ensuing battle, including his brother Tom, who had received two Medals of Honor for capturing Confederate flags in the Civil War. The Sioux Rain-in-the-Face later claimed that he cut out Tom Custer's heart and bit off a piece of it and spit it in his face to avenge an earlier insult. Their brother Boston, brother-in-law James Calhoun, and nephew Henry Reed also fell to the Indians in the debacle.

After Custer's defeat, the Army pursued the Sioux and Northern Cheyennes relentlessly. The troopers of Col. Ranald S. Mackenzie and Col. Nelson Miles campaigned throughout the next winter despite great hardship. By spring nearly all of the fugitives had surrendered.

Crazy Horse came in on May 6, 1877. Sitting Bull, however, eluded the soldiers who were hounding him. He took the remnants of his people to Canada, where they lived peacefully but could not find enough to eat. Many of his followers filtered back to the United States and to the reservation. Finally, in July of 1881, Sitting Bull followed. When he turned in his rifle to Miles he stated, "I was the last man of my tribe to surrender my rifle."

After years of research, Edgar Paxson painted this reconstruction of Custer's end. Custer is at center, in buckskins.

Chief Joseph, who led the Nez Perces on their doomed 1,700-mile trek to seek safety in Canada.

# "I WILL FIGHT NO MORE"

## *The Nez Perces*

During the summer and fall of 1877, eastern newspapers were filled with stories about an Indian chief who led his people on a desperate flight from Army troops in Oregon, Idaho, and Montana. Chief Joseph was hailed by some as the "Indian Napoleon." In fact, Joseph was a peaceful man who wanted only to return to the land of his birth.

When gold was discovered on their land in the Wallowa Valley of Oregon in 1863, some Nez Perces signed a treaty in which they agreed to leave. Elements of the tribe, however, refused to sign and stayed in their homeland. In May of 1877, the Department of the Interior requested the Army remove the Indians by force if they would not leave peacefully. So began a desperate flight that covered over 1,700 miles.

General Oliver Otis Howard gave Joseph, leader of the Wallowa Valley Nez Perces, an ultimatum: Leave the Wallowa within a month or face war. Chief Joseph left the valley for the assigned reservation, but on June 13, some of his young warriors got drunk, slipped away from camp, returned to the valley, and killed four white settlers. In the next two nights, the young warriors killed at least fifteen more whites.

Joseph, knowing that a retaliatory war was now inevitable, gathered his people and pushed east, hoping to escape the army and reach the buffalo hunting grounds on the other side of the Rockies. On the evening of June 16, the Nez Perces camped on the banks of the Salmon River near White Bird Canyon in Idaho. Scouts told Joseph that soldiers were approaching.

In the early morning hours of June 17, Joseph deployed his warriors along the ridges of the hills inside White Bird Canyon. Lieutenant Edward R. Thellar led three groups into the canyon: an advance guard of regulars, a detachment of Oregon volunteers, and a column of ninety soldiers who took up the rear.

They were met by a Nez Perce truce party displaying a white flag. When the volunteers ignored the flag and opened fire, Chief Joseph's warriors returned fire with deadly effect. The volunteers quickly moved to a knoll, but Thellar and his advance guard were trapped under fire in a ravine down below. The column of regulars moved forward into the canyon and set up a skirmish line. Sergeant Michael McCarthy was ordered to take a detail of six men and hold, at all costs, the high, rocky ground to the right.

The Indians pressed forward on foot in a well-organized, relentless attack. The volunteers on the left broke and ran, leaving the left flank of the column exposed. McCarthy, on the right, held his post and continued to fire, but the inexperienced troopers in the column took their cue from the escaping volunteers and turned and ran, leaving Thellar and his advance party cut off at the front. All eighteen of them were soon killed. McCarthy, also abandoned along with his six-man detail, remained in position and beat back an attack.

Meanwhile, Lt. William R. Parnell and other officers followed the men who had fled, trying to rally them to counterattack. Parnell led a small detachment to rescue McCarthy and his troops, who were then fighting their way back out of the canyon. By the time the two groups met, two of McCarthy's men had been killed. Parnell organized his and McCarthy's men, a combined force of fourteen, and executed a disciplined retreat toward the mouth of the canyon. During this withdrawal, McCarthy's horse was shot from under him and he became separated from the others. Parnell returned to rescue another man whose horse had

Amid the bodies of men and horses, Chief Joseph declares an end to his struggle.

been shot, but McCarthy's plight went unnoticed.

McCarthy dashed for a nearby creek where there was a large clump of bushes in which he tried to hide himself. From his cover, he could see the rest of his outfit slowly retreating with Parnell, away from the Indians who were now running past the bushes where he hid. McCarthy next saw that a number of Nez Perce women had moved into the area and were picking clean the bodies of the dead soldiers. To his horror, he noticed that his own boots were sticking out of the brush and had been seen by one of the Indian women. He carefully slipped out of them and crawled farther into the undergrowth.

Bootless, horseless, and without ammunition, he waited for nightfall. When it grew dark, he crawled down the creek bed and continued into the forest and mountains. He wandered through the territory, traveling only at night and hiding during the day. After three days of walking, he made contact with the 1st Cavalry at Mount Idaho. His intrepidity was not to go unnoticed. He and Parnell both received the Medal of Honor for their bravery at White Bird Canyon.

For the Nez Perces, the battle represented the beginning of the longest and most desperate odyssey of the Indian Wars. With General Howard in pursuit, the Indians traveled steadily east, winding their way through the Rockies. They fought pitched battles as they crossed Idaho, first at Clearwater, then at the Big Hole River, and finally at Camas Meadows. As expert Nez Perce marksmen covered his withdrawal, Chief Joseph escaped after each of these battles. Often suffering heavy losses, he led the remnants of his people deeper into the Rockies. They crossed the newly established Yellowstone National Park and made their way to Montana, where they fought again at Canyon Creek. General Sherman, alarmed at the Indians' progress, alerted Col. Nelson Miles to cut off the retreat from the east.

On a cold, clear September 30, Miles's column came upon the trail of the Nez Perces and followed it to Bear Paw Mountain. When the Indian village came into view, Miles ordered the 7th Cavalry, newly replenished after its decimation at the Little Bighorn the year before, to charge directly into the tepees while the 2nd Cavalry stampeded the ponies.

The surprise was not total. They had caught the Indians in place, but the Nez Perces were ready to fight. Warriors found cover in deep ravines carved by water into the hillsides and opened fire, concentrating mainly on the officers and NCOs. Within minutes, all of the advancing officers were either dead or wounded. The charge of the 7th faltered as the dead toppled from their horses and the living dismounted to take cover. Seeing that the charge would fail without leadership, Lt. Henry Romeyn of the 5th Infantry mounted one of the captured Indian ponies and rode forward into the fray to join the embattled cavalrymen.

Romeyn ordered the troopers to remount and follow him. They tore down a steep hill into the fire of the Indian snipers, and Romeyn led them almost upon the Indians before he was shot. The bullet hit on the right side of his chest, breaking one rib as it entered and another as it exited near his spine. Another shot from the fusillade ricocheted off his shoulder and tore his ear. Sergeant Henry Hogan of the 5th Infantry earned his second Medal of Honor of the Indian Wars by risking his life to rescue Romeyn. He rushed forward, picked up the lieutenant, and carried him from danger. (Hogan's first came for actions in the 1876–1877 winter campaign against the Sioux.) Romeyn also received the medal for his courageous charge.

After besieging the camp for five days, Miles negotiated the Indians' surrender. After his three months of keeping the army at bay, Chief Joseph spoke the words that expressed the weariness the Indian felt at trying to defeat an inexorable force: "Hear me, my chiefs! I am tired; my heart is sick and sad. From where the sun now stands I will fight no more forever."

# FIGHTING APACHES
### *The Pursuit of Geronimo*

In 1886, the Apaches were brought permanently within the reservation system—the last Native Americans to be subdued. They had fought in the Southwest for over three centuries against the white man—first against the Spanish, then the Mexicans and Americans. They had earned a reputation as feared and cunning guerrilla fighters. More Medals of Honor, nearly half the total for the Indian Wars, were given for actions against the Apaches than against any other tribe.

The US Army had repeatedly forced the Apaches into the reservation at San Carlos, Arizona, between 1871 and 1886, but the Indians had not been easily contained. Located near Fort Apache in eastern Arizona, San Carlos lay on desert land where farming was difficult at best. The reservation was overcrowded. When rations were short, people went hungry and some starved. For Apaches who left the reservation and became renegades, life offered adventure, riches and livestock from raiding, and a chance to live the old life in hideouts such as the Sierra Madre Mountains of Mexico.

The Chiricahua Apache war chief, Geronimo, was an intermittent resident of San Carlos. The Chiricahuas were ordered to San Carlos in 1876, but Geronimo refused to comply. He was captured and brought there in shackles. A year later, he left to join another chief, Juh, in Mexico. The Mexican army forced them back to the United States and San Carlos. There, Geronimo and his people lived in relative peace on the reservation for several years.

The Apache leader Geronimo strikes a fierce pose in this 1886 photograph.

In the summer of 1881, the Army increased its presence at San Carlos Reservation. Geronimo, nervous about the number of troops in his midst, left with seventy-four of his followers. He returned to lead a raid that released other Apaches while killing the white police commissioner of the reservation. Then he headed for Mexico and the Sierra Madre Mountains.

In September of 1882, Gen. George Crook organized 250 Apache scouts into five companies, put Army officers in charge, and sent them into Mexico to find Geronimo. This Indianized US Army was able to enter land in which no American or Mexican white man had previously traveled. The battles fought within their own strongholds induced the Apaches to negotiate.

Crook returned the Apaches to San Carlos in March of 1884. But again the reservation could not hold them. In May 1885, Geronimo and Nachez, son of the great chief Cochise, and 130 followers left. Crook's border patrols could not prevent the Apaches from raiding back into New Mexico and Arizona. By winter, a new expedition was mounted. Led by Capt. Emmett Crawford, this group rode until a scout found a hostile camp in a Sierra Madre gorge near jagged peaks that formed the so-called Devil's Backbone. They struggled down treacherous pathways into the gorge, but the braying of Apache mules gave them away. The Apaches fled. Troops burned the empty camp and supplies. Suddenly an old woman appeared and told Crawford that Geronimo and Nachez were ready to talk. They arranged a conference for the next day, January 11, 1886.

Mexican soldiers who had been trailing the Apaches interrupted that plan. They came upon Crawford's Apache scouts and, believing them to be Geronimo's people, opened fire. Crawford shouted for them to stop, running forward with Lt. Marion Maus of the 1st Cavalry, who spoke Spanish. The Mexican soldiers held their fire but remained suspicious when they saw the Apaches reloading their rifles. Crawford, Maus, and the Mexican officers proceeded to parlay in the middle of the camp. But suddenly a shot rang out, followed by an explosion of fire from both sides. The Mexican officers fell from their horses, and Crawford had been wounded in the head. Maus took command, and after a blazing two-hour standoff, the firing ceased. An uneasy truce gave both sides time to care for their wounded.

The next day the Mexicans summoned Maus. After six hours of uneasy negotiations, Maus agreed to let them have some horses to carry their wounded out of the mountains. He was then allowed to return to camp and withdraw with his men. The next morning, his group started back up the mountain, carrying Crawford and the other wounded on litters. That first day the climb was so treacherous they covered only three miles. After they had stopped for the night, again an Apache woman entered the camp to say that Geronimo would negotiate.

Maus, scout Tom Horn, and five of the Indian scouts arrived unarmed, as Geronimo demanded, at the prearranged site. Geronimo and his men, however, were equipped with

Left to right: Buffalo Bill Cody, Gen. Nelson Miles, Capt. Frank Baldwin, and Capt. Marion P. Maus, surveying an Indian camp.

Wearing his Medal of Honor, Marion Maus stands for a wedding portrait. The party includes a young officer named John J. Pershing (third row left), later to become the commander of US forces in World War I.

A parley between Geronimo (third from left) and General Crook (second from right) in Mexico, March 27, 1886. Lieutenant Maus, with moustache and white hat, is at center.

Geronimo departs for Florida from Fort Bowie, Arizona, 1895.

rifles and bandoliers. When Geronimo asked Maus why he was in the mountains, the lieutenant replied, "I came to capture or destroy you and your band." Impressed by his honesty, Geronimo shook Maus's hand. The two then arranged for a meeting between General Crook and the Apaches.

Maus led the remainder of his men back to New Mexico, an arduous trip of a thousand miles. Crawford died and was buried along the route. Maus would earn the Medal of Honor for his courage and leadership throughout the bloody attempt to bring in Geronimo.

Crook meanwhile arranged for the Apaches to return to the San Carlos Reservation. However, on the night of March 28, 1886, thirty-five of the Apaches escaped again to Mexico and the Sierra Madre. General Sheridan blamed Crook for the failure and replaced him with Brig. Gen. Nelson Miles.

Commanded by Capt. Henry Lawton, a task force left Fort Huachuca, Arizona, on May 5, 1886, for Mexico with orders from Miles to "capture or destroy" the Apaches. The fleeing Apaches had set fire to everything in their wake. The smoke and the insects that swarmed away from the blaze added to the misery of Lawton's men as they rode through 120-degree temperatures. The Apaches had split up, making them difficult to pursue. Lawton's men followed one trail in a circle back to Arizona, just twenty-five miles from where they had started three weeks earlier.

On May 29, Lawton hoped to send word to Miles of his progress and to request further orders. Twenty-five miles of perilous Apache country lay between Lawton's camp and the telegraph office at Pentano, Arizona. Civilian scouts refused to carry the dispatches unless they were paid an exorbitant fee. Only Dr. Leonard Wood, a Harvard-educated M.D. who had joined Miles's army looking for adventure, was willing to attempt the journey.

Wood had marched twenty miles that day, and then rode twenty-five miles to Pentano, losing the trail several times in the darkness. He arrived at Pentano at 10:00 p.m., delivered and received dispatches, then set out for the return journey four hours later at two o'clock in the morning. He arrived in camp at 7:30 a.m., just as the men were deploying to ride out for the day. Wood fell in line and traveled another thirty miles before he was finally able to bed down.

Miles's orders were to travel south in pursuit of Geronimo until the Indian surrendered. The scorching heat and choking dust of the march across the rugged Apache territory, infested with reptiles and insects, began to take its toll. Most of the men had to be replaced over the next two months. Wood, who was bitten by a tarantula, eventually collapsed with fever and delirium, though he recovered to continue the march. The troops never got close enough to Geronimo to capture him, though once they sneaked up and managed to seize supplies and ponies. The Apaches by this time were also weak and tired from the long trek, and being pursued now by the Mexican army as well.

In late July, Miles sent Lt. Charles Gatewood to join Lawton in Arizona. Geronimo trusted Gatewood, and Miles hoped he could convince the renegade Apache to surrender. Gatewood reached Lawton on August 3, and soon after, Geronimo agreed to talk. He apparently hoped for better terms if he were to surrender to the United States rather than Mexico.

Gatewood dashed that hope when he told Geronimo that the Apaches would have to surrender unconditionally and go to Florida, where his Chiricahua people had already been relocated. He had no choice. With the Mexicans closing in, he agreed to Gatewood's conditions and brought his people, still armed, to Lawton's camp.

On August 28, the Mexican army made its way to the American camp. The Apaches, alarmed, took up arms and prepared to fight. Lawton sent Wood and Tom Horn, the scout, to meet the Mexicans to diffuse the tense situation.

Apaches near Neuces River, Texas, before embarking for reservations in Florida. Geronimo is seated front row, third from right. At center front is Nachez, Geronimo's cohort.

# THE INDIAN SCOUTS

*Alchesay, one of ten Apache scouts who received the Medal of Honor for the winter campaign of 1872–1873.*

When Lt. Col. George Crook forwarded twenty-three Medal of Honor recommendations from his campaign against the Apaches in the winter of 1872–1873, Army officials were incredulous: included were the names of ten Apache scouts who had served with Crook. The War Department could not believe that all ten Indians had exhibited valor, so it rejected the requests. Crook promptly resubmitted all ten names, stating that the Apaches had in fact merited the medal.

Crook had long been impressed with the tracking and fighting skills of the Apaches; against them, he once said, "regular troops are as helpless as a whale attacked by a school of swordfish." But because the many Apache tribes frequently feuded, Crook was able to recruit men from one tribe to fight against those from another.

While the scouts were not cited for any one particular action, one incident from the Arizona campaign was representative of their contribution that winter. Guided by the scouts, the Americans cornered a group of Yavapai Indians at a cave in the Salt River Canyon. Nantaje, an Apache private who knew the area well, led a group of sharpshooters in a surprise attack at the mouth of the cave. During the battle, a Yavapai boy was caught in the crossfire. Nantaje ran from cover and carried the boy to safety. By the end of the day, Nantaje and the other scouts had helped rout the Indians in the cave, seventy-six of whom were killed. The place was henceforth known as "Skull Cave."

In March 1875, the War Department reconsidered Crook's request and awarded the Apache scouts Medals of Honor. After that, the scouts' paths diverged. One recipient, Alchesay (all the Apache scouts were known by only one name), served with Crook for several more years. In March 1886, he rode with Emmett Crawford and Marion Maus in pursuit of Geronimo (see page 68) and led an advance party to the Apache leader. Two years later he led a group of Apache chiefs to Washington, D.C., where they were received by President Grover Cleveland. Alchesay later returned to Arizona and became a successful cattle rancher.

Other Medal of Honor scouts of Skull Cave faded from the official records. Little or no information exists about such recipients as Chiquito, Blanquet, and Elsatsoosu. The fate of the recipient known only as "Jim" was lost until 1927, when his widow applied for his Army pension and reported that he had died almost forty years earlier.

Confusion in the records may also have been responsible for a mix-up in the awarding of a medal. In 1869, the War Department published an order granting the Medal of Honor to Co-Rux-Te-Chod-Ish, also known as Mad Bear, for being wounded by a stray cavalry bullet while chasing an Indian in Kansas. Years later, Mad Bear's commanding officer reported that the medal had actually been earned by, and given to, another Indian with a similar name: Co-Rux-a-Kah-Wadde, or Traveling Bear. The error was never corrected.

The angry Mexicans demanded Geronimo. Wood refused, informing them that the Apache leader would return to the United States. The Mexican leader insisted on talking to Geronimo. In the tense confrontation that ensued, Geronimo, his pistol drawn, told the Mexican commander that he had surrendered to Lawton and would go north to the United States. The Mexicans withdrew. On September 4, 1886, General Miles met Geronimo at Skeleton Canyon, Arizona. The Indians returned briefly to San Carlos before boarding a train for Florida.

Dr. Leonard Wood received the Medal of Honor for his role in the capture of Geronimo. It was only the first act of a long and distinguished career. Wood became a close friend of another adventure-loving easterner, Theodore Roosevelt, with whom he founded the Rough Riders. He later served as governor-general of the Philippines and as the General of the Army on the Joint Chiefs of Staff. In 1920, he nearly became the Republican candidate for the presidency but lost the nomination to Warren G. Harding.

# DEATH AT PINE RIDGE
## *Wounded Knee*

The Ghost Dance religion that sparked the last major conflict of the Indian Wars arose from a mixture of mysticism and hatred for reservation life. The Indian tribes throughout the West believed that a Christ-like Indian Messiah had come to teach the Indians a dance that would suspend them in the heavens with their ghost ancestors, where they would be invulnerable as the white man was buried by new earth down below. The Ghost Dance spread like a prairie fire, but to white authorities it posed a threat to the reservation system. By mid-November 1890, anarchy reigned at the Pine Ridge Agency in South Dakota as the Indians defied the agents' orders to stop the dance. The agents called in the Army, and over six hundred families of the dancers withdrew to far corners of the reservation.

The main act at the Pine Ridge Agency during the winter of 1890–1891 was to take place in December by a small stream known as Wounded Knee. Before that, a sideshow, marking the end of a much longer drama, played itself out. On December 15, Indian policemen from the Standing Rock Agency, which stood near the border of the two Dakotas, tried to arrest Sitting Bull, mistakenly thought to be a leader of the Ghost Dancers. Sitting Bull, the Sioux medicine man who had led the defeat of Custer fourteen years before, was killed in the melee that followed.

Orders had also been issued for the arrest of Big Foot, chief of the Miniconjous, who decided to join the Oglala Sioux at Pine Ridge with 350 of his people. The 7th Cavalry intercepted them near Wounded Knee Creek in South Dakota. The troops surrounded the Sioux, and the Army commander, Col. James Forsyth, posted small but deadly fifty-rounds-per-minute Hotchkiss cannon on the hills above the camp. At dawn the next morning, Forsyth ordered the Indians to surrender their weapons, and they slowly began to comply. When Forsyth saw the heap of old and broken rifles in the center of the camp, he suspected that the Indians were hiding their real weapons. He ordered a thorough search.

While the search proceeded, a medicine man incited the braves to fight, claiming the "powerful medicine" of their ghost shirts would protect them from the soldiers' bullets. A scuffle broke out when a young Indian named Black Coyote protested the seizure of his new

Sitting Bull, whose Sioux people were among the last to resist subjugation by the US Army.

Oglala Sioux engage in a Ghost Dance at Pine Ridge. The mystical religion sprang up in the 1890s and spread among many tribes.

Winchester rifle by waving it in the air. There are nearly as many versions of what happened next as there were survivors of the battle that followed. Some of the Indians said that the inexperienced soldiers panicked and fired when Black Coyote waved his weapon. Others claimed the soldiers fired indiscriminately and without provocation. The officers on the scene, however, reported that the Indians had hidden rifles in the blanket rolls and under women's skirts, and when the soldiers began their search, they pulled the weapons from their hiding places and opened fire.

In the explosive and horrible battle that followed, men clubbed and knifed each other and discharged high-powered weapons at close range. The Indians scattered into surrounding ravines, screaming as they ran. The gunners manning the Hotchkiss guns moved to the attack. Rounds from the rapid-fire cannon cut down men, women, and children as they fled.

A few of the Sioux warriors escaped the first flurry and ran into a ravine that sheltered them from the fire of the cannon. They crawled along in the direction of one of the Hotchkiss guns. When the warriors reached the lip of the ravine they began to pour fire on the crew of the artillery piece. As several of his comrades retreated, Cpl. Paul H. Weinert and other soldiers manhandled the gun in the direction of the ravine. Weinert heard his commanding officer, Lt. Harry Hawthorne, cry, "Oh, my God." The lieutenant fell wounded and landed on his side. Weinert vowed at that moment, "By God, I'll make them pay for that."

# THE BUFFALO SOLDIERS

The Indians of the West called black troopers "buffalo soldiers" because, it was said, the troopers' black hair reminded them of a buffalo's mane. Another possibility for the nickname was the heavy buffalo robes the soldiers wore on winter campaigns. Whatever the origin of the name, black soldiers of the West were regarded by their Indian adversaries as courageous opponents.

Through various campaigns, the buffalo soldiers also earned the respect of some of their comrades. Desertion rates were lower and reenlistments higher in the all-black 9th and 10th Cavalry and 24th and 25th Infantry than in white units. Many black soldiers considered the Army a chance for economic advancement and respect, so the soldiers were well disciplined and took pride in their profession. Their white officers, who at first had feared that appointments to black regiments might harm their careers, swore by them and considered them excellent soldiers. A few specifically asked to be assigned to black units.

Despite the esteem of their own white commanders, the black soldiers faced racism from others. The Army sent them for long stretches to the most remote and least desirable posts. Segregation from white troops was strictly enforced: Many officers ordered the "nigger troops" not to form up close to their white men. Major Eugene Carr took a lower rank with a white unit rather than be assigned to a black regiment. (Ironically, the buffalo soldiers saved Carr's life in a fight at Beaver Creek, Colorado, in 1868.)

Few black soldiers who fought Indians were formally recognized for valor, though they were in the thick of combat and by most accounts conducted themselves admirably. Yet only fourteen black soldiers in all four regiments received the Medal of Honor in over twenty-five years of fighting on the frontier. By contrast, the white soldiers of the 8th Cavalry who saw similar action received eighty-four medals. Men in the white 1st Cavalry received thirty..

The black soldier was never embraced by white society after military service. Sergeant Brent Woods, a former slave who earned the Medal of Honor for actions against the Apaches in New Mexico, is an example. After receiving an honorable discharge in 1902, Woods returned to his native Pulaski County, Kentucky, where he died in 1906. He was buried in an unmarked grave and forgotten for almost eighty years. But through the efforts of Medal of Honor historians, Woods's grave was located, and his remains were moved to a new gravesite with a headstone appropriate for a Medal of Honor recipient. In 1984, the Army gave Brent Woods a full military funeral, seventy-eight years after his death.

*"Buffalo soldiers" of the 10th Cavalry in Montana, 1894. Only one black soldier from this regiment, Sgt. William McBryar, received the Medal of Honor.*

Corporal Paul Weinert (behind gun) and fellow gunners of the 1st Artillery pose with a Hotchkiss gun.

One of Weinert's comrades, Pvt. Joshua Hartzog, rushed to pick up the wounded lieutenant and carry him to safety. Meanwhile, Weinert alone ran the gun farther down the hill to maneuver it into the opening of the ravine. The others in his crew yelled for him to come back, but Weinert paid them no heed. He loaded and fired the single-shot cannon until the gun became too hot to handle. Bullets flew about him. One hit a shell and knocked it from his hand as he was loading the gun, but, fortunately for Weinert, the round did not explode. The wheels of his cannon were pocked with bullet holes after the fight, but Weinert escaped without a wound. His fire drove the Indians from the ravine.

Weinert, who thought he might be court-martialed for acting independently and ignoring the orders to retreat, was happily surprised when his captain grasped him by the shoulders and said, "That's the kind of men I have in my battery." Weinert not only escaped a court-martial—he was awarded the Medal of Honor. Hartzog's dash to save the lieutenant merited him a medal as well. And Lieutenant Hawthorne himself was awarded the Medal of Honor for "distinguished conduct" in the battle.

The battle was an ugly affair. The Indians were ragged and hopeless, and many of them were cut down by cannon fire as they fled in panic: 150 of them were killed, including 62 women and children. But some of the warriors fought with an energy only increased by desperation, and twenty-five soldiers died that day as well. The battle, uneven as it was, brought the same kind of terror to the soldiers as comes to anyone under fire. Some of these men showed great courage in the face of this fear. In all, seventeen men were awarded the Medal of Honor for bravery at Wounded Knee and at the fight that followed at Drexel Mission.

When the news of the fight reached the other Indians at Pine Ridge, over four thousand of them headed for a stronghold fifteen miles to the north of the agency. On December 30,

Soldiers load Indian bodies onto a wagon in preparation for a mass burial.

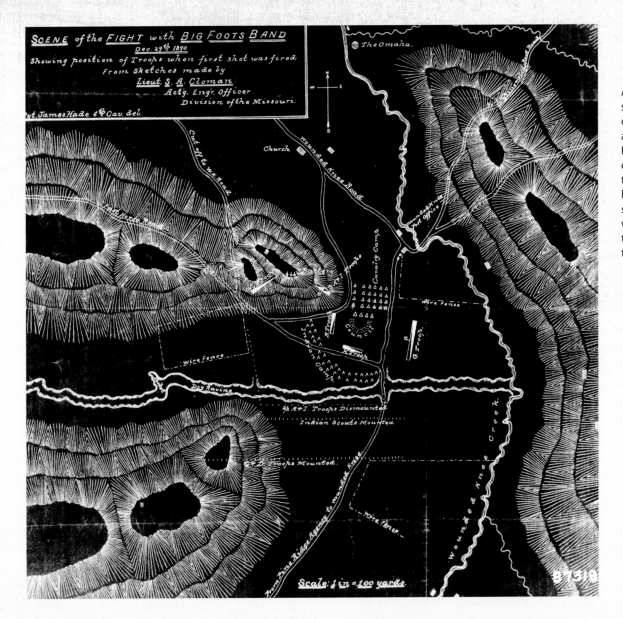

An Army map shows the scene of the massacre at Wounded Knee. Devastating cannon fire from the surrounding hills cut down scores of Indians while cavalry troops swept into the Sioux camp.

they trapped a contingent of the 7th Cavalry at Drexel Mission on the reservation, but the whites were rescued by the "Buffalo Soldiers" of the all-black 9th Infantry, which had marched all night to relieve them. The short-lived rebellion ended on January 15, when General Miles slowly closed a ring of 3,500 soldiers around the Indians' camp at the far reaches of Pine Ridge.

The Ghost Dancers were brought back to the agency, where they lined the ridges as the 7th Cavalry and the 9th Infantry, among others, marched in review past General Miles. The winter wind howled and stirred up yellow dust that nearly obscured the view, and the Sioux watched in silent witness to the end of an era.

The frozen corpse of Big Foot lies in the snow after the massacre.

# CHAPTER THREE

# The Wars of American Expansion

Korea and China, 1871 and 1900
Latin America, 1898-1933
The Philippines and Samoa, 1899-1913

# America Ascendant

*Previous pages*
The US Asiatic Squadron under the command of Cdre. George Dewey destroys the Spanish fleet in Manila Bay, the Philippines, May 1, 1898, in the early days of the Spanish-American War.

*Below*
Two towering figures of the era of American expansion: Alfred Thayer Mahan and Theodore Roosevelt.

T HE US ARMY'S INDIAN-FIGHTING operations in the American West reflected one of the nation's main concerns in the latter half of the nineteenth century. For decades after the Civil War, those concerns remained exclusively domestic: the winning of the West, the ever-accelerating industrialization of the North, the Reconstruction of the South. The United States did not possess a single overseas territory, nor did it desire any. American foreign policy sought only two traditional aims: enforcing the Monroe Doctrine that forbade the extension of European power in the Western Hemisphere, and defending the right of American citizens to conduct lawful trade throughout the world.

The republic's priorities were reflected in the experience of its navy. During the Civil War, the US Navy had become perhaps the most powerful in existence. At the close of the conflict it had 671 vessels in commission, 71 of them ironclads at the forefront of naval technology. Its demobilization was drastic. By 1870 the number of vessels in service had dropped to 52, mostly full-rigged, wooden ships whose steam engines were viewed as auxiliary power. For the next twenty years it would remain at best a third-rate navy, inferior to those of all the great powers and many middling powers as well.

Yet this antiquated little navy was adequate enough to perform the missions Congress intended it for. Ruling the waves had never been among them. In the event of war, the Navy was not to engage the enemy's fleet, but attack his merchant shipping, as it had in the Revolution and the War of 1812. In time of peace, it was to protect American lives and property in unruly areas of the globe and to promote the growth of American commerce and trade.

The Korean expedition of 1871, which led to the first award of the Medal of Honor for overseas combat operations, was meant to serve both these conventional, peaceful purposes. The "Hermit Kingdom" of Korea was the last Asian land with which the United States had not established diplomatic relations. The desirability of such contacts had been demonstrated several years earlier by the massacre of the crew of an American trading ship. It was thought that diplomatic relations might avoid such incidents in the future. Accordingly, Rear Adm. John Rodgers's Asiatic Squadron was

detailed to carry Frederick F. Low, US minister to China, to Seoul to open negotiations. When small boats sent to survey the channel to the city were fired upon by shore fortifications, Rodgers gave the Koreans ten days to apologize. Their refusal to oblige was followed by the landing of a brigade of sailors and Marines. In two days' fighting, the offending fortifications were captured and destroyed. The expedition then departed, conscious of the failure of its mission and the rectitude of its actions. A treaty was not negotiated until 1882.

More than a quarter-century would pass before another Medal of Honor was granted for a combat action abroad. By then, America had turned its attention to the outside world. There were many reasons for this. One was the wave of imperialism that arose in Europe in the late 1870s. Colonies, it was claimed, were profitable; colonies brought prestige; colonies were strategic; colonies were romantic; colonies were a Christian duty. By the 1890s, large numbers of Americans, many holding influential positions, had embraced the imperialist argument. Their susceptibility may have been heightened by the closing of the western frontier, which had disappeared by the beginning of the decade. Some historians have concluded that, psychologically attuned to endless expansion, Americans sought a new frontier beyond the seas.

William Randolph Hearst's newspapers fanned the flames of war after the destruction of the battleship *Maine* in Havana Harbor on February 15, 1898. Modern research blames the explosion on a fire in the ship's coal bunker that spread to a weapons magazine.

Also important in molding opinion was the unofficial public relations campaign conducted by naval officers to convince their countrymen that a strong navy was necessary to protect the foreign trade that was in turn necessary to the national wellbeing. By far the most important naval publication was Capt. Alfred Thayer Mahan's analysis, *The Influence of Sea Power Upon History, 1660–1783*, which appeared in 1890. Mahan used the long maritime struggle between Britain and France as a test case to develop certain supposedly timeless "principles" of naval warfare. Applied to the United States, his principles clearly called for the renunciation of the strategy of commerce raiding; the construction of a powerful battle fleet capable of defeating an enemy to win "command of the sea"; and the acquisition of colonial naval bases.

The American outlook was also affected by events abroad. Brazil purchased a British-built armored cruiser that was adjudged an even match for the entire US Navy, provoking Congress in 1886 to authorize the construction of the first two American battleships. In 1889, a dispute over the right to establish coaling stations in the Samoan Islands led to serious friction with Germany. Then in 1890, the deaths of three bluejackets (as the Navy's enlisted men were known) in a brawl in Valparaiso brought the United States close to war with Chile, whose fleet Americans were shocked to learn was superior to their own. Thereafter, the quickening of interest in the overseas world was paralleled by an expansion of the Navy. By 1898, the United States had six battleships in commission and five more in the yards.

While these developments set the stage for the nation's entry into the Spanish-American War, they were not directly responsible for it. The two principal causes of the conflict were

external. The first was the brutality of the methods by which Spanish colonial authorities sought to suppress the revolution that began in Cuba in 1895, methods that outraged the American sense of humanity. The second was the mysterious explosion of the battleship USS *Maine* while it was on a goodwill visit to Havana on February 15, 1898. Recent research indicates that the explosion was accidental, but at the time almost everyone assumed that the ship had been destroyed by the dastardly dons. At once the cry went up, "Remember the Maine! To hell with Spain!" William Randolph Hearst, especially, inflamed national opinion in his newspapers. President McKinley attempted to brake the rush to war, instructing Ambassador W. L. Woodford to warn the Spanish government that only its promise to free Cuba could avert hostilities. On April 9, after weeks of negotiation, Woodford extracted the promise. It was too late. Under intense pressure, McKinley submitted a war message to Congress two days later.

The fighting in Cuba lasted slightly more than four months. Everywhere, at El Caney, San Juan Hill, and Santiago, American arms were victorious. In the Pacific, Cdre. George Dewey's fleet destroyed the Spanish Philippine squadron in a single engagement. The conduct of operations in many instances was amateurish in the extreme, but this would not become public knowledge until long afterward. In 1898 a jubilant country agreed with Secretary of State John Hay: It had been "a splendid little war."

*Top*
San Juan Hill, east of Santiago, Cuba, scene of the climactic battle of the Spanish-American War on July 1, 1898.

*Above*
Lieutenant Colonel Theodore Roosevelt and his 1st US Volunteer Cavalry, the "Rough Riders," atop San Juan Heights after the battle.

Victory over Spain laid the foundation of the American empire. Cuba, officially promised independence at the outbreak of war, received it in 1903 but under conditions that made the island an American protectorate. The United States also retained all the other Spanish colonies: Puerto Rico, Guam, and, after heated debate, the Philippines. It was in celebration of the annexation of the latter that Kipling wrote the poem "The White Man's Burden," congratulating America on shouldering her imperial responsibility. But the new empire spread beyond the territories won from Spain. It also included Hawaii, annexed during the war; Wake Island, claimed in 1899; and several of the Samoan Islands, divided with Germany in 1900.

Almost at once, Americans were reminded that empires were held together by blood. Insurrections broke out in the Philippines and Samoa in 1899. A year later in China, the antiforeign uprising known as the Boxer Rebellion found US troops fighting beside European and Japanese soldiers in both the defense and the relief of the legations at Peking. The Samoan skirmish lasted only a few weeks, and foreign forces made quick work of the Boxers. The suppression of the Filipino *insurrectos*, though, took two years and cost more American lives than the war with Spain. Nor was it the end of the trouble in the Philippines. The assertion of US authority over the fierce Moro tribesmen of the southern islands would require more than a decade of intermittent campaigning.

Grisly reports of the war in the Philippines reinforced the views of a vocal minority of Americans opposed to empire, but these protests did nothing to check the nation's rise to international power. In 1901 an assassin's bullet brought an early end to McKinley's second term, and Theodore Roosevelt, the hero of San Juan Hill, succeeded to the presidency. The effects of his seven years in office were momentous. A former assistant secretary of the Navy and disciple of Mahan, Roosevelt was the first president to believe that the United States should play an active role in international affairs. His policy, he said, was to "speak softly and carry a big stick." The big stick he had in mind was the US Navy, which he set out to make second only to that of Great Britain, the traditional mistress of the seas.

Primarily to permit the rapid concentration of the fast-growing fleet in either ocean, Roosevelt resolved to build a canal across Central America. The Colombian province of Panama, where the French had made a start, was chosen as the site. When the Colombian senate rejected Roosevelt's canal treaty, he responded by underwriting a revolution that gave Panama its independence and the United States its canal. Work began in 1904 and was completed ten years later.

The canal increased America's strategic stake in the Caribbean. Indirectly threatening that stake was the propensity of regional governments to default on their debts to European investors, a standing invitation to intervention. Roosevelt took characteristically vigorous preemptive action in 1904 by proclaiming a corollary to the Monroe Doctrine. It stated that the United States had assumed the role of hemispheric policeman. The European powers would have no pretext for intervention; in the case of "chronic wrongdoing," Uncle Sam would take charge.

For the next quarter-century, the Roosevelt Corollary provided the basis for repeated interventions in the Caribbean and Central America. Americans called them "banana wars" after the fruit they associated with the region. Roosevelt himself made little use of his corollary. He invoked it only once, in 1905, to accept the debt-ridden Dominican Republic's offer to give American officers control of the collection and disbursement of its customs revenues. (He also reoccupied Cuba from 1906 to 1909 to break what he called "the insurrectionary habit," but that was permitted by the American-authored Cuban constitution.) In 1912, his successor, William Howard Taft, landed Marines to put down a revolution in Nicaragua and left a hundred-man legation guard in Managua. Two years later, Woodrow Wilson, an anti-imperialist whipsawed by his determination "to teach the South American republics to elect good men," began the most extensive interventions of any president by landing troops at Veracruz, Mexico. In 1915, the disintegration of the Haitian government prompted him to send in the Marines, initiating an occupation that would last nineteen years. The Dominican Republic was brought into the fold under similar circumstances the following year.

Soon thereafter, events in the Caribbean were eclipsed by America's entry into World War I. When in 1919 an uprising in Haiti recalled attention to the region, the mood of the country had changed. Warren Harding's campaign promise to end "bayonet rule" in the Caribbean was applauded. Disillusioned by the outcome of their attempt to make the world safe for democracy, most Americans were ready to leave their neighbors to their own devices. The administration of Haiti was reorganized to speed the republic's progress toward independence in 1922. The Marines were withdrawn from the Dominican Republic in 1924; the Managua legation guard followed in 1925.

Roosevelt was the first president to believe that the United States should play an active role in international affairs. His policy, he said, was to "speak softly and carry a big stick."

A US Marine (standing, second from right) and members of Nicaragua's Guardia Nacional, the native *voluntarios*, in 1928.

Ironically, only two years later, civil war in Nicaragua drew the United States into its most controversial banana war. The intervention never became a full-blown occupation, however, and did more to reinforce than retard the trend toward disengagement. In 1933, President Franklin D. Roosevelt inaugurated his "Good Neighbor Policy" toward the Latin American lands. A few months later, the United States formally renounced the right to intervene in their affairs, nullifying the earlier Roosevelt's corollary. The last Marine units left Nicaragua in 1933, and the occupation of Haiti was terminated in 1934. That same year the Philippines were granted commonwealth status and promised independence in 1946. The wars of expansion were over.

The motives that gave rise to these conflicts were primarily strategic and ideological rather than economic. McKinley found his answer to the question of whether to annex the Philippines in prayer. In the Caribbean, Roosevelt and Taft acted to promote stability, not to enrich investors. Wilson emphasized an additional purpose, the development of democracy. No doubt all three realized that an orderly, revolution-free Caribbean would be to the advantage of American business, but that realization did not dictate their policies. There was no significant American investment in Haiti, where the Marines stayed the longest; in Mexico, where there was a huge investment, Wilson acted in opposition to the wishes of the investors, helping to overthrow a president they wanted him to support.

In hindsight it is easy to see that the interventions failed to achieve their objective. American hopes centered on the creation of efficient, apolitical armed forces—the *Gendarmerie d'Haiti*, the *Guardia Nacional Dominicana*, and, in Nicaragua, the *Guardia Nacional*—trained and during their formative years led by US Marines. These forces were supposed to stabilize the operation of the democratic process in their countries by precluding the losers' customary resort to revolution. It did not work that way. Where the forces provided stability they did so, at the expense of democracy, as the instruments of dictatorship. The Dominican *guardia* produced Rafael Trujillo; the Nicaraguan, Anastasio Somoza.

The failure did not stem from lack of effort. American rule was paternalistic and often patronizing but almost painfully well intentioned. The Marines did more than chase rebels and train troops. They set an example of honest administration, built roads and schools, and undertook extensive programs of public health and sanitation. Materially, the occupied lands benefited from their presence. Weighed against the loss of independence, however, the Caribbean peoples found the improvement insubstantial. Perhaps a Haitian put it best in a conversation with a Marine officer who remarked that Haiti would be glad to see the Americans go. The Haitian agreed. "We know that you have helped us in many ways," he added, "and we appreciate that. But, after all, this is our country, and we would rather run it ourselves."

# First Actions in Asia
## Korea, 1871

THE FIRST CONFLICT OF the wars of expansion took place in the Far East. It resulted from the dispatch of a naval force to convey a diplomatic mission under Frederick F. Low to the "Hermit Kingdom" of Korea. Unfortunately, the Koreans preferred to remain hermits.

On May 30, 1871, five ships of the US Asiatic Squadron approached the western coast of Korea. The next day they were fired on by Korean forts. A survey of the three principal fortifications revealed that they could not be shelled into submission but would have to be stormed.

For this purpose, a naval brigade of sailors and Marines was organized under the orders of Cdr. Lewis A. Kimberly. Commander Silas Casey's bluejacket battalion, 542 strong, was drawn from the vessels that could not enter the channel—Admiral Rodgers's flagship (the screw frigate *Colorado*) and the sloops *Alaska* and *Benicia*. It included an artillery detachment of seven twelve-pound howitzers. The much smaller Marine battalion consisted of a hundred men led by Capt. McLane Tilton. Fire support was to be provided by the gunboats *Monocacy* and *Palos*. Overall command of the operation was entrusted to Cdr. Homer C. Blake.

Early on the morning of Saturday, June 10, twenty-two open boats left anchorage to engage the first fort. As soon as the Korean guns had been silenced, the brigade would land abreast of the work on a flat plain, the Marines in the lead. The first part went as planned, but the plain proved to be a knee-deep mud flat. Troops left shoes and socks behind and howitzers sank up to their axles in the muck. It was many hours before the last howitzer could be manhandled to firm ground. The next morning, the approach of the Marines sufficed to put the second garrison to flight.

The last and largest of the forts, christened the Citadel, stood on a conical hill. One-hundred-fifty yards from the fort, the brigade was greeted by a fusillade that proved these Koreans intended to fight. Their fire was inaccurate, though, and ineffective. When there was no longer time for them to reload their muskets, the Koreans began rolling stones down into the storming party.

A company of bluejackets led the rush up the slope. At its head was Lt. Hugh W. McKee, whose father, an Army colonel, had been killed in the Mexican War. Scrambling over the rampart, McKee dropped into the fort, closely followed by Boatswain's Mate Alexander McKenzie, Quartermaster Samuel F. Rogers, and Ordinary Seaman William Troy. The Koreans swarmed over them in hand-to-hand fighting. McKee was speared; McKenzie went down with a sword cut to the

The gunboat *Monocacy* (at left in photo) and screw tug *Palos* sail into a channel near present-day Inchon to provide covering fire for sailors and Marines attacking Korean forts in June 1871.

head, and Rogers and Troy were seriously wounded.

Even as McKee's little band was being overwhelmed, their comrades were clambering into the fort. Ship's Carpenter Cyrus Hayden, the bluejackets' color bearer, planted his flag on the wall. A Korean leveled a matchlock musket at Pvt. Michael McNamara. McNamara wrenched it out of the man's hands and clubbed him to death with it. Quartermaster Frederick Franklin took command of McKee's company.

Private John Coleman tried to reach the wounded McKee, whom the Koreans were dragging into their ranks. They were too many for him, but Coleman did succeed in rescuing McKenzie. By then the superiority of the Americans' weapons had begun to tell, and the Koreans fell back. Two Marines, Cpl. Charles Brown and Pvt. Hugh Purvis, darted forward and hauled down the governor's standard. These six men and those in McKee's party were all to be awarded the Medal of Honor for their gallantry at the Citadel.

A member of McKee's company, German-born Landsman William F. Lukes, a twenty-four-year-old cook, saw a group of Koreans carrying his officer down the eastern side of the hill. Cutlass in hand, he ran toward them, shouting for others to follow. Seamen Seth Allen and Patrick Murphy responded to his call. All three Americans were cut down with swords and spears in a short, savage encounter, but the Koreans abandoned the struggle.

Lukes's action concluded the struggle for the Citadel. Only 3 Americans out of 350 had been killed and 11 had been wounded, Lieutenant McKee mortally. Altogether, fifteen Medals of Honor were awarded for the expedition: nine to seamen and six to Marines.

*Top*
Sailors atop the first Korean fort on June 10, 1871.

*Middle*
Korean corpses strewn near the Citadel.

*Bottom*
Corporal Charles Brown, Pvt. Hugh Purvis, and Capt. McLane Tilton (left to right) aboard the USS *Colorado* with a flag captured at the Citadel.

# China, 1900

A peasant uprising in northern China aimed to purify the country of outside influences by the simple expedient of exterminating all foreigners. Even as the aftermath of the Spanish-American war left Americans fighting in the Philippines (see page 103), the United States found itself drawn into another conflict in Asia.

By 1900, the United States, Japan, and nine European nations maintained legations in China. Diplomatic corps in Peking heard alarming reports of a movement calling itself the Righteous Society of Heavenly Fists. Westerners called them Boxers, and soon requested protection. The first detachment—337 American, British, French, Italian, Japanese, and Russian sailors and Marines—reached Peking on May 31. Eighty-nine Austrians and Germans followed on June 3. The situation deteriorated rapidly.

On June 9, the British prepared troops for an immediate advance on the city. The Chinese government ordered the diplomatic community to leave Peking within twenty-four hours. The diplomats requested an interview with Chinese officials, but when no response came, the German ambassador set out for the foreign ministry. News that he was shot and killed by a Chinese soldier en route convinced the other westerners that they must defend themselves.

The Boxers launched their first attack that same day. Some 1,300-plus foreigners, missionaries, and guards, plus several thousand Chinese Christians, packed into an outlying perimeter created by several abandoned legations. The diplomats had little artillery, but an old cannon barrel was discovered at an iron foundry inside the quarter. Gunner's Mate First

The men of Troop L of the 6th US Cavalry ride along the Great Wall of China just east of the Nan-Kow Pass near the Ming Tombs, circa 1900.

*Above*
Calvin Titus as a West Point cadet.

*Right*
President Theodore Roosevelt traveled to the US Military Academy at West Point in 1902. The presentation of Calvin Titus's medal was the climax of a ceremony to celebrate the academy's centennial.

Class Joseph Mitchell was put in charge of renovating the piece. "It was about 100 years old," Mitchell wrote. "To mount it I took a piece of timber and lashed the gun to the station water carriage. It had no trunnions or sight, but nevertheless it was of good use. I used Chinese and German powder, Russian shell and Japanese fuses with it, and to work the old cannon I fought under every flag in the legation district, and the breastworks of the enemy were leveled rapidly. . . . I had the old gun all by myself, as everyone was afraid it would burst." For his resourceful defense, Mitchell received the medal.

By then, the Boxers had also besieged the International Settlement at Tientsin. The attack was beaten off after heavy fighting from Russians and US Marines. The flow of foreign troops into northern China quickly gathered momentum. Meanwhile, foreign landing parties captured the forts guarding the mouth of the Hai River. Tientsin was captured on July 13–14 by a force of 6,500 men, one-sixth of them American. Nine Medals of Honor were awarded for this engagement.

Finally, on August 3, British Brig. Gen. Sir Alfred Gaselee marched from Tianjin to Peking at the head of an International Relief Expedition of 18,600 men, including 2,500 American soldiers and Marines. Once they reached the city, he called for volunteers to scale the city wall. Trumpeter Calvin P. Titus of the 14th Infantry responded: "I'll try, sir!" Without ropes or a ladder, Titus worked his way up the thirty-foot wall by finding hand- and footholds amid the stones. He came under fire at the top but survived the assault. Titus's gallant action inspired his fellow soldiers, who assaulted and penetrated the city wall.

The defenders had withstood a siege of fifty-five days. The relief of the legations shattered the Boxers' credibility with the Chinese people and for all practical purposes the Boxer Rebellion was over.

# Latin America and the Caribbean
## Cuba and the Spanish-American War, 1898

**B**EGINNING WITH THE SPANISH-AMERICAN War in 1898, the United States projected most of its military power in the Western Hemisphere, especially to the south. Theodore Roosevelt's 1904 corollary to the Monroe Doctrine initiated a decades-long series of military involvements throughout the Caribbean Basin, as America played hemispheric policeman in the face of restive populations, coups, and revolutions from Mexico to the Dominican Republic.

The Spanish-American War moved America onto the world stage. It also vindicated Alfred T. Mahan's theories of sea power. If the US Navy could win command of the sea, cutting the Spanish colonies off from the homeland, victory was assured. In the Pacific the issue was decided within three weeks of the commencement of hostilities by Cdre. Dewey's destruction of the Spanish Philippine squadron at Manila Bay. In the Caribbean, to which Spain sent a cruiser squadron under Rear Adm. Pascual Cervera y Topete, matters were not settled so quickly.

The first Medal of Honor awarded for the "splendid little war" with Spain was earned by Chief Carpenter's Mate Franz Anton Itrich at the Battle of Manila Bay on May 1, 1898. Another fifty-two men received medals for dredging up and cutting the Spanish overseas cables near Cienfuegos, Cuba, under a heavy fire from shore on May 11. Most of the other medals authorized for the conflict were granted for chasing down the Spanish commander Pascual Cervera's cruiser squadron.

Rear Admiral William T. Sampson, commander of the US North Atlantic Squadron, attempted to intercept the squadron off Puerto Rico and Havana. Cervera expected as much and slipped safely into port at Santiago, on the southeastern coast of Cuba, where his ships were discovered on May 28. For Sampson, this was a disappointing development. His squadron was greatly superior to Cervera's, but the only way into Santiago Harbor was through a narrow, mined channel, covered by shore batteries. He dared not risk his battleships. He could, of course, blockade the port, but Cervera might somehow steal out. The solution was to bottle him up by sinking a ship across the channel.

On May 29, Sampson discussed this intention with Assistant Naval Constructor Richmond Pearson Hobson, who immediately volunteered for the mission. A handsome man with strong, symmetrical features and a large handlebar mustache, Hobson was also a peculiar one. Born in Greensboro, Alabama, in 1870, he entered the Naval Academy at the age of fifteen. There his unflinching sense of duty led him to report members of his own class

The Spanish–American War moved America onto the world stage. It also vindicated Alfred T. Mahan's theories of sea power.

for disciplinary infractions. His diligence violated the midshipmen's unwritten code, in consequence of which his classmates stopped speaking to him except on official business. During his senior year they decided that they had misjudged him and invited him back into the fold. Hobson responded by declaring that he had grown accustomed to the existing arrangement and would prefer for it to continue. Graduating first in his class, he was chosen for advanced study abroad and earned a degree from the French *École d'Application du Génie Maritime* in 1893. Upon the outbreak of war he was assigned to Sampson's staff.

Lieutenant Richmond P. Hobson (above) guided the *Merrimac* into Santiago Harbor under heavy Spanish fire before he and his crew were captured and held as prisoners of war. Pictured at top is Hobson's cell in Morro Castle, Santiago, in 1898.

Sampson had already selected a block ship, the 333-foot collier *Merrimac*. Hobson prepared it for sinking, and around two o'clock on the morning of June 3 he took it out of the blockade line. Accompanying him was a skeleton crew of seven enlisted volunteers: Gunner's Mate First Class George Charette, Coxswain Claus K. Clausen, Coxswain Osborne Deignan, Watertender Francis Kelly, Chief Master-at-Arms Daniel Montague, Coxswain John E. Murphy, and Machinist First Class George F. Phillips.

In planning the operation, Hobson had concluded that the approach should be made in darkness and at flood tide, just after the moon set. He had strung ten charges at vital locations twelve feet below the water line on the *Merrimac*'s port side. The charges would be fired by battery-powered electrical circuits that would sink the ship almost instantaneously. A lifeboat was taken aboard to provide the crew with a chance of escape, and a launch was ordered to stand off the channel to pick them up. For his men, who likely would spend some time in the water, Hobson prescribed a most unconventional uniform consisting of woolen underwear, two pairs of socks, a pistol belt (with pistol), and a life preserver.

Approaching the channel at her full speed of nine knots, the *Merrimac* managed to come within five hundred yards of its mouth before the Spanish opened fire. The ship plunged ahead, shuddering from a succession of hits. The steering gear was soon disabled, but her momentum kept her on course. At the predetermined position, Hobson gave the order to set off the charges. He already knew from tests that three of the circuits were dead. Now he was appalled to find that the Spanish fire had shattered so many batteries that only two of the remaining charges exploded. The damage they did would not be sufficient to sink the ship before the tide swung her out of place. An attempt to hold her by anchoring was frustrated when the chains were shot away. Helplessly, Hobson watched as the ship drifted to the side of the channel.

He and his men now found themselves on a slowly sinking hulk under almost point blank fire from rifles, machine guns, shore batteries, and the ships of Cervera's squadron. Afterward Hobson recalled, "The striking of projectiles and flying fragments produced a grinding sound, with a fine ring in it of steel on steel. The deck vibrated heavily, and we felt the full effect, lying, as we were, full-length on our faces. At each instant it seemed that certainly the next would bring a projectile among us. . . . I looked for my own body to be cut in two diagonally, from the left hip upward, and wondered for a moment what the sensation would be."

Incredibly, the entire party survived the sinking of the ship. The Spanish barrage had destroyed their lifeboat, eliminating any possibility of escape, and the next morning they were picked up, clinging to a raft, by a launch containing Admiral Cervera himself. The first word the Spanish officer said as Hobson climbed aboard was "*Valiente!*" ("Brave!"). Hobson and his crew were held as prisoners of war in nearby Santiago. Six weeks after the sinking of the *Merrimac*, they were exchanged for a Spanish officer. All seven of his men received the Medal of Honor in 1899. As an officer, Hobson was ineligible under naval regulations of the time.

*Left*
Hobson, top left, and his crew: Claus Clausen, Daniel Montague, and Francis Kelly (top) and George Charette, Osborne Deignan, George Phillips, and John Murphy (bottom). At center is the sinking of the *Merrimac*.

*Above*
Hobson and his crew attempting to escape from the *Merrimac*.

# "THAT INFERNAL MEDAL OF HONOR"

One of the great ironies of the era of American expansion is that its most enduring figure was recommended for a Medal of Honor but was denied the award. Years later the rejection would still rankle Theodore Roosevelt, Rough Rider and president.

After the Rough Riders' legendary charge up San Juan Hill on July 1, 1898, Lt. Col. Roosevelt became a hero back in America. He was praised for his actions and later recommended for the Medal of Honor. The wave of popularity that greeted him on his return to the United States led to the governorship of New York, the vice presidency, and, upon the assassination of William McKinley, the White House.

But while he would gain the presidency, Teddy Roosevelt was denied the other prize he coveted. In the fall of 1898, the War Decorations Board prepared to reject Roosevelt's case due to a lack of eyewitness statements vouching for his actions on the hill.

Roosevelt, elected governor that November, was livid. He quickly asked his friend, Sen. Henry Cabot Lodge of Massachusetts, to look into the matter on his behalf. "The War Department does not intend that I shall have the Medal of Honor," he wrote Lodge in November. "If I didn't earn it, then no commissioned officer can ever earn it." Lodge reported that the War Department offered a retroactive brevet promotion in lieu of the medal, but Roosevelt was adamant. "Don't bother about the brevet," he replied. "It is the medal for which I care."

The governor asked his former comrades to verify his actions, and soon, written statements from other Rough Riders arrived in Washington. Major General Leonard Wood, a Medal of Honor recipient from the Indian Wars, stated that Roosevelt was one of the first up San Juan Hill and that "his services on the day in question were of great value and of a most distinguished character." Captain Robert Howze, another recipient, noted two occasions on which Roosevelt had displayed "the most conspicuous gallantry" on the hill.

But while the Decorations Board may have looked favorably upon the evidence, the Secretary of War, Russell A. Alger, was offended by Roosevelt's pressure tactics toward the panel. The former Rough Rider was convinced that Alger was bitter over his complaints that the War Department had mismanaged the American logistical effort in Cuba. The conflict came to a head in early 1899 when Alger announced at a White House dinner that Roosevelt would not receive the medal. Roosevelt and Lodge, in attendance that night, were humiliated.

By the end of January, Roosevelt had given up on his quest. "As for that infernal Medal of Honor," he wrote Lodge, "I really wish and ask that you do nothing more about it at all." Amid mounting charges of mismanagement during the war, Alger was dismissed in July. Teddy Roosevelt's Medal of Honor was forgotten.

But being denied the honor only increased Roosevelt's respect for the medal. During his presidency the standards were raised for its bestowal, and a new design for the Army medal was approved and patented for the first time. Roosevelt also set the tone for future presentations in 1905 when he directed that the medal be awarded "with formal and impressive ceremonial," by the president, if possible.

In the 1990s, special legislation was passed that allowed Teddy to be considered for the Medal of Honor. On January 16, 2001, in a ceremony held in the Roosevelt Room of the White House attended by many Roosevelt family members, President Bill Clinton presented the medal to Tweed Roosevelt, Teddy's great-grandson—almost 103 years after Teddy's actions on San Juan Hill.

*Roosevelt (right) with Col. Leonard Wood (to his right) and Maj. Gen. Joseph Wheeler (with beard).*

Richmond P. Hobson came home to find himself a hero. A public peck on the cheek by a cousin at the beginning of a national tour inspired a kissing craze in which he was bussed by an estimated ten thousand women. He retired from the Navy in 1903, entered politics in 1906, and served four terms as a Democratic congressman from Alabama. Thereafter he occupied himself promoting such causes as naval expansion, prohibition of alcoholic liquor ("protoplasm poison," he called it), and the suppression of drug dealing. In 1933 a special act of Congress awarded him the Medal of Honor.

After the failure of the attempt to bottle up the Spanish ships in Santiago, Admiral Sampson called on the Army to flush them out. The seventeen thousand men of Maj. Gen. William T. Shafter's V Corps sailed from Tampa, Florida, on June 14, and began landing near Santiago eight days later. On July 1, they stormed the Spanish outposts at El Caney and San Juan Hill. Twenty-five Medals of Honor were granted for these actions. With the Americans closing on Santiago, the captain-general of Cuba ordered Cervera to try to fight his way out. On Sunday, July 3, 1898, the Spanish squadron was annihilated in a one-sided battle in which not a single American vessel was lost. The defenders of Santiago surrendered two weeks later and an armistice with Spain was signed on August 12.

A depiction of Lieutenant Hobson's capture by Admiral Cervera, with Hobson's portrait and those of other heroes of the Spanish-American War.

# Mexico, 1914

As the new century dawned, other regions in Latin America proved capable of arousing American indignation. In February 1913, Gen. Victoriano Huerta seized the presidency of Mexico in a bloody coup d'état. At home, his initiative provoked a revolution. In Washington, President Woodrow Wilson resolved to force Huerta out, setting the stage for another expansion war, this one in the Caribbean.

Neither initial diplomatic pressure nor an arms embargo expunged Huerta. When Wilson learned that a huge cargo of munitions was approaching the port of Veracruz, on Mexico's east coast, he ordered it intercepted. Plans were prepared to seize the Veracruz customhouse and occupy the city if need be.

The military commandant of the city armed convicts in the city jail and ordered men to the waterfront to repel the invasion. Mexican troops and armed civilians fired on troops in the streets and alleyways. All was quiet as 787 American Marines and sailors disembarked and fanned out through the city.

As one group of US sailors, under Ensign George M. Lowry, approached the customhouse, a Mexican policeman opened fire. In moments, a crackling fusillade from Mexican troops and civilians was heard.

Ensign George M. Lowry, who led a company from the USS *Florida* that seized the customhouse at Veracruz after fierce street fighting.

# CHANGING STANDARDS

The criteria by which the Medal of Honor is awarded have changed greatly over the years. The ambiguity of the original legislation for the Army and Navy medals gave nineteenth-century commanders wide latitude in choosing men "who shall most distinguish themselves by their gallantry in action and other soldierlike [or seamanlike] qualities." In those early years, many were undoubtedly given medals for actions that were not extraordinarily valorous but were in some way commendable. Considering a slew of recommendations for the battle of the Little Bighorn in 1877, Brig. Gen. Alfred H. Terry expressed exasperation with the lack of clear standards for medal-worthy actions. "Medals of Honor are not intended for ordinarily good conduct," he said, "but for conspicuous acts of gallantry." But the years since Appomattox had blurred such a distinction, or at least clouded the record.

The 1890s were, in the words of one medal historian, "the Dark Ages in the history of the Medal of Honor. The old veterans of the Civil War were on the march, storming the halls of Congress in their black slouch hats and pestering the overworked clerks at the War Department." In person or by mail, they sought their own Medals of Honor. Since there was no time limit on awards, a constant stream of requests flowed into the capital. "I believe I am entitled to a medal" was a common line, followed by a brief description of an act from years before. There was usually no extensive review or verification of the action; in some cases, the applicant's word was sufficient. The secretary of war would then direct that a medal be engraved and sent to the veteran.

From 1891 to 1897, over five hundred Medals of Honor were awarded for Civil War actions. The Medal of Honor Legion, a newly formed organization of medal recipients, expressed concern that the generous bestowal of the award was weakening its intended prestige. By the middle of the decade, many Army officials agreed.

On June 26, 1897, Secretary of War Russell A. Alger announced a more uniform method of determining Medal of Honor eligibility, stating that a deed must demonstrate "most distinguished gallantry in action" based on "incontestable proof" of the action. Verification, the Army announced later, had to come from "official reports of the action, record of events, muster rolls, and returns and descriptive lists." All subsequent recommendations were to be accompanied by the testimony of two or more eyewitnesses. Applications for actions taking place after January 1, 1890, could not be made by the prospective recipient himself, only by another officer or soldier having personal knowledge of the action. A year later the department announced that only officers could submit recommendations.

Alger's order also stipulated that recommendations for actions taking place in the future must be forwarded to the adjutant general within one year of their occurrence. It was the first time that the government placed a time limit on medal applications. The deadline did not apply to past actions, however, so Civil War deeds could still be considered. It was not until 1917 that the last two Union veterans, Henry Lewis and Henry C. Peters, got their Medals of Honor. As a result of these guidelines, recommendations for both the Army and Navy medals decreased, and subsequent citations became longer and more complete.

Though medal policy had been clarified somewhat, the liberality of many past awards still vexed some lawmakers and officers. In April 1916, President Wilson signed a law that not only revised medal standards but also allowed the Army to atone for past indiscretions.

The bill provided for the establishment of an "Army and Navy Medal of Honor Roll" and directed that a pension of ten dollars per month starting at age sixty-five be paid to each person who had "been awarded a medal of honor for having distinguished himself conspicuously by gallantry or intrepidity, at the risk of his life, above and beyond the call of duty." This last phrase would set the tone for later Medal of Honor awards for all armed services.

Some veterans were bound to be ineligible for the roll because of the tougher requirements for the medal. The War Department was ready to take a drastic step to correct what some viewed as unwarranted past awards. The opportunity came about in June 1916 when Congress authorized the department to appoint a board of five retired general officers to review every one of the

2,625 Army Medals of Honor awarded up to that time.

Chosen to head the panel was Lt. Gen. Nelson A. Miles, a medal recipient from Chancellorsville, a commander during the Indian Wars, and a past commander of the Medal of Honor Legion. Though Miles and his fellow officers later expressed uneasiness at being asked to rescind awards years after they were given, their concern over the dilution of the medal's prestige apparently superseded those feelings.

In a report filed on February 15, 1917, the Army board removed from the rolls the names of 911 recipients, more than one-third of the previous total. Included were an entire regiment, the 27th Maine, numbering 864 men (see page 37), and the twenty-nine members of the honor guard that had escorted President Lincoln's body to Illinois in April 1865. All these men were judged not to have merited the medal because they did not distinguish themselves in combat and at the risk of life.

The other eighteen were expunged for either lack of supporting evidence or failure to meet the statutory requirements. Dr. Mary Walker was another casualty of the review (see page 40), as were five men who had been Civil War or Indian Campaign scouts, including William F. "Buffalo Bill" Cody. "These men fully earned their medals," the panel reported, but because they were civilians at the time of their actions, they had become officially ineligible.

Some of the canceled recipients were notified that it was now illegal to wear or display their medals. To those who had never received them, such as some from the 27th Maine, such a warning was moot. Others, like Mary Walker, vowed to continue to wear their medals.

With the tightening of standards, however, military officials were left in a bind. Since the Medal of Honor and the Certificate of Merit (revived in 1877 for "distinguished service whether in action or otherwise, of a valuable character to the United States") were the only two awards in existence, how would lesser, but still praiseworthy, deeds be recognized?

The answer was an act that became law on July 9, 1918, creating three additional medals for the Army (and later the Air Force): the Distinguished Service Cross (and later, the Air Force Cross); the Distinguished Service Medal; and the Silver Star. The counterparts for the Navy and Marine Corps, established a year later, were the Navy Cross and the Distinguished Service Medal. Each was intended to honor actions that were notable but not "above and beyond the call of duty."

In a subtle yet important shift away from the Civil War legislation, the act authorized the president to award the new medals, "but not in the name of Congress." That imprimatur, and the attendant prestige, was reserved for the nation's highest honor. In later years, with the creation of other military awards, the Medal of Honor retained its place as America's premier military decoration, atop what became known as the "Pyramid of Honor."

Most of the changes concerning the Medal of Honor have dealt with the Army version. For almost a hundred years, the Navy regulations were basically unchanged. The phrase "seamanlike qualities" in the original legislation enabled the service to award its medal to sailors for peacetime bravery "in the line of their profession," such as rescues at sea. Finally in 1963, Congress decreed that the Navy medal could only be given for combat actions. (The Navy has never revoked past awards for statutory ineligibility, but several sailors lost their medals because of subsequent dishonorable conduct, such as desertion.)

Other features of the medal-awarding process have also been refined. The time limit between an action and the awarding of a Medal of Honor for it has occasionally been changed; today, for all services, the recommendation must be made within three years and the medal must be presented within five years. Congress can extend the limits by special statute, allowing for reconsideration of a case if new evidence warrants it.

The review process for a Medal of Honor recommendation in modern times is quite strict. A field commander's report goes through the chain of command to the awards board of the respective service, then to the service secretary, then to the secretary of defense, and finally to the president. At any point the medal can be denied. But if the president approves the recommendation, it has passed the strenuous test of verification and is judged worthy of the nation's highest award.

Lowry's company braved deadly machine-gun and sniper fire before reaching the customhouse and securing it. Another company of sailors arrived and took control of a warehouse filled with bales, sacks, and barrels of cotton, rice, sugar, rum, and molasses. Their commander, Ensign Paul Foster, had them load the stores onto hand trucks, creating a mobile breastwork they rolled into the street as protection for their advance. By noon the next day, American forces were in control of the city. In the two days' fighting, seventeen men were killed and sixty-three wounded. Mexican casualties were approximately eight hundred dead and wounded. On November 21, 1914, Huerta surrendered the presidency of Mexico.

Ensigns Lowry and Foster both received the Medal of Honor for Veracruz, along with fifty-three other men. Never before or since were so many Medals of Honor awarded for a single engagement; in fact, many regarded the number as extravagant.

*Left*
Troops raise the US flag over the Hotel Terminal on April 27, 1914, after the fall of Veracruz to American forces.

*Right*
Ensign Paul Foster (seated at desk) later acted as provost marshal of Veracruz, earning the sobriquet "Boy Poo-Bah of Veracruz."

# Haiti, 1915–1920

Scarcely a year after the landing at Veracruz, the United States intervened in Haiti. American policymakers had long been distressed by affairs there, where coup seemed to follow coup. To the Wilson administration, the latest of the Haitian revolutions seemed a golden opportunity to set the country straight.

*Caco*, the Haitian name for a native bird of prey, referred to part-time bandit-soldiers who lived in the jungly highlands of central Haiti. For generations, the cacos had been a crucial force in Haitian politics. For a certain sum, and permission to loot, they could be hired to replace one president with another. Haitians regarded this as "a well understood system for changing governments." To Americans, the cacos were an unruly influence on the political process and needed to be disarmed or removed.

On September 18, 1915, a band of cacos fired on a Marine patrol. A month later, a patrol of forty-four mounted Marines was ambushed after sundown by four hundred cacos. The time for action had come. By mid-November, aggressive patrolling had dispersed all but the hard core of cacos, who had retreated to Fort Rivière, atop a mountain deep in the hinterland.

Major Smedley Darlington Butler determined to take the fort. Butler was a colorful character. He had fought in Cuba, been wounded and cited for bravery in the Boxer Rebellion in China, and served on almost every coast of Central America, playing a leading role in Nicaragua in 1912. On November 17, Butler and his men dragged machine guns up the steep slope of the mountain to the fort. An open drain proved the only access. As Butler and his men emerged from the drain, a screaming throng of sixty or seventy cacos rushed toward them, some brandishing clubs. Fast work with .45s felled the caco leaders. In fifteen minutes, the Marines had control of the fort. Butler, Sgt. Ross L. Iams, and Pvt. Samuel Gross each received the Medal of Honor for their efforts that day.

For several years after the capture of Fort Rivière, something approaching peace prevailed in Haiti. Late in 1918, however, the emergence of a dynamic new leader, Charlemagne Péralte, brought the cacos back to life. Sergeant Herman H. Hanneken proposed to trap Péralte. For a bribe, a prominent citizen, Jean-Baptiste Conze, agreed to pretend to join the cacos, raise his own band, and gain Péralte's confidence. Hanneken strengthened the deception by "attacking" the band and "injuring" Conze.

The ruse worked. Word arrived that Péralte planned to attack the town of Grand Rivière du Nord, with Conze's band, on the night of October 31. Hanneken ordered Marines into the town, then set up an ambush. Soon, some seven hundred cacos approached the town, but Péralte was not among them.

Hanneken and his second-in-command, Marine Cpl. William R. Button, decided to try to reach Péralte's camp. With incredible daring, they bluffed their way through six caco checkpoints and entered the camp. Fifteen feet away from where Péralte stood, Hanneken drew his .45, and shot him. Back in the town, the Marines were equally successful. During the night, the caco attack on Grand Rivière was shattered.

In the morning, Péralte's body was brought down the mountain to convince any remaining doubters that the cacos were finished. Hanneken and Button each received the Medal of Honor, and by the end of 1920, Haiti was at peace again, at least for a while.

Major Smedley Darlington Butler was a double recipient of the Medal of Honor.

Sergeant Ross L. Iams earned the Medal of Honor in action at Fort Rivière.

Sergeant Herman H. Hanneken earned the Medal of Honor for his daring near Fort Rivière.

Medal of Honor recipient for the Dominican campaign, 1st Sgt. Roswell Winans.

# The Dominican Republic, 1916-1924

The United States was equally concerned about developments on the other side of the island, in the Dominican Republic. In April 1916, Gen. Desiderio Arias, a leader of the anti-American faction, revolted against pro-American President Juan Isidro Jimenez. Rear Admiral William B. Caperton landed troops to maintain order. Jimenez refused to attack his own people and resigned from office. General Arias had retreated to Santiago, in the north. Colonel Joseph H. "Uncle Joe" Pendleton assumed command of the Marines to rout him.

On June 26, 1916, Pendleton led 837 men of the 4th Marines inland around the hills from Monte Cristi; a smaller force of bluejackets and Marines moved out through the hills along the railroad from Puerto Plata the same day. The next day, his men dispersed a body of rebels dug in on two hilltops near Las Trencheras. Then, the Puerto Plata column broke through another enemy force outside the railroad tunnel at Alta Mira. The decisive action of the campaign was fought by Pendleton's command at Guayacanas on July 3.

The rebels had entrenched in heavy underbrush on a ridge across the Marines' path. Gunners dragged heavy Colt and Benet-Mercier machine guns through dense scrub to within two hundred yards of the rebel trenches. Corporal Joseph A. Glowin set up behind a fallen tree trunk and fired until he was injured twice. Nearby, 1st Sgt. Roswell Winans sprayed the trenches until his Colt jammed. Heedless of the rebel fire, he gestured toward the front and ordered a skirmish of Marines to follow him. The rebels fled as the advance neared their trenches. On July 6, Arias laid down his arms. Both Glowin and Winans were awarded the Medal of Honor for their intrepidity.

The third and last Medal of Honor awarded for the Dominican campaign was issued to 1st Lt. Ernest C. Williams. The Americans had issued a general disarmament, which Marine

Marines in the Dominican Republic during the pursuit of Arias's rebels, 1916.

units enforced throughout the Dominican Republic. One provincial governor, Juan Perez, refused to disarm. He held the provincial *fortaleza*, a walled masonry compound that served as both a government house and fort, at San Francisco de Macoris. Williams was assigned to remedy the situation.

Williams and two companies of Marines approached the fortaleza after dark. He led a dozen men in a dash for the open gate. Startled defenders wounded eight of his party, but Williams and the others got through. Their comrades surged forward, and in ten minutes it was all over.

# Nicaragua, 1927–1933

In 1912, President William Howard Taft sent US Marines to put down an uprising in Nicaragua, and left a unit of a hundred Marines to protect the American legation in the capital, Managua. By the mid-1920s, the United States was winding down its Caribbean commitments. In 1925, the legation guard withdrew from Managua. Hardly had the Marines departed, however, than the Liberal party leader Gen. Jose M. Moncada launched a revolt against the Conservative government. America landed peacekeeping forces, and in 1927 former Secretary of War Henry L. Stimson was sent to Nicaragua to negotiate a ceasefire.

Stimson promised the warring parties that if they would disarm, the United States would supervise free and fair elections in 1928. Both the Conservatives and Liberals agreed. One relatively junior Liberal leader, Augusto C. Sandino, however, did not. On July 16, 1927, he began what would be the last of the "banana wars."

Sandino and his followers, the Sandinistas, established their anti-American insurrection

Medal of Honor recipient for the Dominican campaign, 1st Lt. Ernest Williams.

US Marines capture a flag from Augusto Sandino's forces in Nicaragua.

# MEDAL OF HONOR DESIGNS

The current Army, Navy, and Air Force Medal of Honor designs are the products of almost a century of revision, both to preserve their singularity and to satisfy the changing wishes of military officials.

Cast from the same dies during the Civil War, the original Army and Navy medals have remained the models for their later incarnations. Both feature "Minerva Repulsing Discord" at the center and different suspension ribbon attachments particular to each service. These two medals, with only a change in the Army ribbon in 1896, were presented for the rest of the nineteenth century.

The widespread imitation of the Medal of Honor design by veterans groups, most notably the Grand Army of the Republic in the late 1800s, caused Army officials to consider a new design for their medal. Conceived by Brig. Gen. George Gillespie, a Civil War recipient, and approved in 1904, the new Army design was a five-pointed star, with a profile of Minerva at the center, surrounded by a green enameled laurel wreath. The Army eagle now rested on a bar reading VALOR. Supporting the medal was a blue silk ribbon, spangled with thirteen stars.

Gillespie received a patent for his design, which he turned over to the secretary of war and his successors. After the patent expired in 1918, Congress passed a law forbidding the unauthorized duplication of military medals.

Meanwhile, the Navy, which had awarded scores of Medals of Honor for peacetime bravery, created a different model for actual combat action in 1919. The Maltese cross designed by Tiffany & Company of New York bore the American eagle surrounded by four anchors. It was attached to a blue, starred ribbon with a bar that inexplicably bore the British spelling of VALOUR.

Only a handful of men, mostly from World War I, received this type of medal. Non-combat acts of valor continued to be rewarded by the star design of the Medal of Honor, now with a ribbon similar to the Army model. In 1942, Congress eliminated the Tiffany cross, and once again all naval personnel were eligible for only one Medal of Honor, the original star. The cross remains the rarest Medal of Honor model and represents the only time that the military deviated from its star design.

*Current US Army, US Navy, and US Air Force Medals of Honor.*

The naval star and the 1904 Army design were the models awarded during World War II. The medals were attached to a blue ribbon with a clasp, making the Medal of Honor the only American combat award that is draped around the neck. The neck ribbon was the last alteration of the modern Army and Navy medals.

In both world wars, Army Air Corps pilots received the Army Medal of Honor. Even in Korea, after the Air Force had become a separate service, its men continued to receive the Army design. In 1963, the Air Force created its own medal, first presented to Vietnam fliers. The Air Force Medal of Honor is similar to the Army medal, with the head of the Statue of Liberty replacing Minerva and a ribbon attachment more specific to that service.

One need not wear his Medal of Honor to be identified as a recipient. Military men on active duty wear a blue ribbon bearing five stars on the left breast of the uniform, always above all other decorations. A starred rosette is worn in the lapel by civilians.

*Top (left to right): Original Navy medal, 1862; original Army medal, 1862; Army, 1896.*
*Bottom (left to right): Army, Gillespie,1904; Navy, 1913; Navy, Tiffany Cross, 1919.*

Augusto Sandino, who led an insurrection against US forces in Nicaragua.

Corporal Donald L. Truesdell (left) receives the Medal of Honor. Truesdell later became a marksmanship instructor in World War II.

in the upland jungles, then attacked the US Marines at the village of Ocotal in the summer of 1927. Months of skirmishes followed until aerial reconnaissance located their headquarters.

On December 19, the Marines attacked, but instead of the two hundred to five hundred Sandinistas they expected, they were ambushed by one thousand. The Marines fell back to the village of Quilali. They set about improvising an airstrip for evacuating the wounded and bringing in reinforcements and supplies. The squadron's mechanics modified one of its 02U-1 Vought Corsair biplanes with landing gear from a DeHavilland DH-4, deemed more suitable for the expected rough landings. First Lieutenant Christian F. Schilt, a former enlisted man who had placed second in the Scheider International Seaplane Race in 1926, volunteered to pilot the craft.

Between January 6 and 8, 1928, Schilt made ten flights into Quilali, evacuating the wounded and bringing in 1,400 pounds of supplies. Every flight was a risky adventure. The Sandinistas fired mercilessly during every landing and takeoff. And because the Corsair lacked brakes, every landing meant that men on the ground had to run out and grab the plane's wings before it reached a ravine at the end of the bumpy, five-hundred-foot runway. Schilt's heroism was rewarded with the Medal of Honor.

Elections took place in 1928, as promised, and General Moncada won in a landslide. Sandino denounced him as an imperialist lackey, and vowed to continue to fight. Sandino appreciated the potential of the press. By this time, he had cultivated it to achieve international renown and even become an inspiration to revolutionary movements throughout Latin America. Stimson reasoned that attempting to eradicate the Sandinistas totally would require too great a military effort than it was sensible for the United States to make. He therefore ordered the US Marines to train the Nicaraguan *Guardia Nacional* to take over the country's defense.

Corporal Donald LeRoy Truesdell was on patrol when a rifle grenade fell from its carrier and struck a rock, igniting the detonator. Truesdell rushed for the grenade to get it away from his men, but it exploded in his hand. He saved his patrol from death or injury, but lost his right forearm. The Medal of Honor he received was the first one he had ever seen.

On January 1, 1933, Juan Sacasa assumed the country's presidency, and the next day the Marines left Nicaragua according to plan. Sandino initially agreed to disband his army in exchange for concessions, but friction ensued. Sacasa proposed further negotiations, and on February 21, 1934, Sandino and several of his lieutenants dined with Sacasa at the presidential palace. As they were leaving, they were mowed down by machine-gun fire, under orders of Gen. Anastasio Somoza. Two years later, Somoza deposed Sacasa and established an authoritarian regime that would rule Nicaragua until the overthrow of his son, Anastasio Somoza DeBayle, by a new generation of Sandinistas in 1979.

# A Restless Colony
## The Philippine Insurrection, 1899–1913

THE VICTORY OVER SPAIN was destined to have a bloody aftermath half a world away from the Caribbean. In the glow of its triumph, the United States decided to annex the conquered Philippines. A violent insurrection ensued, led by a young Filipino named Emilio Aguinaldo. Back home, after the initial outburst of indignation at Filipino ingratitude, few people paid much attention to the struggle, and most of those who did disapproved of American involvement. Major General Adna R. Chaffee, appointed to command in the islands in 1901, told his civilian superior, Governor-General William Howard Taft, that there was no glory in the Philippines.

In contrast to the Spanish-American War, the insurrection in the Philippines was neither splendid nor little. At peak strength, US forces in the islands numbered sixty-nine thousand men. By July 4, 1902, when President Theodore Roosevelt officially declared the conflict at an end, one thousand Americans had been killed in action and three thousand wounded. (The last medal of the conflict would be earned in 1913 during the Moro Rebellion.)

The nature of the Philippine campaigns differed sharply from previous American wars. The tropical climate was hot and humid. During the five months of the rainy season,

US soldiers in the Philippines await battle.

US soldiers in action during the Philippine Insurrection.

drenching downpours fell two out of every three days. Disease felled as many soldiers as bullets. Malaria was a fact of life. After the first few battles, the contest became a guerrilla war, a type of conflict guaranteed to embitter regular troops. And, bitterness was compounded by racial prejudice against the Philippine people, whom President William Howard Taft referred to as "little brown brothers" in what was regarded as a polite reference.

Corporal Frank L. Anders, who had grown up as an Army brat and been held during his christening by an officer of Custer's cavalry, was one of the twenty-five sharpshooters picked to scout out a planned offensive on the rebel-held city of San Isidro. Arthur W. Young, a civilian volunteer and former frontiersman, organized a detachment of scouts and picked Anders for his unit.

Keeping well ahead of the main body, Young set a blistering pace toward San Isidro. On the morning of May 13, all except ten of his men were too fatigued to go on. Young led them forward, accompanied by two officers who had joined the detachment the previous day, Cpts. William E. Birkhimer and J. F. Case. At around nine o'clock, the scouts approached the town of San Miguel de Mayumo only to find three hundred Filipino *insurrectos* blocking their path. Their entrenched position made a frontal assault necessary. Young sent Case to bring up reinforcements, but announced, "We are not waiting for support. We are going forward."

They did just that. Sending five men to try to work around to the left, Young led Anders and four others straight toward the insurrectos. Birkhimer went with them. They advanced in short rushes, the sharpshooters covering one another. It took half an hour to cross the 150 yards to the enemy position, and when they reached the entrenchment, they found only forty-nine dead insurrectos.

The other men rejoined them there, and the detachment pushed on another two hundred yards toward a bridge crossing to the town. The insurrectos met them there and charged. The Americans crossed the bridge into San Miguel; six were cut down by the scouts' fire and the others fell back, but Young was mortally wounded. His men carried him across the bridge into San Miguel, where they occupied the church in anticipation of a counterattack. For four hours, from 10:00 a.m. to 2:00 p.m., the scouts held the enemy at bay. Shortly thereafter, the approach of American reinforcements caused the Filipinos to retire.

All of the men, including Anders, who had followed their commander in the attack on the insurrecto entrenchment, received the Medal of Honor: Cpl. Frank Anders, Captain Birkhimer, and Pvts. Willis H. Downs, Gotfred Jensen, Edward E. Lyon, and Peter H. Quinn. Happily, the passions of the insurrection war eventually faded; the Filipino-American friendship that grew up in its aftermath would be affirmed forty years later, when a more terrible contest would engulf the Pacific.

Corporal Frank L. Anders, who earned the Medal of Honor during an attack on Filipino insurrectos.

US soldiers and captured insurrectos at the cathedral in the Walled City, Manila.

# CHAPTER FOUR

# World War I

## 1914-1918

# The First World War

The First World War erupted with the crack of a Serbian assassin's bullet, killing Archduke Franz Ferdinand of the Austro-Hungarian Empire. In one cataclysmic week, from July 28 to August 5, 1914, Austria-Hungary declared war on Serbia; Russia mobilized in support of its Balkan ally; Germany declared war on Russia and its key ally, France, and marched into strategically vital Belgium; and Great Britain declared war on Germany for violating Belgium's neutrality. In the ensuing weeks and months, European powers dragged in their colonies across the globe while the opportunistic joined the side of the alliance they judged most likely to win. In the next four years, over thirteen million soldiers and civilians were to die in the conflict.

The United States proclaimed neutrality at first. Said President Woodrow Wilson, "It is a war with which we have nothing to do, whose causes cannot touch us." But over the next thirty-three months, the American president and people slowly changed their minds. The US government came to fear for the future of the United Kingdom and the balance of power it had maintained to America's advantage. More crucial to popular sentiment, the new technology of warfare made the American vision of neutrality obsolete.

On May 7, 1915, a German U-boat torpedoed and sank the British passenger liner *Lusitania,* killing over 1,000 people, 128 of them Americans. For a time, the United States flamed with war fever. It cooled only when the German government promised to rein in its submarine fleet. But by 1917, Germany felt compelled to break a tight British blockade, which was strangling its imperial war machine. In February, Germany resumed unrestricted submarine warfare. In March, its submarines, without warning, sank five unarmed American merchant vessels. On April 2, President Wilson called for war. The Senate agreed, 82-6; the House followed on April 6 by a 373–50 vote.

The United States entered a deadly standoff that had been raging with exhausting brutality. Lines of fortified trenches scarred northern France and Belgium. Around them, soldiers died by the thousands in massed infantry assaults that moved the line only a few feet forward or back. Ten days after the United States declared war, the French launched yet another futile attack near Reims and in ten more days had gained nothing but another 187,000 casualties.

Attempting to tip the balance, both sides produced progressively more ruthless weapons of destruction. Machine guns were the biggest killer. At the onset of war, France had 2,500 machine guns; by the armistice it had built and deployed 314,000. A single gun could wipe out dozens of charging

*Previous pages*
Men and tanks of the US 1st Infantry Division advance against German machine-gun positions near the Villers-Cotterêts Forest, July 1918.

*Below*
Archduke Franz Ferdinand (far right) and his wife Sophie in Sarajevo, June 28, 1914, moments before they were both assassinated by Serbian terrorist Gavrilo Princip.

men in moments. Other relatively new agents of death were hand grenades, trench mortars, aerial warfare, tanks, and poison gas. In one twenty-minute gas bombardment at Ypres in 1915, fifteen thousand men died or were left to spend the rest of their lives as gasping invalids.

The new destructive power had taken an enervating toll on both sides by the time the United States entered the war, but the Allies were in worse shape than their enemies. Low morale following the French failure in the Champagne offensive led to a series of mutinies in the French army. Germany's revival of submarine warfare was having its intended effect on British shipping, the principal Allied resource. And in Russia, antiwar rumblings grew louder until in November 1917 they sparked a revolution that resulted in a separate peace. The entry of the fresh, enthusiastic doughboys, backed by the industrial might of the United States, could not have come at a more opportune time.

German troops marching off to war accept flowers from an admirer. Germany mobilized eleven million men to fight in the Great War.

In March 1917, the US Army consisted of about two hundred thousand men. During the war, that number leaped to four million, over half of them draftees. One and a half million American soldiers ultimately saw combat in France and another half-million supported them. But this was a slow process. Drafting, training, equipping, and moving large numbers of troops across the ocean was a gargantuan task. It took eight months for the Americans to join the fighting. By May 1918, only the first half a million troops had arrived in France. And they were still engaged in training or were occupying quiet sectors. Until June, the support they gave the Allies was moral.

That all changed, though, once they became engaged. In the last five months of the war, forty-nine thousand doughboys gave their lives in the Allied cause; over two hundred thousand more were wounded. An additional sixty-three thousand died in the influenza pandemic that scourged military compounds.

Commanding the American Expeditionary Forces (AEF) was John J. Pershing. Called "Blackjack" because of his iron will and steely discipline, his powers were sorely tested in creating an army from scratch. He took command of American forces in Europe in 1917. He had orders to cooperate with the Allies but to build the AEF as a distinct and separate unit. This conflicted with the plans of Marshal Ferdinand Foch, commander of French and British operations on the western front, who implored Pershing to turn over his forces to the unified

# JOEL T. BOONE

On July 19, 1918, Lt. Cdr. Joel T. Boone displayed valor in the battlefield while serving as a medical officer with the 6th Regiment, US Marines. Leaving the shelter of a ravine near Vierzy, France, Boone ventured into an unprotected field under heavy enemy fire, through a mist of gas, to administer first aid to wounded Marines. When his medical supplies were exhausted, he went back through the heavy fire and gas to replenish his supplies and help save more lives. Boone repeated this heroic act later that same day.

Boone served in many capacities as a medical officer for the Navy, including as a physician in the White House, and also served in World War II and the Korean War, making him one of the few individuals to have served in all three conflicts. He is one of the most highly decorated medical officers in the history of the armed services, having been awarded the Distinguished Service Cross, the Silver Star (six times), the Bronze Star, and the Purple Heart, among many other awards. But it was the Medal of Honor he earned that day in France.

*Acting Secretary of the Navy Franklin D. Roosevelt pins the Medal of Honor on Lieutenant Commander Boone at the White House in 1919.*

command to be deployed where Foch deemed them most needed. For the most part, Pershing held firmly to his orders.

Only during the darkest days of the German offensive on the Marne in the spring of 1918 did American troops fight under foreign command. One of the battles of that offensive, at Château-Thierry in June 1918, was the Americans' first significant engagement—and their first victory. In one month of heavy fighting, the US 2nd Division, fighting under French command, halted a major German advance, then pushed the enemy out of Belleau Wood. Two Marines and two Navy medics earned Medals of Honor in that action. Germany's defeat in the Aisne-Marne offensive eased the pressure on the Allies considerably. Morale rose, and Pershing reclaimed his troops for the separate US Army.

On September 26, following three months of small engagements, the Allies launched a great counteroffensive along the entire front. The AEF took the eastern sector, centered upon the heavily defended Argonne Forest. Pershing deployed every American division at his disposal—1.2 million US troops in total. Their goal was to cut off the main German supply line feeding the western front.

The Germans fought desperately, employing their advantages in position, artillery, and experience. But the Americans overpowered them in numbers and audacity. In six weeks of brutal fighting, the AEF captured the Argonne, taking sixteen thousand prisoners in the bargain. Eighty-two men earned the Medal of Honor in the engagements.

On November 11, after a week of strikes, mutiny, and revolution among its allies, Germany surrendered. The peace negotiations at Versailles, France, were a fiasco from the start. Wilson had convinced the German government to sue for peace on the basis of his "Fourteen Points"—including "open covenants of peace, openly arrived at," free trade, mutual armament reduction, and adjustment of colonial claims to give equal weight to the desires of the native populations. Wilson had not bothered to get the Allied governments to agree to these terms—

nor would they now. Even the US Congress opposed many of the points. Wilson called for a lenient peace, to bring Germany into the society of democracies, but Britain and especially France insisted on unconditional surrender. With casualties running in the millions and destruction of property in the billions of dollars, the French and British demanded huge reparations, regardless of Germany's ability to pay.

Wilson had envisioned an enlightened treaty that would spell the end of all war. But so different was the document he came back with than his original promise that the nation turned away from it in revulsion. On November 19, 1919, the US Senate rejected the Versailles Treaty and the League of Nations it created. In the economic and social heydays of the 1920s, the United States tried to distance itself from the quarrelsome continent where thousands of its young men lay buried.

A soldier boy of the 71st Regiment Infantry, New York National Guard, saying goodbye to his sweetheart as his regiment leaves for Camp Wadsworth, Spartanburg, South Carolina, where the New York Division trained for service.

Unrestricted German submarine warfare took a frightful toll on Allied shipping. Here survivors of a U-boat torpedo attack slide down ropes from their crippled craft to board waiting lifeboats.

# OVER THERE

The beleaguered Allies, many of whom had been fighting for over three years, cheered the arrival of American forces in France in 1918. The doughboys' high spirits proved the decisive factor in overcoming the same miserable conditions that had bled other nations dry. They tipped the balance of power in favor of the Allies.

A cover for inspirational sheet music likening General Pershing to the father of his country.

US soldiers in a trench put on gas masks to protect themselves from poisonous gas.

American tanks in the Argonne, 1918.

# ADVANCE ON THE MARNE
## *Belleau Wood*

In the late spring of 1918, French morale reached rock bottom. After nearly four years of incessant, grinding war, victory seemed as far out of reach as ever. The US declaration of war was now more than a year old—and still the Americans had made no significant contribution on the battlefield. Then in early June, in an obscure little forest called Belleau Wood, the US Marines stopped, and then reversed, a week-long German advance on the Marne River. A French staff officer, seeing the doughboys arrive at the front, declared: "The spectacle of those magnificent youths . . . contrasted strikingly with our regiments in their faded uniforms, wasted by so many years of war. . . . Life was coming in floods to reanimate the dying body of France."

Shot and shell were not the only means of destruction on the battlefields of France. Here, soldiers administer aid to victims of a gas attack at Jaulny, France.

On May 27, 1918, a thunderous barrage of gas and high-explosive shells signaled the start of Germany's major offensive in the Marne region. Thirty German divisions punched through the French lines at the Chemin des Dames and began to push toward Paris. By June 1, they had less than forty miles to go. The French were in disarray; the enemy had scored tremendous victories, including the capture of over sixty-five thousand prisoners. In a tense meeting of the Allied Supreme War Council, French Premier Georges Clemenceau blamed the massive defeat on General Pershing's unwillingness to throw his troops into the fight. Pershing thought otherwise; he laid the blame on the Allies' stubborn commitment to trench warfare. As much as his French counterparts, however, he feared the loss of Paris— and with it the loss of the war. On May 30, Pershing dropped his insistence on a separate US Army and temporarily turned over his first five divisions to fight under French command. Hours later, the US 2nd Division was ordered to head for the very center of the German advance at Chateau-Thierry.

The 2nd Division of US regulars was a "bastard" division: half Marine, half Army. Though they were called regulars, not even a quarter of its men had been in the service for more than a year. Most, Army and Marine alike, had enlisted in the flush of patriotism that followed the US declaration of war. But they were more than ready to take on the Germans, having spent the last four and a half months in France training and patrolling away from the front.

Two days and several changes of orders later, the division stood on the battle line. On June 4, the Marine brigade halted the Germans at Belleau Wood. So far, however, action had been light. By June 6, they were ready to go on the offensive. They eagerly accepted orders to flush the Germans out.

The 49th and 67th Rifle Companies of the 5th Marines led the attack. Their objective was Hill 142, a commanding position overlooking the wood. To secure it they would have to defeat two German battalions backed up by three machine-gun companies hidden in the trees. At 3:45 a.m., the Marines headed up. For the first fifty yards they advanced easily, protected by the morning fog. Then, as the sun cut through, the machine guns from the hill opened up. A number of Americans fell; many more hit the ground in fear. For several minutes the Marines halted. Then, the initial shock over, they rushed the wooded ridge.

Marine Gunnery Sergeant Ernest A. Janson, who received two Medals of Honor under two different names.

Gunnery Sergeant Ernest Janson, a thirty-nine-year-old career man, urged his platoon into the forest. Janson was a man as mysterious as he was brave. In 1910, after eleven years in the Army, he left the service and enlisted with the Marines as a buck private under the name of Charles Hoffman. He never explained why.

No explanations about names were required in Belleau Wood on June 6, 1918, however. Janson's job was to take the hill. He and his comrades in 49th Company ran from clearing to forest to ravine, taking machine-gun fire and giving more than their share of casualties in return. In just over two hours, they not only reached their objective, but, because of a map-reading error, they overran it by six hundred yards. By midmorning, they had begun consolidating their position on the hill.

Janson was in the midst of organizing a strong point on the north side of the hill when the enemy counterattacked. Experts at infiltration, the Germans penetrated within twenty feet of the Marines unobserved. Then Janson spotted a dozen Germans armed with five machine guns crawling through the thick underbrush. The sergeant shouted a warning to his company, then rushed their position before the enemy could recover their momentum. Singling out the two leaders, Janson bayoneted both. The others dropped their machine guns and ran. Company commander Capt. George Hamilton, who had witnessed the incident, credited Janson's quick action with saving 49th Company and keeping American possession of the hill. The sergeant had also earned a Medal of Honor, with two citations, and the confusion about Janson/Hoffman's name went down in history. Under the dual arrangement for members of the Marine brigade serving in the First World War under Army command, Medal of Honor recipients received two awards—one from the Army, one from the Navy. Janson's two citations

German prisoners, captured by Americans, at Belleau Wood.

carry separate names. The Army medal went to Ernest Janson, the Navy medal to Charles F. Hoffman.

With Hill 142 securely in American hands by midafternoon June 6, the Marines struck into Belleau Wood itself, but they could not break through to their objective, the village of Bouresches on the forest's southwest corner.

The job fell to 96th Company. To reach Bouresches, the company had to cross an open wheat field directly in front of a line of German trenches, machine-gun emplacements, and sharpshooter pits nestled just inside the wood. By the time the 96th had crossed the seven-hundred-yard field, only thirty remained in good enough shape to fight. One was Gunnery Sgt. Fred Stockham. A ten-year veteran of the Marine Corps who had seen combat in Nicaragua, Stockham urged on the green recruits under him. Fighting in the streets of Bouresches, nine more Marines fell. But Stockham and the others under the command of Lt. Clifton B. Cates pressed forward. With only twenty-one men left on their feet, they took the village. For that day's action, Stockham won a division citation and the Croix de Guerre with gilt star.

Americans and their German prisoners.

The 96th held on to Bouresches for three days until it received desperately needed relief. For four days, the company stayed in support, the closest thing to a rest the Germans and the thin Allied line would give them. On June 13, somewhat revived and reinforced by their treated wounded, they were ordered back to the mile-square wood, two-thirds of which now lay under Marine command. But the battle was not over.

At midnight, just as the 96th was arriving on line, the Germans launched a powerful counterattack. The Germans directed a five-hour barrage of high explosives, artillery shells, and mustard gas into the thinning, gouged-out forest. The 96th, caught in the blast before it could properly entrench and prepare itself, lost half its men, most to gas. Many gas masks proved defective, others were rendered useless by shrapnel. Sergeant Stockham was evacuating wounded and gassed Marines through the barrage to the dressing station when shrapnel from a high explosive shell ripped through the mask of the man he carried. He pulled off his own mask and placed it on the wounded man while taking him to the aid station. He then returned to the front, maskless, to pull out more wounded. Choking and gasping from lack of air, he made several more trips. Then he collapsed, destined to die the horrible death of the gas victim nine days later.

As Stockham was carried from Belleau Wood, the Marines threw back the German counterattack. On June 25, the Americans staged their final assault and took the wood completely. The Marine brigade had defeated four enemy divisions in their three-week battle.

Twenty-one years went by before Stockham was awarded a Medal of Honor for his sacrifice. Lieutenant Cates had submitted a formal recommendation the night of the incident, but

The village of Vaux, near Belleau Wood, decimated by American artillery fire.

like all the citations that chaotic night, it was lost before reaching division headquarters. Stockham's comrades would not let the matter drop. At a company reunion in the 1930s, they voted to press the claim, even though the final extension for granting medals for World War I had lapsed. Cates, who was soon to become commandant of the Marine Corps, prevailed upon some acquaintances in Congress to make a special case of Sergeant Stockham, whom Cates called "the bravest man I ever knew." On July 15, 1939, President Franklin D. Roosevelt signed into law a special resolution passed by both houses awarding the medal to Gunnery Sgt. Fred Stockham.

# SURVIVAL IN THE ARGONNE
## *The Lost Battalion*

After the Allies beat back the German assault on the Marne, attention turned to eastern France. First the Allies reduced the Saint-Mihiel salient in September 1918. Then the Americans, fighting under General Pershing, launched an attack against enemy positions in the Argonne Forest.

The most legendary American unit to emerge from the Meuse-Argonne campaign was the so-called "Lost Battalion." Like all legends, however, the story of the stranded outpost that held out for a week against concerted German attack has been mixed heavily with myth. The very name "Lost Battalion" is a misnomer. The unit, which was made up of parts of three battalions plus support personnel, knew precisely where it was, and so did its superiors. The name was coined by a wire-service editor in the United States. Reading a dispatch on the plight of the besieged task force, he penciled in the term "lost"—not, he later explained, meaning confused, but rather "being done for, of being in a hopeless situation." In that sense, he came very close to being right.

The First Army began its drive on the forbidding Argonne Forest on September 26, but bogged down after only a few miles. The forest itself was the principal enemy. A nearly impenetrable tangle of trees and underbrush, strewn with ravines and rock-covered hills, the wood gave cover to dozens of German machine gunners and snipers, while it fiercely resisted penetration by the Allies' heavy weapons. As Pershing threw his troops into the forest in waves, the well-hidden and entrenched Germans picked them off with devastating ease. By October, the Argonne Forest had become the black spot on the Allied line.

On the evening of October 1, Gen. Robert Alexander, commander of the 77th "Statue of Liberty" Division, drew up yet another plan to crack the Argonne from the south. His sector was holding up the American advance line. More critically, his troops were growing weaker with each rebuffed assault. He needed to break the German defense soon. All attempts to flank the wood having failed, Alexander ordered a three-pronged drive right through the middle. The center of the attack would be the 308th Infantry. The advance battalion would be the 1st, under Maj. Charles Whittlesey.

At 8:10 a.m. on October 2, the 77th headed into a driving rain. Between the weather and the woods, the men could barely see where they were going. From their hiding spots in the forest, however, German machine guns and artillery could get an easy fix on the stumbling and crashing Americans. Whittlesey's battalion trudged forward slowly but steadily, casualties mounting at a frightening pace as it advanced farther and farther ahead of its flanks. At 10:00 a.m., the major phoned headquarters to protest his orders. The battalion would be cut off if it continued, he warned. He urged a halt until the flanks caught up. Alexander issued a curt reply: The objective must be attained that day.

In the early afternoon, three companies of the 2nd Battalion under Capt. George G. McMurtry were ordered to aid Whittlesey. This time the going was much easier, the Germans having turned their full attention to the flanks. Congratulating themselves on their good fortune, the Americans crossed the line and made for their objective, five hundred yards up the hill.

An infantry attack in the woods at Argonne Forest.

In an elongated pocket on the hillside, just beneath the road, Whittlesey called a halt. The position was fairly secure, protected by thick forest and the slope of the hill, with a creek providing fresh water only fifty yards below. It seemed the safest place to set up camp until the flanking forces joined them. Whittlesey set up a "runner chain," a relay team of soldiers who would carry messages to headquarters. Then he positioned the companies and ordered them to dig in. A quick head count showed that of about seven hundred men from the 308th that began the assault, fewer than six hundred were now present for duty.

Back at headquarters, concern grew. Neither flank had gained any ground; indeed, in some areas they had lost territory. Whittlesey's task force was alone, and Alexander decided to send it more help. He ordered another battalion to the position. Moving across the wretched terrain in total darkness, however, all but one company got lost, and that one lost two of its squads. Only seventy-nine men from Company K, under Capt. Nelson Holderman, reached the outpost. They were the last Americans to make it in or out for the next five days. By sunrise the Yanks were surrounded.

October 3 opened with an artillery barrage from a German regiment holding the crest of the hill above the Americans. Whittlesey had chosen a good position. The angle of the pocket tilted against the guns' trajectory. Shells fell all around, but few made it into the perimeter. Trench mortars and potato masher grenades followed with greater accuracy but little effect, since they were most lethal in an enclosed space. The deadliest enemies were machine guns—and time. The men had rations and medical supplies for only one day, ammunition for not much more. Their water supply depended on free access to the brook below them—which a German machine gun now monitored closely. Without relief the task force would become ever more vulnerable to infantry charge.

To build their manpower, Whittlesey sent Company E back down the hill to find and bring back two companies that headquarters had held for reserve. A little more than an hour later, eighteen of Company E's fifty men staggered back to the outpost. Most were wounded. They had been ambushed by English-speaking Germans. The runner chain had likewise been annihilated. Now the only

After capturing the German second-line trenches in a section of the Argonne Forest, these American soldiers enjoy a needed rest.

means of communication with division command was the battalion's six carrier pigeons. Whittlesey dispatched one reporting his position and requesting immediate aid.

At dawn on October 4, 1st and 2nd Battalions reported 82 killed and 140 wounded since arriving in the pocket. There were only three enlisted medics to minister to the wounded, and they had already run out of bandages and most other supplies. The seriously wounded were lying in foxholes and behind fallen trees—anywhere that might afford them a bit of protection and keep their moans at some distance from the already skittish defenders. Whittlesey and McMurtry walked among the men, trying to give them some assurance that they had a reason to hang on, but it was not easy. The major had sent off three pigeons, without any indication that the messages had been received. Patrols dispatched to the right and left found no sign of allies on either flank. Those sent down the hill never got more than halfway. With relief no closer, at 5:30 a.m. the second day's assault began.

At headquarters, Alexander was doing everything he could to send help to the besieged unit. He ordered two reserve companies to join the battalions in the pocket, but they were turned back, decimated by German fire. A message from Whittlesey at midmorning reported that after beating off a concerted attack earlier in the day, his effective strength was down to 235, and those were suffering from hunger and exposure. The wounded, without tents, blankets, or even coats to ward off the cold were in especially bad shape. "Cannot support be sent at once?" he implored. Alexander phoned the division's artillery commander and told him to train his guns on the Germans on the hill above the pocket. At 1:15, the American guns let fire.

The next four hours were by all accounts the worst of the entire siege. Somehow the artillery commander got the wrong coordinates. Believing they were pinpointed on the Germans, the gunners sent a massive barrage directly onto the Americans. Men, at first elated to hear guns barking from the south, scrambled in a panicked race to escape the fusillade. Nearly all of what was left of Company E was captured when its lieutenant tried to lead it to a safer position. Eighty others were killed or wounded.

The normally calm Whittlesey rushed to his command post and dashed off a message to headquarters: "Our own artillery is dropping a barrage directly on us. For heaven's sake stop it." The frightened bird keeper released the first pigeon before he had attached the message. That left only one bird. He clipped on Whittlesey's note, tossed the pigeon into the air, and watched with breath held as the confused bird flew to the nearest tree and perched. Only by throwing stones at it could Whittlesey persuade the pigeon to fly through the artillery barrage. Once the message was airborne, he could only pray that it would make it to the base.

The major gathered a party to evacuate the wounded to a place that afforded some modicum of cover from the

Captain Nelson Holderman, 307th Infantry, one of the last Americans to reach the Lost Battalion before the siege began.

American soldiers go on the attack in the Argonne Forest.

Cher Ami, the carrier pigeon that brought a critical message to the rear and lost a leg in the process.

Second Lieutenant Erwin Bleckley sketched a map of German positions near the Lost Battalion. Note the half wings of an aerial observer on his blouse.

falling shells. After that, he resumed his tour of the defense. The men took heart from the sight of Whittlesey and McMurtry walking steadily among them, issuing reassuring words, promising the attack would soon end. The leaders' fortitude was all the more impressive since both were wounded. McMurtry, whose kneecap had been blown away, moved with considerable pain.

At 4:00 p.m. the last pigeon, by then badly injured, reached division headquarters, and the horrified commanders called an immediate halt to the shelling. It was too late to spare the outpost, though. In addition to killing and wounding dozens of Americans, the four-hour barrage had wiped out their cover. The halt in the artillery assault was thus followed immediately by the most accurate German machine-gun and grenade attack so far. Behind it came the enemy's first concerted infantry rush. Twice the Germans made it across the road to the very edge of the perimeter before the Americans knocked them back. Heavy fighting continued for the rest of the day. At nightfall the battalions still remained in command of the position, though by their fingernails.

After a night of renewed rainfall, the morning of October 5 finally brought some relief. A thick ground fog blanketed the pocket, preventing the Germans from launching their usual dawn artillery and machine-gun attack. Hunger, cold, and diminishing morale were now the principal enemies. Men licked up coffee grounds, seeds, anything edible they could find. They rummaged through the pockets of their dead comrades in a mostly futile search for food. Others, too weak even to forage, huddled shivering in foxholes. Perhaps most damaging to the morale of the men, many of whom were desperate for water, was the constant rush of the brook below. Whenever the Germans heard the clank of a bucket or helmet against the streambed, they sprayed the area with machine-gun fire. So many men died making unauthorized water runs that Whittlesey had to post riflemen along the path leading to the creek with orders to shoot anyone seen going that way.

Overhead the Lost Battalion could hear airplanes searching for its position. Now and then the defenders noted the thump of falling parcels. But none fell within retrievable distance. The starving Americans did not have to guess the contents of the airdrops; the enemy let them know in sickening detail. "Ham!" they called out in English. "Chocolate, biscuits, butter!" The Germans surrounding them were eating better than they had in years. Messages of encouragement sent from headquarters by plane fell even farther afield—one was picked up by a reserve unit some seven miles to the rear.

The pilots did their best. Two of them, Lts. Harold Goettler and Erwin Bleckley, flying a two-seater observation plane, made a number of extremely low passes over the area trying to pinpoint the battalion despite crippling antiaircraft fire by the Germans on top of the hill. These pilots had no more luck than any of the others in getting supplies to the outpost, but Bleckley was able to map out the enemy gun positions before he passed out from wounds. After taking a number of direct hits, Goettler somehow coaxed the biplane to a rough landing inside French lines. When the Allies reached the cockpit, however, they found the pilot dead. Bleckley died a few minutes later. Both men were awarded the Medal of Honor posthumously.

With the help of Bleckley's map, the 77th Divisional Artillery readjusted its sights. Once the mist cleared, the Germans were the ones to feel the power of the American guns. The barrage hit them just as they were massing for an attack. It probably saved the task force from being overrun. When the Germans were finally able to regroup and launch their attack late that afternoon, they were a greatly weakened force. Once again the defenders beat them back.

Meanwhile, beneath them, the 308th's commander asked to be relieved rather than send his decimated forces on another suicidal attempt to break through to the stranded 1st and 2nd Battalions. Alexander relieved him and ordered the 3rd Battalion up again.

Day four of the siege was an even crueler version of those that had preceded it. The enemy brought in flamethrowers in a desperate move to finish off the Americans. The liquid fire actually did little real damage in the defoliated pocket, but it was nearly the last straw for the terrified defenders. Whittlesey had to spend every waking moment now encouraging his men to hold on. The sounds of a major battle were getting closer, he told them; they would soon be free. Few any longer believed him. They fought on, but for the first time they lost ground. That night Whittlesey's greatest fear began to materialize. Nine men sneaked out from the perimeter to get some airdropped parcels and were captured. His command was coming apart.

October 7, as men down at headquarters discussed the meaning of the news they had just received of Germany's preliminary bid for peace talks, the soldiers in the pocket wrote farewell notes to their families. There were no writing supplies, so they scrawled their letters on shirttails and old bandages, using mud or even blood for ink. They had been without food or water for three days of nearly constant warfare. Around them the bodies of their dead comrades had begun to putrefy. They had no idea that on the crest of the hill the Germans, too, were ready to quit. The 77th Division's persistent assault on the Argonne was draining the enemy badly. The German division commander ordered the regiment besieging Whittlesey's outpost to prepare to move out that night with or without a victory.

At the German regiment's command post, the officers discussed how they could avoid the blotch of a defeat on their records. They tried a bold gambit. Picking out one of the prisoners captured the night before, they sent him back to the pocket with a message calling for the task force's surrender. "The suffering of your wounded men can be heard over here in the German lines," it read, "and we are appealing to your human sentiments. A white flag shown by one of your men will tell us that you agree . . ." Whittlesey, McMurtry, and Holderman read the message a couple of times. Then, for the first time in days, they broke into genuine smiles. "We've got them licked or they wouldn't have sent this," McMurtry grinned. Whittlesey crumpled up the message.

Word of the German demand spread rapidly through the pocket. The appeal to humanitarianism infuriated men who had watched their buddies die and their unburied bodies rot. Men who had not spoken for days joined in a chorus of abuse aimed at the German line. The enemy answered with their most determined assault yet. The Americans, revived by their anger, fought back. Wounded men limped out of their foxholes to the front line and fired guns that had long been silent. Those who could not get to their feet loaded ammunition. Holderman went nearly wild with rage, standing in the open and blasting away at the enemy, whooping whenever he scored a hit. After an hour of this unexpected punishment, the enemy called retreat and ran back up the hill.

First Lieutenant Harold Goettler, Bleckley's pilot, was able to land his plane behind Allied lines before succumbing to his wounds.

Captain George G. McMurtry, a former "Rough Rider," led three companies of the 2nd Battalion, 308th Infantry, in support of Major Whittlesey's men.

The survivors of the Lost Battalion in October 1918, shortly after their rescue.

Major Charles Whittlesey receives the Medal of Honor on Boston Common, December 24, 1918.

That afternoon, the 77th Division finally crossed the German line. At 6:00 p.m. a patrol from the 307th Infantry made it into the wretched perimeter. A messenger reported to Whittlesey that there was a captain on the road who wanted to see him. With effort, the major rose from the ground, telling McMurtry he need not bother getting up. An enlisted man asked, "Is it safe now on the road?" Whittlesey muttered, "I guess so" and slowly walked out. A few minutes passed before McMurtry realized what that meant—the road had not been safe since they got there. They were relieved.

The resistance of the Lost Battalion carried a tremendous cost. Of the more than 600 men who entered the pocket, only 194 marched out October 8. One hundred seventy were dead; the rest were carried out on stretchers, many to die of their wounds in Army hospitals. Holderman's medical report revealed ten separate wounds—two listed as severe—in both legs plus his right arm, left hand, right foot, pelvis, and face. McMurtry had a shattered knee and a number of surface lesions. Both, however, along with a number of their men, volunteered to go back on the line just as soon as they had downed a good meal. And both men would later receive the Medal of Honor for their courage during the long siege.

Whittlesey, too, had wounds on his body; but none were as severe as the mental anguish he felt from the many orders he had given and patrols he had sent off to their doom. In later years that anguish grew amid misguided accusations that he had brought on the siege by pursuing the Germans overzealously, overstepping his orders. The memory of the week in which he earned the Medal of Honor would not let him go. In 1921, Charles Whittlesey boarded a vacation liner to Cuba and jumped over the side. His body was never found. His friends pronounced him "a war casualty."

# THE LAST DAYS

## *Lieutenant Furlong's War*

Just as the machine gun was the most significant weapon of the war, more Americans received the Medal of Honor for charging machine-gun nests than for any other kind of action. To many, such an act might seem the height of courage—or madness. For one American soldier fighting in the last weeks of the war, it was just part of the job.

When Dr. Harold A. Furlong was asked why, as a young lieutenant, he took on an enemy emplacement of four machine guns and more than twenty soldiers, he seemed surprised that it even merited a question. "There was no choice to do anything different," he said. "The machine gunners had to be stopped. . . . I had no idea that it was a heroic deed. . . . The machine guns were silenced. I was grateful and so were my compatriots."

Lieutenant Furlong was at the front line on November 1, 1918, the first day of the final stage of the Meuse-Argonne offensive. He had trained for that moment for four years: first, in the required military science course at Michigan Agricultural College; then, after the United States declared war, at the First Officers' Training Camp; and, once he enlisted, another eighteen months at Army camps. Not until June 16, 1918, did he debark in Europe, ready for war.

After a few weeks on the battlefield in the Saint-Mihiel offensive, Furlong received orders to report to the AEF school at Gondrecourt for more training. There, Furlong took a class on the fine points of attacking machine guns. That course "probably saved my life," Furlong said later. When Furlong returned to his unit at the end of October, he learned he had been promoted to first lieutenant. He was ordered to ready his platoon for an assault on November 1 on the German line at the Bois de Bantheville.

Several hours before the assault, the 3rd Battalion got orders to move up to the jump-off point. Furlong recalled vividly the next events.

> From the edge of our position, there was a clear space in front. Crossing that open space caused many casualties. The German front was just beyond the open area and their guns had clear shooting on the advancing men. We finally reached a position only a few yards from tremendous bombardment. The noise was deafening. We followed our barrage dangerously close. I left First Lieutenant Jared Jackson to look over my platoon and learned later that he was killed by a sniper moments later. I was appalled to see how many of our men had been killed.

Furlong checked his platoon for casualties, regrouped his men, and then led them against the fiercely resisting enemy line.

> On my reconnaissance, I could see a country road that crossed out front and, on the side toward the enemy, there was a small elevation. I ran, zigzagging to the protection of the slight rise and crawled along until I reached four of my men. There was a deep shell hole about twenty-five feet in front of us and I said that we must get to the hole. No one moved. I bounded up, ran to the protection of the hole and, from there, into the edge of the woods. Corporal John W. McKay followed me. . . . The Germans had sighted our location and turned a machine gun in that direction, which kept the other men from following.
>
> When I entered the woods, I saw a machine gun emplacement that had been wiped out by our artillery. There was a path, apparently made by the Germans who had been servicing the gun. Down the path, we could see the heads and shoulders of Germans who were firing

First Lieutenant Harold A. Furlong earned the medal for overtaking an enemy machine-gun nest and capturing twenty German enemy soldiers.

another machine gun at our men. I lifted my rifle, cursed at McKay to jolt him back to reality, and started to shoot. We both fired at all the Boche that we could see firing the machine gun. Our firing was accurate and we saw the Germans slumping down and [all four of] the machine guns stopped firing . . . I did not know how many men I (we) killed or wounded. . . . I started forward; McKay signaled to our men to advance. There were probably 10–15 Germans milling around when McKay and I walked into their midst. I had my pistol in my hand and the Germans seemed so surprised that they made no move to shoot McKay or me. My men stormed into the emplacement and took over the captured German prisoners. . . . The entire incident with the machine guns lasted less than ten minutes.

Including the wounded, Furlong sent twenty prisoners back to the compound. Then, without so much as a breathing spell, he resumed the assault.

Our barrage was advancing and I knew we had to follow as closely as we could . . . [Our colonel] told me that Jared Jackson was dead and he put me in command of the company. With what men I could gather around me, we started through the thick woods. I had not been wounded but, in making my way through the thorns, I was soon covered with blood and felt like I had been attacked by a thousand cats. We reached our objective and stopped. Our part was temporarily over, but other units of the 353rd passed us and went on to our second objective. . . . When we lay down on the ground to rest, I found that I was shaking like an aspen leaf. But not from fear, just from nervous exhaustion and fatigue.

Furlong remained adamant that what he did that November day was part duty, part training, part luck, and in no way the result of any special quality he possessed. The Army command did not see it that way. Three months later, he was on occupation duty in Germany when a courier approached him and told him to report at once to regiment headquarters. There, regiment commander Col. James Reeves handed him a sheet of paper. It was an official order from General Pershing, commander of the AEF, to report to his headquarters in Chaumont to be decorated with the Medal of Honor.

*Below*
German machine gunners in a trench near Reims, France.

*Below right*
War graves on a battlefield in northern France. First Lieutenant Jared Jackson was buried in a gravesite much like this one, at the Bois de Bantheville.

# SERGEANT YORK

The American guards were astonished as the tall, red-haired corporal marched his prisoners into camp. They had seen large groups of captured Germans before, but nothing like this. The date was October 8, 1918, in the first month of the Meuse-Argonne Offensive. Alvin Cullum York, a sharp-shooting black-smith from the Tennessee hamlet of Pall Mall, was about to become Sergeant York, the greatest hero of the Great War.

York's colonel visited the site where York had fought, counted the German bodies and abandoned guns, and talked to other Americans who were on the scene. They explained that after capturing several Germans they had been pinned down by machine-gun fire from the top of a ridge. York had pressed forward alone, shooting enemy soldiers whenever they appeared over the trenches. At last a German major promised to order his men to surrender if York would stop picking them off. In less than three hours, Corporal York had single-handedly killed twenty-five Germans, silenced thirty-five machine guns, and taken 132 prisoners.

York was quickly promoted to sergeant and awarded the Medal of Honor. He became the toast of Europe, lauded by President Wilson in Paris and by people all across the continent. Marshal Ferdinand Foch told him, "What you did was the greatest thing accomplished by any private soldier of all the armies of Europe."

York was an unlikely war hero. He had registered for the draft as a conscientious objector, explaining that the Bible forbade killing. At boot camp, his captain quoted various scripture passages concerning righteous war, which, he argued, were applicable to the conflict at hand. After much deliberation, York pronounced himself satisfied and went off to France.

America was waiting for Alvin York when his troopship pulled up to a Hoboken dock on May 22, 1919. Rushed by photographers, dignitaries, and spectators, he was whisked to the Waldorf-Astoria Hotel and given a suite adjacent to the one reserved for the president. Then came a staggering line-up of public appearances. At the stock exchange, trading was suspended and members paraded York around the floor on their shoulders. Earlier he had expressed a desire to see the city's famous subway system; transit officials obliged with a tour in a private car. York admitted, "New York is certainly a great city, but it do tire a fellow out some." He and his congressman

*Alvin York's mother welcomes him home to Pall Mall, Tennessee, May 30, 1919.*

traveled to Washington, where he was applauded on the floor of the House of Representatives. After making the rounds of the capital, York said that he had "seen it all."

York was deluged with offers for lectures, tours, and books, but wanted none of it. "This uniform ain't for sale," he said, and boarded a train back to Pall Mall. There he was paraded through town in a caravan of automobiles and mules. To his beloved mother and neighbors, the national hero was still "the same old Al."

It took another world war to draw Sergeant York back onto the public stage. At age fifty-four he registered for the draft at the same country store where twenty-five years earlier he had signed up as a conscientious objector. "If they want me for active duty, I'm ready to go," York declared. "I'm in a mighty different mood now from that other time." Though he was never called, York served as head of the local draft board and sent two of his sons off to war.

A series of strokes in the 1950s confined him to a wheelchair, and on September 2, 1964, Alvin York died in a Nashville veterans' hospital.

# WARRIORS ALOFT
## *The Air Aces*

The air aces of World War I displayed a special kind of courage. Attacking alone, with no place to take cover, in a machine that was often as deadly as enemy bullets, the aviator had to possess the fearlessness of a lone wolf. The best, like Eddie Rickenbacker, combined daring with prudence. Others, like Frank Luke, were determined to engage the enemy no matter what the cost.

The airplane had been in existence barely more than a decade when the war began, but development of air power surged after that. In the first year of the war, the role of the aviator was limited to observation. He was seen as "a useful extension of the traditional cavalry scout." Any "dogfights" were semi-comical affairs, with pilots hanging out of their planes trying to shoot one another with their revolvers or just shaking their fists angrily. In 1915, however, a Dutch inventor named Anthony Fokker, working for the Germans, invented a gear to synchronize machine-gun fire with the turning of the propeller blades. After that, guns could be mounted in front of a pilot's seat. The era of aerial combat had begun.

When the United States entered the war, it was woefully behind the European powers in aviation technology. There were less than 250 American planes, but 180 American pilots were already fighting in a volunteer force called the Lafayette Escadrille. From 1917–1918, the American Air Service played only a marginal role in the war, but its dashing fliers captured the nation's imagination.

The man who became best known in the households of America was "ace of aces" 1st Lt. Eddie Rickenbacker. To earn the sobriquet "ace," a pilot had to shoot down five enemy

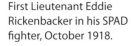

First Lieutenant Eddie Rickenbacker in his SPAD fighter, October 1918.

Eddie Rickenbacker of the celebrated "Hat-in-the-Ring" squadron claims another German victim.

planes. Rickenbacker downed twenty-eight (two unconfirmed) in only five months of combat. Twice his plane was crippled, forcing him to crash-land; he also needed an operation for an ear infection caused by flying at high altitudes. But Rickenbacker never received a scratch in combat.

Fatherless at twelve, Rickenbacker quit school to help support his family and soon became an auto mechanic. After putting in twelve hours a day on the job, at night he studied for a correspondence degree in engineering. In 1908, at the age of seventeen, he became a test driver. By 1910 he was making $40,000 a year as America's top racer.

When Congress declared war, Rickenbacker immediately wrote the Army to propose the development of a flying squadron made up of racecar drivers. Their knowledge of combustion engines combined with their quick reflexes and speed-driving skill made them perfect candidates for mastering the new air technology, he said. The Army rejected the idea but made a counterproposal. Would Rickenbacker go to Europe to be a driver for General Pershing? Rickenbacker said yes, but he still intended to become a flier. Once overseas, Rickenbacker thought he could switch easily to the air service. Pershing thought otherwise. He was quite happy with his new driver and consistently rejected Rickenbacker's requests for transfer.

# THE MEDAL IN PEACETIME

Since its creation in the 1860s, the Medal of Honor has usually been considered a wartime decoration—a symbol of the highest achievement of men in the terrible field of arms. Yet the long history of the medal includes almost two hundred awards for gallantry performed when the nation was at peace. The peacetime awards have been bestowed for various reasons, some formulaic, some as individual as the recipient himself. Most are founded in the emergencies that arise in a peacetime Navy, as the inevitable consequence of life at sea. Others are "special legislation" awards bestowed by Congress for courageous, nonbelligerent actions of military men. Still others, while called "medals of honor," are not the award as it is generally understood.

The first set of these, and the ones most clearly defined as military Medals of Honor, are those bestowed by the Navy. The purpose for awarding them was set forth in the original medal legislation of December 1861. The Navy bill called for Medals of Honor to be awarded for gallantry in action "and other seamanlike qualities." Later, this was clarified to include "deeds of gallantry and heroism in times of War and of Peace." The Senate register of medal citations records that these awards "recognized bravery in saving life, and deeds of valor performed in submarine rescues, boiler explosions, turret fires, and other types of disaster unique to the naval profession."

Approximately 180 naval peacetime Medals of Honor were awarded from 1866 to 1940. In almost all cases, these medals involved gallantry by seamen at the risk of their lives. The recipients include such men as Henry Williams, who in 1879 went over the stern of the USS *Constitution* to perform "important carpenters work upon her rudder" in a heavy gale. They also include others: John F. Auer and Matthew Gillick, who "rescued from drowning a French lad who had fallen into the sea from a stone pier" near the USS *Lancaster* as that ship rode in Marseilles Harbor on November 20, 1883; Watertender John King, who earned the Medal of Honor twice for heroism during boiler explosions aboard the USS *Vicksburg* in 1901 and the USS *Salem* in 1909; the divers who rescued the crew of the submarine *Squalus* in 1939; and Ensign Thomas J. Ryan, who pulled a woman from the wreckage of the Grand Hotel in Yokohama, Japan, when an earthquake struck that city in September 1923.

During the early twentieth century, the Navy sought to distinguish its peacetime and wartime recipients by awarding medals of two different designs. In 1919, Congress approved the "Tiffany cross" Medal of Honor for naval combat awards, retaining the old medal design for noncombat awards. In 1942, however, another act of Congress restored the dual status of the old design. Since then, no naval peacetime Medals of Honor have been bestowed, nor are any likely to be in the future: An act of Congress adopted on July 25, 1963, specified that the naval Medal of Honor was to be awarded only for combat actions. Different naval awards are now bestowed for gallantry outside of combat.

The "special legislation" awards were Medals of Honor bestowed by special acts of Congress. The nature of these awards has been complicated by the fact that throughout American history, Congress has awarded "congressional gold medals" or "congressional medals of honor" to many citizens for special acts or contributions to American life. These gold medals are not the military Medal of Honor, but the similarity of nomenclature has been a source of confusion. Often the difference can be understood only by the use of two words: "a" medal of honor as opposed to "the" Medal of Honor. Sometimes, the only decisive piece of evidence as to whether an award is *the* Medal of Honor is the thing itself—the design of the medal bestowed.

"Special legislation" awards of *the* Medal of Honor have been made to military men turned explorers: Commander Richard Byrd, Machinist Floyd Bennett, and Reserve Col. Charles Lindbergh. Another is a "lifetime of service" award to a man who contributed mightily to the service, yet whose name is almost forgotten to modern Americans: Maj. Gen. Adolphus W. Greely. Another medal, created by special legislation, was probably not intended to be *the* Medal of Honor: the award to Col. Billy Mitchell, the prophet of American military aviation. The inclusion of his name in the official congressional compilations of the Medal of Honor, however, has stirred controversy since the award was bestowed in 1946.

Other congressional gold medals are less controversial. Most of the earlier gold medals went to military heroes. The first recipient was George Washington, for his "wise and spirited conduct" in the siege of Boston; his medal was approved on March 25, 1776, even before independence from Great Britain was declared. The practice of giving gold medals to military figures became less frequent with the establishment of the Medal of Honor during the Civil War, but in the twentieth century, congressional gold medals have been awarded to other military men: Gens. John J. Pershing, Douglas MacArthur Jr., George C. Marshall, and Adm. Ernest J. King, to name a few. More frequently, gold medals have recognized the special contribution of citizens from all walks of American life. Medals went to George M. Cohan for his patriotic songs ("Over There," "A Grand Old Flag"); to Robert Frost for his poetry; to John Wayne for his acting and "service to the Nation"; and to Bob Hope, Walt Disney, Marian Anderson, Roberto Clemente, and other notables. In addition, foreigners such as Winston Churchill, Simon Wiesenthal (for his "contribution to international justice through the documentation and location of war criminals from World War II"), and Canadian Ambassador Kenneth Taylor (who aided the safe return of six American embassy officials during the Iranian hostage crisis of 1979–1981) have been awarded congressional gold medals.

Another honor, the Presidential Medal of Freedom, is awarded annually by the president to a number of individuals. The Presidential Medal of Freedom is the nation's highest civilian honor and has no specific connection to combat or military service. It is presented to individuals who have made especially meritorious contributions to the security or national interests of the United States, to world peace, or to cultural or other significant public or private endeavors. Recipients are luminaries in all walks of life, from education to politics to sports figures. It was established by President Kennedy in 1963 and may be awarded to non-US citizens.

There is one more set of actual Medals of Honor that, while bestowed in peacetime, are inseparably linked to war: the medals to the Unknown Soldiers. Since World War I, the United States has interred an Unknown Soldier from each of its wars at Arlington National Cemetery. After each conflict, the body of an American soldier whose identity could not be determined has been selected for this purpose. The soldier, "known but to God," represents the supreme sacrifice of all Americans who died in that war. On Armistice Day 1921, President Warren G. Harding affixed a Medal of Honor to the

*Military officers lower the casket containing the Vietnam War's unknown soldier into the ground at Arlington National Cemetery. Ronald Reagan, at left, watches with his hand covering his heart.*

flag-draped casket of the American Unknown Soldier from World War I. Further special legislation awarded the medal to the World War I unknowns of Belgium, Great Britain, France, Italy, and Romania—the only foreigners not serving in US forces ever to receive the award. The Medal of Honor was also bestowed upon the American Unknown Soldiers of World War II and the Korean War. And on May 28, 1984, after more than a decade of official peacetime, President Ronald W. Reagan bestowed the Medal of Honor upon the Unknown Soldier of the Vietnam War.

The peacetime Medals of Honor were awarded for gallantry and intrepidity in special circumstances. Some were for specific actions; some were symbolic. Taken together, they represent only a small fraction of the total number of Medals of Honor America has awarded. All of them, however, hold true to the most fundamental principle of the Medal of Honor: they recognize actions by military men above and beyond the call of duty.

"I saw tracer bullets go whizzing and streaking past my face," the ace recalled.

Quite by accident, Rickenbacker found a powerful advocate. Driving along the front, he came upon a broken-down car and stopped to fix it. Its grateful passenger, Col. Billy Mitchell, a top commander of the American Air Service, asked Rickenbacker what he could do in exchange. In January 1918, Rickenbacker received his commission as an air service lieutenant.

Rickenbacker joined the 94th Aero Squadron—the "Hat-in-the-Ring Squadron"—on March 4. Ten days later he flew his first mission. On March 29, he scored his first victory, the fourth by an American serving for the United States. And on May 30, he shot down his fifth enemy plane, becoming the second American ace.

The qualities that marked Rickenbacker as a star among aviators were at odds with the popular image of the impetuous fighter pilot. He was cautious, deliberate, even scientific in his approach to combat flying. He would avoid a fight when the odds were greater than two-to-one on the side of the enemy, but stay awake nights thinking of ways to improve the odds. He had no blood lust for the Germans, once saying "the pleasure of shooting down another man was no more attractive to me than the chance of being shot down myself."

On September 24, Rickenbacker received his captain's bars and command of the Hat-in-the-Ring Squadron. He celebrated the next day by scoring his first of six double victories.

Midmorning on September 25, the day before the scheduled start of the Meuse-Argonne Offensive, First Lieutenant Rickenbacker flew out alone across German lines near Verdun. Below him he sighted a pair of German LVG two-seater photographer aircraft heading in the opposite direction. They were guarded by five Fokkers—fast, high-flying fighter planes. Rickenbacker slipped by above them without being noticed. Then he turned his aircraft around, switched off his engine, and glided silently down toward the rear Fokker. Drawing near, he fired a long burst. The German machine plummeted to the ground.

Surprised by the sudden attack, the four remaining Fokkers panicked and broke formation. Rickenbacker had intended to make a quick escape after the first strike, but he changed his mind as he watched the Fokkers diving wildly right and left, leaving the LVGs unprotected. He changed course again and headed for the nearest two-seater.

The observer in the rear seat of the plane opened up on Rickenbacker with his machine gun, but its fire fell short. To escape the enemy gun as he closed in, Rickenbacker went into a dive until he fell below the LVG, then circled up on the enemy. But the LVG pilot was ready for him. He pulled around, putting Rickenbacker right back in the gunner's path. Rickenbacker had to pull up sharply. In the meantime, the second LVG got on his rear and opened fire. "I saw tracer bullets go whizzing and streaking past my face," the ace recalled. Again he had to zoom out of range and try again.

Several times the scenario repeated itself. Fortunately for Rickenbacker, the Fokkers continued to struggle ineffectually to resume formation. But the battle pulled him ever farther into enemy territory. He eventually decided to give it one more try. Waiting until the LVGs were parallel to each other, Rickenbacker burst up from the side and began firing.

"The nearest Boche passed directly through my line of fire and just as I ceased firing I had the satisfaction of seeing him burst into flames," he recounted. "Turning over and over as he fell, the LVG started a blazing path to earth just as the Fokker escort came tearing up to the rescue. I put on the gas and headed for home."

A dozen years later, the Army rewarded him for this day's work by presenting him with a Medal of Honor. That honor crowned a stack of medals that included the Distinguished

Service Cross with nine oak leaf clusters, the French Legion of Honor, and the Croix de Guerre with four palms.

The reason for Rickenbacker's zeal September 25 was his grim discovery the night before that the 94th Squadron had been overtaken in official victories. That had never before happened to the Hat-in-the-Ring. The challenger was the upstart 27th Squadron, which had joined the flight group only three months before. It had jumped into the lead because of the extraordinary record of its top ace, 2nd Lt. Frank Luke.

Luke and Rickenbacker were like night and day. Brash, boastful, and audacious, Luke had few friends and considerable trouble adapting to military life. Impatience and showing off marred his performance in training, resulting in barely passing marks. But once Luke began knocking observation balloons out of the sky, it became apparent to all that he was, in Rickenbacker's words, "the most intrepid fighter that ever sat in an airplane."

The *Drachen* balloons that Luke hunted were two-hundred-foot cigar-shaped bags of hydrogen, attached to the ground by a two-thousand-foot cable running from a truck-borne

Second Lieutenant Frank Luke pulls away in his SPAD as an enemy balloon bursts into flames on September 29, 1918.

Second Lieutenant Frank Luke ran 1st Lt. Eddie Rickenbacker a spirited race for the honor of being called the "ace" of the American fliers overseas.

winch. Placed at strategic intervals a couple of miles behind the front, they gave the enemy a complete view of Allied positions and movements. Their crews then called down the exact coordinates for artillery fire. Because of this deadly power, the air service made destroying Drachen its top priority.

Attacking huge, flammable targets would seem an easy job, but it was more difficult and dangerous than taking on a warplane. The Drachen were surrounded by antiaircraft batteries and a half-dozen or more machine guns. Above, Fokkers patrolled the balloon line. The attacker had to come in perilously low, hit the bag at the top where the hydrogen concentrated, and position the bullet holes in a tight enough mass to open a large enough leak to set off a hydrogen-oxygen explosion. During the onslaught, the balloon crew would lower the bag rapidly to the ground, exposing the attacker to progressively closer fire and greater risk. The terrors were so considerable, Rickenbacker testified, that only those pilots who were blind to danger sought out balloon combat.

On September 12, in the Saint-Mihiel region, Luke knocked down his first balloon. Two days later he brought down another pair in two flights, disabling both of his planes in the process. When he limped back to base and demanded a third plane so he could go after yet another balloon, his superior, Capt. Alfred Grant, put his foot down. "Balloons or no balloons, we must have discipline," he said.

Grant, however, confronted an irresistible force. Once Luke had tasted victory, he was insatiable. He would sneak out, attack a few balloons, spend the night away from base, and then go after some more on his way back.

Luke burst three more balloons on September 15. By this time he had perfected his technique. He made his assault at dusk, when the Drachen made a huge silhouette in the sky but his small SPAD could barely be seen. The dangers were great, since planes then had no night-flying equipment and the only airfield lights were flares that burned only for a short time. But Luke's flying skill was so finely tuned that these hazards were of little concern to him.

The day after his triple victory he gave a demonstration of his new technique to his now-impressed comrades. As he walked toward his plane, he pointed to two Drachen in the distance, about four miles apart. "Keep your eyes on those two balloons," he said. "You will see that first one there go up in flames exactly at 7:15 and the other will do likewise at 7:19." Observers, including Rickenbacker, saw two tremendous flames in the sky at precisely those times.

While Luke concentrated on wiping out the German army's balloon fleet, he was being protected from enemy attack planes by his wingman and only close friend, Lt. Joseph Wehner. Three times Wehner saved Luke's life by drawing the fire of the oncoming Fokkers. While

Luke pressed the attack, seeing nothing but the target in front of him, Wehner shot down or destroyed enemy planes zooming in on the "balloon buster."

September 18 was Luke's most spectacular day in the air. In less than ten minutes he destroyed five enemy aircraft to take over as America's top ace. But for Luke, it was a hollow victory. As he pulled away from a burning balloon, he realized that Wehner had disappeared. He knew his friend would not have abandoned the fight. He shot down three enemy airplanes in revenge.

Seeing the obvious strain of his friend's death on Luke, commanding officer Lt. Col. Harold Hartney ordered the ace to take a ten-day leave. A week later, Hartney was shocked to discover on his desk a combat report describing the shooting down of a Fokker, signed by Luke. No one had even seen him come back.

After the death of Wehner, Luke flew alone. He was less in control than ever. He defied orders, took greater chances, and remained away from the base for long unauthorized periods. Despite Luke's continued victories, Captain Grant grounded him. "Luke is going hog-wild," he told Hartney. "He thinks he is the whole Air Service." Hartney, however, decided that Luke deserved the chance he had been demanding to fly as a "lone wolf" from an advance field near Verdun. The commander gave him approval, and on September 29, Luke flew off.

After flying over an American balloon company to drop a note that read, "watch for burning balloons," Luke flew into German territory. The American ballooners cast their eyes skyward. One by one, three Drachen exploded. That was the last his countrymen saw of Frank Luke.

Hoping his star pilot was simply up to his old tricks, Grant told Rickenbacker that if Luke ever did show up he would "court-martial him first and then recommend him for the Medal of Honor." In November he gave up the wait and put Luke in for the medal. In only eighteen days, the twenty-one-year-old pilot had scored eighteen confirmed victories. Hartney credited him with at least another ten for which there had been no witnesses. In Rickenbacker's estimation, Luke was "the greatest fighting pilot in the war."

No word of Luke was heard until after the armistice. Then a graves registration officer discovered, in the village of Murvaux, the grave of an American aviator: early twenties, blond hair, heavy build, medium height. The villagers reported he had been shot down September 29 after destroying three balloons and two Fokkers. His SPAD was hopelessly crippled from counter fire, but the American maneuvered his falling plane over a German trench and opened fire with his machine gun, killing eleven soldiers and wounding numerous others. Even after he had crash-landed, he fought on. With German riflemen drawing near he pulled out his pistol and held them off until he died of his wounds.

At the eleventh hour of the eleventh day of the eleventh month, the Great War ended. Unlike Frank Luke, 1st Lt. Eddie Rickenbacker was there to see it. In a rare defiance of orders, Rickenbacker snuck up to the front in his SPAD to get a bird's-eye view of the ceasefire. "There were some shots fired at me," he said, "but at the appointed hour all shooting ceased, and then slowly and cautiously, soldiers came out of the German and American trenches, throwing their rifles and helmets high into the air. They met in no-man's land and began fraternizing just as a group of school kids would after a football game—happy in the realization that they would not be killed in this terrible conflict. It was fantastic to them, and to me, to know that the war was over."

Luke flew into German territory. The American ballooners cast their eyes skyward. One by one, three Drachen exploded.

# CHAPTER FIVE

# World War II

## 1939-1945

# The World at War

**T**HE WAR THAT WAS to thrust America to the forefront of world affairs began when the country was preoccupied with troubles of its own.

In the dark years of the Great Depression, the United States was engulfed in joblessness, poverty, and civil disturbances. Even in the 1930s, Americans could not ignore the waves of violent change that were washing over Europe and Asia. One by one throughout the decade, democracies succumbed to the rule of dictators. Free people bowed to servitude; oppression and silence became the fate of those who had once spoken openly; death awaited millions opposed to the new order. To Americans who listened to the voices from abroad, the hysterical chants signified a world gone mad.

The seeds of the Second World War were sown at the moment that marked the end of the first. An American observer of the negotiations at Versailles said the scene reminded him of ancient times "when the conqueror dragged the conquered at his chariot wheels." After the German delegation signed the treaty on June 28, 1919, they walked from the hall and broke the pen they had used to sign the document. The treaty saddled Germany and its allies with all responsibility for the war and became a hated symbol of the humiliation Germans felt in defeat, a defeat made especially bitter because many felt they had not truly been conquered in over four years of fighting on the battlefield.

The Allies saw the peace process as a chance to make certain their enemy would not rise again, but the harsh demands the treaty made on Germany and its allies would soon lead the world toward a new and more dreadful conflict. The treaty divested Germany of large sections of territory. The most galling provision of the pact left them liable for crushing reparations payments. The first reparations installment left the country economically prostrate. By 1923, inflation was so severe that a US quarter was valued at one billion marks. Though international aid helped restore the German economy, it did not reverse an enduring psychological effect: the German tendency thereafter to trace every economic ill directly to the Versailles treaty.

Germany and other countries in Europe became fertile soil for dictators to plow. Demagogues attracted people who had been uprooted and alienated from their past by the Great War. In Italy, Benito Mussolini seized power, leading his Fascists on an audacious march on Rome in October of 1922. Afraid to send the Italian army against him and risk civil war, King Victor Emmanuel III asked Mussolini to form a cabinet.

Russia, too, succumbed to a new autocratic rule. Between 1917 and 1921, the Russian state had been convulsed by a civil war. Thirteen million Russians had died from war, famine, and disease during the fighting between the Communist Red Army and the counter-revolutionary White Army. The Reds prevailed and the Soviet Union soon became an antagonistic, insular nation that, under Joseph Stalin, turned increasingly inward in an effort to develop its industrial might. The rest of the world learned that Stalin was purging all potential opponents to

*Previous pages*
Landing of US troops on
Omaha Beach, D-Day, 1944.

# BRAVERY IN ITALY

On February 1, 1944, when a heavy attack was launched against his battalion near Cisterna, Italy, Pfc. Alton Knappenberger crawled to an exposed knoll and killed two members of the German crew, wounding the third. Two Germans then crawled near him and threw grenades, but Knappenberger killed them both. Still under attack, he fired at all the armed enemy he could locate. With his ammunition spent, he crawled through steady fire, removed rifle clips from the belt of a casualty, and resumed firing. His brave actions disrupted the enemy attack for over two hours.

On February 8, 1944, near Carano, Italy, Cpl. Paul Huff led a reconnaissance patrol under heavy German fire. Huff moved ahead of his patrol and drew enemy fire on himself. Realizing the danger to his patrol, he advanced alone through a minefield, crawled to the closest emplacement, and wiped out the enemy crew while completing his mission of surveying the strength and location of the enemy company, which enabled a patrol to later rout the company. Still under fire, he returned to his patrol and led his men to safety.

Both men earned the Medal of Honor for their heroic actions during that week in Italy.

*Corporal Huff (left) and Private First Class Knappenberger (second from left) are awarded the Medal of Honor by Lt. Gen. Mark W. Clark (right) in Italy in 1944.*

his plans, killing them or sending them to die in labor camps. Eight million were expunged in a graphic exhibition of totalitarian power.

In Germany in 1919, thirty-year-old Adolph Hitler became one of the first members of the newly formed German Workers party, later known as the *Nationalsozialistische Deutsche Arbeiterpartei*. The world would come to know these members as the Nazis. The group's first attempt to seize control of the state by violence ended in failure and imprisonment in 1923. While in jail, Hitler wrote a book—*Mein Kampf*, a militaristic, anti-Semitic, and paranoid rant that would give form to his vision of the future. After his release, he altered his tactics, turning to elective politics. The German people responded by voting for Hitler's Nazi party in steadily increasing numbers. By the elections of 1932, it was Germany's largest party, capturing 37 percent of the vote. Hitler demanded and received the title of chancellor, then consolidated his power through a series of legal and extralegal moves, emerging as the unchallenged *führer* of Germany.

Hitler's first priority was to build the "mighty sword" of the military. His second was to seize *Lebensraum*—living space—which he took in installments, at first by bombast, bluff, and threat, and later by military force. On March 7, 1936, Hitler moved his army into the demilitarized Rhineland. The world did nothing, even though Hitler later admitted that if the French army had challenged them, the Germans would have been forced to retreat. Feeling himself free of constraints, Hitler accelerated the build-up of his military machine. He annexed Austria in March 1938. In September of that year, British Prime Minister Neville

President Franklin D. Roosevelt, whose confidence and vision helped the nation through depression and world war.

Chamberlain, who had consistently appeased the Germans, betrayed Britain's commitments to Czechoslovakia when he signed a document at Munich allowing the Germans to enter the Sudetenland in exchange for Hitler's promise of peace. Chamberlain returned to London and proclaimed that he had made "Peace with honor. Peace for our time." Hitler ignored the accord and occupied the rest of Czechoslovakia in March of the following year.

The final obstacle to Hitler's plans for European conquest was removed when the Germans and the Russians signed a nonaggression pact in the summer of 1939. The two countries proceeded to attack and dismember Poland on September 1, 1939. Unwilling to surrender yet another country to the policy of appeasement, Britain and France declared war on Germany on September 3.

After nine months of winter quietude, the German *Blitzkrieg* knifed to a series of stunning victories in Norway, Denmark, Holland, and Belgium. The German tanks then skirted the "impregnable" Maginot line of France and took Paris in thirty days. In May 1940, the British just barely succeeded in evacuating their army from the beaches of Dunkirk as France fell. Now only the valiant fighter pilots of the Royal Air Force (RAF) stood between Great Britain and German occupation. The RAF turned back the German air assault in the Battle of Britain, providing the free world its first bit of good news, but the British fought alone in defense of their small island.

In the Pacific, the Japanese had outlined their own version of *Lebensraum* with the Tanaka Memorial, a plan for expansion devised in 1927. Their burgeoning industrial complex and growing military machine demanded raw materials that the home islands and their minor Pacific colonies could not supply. World War I left the traditional colonial powers enervated and preoccupied with their own problems in Europe, and the Japanese seized the opportunity to fill the vacuum with their own brand of imperialism.

In September 1931, the Japanese used the pretext of a dynamite explosion in a Japanese railroad yard in Manchuria to invade the region. Then they pushed farther into China, destroying property and raping and murdering as they went. In Nanking alone, Japanese military forces slaughtered over forty thousand unarmed people. By October of 1938, Japan had a stranglehold on nearly half of China, including most of the major cities.

They set up a "New Order" for an Asian "Co-Prosperity Sphere," the blueprint for a Japanese-controlled empire that called for conquest from Manchuria to New Guinea. Only one obstacle remained to the Japanese drive to secure hegemony over the entire Pacific: the United States and its powerful navy of 171 warships.

The United States spent the years between the wars gripped by a profound desire to avoid future military involvement in Europe. President Woodrow Wilson went to the peace talks in 1919 with the fervent belief that the world must join together in a League of Nations to preserve the peace. He returned home to a country that repudiated his vision. The United States was the only one of the "Big Four" Allies (France, Great Britain, and Italy being the other three) that did not ratify the treaty or join Wilson's league.

America turned away from Europe and its problems in the 1920s, then became preoccupied with the depression of the 1930s. Isolationism became an explicit policy with the Neutrality Act of 1935, which prohibited loans to belligerent countries, proclaimed an arms embargo on all nations at war, and banned travel by US citizens to warring countries. After Germany attacked Poland in 1939, President Roosevelt attempted to lift the provision of the act forbidding the sale of arms. In the three days following Roosevelt's appeal, the isolationists held mass rallies featuring speakers as diverse as Charles Lindbergh, socialist Norman Thomas, and former president Herbert Hoover. They deluged Congress with over one million pieces of mail. But it was the interventionists who prevailed, and the Neutrality Act of 1939 allowed belligerent nations to buy weapons on a cash-and-carry basis. Since Britain controlled the Atlantic Ocean, this effectively excluded the Germans and Italians from American help.

The lifting of the arms embargo ignited the American war machine, which started slowly, then gathered steam. Defense spending accelerated rapidly, and in August 1941 Congress authorized a military draft.

The United States responded to Japanese aggression in China by moving the Pacific fleet from San Francisco to Pearl Harbor, Hawaii, and shutting off shipping to Japan military goods such as aviation gasoline and high-grade scrap iron. The Japanese perceived the US moves as a threat to the New Order in Asia and signed a tripartite alliance with Germany and Italy in September. In spring 1941, the Japanese invaded Indochina. The United States froze

Only one obstacle remained to the Japanese drive to secure hegemony over the entire Pacific: the United States and its powerful navy of 171 warships.

IT CAN HAPPEN HERE!

-UNLESS WE KEEP 'EM FIRING!

A wartime poster reminds American home-front workers of the high stakes involved in the conflict.

all Japanese assets and extended embargoes to all trade, including the export of oil.

The Japanese, with less than a year's supply of oil to feed their military machine, were faced with a stark choice: give up dreams of empire or go to war with America. The militarist Hideki Tōjō, who had been named prime minister in October of 1941, later explained their decision by saying, "Rather than await extinction it were [sic] better to face death by breaking through the encircling ring and find a way for existence." The Japanese negotiated with the United States until the day before attacking Pearl Harbor, all the while planning the operation in minute detail.

The first strike came on December 7, 1941, a day that President Roosevelt said would "live in infamy." Japanese torpedo bombers swooped in on Pearl Harbor at altitudes as low as forty feet and launched torpedoes. Dive bombers swarmed down and dropped armor-piercing and high-explosive bombs before the ships' gunnery crews could react. High-level bombers, deployed in a line above the battleships, delivered their payloads.

That first blow left America stunned and reeling. Six battleships, three cruisers, and numerous small vessels were either sunk or crippled in less than two hours. The United States lost 265 airplanes; some 2,403 men were killed and 1,178 wounded. Time was needed to recover, but time was not available. Guam and Wake Island fell almost immediately and the Philippines followed in May 1942. The Germans and the Italians declared war on December 11, forcing America to fight on two fronts over two oceans.

Pearl Harbor induced the once-isolationist United States to make a total commitment to fight and win a global war. America had agreed with Britain to defeat Hitler first, but the

Japanese could not be ignored. Roosevelt promised, "American armed forces must be used at any place in all the world." At the beginning of 1942, that seemed to be little more than false bravado. Gerry Kisters, an early draftee and later a Medal of Honor recipient, recalled being issued a World War I bolt-action rifle and a pie-plate helmet when he arrived at his mechanized unit in Fort Bliss, Texas, where "the men who were supposed to train us had been taken off horses. They didn't know any more about what they were doing than the fellows that had just come in." Matt Urban, fresh from the Reserve Officers' Training Corps and destined for the Medal of Honor for actions in France, recalled training with dummy wooden guns right up to the time his 9th Division shipped out for North Africa.

The war machine that started so slowly was transformed into a juggernaut in extremely short time. US industry matched and exceeded heretofore unimaginable goals of production. The costs were enormous, but the country absorbed a bill of $288 billion and actually prospered. By 1945, US industry had supplied nearly three hundred thousand aircraft, over seventy thousand ships, nearly a hundred thousand tanks, and the ultimate weapon, the atomic bomb.

The war produced an unprecedented degree of cooperation among the branches of the American armed forces. The Army Air Corps battered the enemy into submission as the Navy carried supplies and men to the beaches. If a new kind of craft were needed to get the troops ashore, it was invented and rushed into production. Seemingly overnight, the Seabees built new airstrips in the Pacific, and the combat engineers built bridges and whole ports in Europe.

America clearly possessed the industrial might to create a giant arsenal, but putting it to use required that enormous logistical problems be solved. The Army and Marine infantrymen who waded ashore went into battle as the best supplied fighting men in the world. For each man in the field, there were three in the rear echelon seeing to his needs. The United States shipped more of everything to its men: more weapons, more medicine, more filing cabinets, more cigarettes—a total of 450 tons of supplies per day for every division in the field. Soldiers were deposited on European shores by the largest armadas in history. War correspondent Ernie Pyle wrote that the strength of America was "appalling even to those who [made] up the individual cells of that strength." In both Europe and in Asia, that muscle would be used to defeat powers that had rolled, seemingly at will, to victories, and it would defeat them both at once.

World War II changed the world irrevocably. Over thirty million people died, with the worst of the brutality unleashed not against soldiers, but civilians. Total war brought estimated death tolls of over a million in the siege of Leningrad; 135,000 in the bombing of Dresden; 83,000 in one firebombing of Tokyo. As the Allies rolled into Germany they found the Nazi death camps. The worst nightmare could not match the reality of the Holocaust, which in George Steiner's words "altered our sense of the limits of human behavior." Six million Jews had been systematically exterminated.

The nuclear age arrived precisely at 8:15 a.m. on August 6, 1945, in Hiroshima, when seventy-eight thousand were killed by one bomb. Atomic weapons forever changed war and politics. Two giants stood astride the world after the war: the Soviet Union, which despite the loss of twenty million people had emerged stronger than before, and the United States, which had begun the war in profound isolation and had emerged an international power that could not again turn its back on the rest of the world.

US industry matched and exceeded heretofore unimaginable goals of production.

Yet, at the beginning, during those darkest hours when the Japanese were knifing through the Pacific, there was doubt. Wrote James Jones, the "Japanese, with their warrior code of the *bushidō*, had been in active combat warfare for ten years; the Germans almost as long." He wondered if the United States could "evolve a soldier, a *civilian* soldier who could meet them man to man in the field. Not everyone was sure we [could]." All of the technology and production the United States might muster would mean nothing if the country could not produce men with the will to prevail. The United States found them in the ranks of the career officers and also in the ranks of the draftees—farm boys, students, and city kids. More than 16 million served in uniform; 405,399 died; 471 have received the Medal of Honor.

They were ordinary Americans. Most of the young men who fought were born during World War I or shortly after. In childhood they had known want during the Depression. When they reached adolescence they were met with uncertainty and rumors of war. And when they came of age they were plunged into the worst conflict in history. It must have seemed to them that they were not born for happiness. Yet they endured.

The Medal of Honor recipients among them symbolized the strength and adaptability of the American civilian soldiers. They listened for every bump in the night on the steaming jungle islands, and they dug into the iron-hard ground of the Ardennes in winter. They sweated out depth charges deep under the sea and peered anxiously for *kamikaze* suicide planes from the bridges of destroyers. They bounced on a carpet of flak at twenty thousand feet in heavy bombers and outmaneuvered Japanese "Zero" fighter planes from the cockpit of their own swift fighter planes. Some died so that others could live. Others lived against all odds.

# DAY OF INFAMY

## *Pearl Harbor*

The dive bombers that shattered the peace of a beautiful Sunday morning at Pearl Harbor plunged the United States into global war. The attack was a complete surprise; in a few moments, the seven battleships lined up in a neat row off Ford Island in the harbor were ablaze, their crews desperately battling to keep them afloat as more bombers and torpedo planes swarmed to the attack. Only the quick action of a few men saved the US Navy from more complete destruction.

Commander Samuel Fuqua, a sailor who had grown up in Laddonia, Missouri, had just finished Sunday breakfast in the wardroom of the battleship USS *Arizona* when the air-raid sirens sounded. He turned to the man who had just been relieved as officer of the deck and inquired if the sirens signaled a drill. The officer was unsure. Fuqua called the bridge to find out what was happening. When no one answered he went topside to see for himself. He heard planes overhead as he emerged from a hatch and walked around a rear turret.

The next thing Fuqua remembered was picking himself up from the deck. He had been felled by the blast of torpedoes blowing holes in the hull of the *Arizona*. When Fuqua regained consciousness, he found himself lying next to a gaping shell hole in the deck. He staggered to his feet and saw high-level bombers dropping their bombs, which "looked like bowling balls as they came down." They struck everywhere along the ship, piercing the steel deck and exploding below. The engine room, the boilers, and the oil tanks exploded. The wounded struggling up from the lower decks added to the chaos. Some of them were on fire and some

Commander Samuel Fuqua, whose cool and courage saved many sailors aboard the USS *Arizona* as it burned and sank in Pearl Harbor.

had been blinded. A few of the wounded, driven by pain, attempted to leap overboard, but Fuqua and uninjured members of the crew knocked them unconscious to keep them from jumping and surely drowning.

Fuqua saw that oil on the surface of the water had ignited. Battleship Row was an inferno. He organized firefighters to keep the flames away from the wounded lying on the quarter-deck—the open stern of the ship's main deck.

Then a bomb struck the *Arizona* next to the bridge. It penetrated the forward magazine of ammunition and the ship "erupted like a volcano." Debris and bodies flew in all directions. Rear Admiral Isaac Kidd and the ship's captain, Franklin Van Valkenburgh, were among the estimated one thousand killed in that one terrible explosion. From the shore, observers could see the ship lifted up and broken by the force of the blast before settling back deep in the water.

Fuqua rushed forward to battle the fires near the captain's bridge, but a tower of smoke already rising from the ship signaled that the *Arizona* was past saving. As more wounded poured back to the quarterdeck, Fuqua attempted to protect them by keeping the fire from spreading farther aft. Despite the desperate situation, he worked calmly, putting the wounded aboard undamaged lifeboats to be transported to the relative safety of Ford Island.

A view from a Japanese plane shows aircraft attacking American vessels at Ford Island on the morning of December 7, 1941. A Japanese bomber is shown in the lower right foreground.

USS *Arizona* as it burned and sank in Pearl Harbor.

Captain Cassin Young chats with Adm. Chester Nimitz after being presented with the Medal of Honor aboard the *Vestal*, April 18, 1942.

The blast in the *Arizona*'s magazines was so powerful that it hurled nearly a hundred men overboard from the *Vestal*, an ammunition tender that was moored alongside the battleship. One of those thrown into the water was the ship's captain, Cassin Young. Tons of debris from the *Arizona* covered the *Vestal*'s deck, and the ship was on fire from numerous bomb blasts. The *Vestal*, listing precariously, was still tied to the blazing *Arizona*, and the oil-covered water between the ships was blazing as well. Sailors remaining aboard the *Vestal* began to abandon ship.

Commander Young swam to the gangway and emerged from the water just as some of his crew had started to clamber down. Covered with oil from the slick, he blocked their path and shouted, "Where in the hell do you think you're going?" When they said that they were abandoning ship, Young ordered them back to their stations, bellowing, "You don't abandon ship on me!" The *Vestal* was cut free from the wreckage of the *Arizona*. The steering gear had been blown away, but with the help of a tugboat and the *Vestal*'s own engines, Young got underway. The *Vestal* cleared the *Arizona* but soon began to sink. Young ordered the tug to pull the *Vestal* onto shore, where he beached the still-salvageable ship on a coral reef.

Almost all the other ships in the harbor near the *Arizona* and *Vestal* were also in danger of sinking. The *West Virginia* had been damaged by three torpedo blasts and took on so much water that it was listing dangerously. On the bridge, Capt. Mervyn Bennion quickly ordered counter-flooding on the side opposite the list and righted the ship, but more torpedo planes struck.

Captain Bennion had just moved to the starboard side of the bridge when Japanese high-level bombers made a direct hit on his ship and on the nearby *Tennessee*. Shrapnel from the blast struck Bennion in the abdomen; but he refused evacuation from the bridge as his crew fought the flames that engulfed the deck. As the fire spread, he ordered his men to leave him, but they refused. Bennion continued to think of the welfare of his ship, receiving reports and issuing commands until he finally lost consciousness. He died shortly after.

Back on the *Arizona*, Samuel Fuqua realized that Captain Van Valkenburgh and Admiral Kidd had been killed. He took command, but the ship's back was broken and the guns were no longer firing. Fewer than 200 of the 1,400 men aboard had survived those first few moments. Fuqua gave the order to abandon ship three hours after the beginning of the attack. The *Arizona* settled into the water, its burning hull now a tomb for over 1,000 men whose bodies were never removed.

Fuqua, who had shown cool and effective leadership in the midst of the blazing chaos, was the only man aboard the *Arizona* who lived to receive the Medal of Honor. Admiral Kidd and Captain Van Valkenburgh were awarded the medal posthumously, each for "devotion to duty, extraordinary courage, and complete disregard of his own life." Another posthumous medal went to Mervyn Bennion, whose only concern was for his ship and his men as he lay dying on the bridge. Eight others at Pearl Harbor were awarded the Medal of Honor posthumously. Cassin Young, who received his Medal of Honor for saving the *Vestal*, lived through the action only to die aboard the *San Francisco* on November 13, 1942, during the Naval Battle of Guadalcanal. In all, fifteen men were awarded the Medal of Honor for acts of valor at Pearl Harbor, the fiery beginning of World War II for the United States.

The *Vestal* lies beached on a coral reef after the Japanese attack.

# DEFENDING THE PHILIPPINES
## *Bataan and Corregidor*

For the Japanese, control of the Philippine Islands was crucial. Wresting the archipelago from its American and Filipino defenders would give the empire clear passage to the raw materials of the southwest Pacific. The Americans, who had held the islands in protectorate since the Spanish-American War, fought a desperate holding action under the command of Gen. Douglas MacArthur. His gallant soldiers, furnished with outdated equipment and cut off from resupply, bore the full weight of Japanese carrier attacks and amphibious landings as they waited for help that would never come.

When Japanese high-level bombers caught the planes of the US Army Air Corps on the ground at Clark Field in the Philippines a full ten hours after the attack on Pearl Harbor, they effectively sealed the fate of the Philippine Islands. The Japanese destroyed eighteen of thirty-five B-17 bombers and fifty-six fighters in that first strike. The US Navy pulled its Asiatic Fleet out of the Philippines the next day, and the remainder of the B-17s flew south to Australia on December 15.

General Douglas MacArthur (left) sits glumly in a tunnel on Corregidor Island with his chief of staff, Maj. Gen. Richard K. Sutherland, during the Japanese conquest of the Philippines.

Mess Sergeant José Calugas, whose artillery skill held off advancing Japanese on the Layac Road, near Bataan.

General Douglas MacArthur and his army remained to oppose the Japanese invasion. Small landing parties of Japanese came ashore at six different beaches on Luzon as a preliminary to the main invasion, which came December 22 and 23 at Lingayen Gulf on the west of the island.

In order to buy time, MacArthur declared open the capital city of Manila and abandoned it to the Japanese. The Allies staged a fighting retreat to the Peninsula of Bataan, across Manila Bay from the city.

The retreat called for Army units to leapfrog past each other as one unit protected the retreat of others by fighting the Japanese at the rear. It was brilliantly executed despite the inexperience of the troops. Eighty thousand men and their artillery gained the peninsula by January 6, 1942.

MacArthur set up headquarters on Corregidor, a fortress island at the tip of Bataan. His soldiers, who called themselves "The Battlin' Bastards of Bataan," gave ground over the next three months, but they made the Japanese pay in blood.

By the time of the surrender of Corregidor on May 6, MacArthur and his family had escaped to Australia under direct orders from President Roosevelt. (They left Corregidor in the PT boat of Lt. John Bulkeley, who received the Medal of Honor for his many daring missions in the Philippines in the months from December 8, 1941, to April 10, 1942.) In ordering MacArthur to leave his command, President Roosevelt and Gen. George C. Marshall, his Army chief of staff, made a political calculation. They reasoned that an inspirational figure planning a return to his command from Australia was a much more potent force than a dead hero in the Philippines. In Australia, General MacArthur was presented with the Medal of Honor. MacArthur had been personally courageous in the face of bombing attacks on Corregidor, but he did not get the medal for any single specified act of bravery. His award is one of the few of the war that could be described as "symbolic," in large part because MacArthur's Philippine army was an inspiration to the American people during those dark days.

MacArthur himself acknowledged this when he accepted the medal, saying that he felt it was "intended not so much for me personally as it is a recognition of the indomitable courage of the gallant army which it has been my honor to command." (MacArthur's medal came seventy-eight years after his father, Arthur, earned a Medal of Honor for rallying Northern troops on November 25, 1863, at Missionary Ridge, Tennessee, during the Civil War. The MacArthurs and the Roosevelts, Teddy and Theodore Jr., are the only father-son duos to receive the medal.

The Philippine Scouts comprised a large part of MacArthur's gallant army. They were Filipino soldiers who had been trained under American supervision, equipped with American weapons, and commanded by American Army officers. Mess Sergeant Jose Calugas served in Battery B, 88th Field Artillery, Philippine Scouts, one of the units assigned to cover the retreat of Americans and Filipinos down the Layac Road to Bataan.

On January 6, Sergeant Calugas had set up his field kitchen under some trees near the settlement of Culis. He finished serving breakfast and was leading a detail of KPs to fetch water for the cleanup. Suddenly, Japanese artillery rounds landed all around the men.

Japanese fighter planes followed, bombing the guns of the 88th, which were deployed in the woods and hills about nine hundred yards north of the mess area. Calugas and the other men dove for the safety of some nearby caves and stayed hidden there throughout the morning-long barrage.

At 2:00 p.m., the Japanese were still firing, but the American guns had fallen silent. Calugas walked to a clearing and surveyed the scene as Japanese airplanes dove and the hillsides erupted in orange flashes and black smoke. When he heard that one of the 88th's batteries had been knocked out and the crew killed, Calugas rounded up volunteers to go with him to investigate. With carbines and .45-caliber pistols in hand, sixteen men followed Calugas toward the batteries. Calugas never knew what became of his tiny force. Some of the men were killed or wounded and some of them may have run away, but by the time the sergeant reached the gun emplacement, he was alone.

The gun had been hit and had toppled into a bomb crater. All of its crew were killed or wounded. Although Calugas was a mess sergeant, he had been trained in combat arms and was a typically versatile and resourceful Philippine Scout. He could not right the cannon himself, so he found one of the wounded gunners and rounded up other men from a nearby emplacement to help. Together the men lugged the gun back into place and put it in firing order. Another man climbed a tamarind tree to act as spotter. From his perch, he could see the Japanese attack force moving forward less than a mile away. As the spotter directed his fire, Calugas aimed, loaded, and discharged the gun. In Calugas's words, "We kept this up about two hours. Then, they must have called for more planes to try and spot our gun. The enemy was not making any progress at that time because our shooting was very good." Each time the Japanese planes appeared, Calugas and his makeshift crew stopped firing and dived for cover in the jungle, hoping that the plane would not be able to locate the gun. This cat-and-mouse game continued until Calugas ran out of shells.

The mess sergeant's deadly accuracy stopped the enemy advance until the next day, when Japanese reserves arrived. Calugas's barrage had given the 88th valuable time to regroup and fight on.

After the battle, Calugas returned to his duties as a mess sergeant. Shortly after the action, he heard himself praised on "Voice of Freedom" radio for his valor at Culis. Three years were to pass, however, before he would receive the symbol of that valor. He was taken prisoner in the general surrender of Bataan on April 9. The seventy-five thousand survivors were forced to march from Mariveles in the south to a railroad siding at San Fernando, some forty-five miles away. Exhausted and hungry after four months of hard fighting on half-rations, many of the men also came down with dysentery and malaria. Under a blinding tropical sun, their Japanese captors denied them food and water during the ordeal that became known as the Bataan Death March. Those who fell from the ranks were shot and left on the road by Japanese death squads. An estimated 7,000–10,000 died, 2,300 of them Americans. The captives were sent by boxcar to Camp O'Donnell, northwest of Clark Field, where they were interned. Calugas survived two savage beatings during the Bataan Death March and spent three years in a Japanese prison camp before Gen. George C. Marshall draped the blue ribbon of the Medal of Honor around his neck on April 30, 1945.

One of the scouts' American officers was 2nd Lt. Alexander Nininger, a Georgia native who had graduated from West Point in 1941. Nininger was on his first assignment after

Each time the Japanese planes appeared, Calugas and his makeshift crew stopped firing and dived for cover in the jungle, hoping that the plane would not be able to locate the gun.

American prisoners Samuel Stenzler, Frank Spear, and James Gallagher (left to right) rest during the Bataan Death March.

being commissioned. He and his unit raced to build a line of defense as the Allied forces tried to seal off the Bataan Peninsula from Japanese attack. Nininger's men cut trees and constructed fortifications in the swamps near the town of Abucay, on the eastern coast of Bataan.

The Japanese attack, however, came to the west of Nininger's position, near the spine of low mountains that ran down the center of the peninsula. The Americans and Filipinos pushed back the first onslaught, but more than a thousand Japanese snipers infiltrated the Allied defense line during the struggle.

Nininger volunteered to leave his company and join the reserve units that had moved up to reinforce the Allied line at the point of the Japanese assault. When Nininger arrived at the front line on January 12, he found that the Japanese had overrun the Allies' foxholes and were now occupying them, firing at the Allies from the Allies' former positions. Nininger loaded himself with grenades and led a counterattack through a hail of fire. Shrapnel from Japanese artillery raked the dirt around him. The rest of the soldiers following the young lieutenant faltered in their attack and sought cover, but Nininger sprinted on. Hit by a bullet, he fell to the ground but then crawled forward and threw his grenades. When a medic caught up with him and tried to administer aid, Nininger broke away to renew his one-man assault.

In sight of his comrades, Nininger attacked another Japanese foxhole. He was again hit by rifle fire, but even that did not halt his advance. When three Japanese soldiers charged with bayonets, Nininger killed them with his .45. Then at last, he succumbed to his wounds.

Nininger was the first of 37 men of his 424-man West Point class to die in World War II. The first to die was also the only one to be awarded the Medal of Honor.

# TURNING THE TIDE
## *The Tokyo Raid and Midway*

The first five months of the Pacific war were unremittingly bleak. But that was to change in April 1942, when Lt. Col. Jimmy Doolittle led a carrier-based force of B-25 bombers on a daring raid over Japan. The damage to the Japanese was slight, but the mission provided an enormous morale boost for America. Two months later, the Japanese launched a carrier strike force for an invasion of the US base on Midway Island at the far western end of the Hawaiian chain. Navy planes from American carriers and Marine planes based on Midway were launched to meet the threat.

When the long-awaited moment finally arrived, Doolittle revved his airplane's engines to top RPMs and waited for the signal to take off from the deck of the aircraft carrier *Hornet*. The signal came when the bow of the ship was on its upward rise. He began his slow taxi to the end of the short runway, only 467 feet away. Once his wheels left the deck, the crews in fifteen B-25s still on the aircraft carrier could see the entire top of his bomber as it strained upward in a steep climb. Gaining altitude and speed, Doolittle set course for Japan.

Jimmy Doolittle, a forty-five-year-old former stunt flier and racer, had helped Col. Billy Mitchell in the bombing demonstration that brought attention to the offensive potential of aircraft. Because of his age and his position on the staff of Army Air Corps Chief Hap Arnold, Doolittle was not supposed to fly to Tokyo. It was his job to organize the mission, train the pilots, and modify the aircraft so that they could take off from the short distance of an aircraft carrier's runway. His request for permission to lead the raid was at first refused flatly. He continued to plead his case, pointing out that he knew more than anyone else about the planes, the crews, and the mission. He finally won Arnold's grudging assent.

The *Hornet* took the flight of bombers as close to Japan as safety would allow. The original

Lieutenant Colonel Jimmy Doolittle and his crew: (from left) Lt. Henry Potter, Doolittle, Staff Sgt. Fred Beamer, Lt. Richard Cole, and Staff Sgt. Paul Leonard.

nal plan had called for takeoff 400 miles from Japan, but that strategy was scuttled when the carrier was spotted by a Japanese patrol boat. The planes left on their historic mission a day earlier than had been planned and a full 668 miles from Tokyo.

Each of the B-25s carried a five-man crew, four five-hundred-pound bombs, and extra gasoline tanks for the long one-way journey, a total of thirty-one thousand pounds. For three weeks, Doolittle and his pilots had practiced taking off within the limited number of feet required on an aircraft carrier, but that was on the ground and under ideal conditions at Eglin Field, Florida. A fully loaded B-25 had never before taken off from the pitching and rolling deck of a carrier, which was designed for much smaller fighter planes and torpedo and dive bombers.

As he neared
Tokyo, Japanese
Zero fighter planes
spotted him, but
he plunged even
closer to the earth,
escaping the
enemy fighters
by allowing his
plane's camouflage
to blend into
the terrain.

After Doolittle's plane left the deck, there came fifteen takeoffs, each as heart-stopping as his. Once airborne, each plane sped toward the target on its own; to wait for a formation would waste fuel. They stayed low over the water, flying straight for Japan. Success demanded nearly perfect timing and better luck. As Doolittle said, it was "in the laps of the gods."

Flying at two hundred feet, Doolittle reached the coast five hours after takeoff. As he neared Tokyo, Japanese Zero fighter planes spotted him, but he plunged even closer to the earth, escaping the enemy fighters by allowing his plane's camouflage to blend into the terrain. He came in "hugging the deck" over Tokyo, found the target, then popped up to 1,200 feet to drop his bombs. (A book and movie about the raid were entitled *Thirty Seconds Over Tokyo*. Doolittle later said that they were over the city longer than thirty seconds, "but it brings up the point that we did not tarry.")

Although he was exposed to antiaircraft guns, no more fighters found him as he set course for China. The plan had called for the bombers to fly to the mainland, where they were to land at an airfield called Chuchow. However, fierce headwinds encountered on the flight into Japan had caused the planes to use more fuel than anticipated. As the B-25s approached the coast of China, they met dense clouds and rainstorms. The fuel gauges soon neared empty, and the pilots all arrived at the same hard realization: They would have to choose between ditching, or, if they could reach land, either bailing out or crash-landing.

Doolittle's fuel lasted until he was over the mainland. He and the other four men of his crew all managed to parachute safely into Chinese territory and return home. Others were not so fortunate. Two planes crash-landed in Japanese-occupied territory, and three of the eight surviving crewmembers were summarily executed. Another man starved to death while in Japanese custody. The four survivors remained prisoners until the end of the war. Of the eighty men who began the mission, six died, either in captivity or in crash-landing. One plane landed at Vladivostok in the Soviet Union. Its five crewmembers were interned together at various places inside Russia until May 29, 1943, when they escaped over the Persian (Iranian) border. Their B-25 was kept by the Soviets.

When Doolittle discovered that all of his planes were lost and that two of his crew had been captured by the Japanese, he thought the mission had been a costly failure. Later, realizing the raid had struck a great psychological blow at the enemy and raised the spirit of America, he revised his estimate, saying, "The mission gave the American people the first piece of good news they had had. It caused the Japanese to question their warlords, who had said that Japan would never be attacked."

After he returned to Washington, Doolittle discovered while riding in a staff car with General Arnold and Gen. George C. Marshall that he was to receive the Medal of Honor. When he protested that he did not deserve it, General Marshall turned to him and said gravely and quietly, "I think you do."

Less than two months after the Doolittle raid, a Japanese four-carrier strike force bore down on Midway Island. On June 4, 1942, it launched 108 dive bombers and Zero fighters to destroy the American forces at the island's airfield. Awaiting them were two squadrons of mostly inexperienced Marine pilots flying mostly obsolescent planes. Major Lofton Henderson's dive-bomber squadron consisted of just twenty-seven serviceable planes: sixteen modern SBD Dauntless bombers and eleven outdated SB2U Vindicators. One of the pilots of Maj. Floyd B. Parks's fighter squadron said that anyone flying their old F2A Brewster

American soldiers in World War II battled across the globe, on land, sea, and in the air. A Navy Dauntless dive bomber prepares to attack Wake Island in the central Pacific, 1943.

fighters into combat against Japanese Zeros was "lost before leaving the ground." The pilots called the planes the "Flying Coffins."

On June 4, twenty-five Marine fighter pilots in Brewsters rose up to meet the Japanese aerial armada. Fifteen of the Americans were shot down in the dogfight without registering a single kill as the Japanese pummeled the airfield. Henderson's two-man dive bombers, meanwhile, flew out to attack the Japanese fleet. When the slow-moving planes tipped into their dives, they were easy targets for the Zeros and for Japanese antiaircraft gunners who waited on the carriers.

Henderson's squadron included an untested young pilot from Minnesota named Richard Fleming. In the first few moments of the bombing run, he saw Henderson's lead plane burst into flames after taking several hits from the carrier *Akagi*'s guns. Fleming and the rest of the squadron took over for the commander and dived toward the targets, straight into heavy clouds of antiaircraft fire. Fleming's gunner said the shrapnel hitting the dive bomber sounded like "buckets of bolts" being thrown into the propeller.

The standard operating procedure for a dive-bomber called for releasing bombs at 1,500 feet, but with his plane bouncing from antiaircraft bursts, Fleming plunged to within 400 feet of the carrier. He dropped his bombs, narrowly missing the deck, and somehow managed

Marine Captain Richard Fleming followed his bombs into the Japanese cruiser *Mikuma*.

to pull out of the dizzying dive. Both he and his gunner were wounded by the firing, but they survived the daredevil attack. His ground crew on Midway counted 179 holes in the plane after his return.

The dive bombers recorded several near misses but did not hit any of the carriers. Their mission was not in vain, however. The arrival of these land-based dive-bombers convinced the leader of the carrier strike force, Admiral Chūichi Nagumo, to send his planes again against the landing strip at Midway Island. The Japanese planes were loaded with high-explosive bombs for the airfield rather than the armor-piercing variety designed to destroy ships. Before the planes took off, Nagumo received word from one of his surveillance planes that American carriers were within striking range. He hastily ordered the bombs changed. Just as the Japanese were re-arming their planes, torpedo bombers from the US carriers *Hornet*, *Yorktown*, and *Enterprise* attacked.

These brave carrier pilots had flown beyond the fuel capacities of their fighter escorts, and thus came in without protection. The Japanese Zeros and antiaircraft fire tore them apart. Of the forty-one planes of the three torpedo squadrons, thirty-five were shot down.

Again, the price was high but brought a valuable return. The Zeros stayed near the water for the fight with the torpedo planes, leaving their carriers exposed to US Navy dive bombers, which attacked from fourteen thousand feet. The dive bombers ripped great holes in the carriers *Akagi*, *Sōryū*, and *Kaga*. Gasoline explosions erupted, and all three Japanese carriers were destroyed. The fourth Japanese carrier, *Hiryū*, was attacked and sunk later, but not before its dive bombers were unleashed against the USS *Yorktown*, badly damaging it. A submarine sank the crippled *Yorktown* the next day.

On June 5, Fleming led the remaining planes of the squadron (now reduced to only twelve of the original thirty-six) in an attack against the heavy cruisers *Mogami* and *Mikuma*. He repeated his bold strategy of the day before, piloting his bomber into a screaming dive. Another pilot saw Fleming's plane spit out black smoke after being hit by antiaircraft fire early in the dive. At 350 feet, Fleming released his bombs, then followed them down. No one knows if his action was intentional, but the plane crashed directly into the *Mikuma*. The resulting flames were sucked into the

The wreckage of Fleming's plane is strewn over an aft gun turret of the ship.

air intake of the ship and ignited gas fumes in the starboard engine room, killing the Japanese crew.

The captain of the *Mogami*, A. Soji, observed Fleming's dive against the *Mikuma*. He later remarked, "I saw a dive-bomber dive into the last turret and start fires. He was very brave."

All of the pilots who fought the decisive battle of Midway were "very brave." The battle turned the tide of war in the Pacific, halting Japanese expansion. Yet of all the courageous pilots who sacrificed their lives during the battle, only Capt. Richard Fleming was awarded the Medal of Honor. He stands as a symbol of all those who faced death squarely and did their duty "with dauntless perseverance and unyielding devotion." The stage was set for America to go on the offensive.

Dive bombers attack the Japanese fleet at Midway. Four enemy carriers and one cruiser were destroyed on June 4–5, 1942.

# SOUTH PACIFIC

## *The Naval Battle of Guadalcanal*

Japanese bombers stationed on Guadalcanal in the Solomon Island chain put Allied New Caledonia and Australia in jeopardy. The Americans took the offensive for the first time in the war when the Marines landed on Guadalcanal and took the airfield on August 7, 1942. The US Navy lost so many ships trying to defend and supply the Marines that the narrow strip of water between Guadalcanal and Savo Island became known as "Ironbottom Sound."

The Japanese wanted desperately to land a killing blow against the Americans who hung on to their sliver of Guadalcanal. On the night of November 12, a major Japanese force sailed to the "Slot" (the US sailors' nickname for the passage of water in the midst of the Solomon Island chain), intent on shelling the Marines. The Japanese fleet was composed of two columns, each headed by a battleship protected by a screen of light cruisers and destroyers, twenty ships in all. The only American ships in the area ready to meet them were two heavy cruisers, three light cruisers, and eight destroyers, all under the command of Rear Adm. Daniel Callaghan.

Setting out from Guadalcanal at dusk on the twelfth, Callaghan's ships sailed in single column through Ironbottom Sound in the early morning hours of Friday the thirteenth.

Admiral Daniel Callaghan (top) and BM Reinhardt Keppler (above) both died aboard the *San Francisco*.

The USS *San Francisco* (background) spews smoke after a Japanese plane crashed into it on November 12, 1942. At left is the USS *President Jackson*.

Callaghan, aboard the flagship cruiser USS *San Francisco*, reasoned that his only hope of defeating the superior force lay in executing some bold and unlooked-for stratagem. Discarding orthodox battle strategy, he ran the gauntlet between the two Japanese battleships and their cover of smaller ships, exposing his column to fire from both sides. The opposing forces sailed into chaos. US ships zigged and zagged to within yards of the enemy, sometimes nearly colliding with each other or with enemy ships as they took evasive maneuvers. Ships from both sides occasionally fired on their own during the melee. The noise of the guns and the explosions of the hits at such close range were deafening. Searchlights flashed about wildly and gunfire lit the night sky.

The *San Francisco* was in mortal danger from the first exchange of fire. The Japanese battleships found the range immediately, and shells simultaneously struck each side of the ship. Explosions rocked the superstructure, killing Admiral Callaghan and his staff on one bridge. At the same time, the ship's captain, Cassin Young (who earlier had received the Medal of Honor at Pearl Harbor), was killed when the Japanese scored a direct hit on his bridge.

Three decks down on the ship, below the water line, Lt. Cdr. Herbert Schonland, the damage control officer, had his hands full. Since all lights were extinguished at the first salvo, Schonland and his crews had to rely on hand-carried lanterns. Japanese shells had torn open holes all along both sides of the ship; fires were breaking out everywhere. One fire raged in the Group 2 magazine below one of the forward turrets and threatened to blow the ship to bits. Schonland directed a party to open sea valves and flood the fire. When a direct hit killed twenty men in the repair party, Schonland sent another group of men, which succeeded in putting out the fire. In the midst of fire, shelling, darkness, and confusion, Schonland toiled calmly on.

Boatswain's Mate First Class Reinhardt Keppler, a son of German immigrants from Washington State, was one of those battling the fires. Leaving one of the crews, he attempted single-handedly to extinguish a large fire in the ship's hangar. Keppler walked steadily into the blaze, cutting his way through the flames with the jet of a fire hose. Oblivious to the constant rain of enemy shellfire, he advanced into the heart of the fire. Although critically wounded by shrapnel from one of these shell bursts, he refused to leave his duties. He extinguished the fire in the hangar and went on to fight new fires until he collapsed from loss of blood.

The ship was by now listing at a thirty-five-degree angle. Lieutenant Commander Schonland realized that until he stopped the flow of water, he would be unable to counterflood the ship to correct the list. He assembled a party and led it up to the second deck and water line. The three-foot-high circular walls around the hatches had dammed the water and kept it at waist-deep level. Seawater poured in through holes in the ship's hull that, Schonland remembered, "you could have walked through." Lantern light revealed the gruesome sight of dead bodies and torn limbs floating on the surface of the oily water. Schonland and his men waded to the hull of the ship and stuffed mattresses into the holes, effectively slowing the rush of water. Schonland then ordered the crew to evacuate the ship's sickbay. Opening the sea valves to flood that

section of the ship, he countered the weight of the water on the other side of the ship. When the ship righted, he and his repair party groped underwater to open flush valves manually, first on one side and then the other.

During this desperate balancing act, Schonland heard from the officer of the deck, Cdr. Bruce McCandless, that both the admiral's flag bridge and the captain's navigational bridge had been destroyed. Both officers and their staffs were presumed dead, making Schonland the ship's commanding officer. Instructing McCandless to follow the admiral's plan of battle, Schonland remained below and attended to the urgent task of fighting the flooding and fires threatening his ship. At one point he was directing the efforts to extinguish twenty-five simultaneous fires while bringing the ship to an even keel.

After one half-hour of desperate battle, the *San Francisco* sailed beyond the range of Japanese guns. The Naval Battle of Guadalcanal cost the Navy eight ships, including the cruisers *Juneau*, which was sunk later that day by a submarine, and *Atlanta*, which had to be beached. The Americans destroyed one Japanese battleship and two destroyers, but more important, they prevented the Japanese ships from bombarding the hard-pressed Marines on Guadalcanal.

The badly damaged *San Francisco* limped back to port carrying four men who would be awarded America's highest medal for bravery in action, more than on any ship for a single action in World War II. Reinhardt Keppler, who died a few days after the battle, was awarded the Medal of Honor posthumously for his selfless battle to save the ship from fire. Commander Herbert Schonland, who had kept the *San Francisco* afloat, and Cdr. Bruce McCandless, who had guided her to safety, both received the medal. Admiral Callaghan, architect of the bold stroke of strategy that had halted the Japanese advance and saved the Marines on Guadalcanal, was awarded the medal posthumously.

*Above*
The *San Francisco* enters San Francisco Bay after the long return voyage from Guadalcanal.

*Above left*
On board the USS *San Francisco* are two senior ship's officers who had survived the Battle of Guadalcanal. At left is Cdr. Herbert Schonland, who assumed command after the ship's captain was killed and who led damage-control efforts. At right is Lt. Cdr. Bruce McCandless, the ship's communications officer, who took over and navigated the *San Francisco* to safety. Both Schonland and McCandless received the Medal of Honor for their actions during and immediately after the battle.

# BOMBERS OVER EUROPE
## *The Mighty Eighth*

Despite the stunning Japanese attack on Pearl Harbor, America and its allies weighted their attention toward the defeat of Germany, the most powerful of the Axis nations. US ground forces were woefully unprepared to take the offensive, so the first US contribution in Europe would have to be in the air. The Eighth Air Force arrived in England in the spring of 1942 to begin daylight strategic bombing raids against Germany.

Technical Sergeant Forrest Vosler of the Eighth Air Force, a native of upstate New York, said that it took him just one flight over Germany to be "absolutely sure [he] was doomed" and that he should "sit down and write [his] folks a last letter." His fourth mission as a radioman/gunner for the 358th Bomber Squadron of the 303rd Bomber Group nearly proved him correct.

As Vosler's B-17 neared Bremen on December 22, 1943, flak destroyed one of its four engines. After unloading bombs, the plane wheeled 180 degrees to begin the return trip to England. Then flak hit a second engine, forcing the craft to drop out of formation and fly at

Technical Sergeant Forrest Vosler (fourth from left) and his crewmates with their B-17 bomber during training in Pyote, Texas, summer 1943.

the mercy of the German fighters below, who awaited crippled B-17s like sharks in a feeding frenzy.

Just after Vosler saw two other bombers explode and disintegrate, a 20mm shell from a German Messerschmitt fighter exploded into his compartment. Hot metal burned into his legs, arms, and chest. Vosler remembered: "I couldn't control my hands. I was so nervous I couldn't have held the gun. Then things happened. My whole life . . . went past me in seconds. . . . I'm not talking about skimming. Getting up in the morning, doing the whole routine." The fear of death left him, though, to be replaced by a feeling that he "might as well die standing up." He climbed back into his turret and fired his machine gun until another 20mm shell exploded near him; this time particles sliced into his chest and eyes. Fortunately, the German fighters had to turn back before they could finish off the crippled plane. Although seriously wounded, Vosler helped the badly wounded tail gunner before receiving aid himself.

A B-17 of the 96th Bomber Group unloads over Bremen, Germany, as contrails from the other planes streak the sky.

The pilot struggled to keep the plane airborne until it reached the English Channel while Vosler repaired the radio, which had been knocked out during the attack. He transmitted a distress signal to a British base as the plane ditched into the channel. While the plane began to sink, the crew scrambled out onto a wing and the unwounded readied a raft. In doing so they left the tail gunner standing unattended for a few seconds. Vosler saw the gunner pitching forward into the water. Despite the great pain from his own wounds, he grabbed the falling man and held him up with one hand while holding the plane's wire radio antenna with the other. The others scrambled to Vosler's aid and helped both wounded men aboard the raft. Vosler's radio transmission had alerted boats in the channel, and the men were rescued by a Norwegian fishing boat two hours later.

At first, Vosler thought that the blood he saw flowed from an external wound, but the blood was on the retinas of his eyes. For eight months he was totally blind. One eye was removed in an operation, but doctors held out hope that he might regain sight in his other eye. President Roosevelt delayed the ceremony in which Vosler was to receive his medal, waiting for the heroic Airman to regain his sight. Eight months later, Vosler was indeed able to see the president as he spoke to him in the Oval Office.

A few months before Vosler's heroism, the Eighth Air Force was called upon to perform an unusual mission over Romania. General Louis H. Brereton, the commander of the Ninth Air Force, called the raid on Ploiești of August 1, 1943, "the most difficult assignment ever given an air force." The plan called for 178 B-24 Liberator bombers to fly 1,400 miles from Benghazi in Libya to the Ploiești oil fields in Romania, attack at treetop level, and return on a carefully synchronized schedule, all without the support of fighter planes, which lacked the range to accompany them.

The mission went wrong from the beginning. Three successive lead planes of the mission-leading 376th Bombing Group crashed early en route. The reasons for the crashes were never discovered. Everyone had been ordered to keep radios off, so all watched in silence as the bomber carrying the lead navigator spiraled down into the Mediterranean. The 376th's group

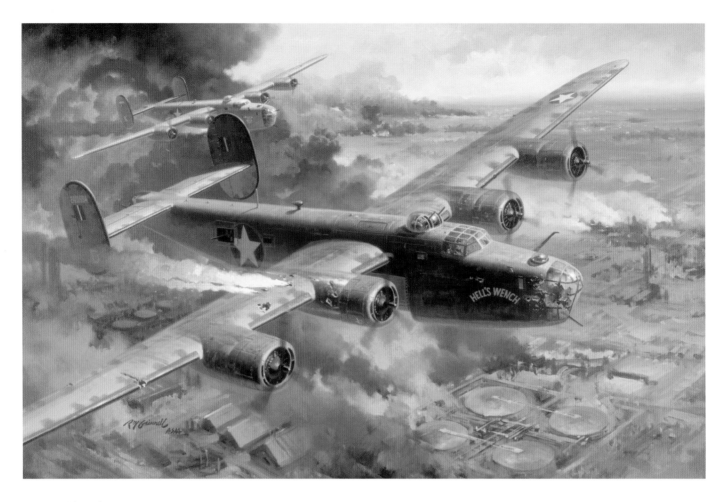

*Fire Over Ploesti* by Roy Grinnell depicts the bombing raid on an oil refinery at Ploiești, Romania, on August 1, 1943.

leader, Col. Jack Compton, who was carrying mission leader Brig. Gen. Uzal Ent, moved up to take the first position. Compton's navigator was inexperienced, and this would prove crucial later in the mission.

As the bombers approached the Alps, they ran into heavy clouds. The 376th and the second bombing group, the 93rd under Lt. Col. Addison Baker, climbed over the cover while Col. John Kane took his 98th under the clouds. Kane lost track of Compton's group and circled the Danube until Col. Leon Johnson's 44th Bombing Group helped him right his course. All groups maintained radio silence, but now the two groups were twenty minutes behind time in the unforgiving schedule.

The first two groups descended to fifty feet for their approach on the target. Compton's lead plane came to a landmark, a railroad crossing, which Compton and Ent mistook for the crossing that led to Ploiești. The young navigator was convinced that the crossing was the wrong one, but Ent overruled him. The bombers of the first two groups sped on—but toward Bucharest instead of Ploiești. By the time the commanders discovered the error, it was too late for the two groups to return to their course for their bombing run. General Ent broke radio silence to give the order for them to approach the target from the more heavily defended south. All of the planes of the two groups were also compelled to abandon their assigned targets and bomb any "target of opportunity."

Approaching Ploiești, the bomber groups flew into a wall of fire and split into squadrons. Most of the 376th swung east in a wide end run to come at Ploiești from the northeast, while the 93rd continued straight through the defenses. Three miles from the 93rd's selected target, antiaircraft fire hit the lead plane flown by Lt. Col. Addison Baker and his copilot, Maj. John Jerstad. Flames licked down the sides of the fuselage and onto the wings. Even as their aircraft turned to a ball of flame, Baker and Jerstad continued to the target, jettisoning their bombs to stay airborne. They passed up an open field where they might have crash-landed, hoping to lead the squadron to the target. Moments later the bomber exploded and plummeted to the ground near the refinery. The rest of the squadron had already begun its successful bombing raids.

US Air Force B-24s fly over Ploiești, Romania, after the oil refinery bombing raid.

Meanwhile, the 389th, the last group in the formation, flew toward a separate target, another refinery in Campina, eighteen miles from Ploiești. On the low-flying approach through a valley, the B-24 of 2nd Lt. Lloyd Hughes was hit by ground fire, and its gas tanks began spraying fuel. Hughes continued the attack and released his bombs on target. The leaking gasoline caught fire, and Hughes prepared to crash-land in a dry creek bed. At the last moment he tried to pull up to avoid hitting a bridge, but a wing caught and sent the plane cartwheeling in a fiery crash, killing Hughes and six of his crewmen. (Two men were thrown free when the plane flipped, and they miraculously survived the crash.)

By the time Kane's and Johnson's bomber groups, the 98th and the 44th, arrived at Ploiești, their assigned targets were already engulfed in flames caused by the first two groups. Johnson later remarked, "It was more like an artist's conception of an air battle than anything I had ever experienced. We flew through sheets of flames, and airplanes were everywhere, some of them on fire and others exploding." Kane and Johnson realized that the billowing smoke and fire were no guarantee that the all-important plants containing refining machinery had actually been destroyed. The 98th and 44th, therefore, stayed on course to confront the alerted defenses. As their aircraft neared the target area, sudden explosions from delayed-action bombs rose three hundred feet into the air. A carpet of antiaircraft fire exploded below and around them, and German fighters waited above, biding their time until the American bombers climbed from the blazing target area. The turbulence from the heat of the fires rocked the planes so violently that in each of the bombers pilot and copilot strained together to keep the plane on course. Yet Johnson's 44th, the last group to enter the inferno, scored direct hits on the refinery plants.

The trip back to North Africa was a race for survival. The battered aircraft had to fend off fighter attacks all the way out of Romania and over the Mediterranean. Only 92 of the 178 planes completed the 1,400-mile return leg to Benghazi. Others were forced to land in Sicily, Cyprus, and Turkey. The mission cost the air corps 54 planes lost and 532 Airmen killed, taken prisoner, or missing. The daring raid destroyed 42 percent of the refining capacity at Ploiești, but the long-range effects were questionable because the Germans repaired the plants immediately.

Major John Jerstad volunteered for the Ploiești raid even though he had flown enough missions to be eligible to return home.

Of the five men awarded the Medal of Honor for that mission, only Kane of the Ninth Air Force and Johnson of the Eighth lived to receive it. Baker, Jerstad, and Hughes of the Eighth never wavered from their missions while knowing that it meant almost certain death. Before the war ended, thirteen other men of the Eighth received the Medal of Honor.

# WAR OF ATTRITION
## Sicily and Italy

The American infantryman met his German counterpart face to face for the first time with the Operation Torch invasion of North Africa on November 8, 1942. The green GIs were defeated soundly at the Kasserine Pass in Tunisia but regrouped and helped drive the Germans from Africa. The victory in Africa was viewed as a prelude to a great confrontation in Europe—the second front that would relieve pressure on the Soviet Union and begin to drive toward Germany. Allied dreams of a quick campaign through the "soft underbelly" of the south, however, turned into the nightmare of an offensive bogged down in the mud and mountains of Italy. Salerno and Cassino, Anzio and the Gustav line—these names became synonymous with grinding frustration as the Allies had to slug it out with the Germans for every foot of Italy.

Gerry Kisters was, by his own admission, a terrible garrison soldier. He was too independent and sure of himself for an inexperienced draftee, and he spoke his mind. Yet these were the very qualities that made Kisters an exceptional combat soldier as an advance scout for the 91st Reconnaissance Squadron. The advance men, in their armored cars and jeeps, were the first to move ahead after an air or artillery bombardment. They scouted, cleared roads of obstructions, and defused mines and booby traps. It was a dangerous job. Reconnaissance men were granted more autonomy than the average GI because they had to think quickly.

In Tunisia, near the end of the North Africa campaign, Kisters, now staff sergeant, was the point man for an armored column moving from Mateus to Ferryville. The fields on both sides of the road were heavily mined, so the vehicles were forced to lumber straight down the road. Near a small creek up ahead, Kisters found the road blocked by captured British vehicles. Spotting two German soldiers hiding in a nearby culvert, he threw grenades in their direction. Then he spied a German 88mm artillery piece hidden on a hill just behind the creek, the muzzle trained on the road where the American armor would approach.

Kisters sneaked around the hill to the rear of the artillery emplacement. He threw three grenades, wiping out the unsuspecting artillery crew. That day Kisters earned the Distinguished Service Cross.

Kisters described his actions in combat as "battle fever." "You get so caught up in an action," he explained, "that the danger you're in doesn't really penetrate. You want to do the job . . . and you're going to do it, come hell or high water. You've stuck your neck out so far, it's as dangerous to go back as to go forward . . . maybe more so."

That was the case on July 31, 1943, when Kisters and his unit were assigned to take out a roadblock on a winding mountain road near Gagliano, Sicily. Kisters and a newly arrived second lieutenant rode in the lead jeep at the head of a column of the 91st's vehicles. At each turn in the road, they halted the column, edged around the bend, and nervously surveyed the terrain ahead for any sign of Germans. At one of these bends, machine-gun fire surprised them but fell short.

The two crept toward the closer of two machine-gun nests, and lobbed their grenades at the German gun. The crewmen surrendered and were taken prisoner. The second machine gun opened up from its position on a higher ridge, raking them with fire. Kisters left the lieutenant guarding the prisoners and advanced alone.

Allied dreams of a quick campaign through the "soft underbelly" of the south, however, turned into the nightmare of an offensive bogged down in the mud and mountains of Italy.

Now out of grenades and armed with only a carbine rifle, he crept close to the gun as German snipers, hidden in the mountains, found his range. He was hit by a ricocheting bullet that "damn near tore my leg off," but he went on, dragging his useless leg while firing steadily at the machine-gun crew. Snipers grazed him twice more in the legs, but he continued to crawl forward painfully. As he closed in on the emplacement, he saw the crew above him scrambling to remove sandbags in order to lower their gun and aim it at him. He fired through the gap in the sandbags and killed the crew.

Just then, another sniper's bullet ripped into his arm "like a sledgehammer" and knocked him out. When he came to, his own men had advanced and routed the snipers. Kisters was carried from the mountain by the Germans he had captured in the first machine-gun nest. He had suffered seven bullet wounds, but his feat brought him a Medal of Honor.

He was shipped home on the *Queen Elizabeth*, which had been pressed into service as a transport for the wounded. The ship also carried German prisoners to prison camps in the United States. One of the Germans aboard the huge liner escaped, and the heavily bandaged Kisters, who was born of German immigrants, awoke from a nap with an American M.P.'s pistol pointed at his head. The man who had earned the DSC and the Medal of Honor had been mistaken for a German soldier.

Charles Kelly was another soldier who did not shine until he shipped overseas. His first months in the Army were even more inauspicious than Kisters's. Numerous minor scrapes with the discipline code, and the more serious charge of making an AWOL trip home, made him ineligible for the paratroopers he had been training with. He was shipped to Camp Edwards, Massachusetts, where he hooked up with the North Africa–bound 36th Division. As Kelly put it, "The only way I could get overseas was to screw up."

Kelly's first real combat came during the invasion of Salerno in Italy, where he found himself and his unit pinned down under heavy fire. Kelly advanced, reasoning, "I had enough ammunition so I said, 'The hell with it. I'm going forward.'"

Kelly was a commander's dream. He volunteered to lead patrols whenever someone was needed. On September 13, 1943, he joined a patrol near Altavilla, Italy. Kelly's company was drawing fire from a nearby hill that was supposed to be in American hands but was held by Germans. Kelly led an attack, fighting until he ran out of ammunition for his Browning Automatic Rifle (BAR).

He returned to the mayor's house in Altavilla for more ammunition. It was being used by the Americans as an arsenal, and was under heavy German attack when Kelly arrived. He entered the house, and in the next twenty-four hours, became a one-man army—and a legend. He fired his BAR until the barrel grew red-hot and the gun useless. He used a Tommy gun until he could find no more ammunition for it, then fired another BAR until it, too, overheated. On the third floor, he found an astounding array of weapons at his disposal. Other Americans fell around him during the heated battle, but Kelly seemed to be invulnerable as he moved from window to window. He fired four rounds from a bazooka before it ran out of ammunition. He tossed an incendiary grenade on the roof of a nearby house the Germans were using for cover. When he noticed some German troops advancing on the mayor's house from an adjoining alley, Kelly pulled the firing pins from several 60mm mortar shells and dropped the live rounds out the window. The explosions rocked the foundation of the house.

Just then, another sniper's bullet ripped into his arm "like a sledgehammer" and knocked him out.

*Above*
Medal of Honor recipient Sgt. Charles "Commando" Kelly (right) holds a Vets for Ike birthday cake for General Eisenhower in New York City in 1952. At left is Clyde A. Lewis, former National Commander of the V.F.W.

*Above right*
Charles Kelly on March 11, 1944, in the Maddaloni area of Italy.

He then spotted a 37mm antitank gun in the courtyard. Though he had never fired one before, he loaded and aimed it at a nearby church steeple where he had seen snipers and pulled the lanyard. The round hit the top of the garden wall just beyond the muzzle of the gun, and the impact threw Kelly against the wall of the house. Luckily, he had loaded it with an armor-piercing shell and not a high-explosive round or the blast would have killed him. He raised the muzzle to clear the wall and blasted the church steeple, then continued firing until he was out of shells.

When the American troops started their withdrawal, Kelly volunteered to stay behind and cover them. Later, when he joined up with the unit, one of his buddies told him that they had already made plans to go back and "try and find your body."

"Commando" Kelly was harder to kill than that. He survived seven more months in combat, including some vicious fighting at the Rapido River in January of 1944. The only thing that stopped Kelly was his own government, which brought him back to the United States for a war bonds tour. The one-time AWOL returned to Pittsburgh in May 1944 for a parade and a tumultuous ovation. This time he wore the Medal of Honor.

Kelly had grown up in a large family in a tough part of Pittsburgh. He and his nine brothers had slept in shifts in a house without electricity or plumbing, so he knew something about hardships when he joined the Army. He also knew about the protection and love a tightly knit group of brothers provided for each other. Kelly received the Medal of Honor, in part, because he extended that fraternal feeling to his buddies in the 36th Infantry: "You live with me and you become a family . . . just like brothers. If one of them gets hurt, you're mad. That's it. We were a family. [If] they hurt them, they hurt me."

# LIBERATION
## *The Battle for France*

On D-Day, June 6, 1944, the greatest armada in history sailed across the English Channel to the shores of Normandy. The Allied invasion of Europe marked the beginning of the end for the German war machine. Between D-Day and the end of June, nearly a million men landed in France, but the Germans kept them bottled up within a hundred-mile front in northern France for more than a month. The fate of the entire invasion rested on the shoulders of the soldiers who were asked to break out from the narrow front and to push through the Germans at the village of St.-Lô.

One of the key players in the successful fighting that pushed the Germans back from St.-Lô was Capt. Matt Urban. Urban, a native of New York, was already highly decorated for his actions with the 60th Infantry, 9th Division in Tunisia and Sicily. He spent the six-month period before D-Day training in England. On D-Day plus four the 9th waded ashore. Urban led his company in fighting through French hedgerows, tree- and vine-covered banks of dirt that for centuries bounded the open fields of the northern French farming country. Each field had to be taken separately by the Americans, who battled to root out German machine guns and tanks dug in behind the natural walls of the hedgerows. Each hedgerow taken meant another hedgerow to attack at the end of the next field.

On June 14, in one such field near Renouf, France, heavy fire from two tanks pinned down Urban's company. When his bazooka man was wounded, Urban picked up the weapon. One of his men carried ammunition for him. Under withering fire the two worked their way up to and around the hedgerow. They crawled to within fifteen feet of the tanks and destroyed them. Later in the same day, a 37mm tank shell narrowly missed Urban and hit the hedgerow just behind him. "It splattered . . . [and I] took it in the left leg." Badly wounded, he refused evacuation until the next day because he knew he and his men had only another quarter of a mile to go to secure the area.

Three weeks later, while recovering in a hospital in England, Urban heard that the 9th was suffering very heavy casualties and that many of its officers and sergeants had been killed. He left the hospital, crossed the English Channel on a troopship, and hitched rides to the front. He arrived leaning on a homemade cane, just as the US bombers were striking targets for the beginning of Operation Cobra—the planned break-out at St.-Lô, less than twenty-five miles inland from Utah and Omaha beaches where the US Army had stormed into France nearly a month and a half before.

He found some of the 9th Division troops in disarray, huddled in shell holes with their tanks in flames just a hundred yards in front of them. Although the men were not Urban's own, he ordered them to follow him, leading them forward until they came to two tanks,

"If one of them gets hurt, you're mad. That's it. We were a family. [If] they hurt them, they hurt me."

one smoking and in ruins, the second usable with the driver still inside but with no gunner atop it. The entire area was under intense fire from the Germans who, after the bombing, had reorganized in a dominant position on a long, sloping hill. With no radio or mortars and no time to get them, Urban knew that he had to make do with what he had—the disabled but still usable tank. After a lieutenant and a sergeant were killed trying to man the turret gun, Urban decided, "I'm not going to send any more of these guys . . . to certain death," so he "crawled like a snake" up the tank and dropped in as machine-gun bullets ricocheted off the steel plate.

Barely able to believe he was still alive, he realized he had to stick his head up to fire the machine gun. Later recalling that he was certain he was going to die, Urban remembered a sensation of living "years of life in five to ten seconds." He said a quick prayer, then came up firing the .50-caliber machine gun. The Germans were stupefied when Urban opened fire, some of them "actually standing up." The driver began to move the tank forward and the men, "yelling like Geronimo," advanced with it. "We had them," said Urban. The German line of defense cracked.

Back with his own unit, Urban was made battalion commander when the commanding officer of 2nd Battalion was killed by artillery. Urban was wounded again on August 15, when he was hit by shrapnel in the lower back and chest. Again he refused evacuation.

On September 3, Urban led the battalion's attack to establish the crossing point over the Meuse River. A battalion leader normally commands from the rear echelon, but Urban personally led the attack because of his belief that a good leader stayed in the thick of the action—in front of his men.

Machine-gun fire smashed into the center of his throat as he scrambled across open terrain to relieve three trapped men. Braving heavy fire, his men brought him out on a litter. As he drifted in and out of consciousness from loss of blood and the shock of his terrible wound, Urban saw his battalion chaplain administer last rites and saw a surgeon shake his head bleakly when asked whether Urban would survive.

Urban fought off death and spent seven months in hospitals in England. The neck wound, his seventh wound of the war, kept him out of further combat. Urban fought a different kind of battle to learn to speak again. A series of operations restored somewhat his mangled larynx. With speech therapy and the same grit and determination he had evidenced at St.-Lô and the Meuse, he slowly recovered his power of speech.

Matt Urban had to wait nearly forty years to receive the recognition due him. Letters pertaining to the recommendations for his

Aerial view of St.-Lô, France, after saturation bombing (3,400 tons of bombs) by the 9th US Air Force in July 1944. Operation Cobra was instrumental in the breakout from the Normandy beachhead.

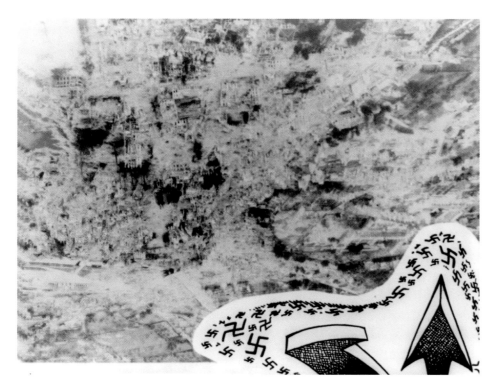

award were lost because his unit was overrun shortly after Urban was wounded at the Meuse, the witnesses to Urban's actions captured. Thirty-five years later, Urban mentioned in a casual conversation with a Veterans' Administration representative that he thought he had once been recommended for the Medal of Honor. The man made an inquiry, and Warrant Officer Carl Hansen of the Pentagon's Awards Office took up the case.

In 1979, Urban picked up the phone and heard Warrant Officer Hansen say, "Colonel Urban . . . I have some great news for you." Hansen had found a long-lost letter recommending Urban for the Medal of Honor. The Medal of Honor was his twenty-ninth combat decoration, and with it Matt Urban joined the ranks of America's most highly decorated World War II soldiers.

Audie Murphy is perhaps the best known of this elite group. Murphy was born in Hunt County, Texas, to a family of sharecroppers. His youth in the Depression was hard: "Poverty dogged our every step," he later wrote. His father deserted the family when Murphy was still quite young, and his mother died when he was sixteen. He took odd jobs until the war came, then tried to enlist in the Marines. The recruiter looked over the skinny, small youth and told him he did not measure up to corps standards. Murphy then tried the paratroops, who also rejected him, before settling for a place in the "unglamorous" infantry.

At first, the Army found him a dubious soldier. His commanding officer in boot camp tried to make him a cook. Murphy swore he would go to the guardhouse first. Another officer wanted him to work in a post exchange. Again he resisted and finally was allowed to ship overseas as a combat infantryman.

He began the war in North Africa as a private and proved to be an adept and resourceful fighter. He advanced through the ranks, saw action in Sicily and Italy, and was a much-decorated second lieutenant by the time he went into action on January 26, 1945. Murphy and the men of his casualty-depleted Company B, 15th Infantry, 3rd Division, were in the forefront of an American attack on a German position in the village of Holtzwihr, France. Told to wait for support, they tried to dig into the snow-covered frozen ground at the edge of a forest about a mile away from Holtzwihr. With them were two armored tank destroyers, each with a turret cannon and a .50-caliber machine gun.

At two in the afternoon, six German tanks rumbled out of Holtzwihr, fanned out in the open field that lay in front of Murphy's position, and ground their way toward Company B. Enemy infantrymen, wearing white camouflage cover, followed the tanks. As the Germans advanced, one of the American tank destroyers slid into a ditch while maneuvering for firing position, its cannon now pointed at the ground uselessly.

The German tanks opened fire on Murphy and his men. A round burst in the trees above his machine-gun squad, killing the men and disabling the gun. Another round blasted into the second tank destroyer and set it afire. Survivors from the crew poured out the hatch and ran to the rear.

Second Lieutenant Audie Murphy was among the most highly decorated combat soldiers to fight in World War II.

When the Germans were virtually on top of him, Murphy called in artillery fire on his own position.

By radio, Murphy called for artillery fire. When the rounds fell behind the advancing tanks, he designated coordinates closer to his own position. American artillery rounds began to find the ranks of German infantry, but the tanks pressed on, spraying the Americans with machine-gun fire. Murphy ordered his men to fall back.

He now faced the advancing Germans alone. He fired his carbine at the infantrymen until he ran out of ammunition, then jumped up on the burning tank destroyer and blasted away with its machine gun. When the Germans were virtually on top of him, Murphy called in artillery fire on his own position. The barrage turned back the attack. Miraculously, Murphy survived heavy pounding by his own artillery, crawling down from the tank destroyer with only a slight shrapnel wound in the left leg. The tank destroyer exploded shortly after Murphy limped away toward the rear. There he rejoined his men and organized them for a successful counterattack against the Germans.

Murphy fought for three more months, until the German surrender. On June 2, 1945, he received the Medal of Honor, the most prized of his World War II decorations.

# NIGHTMARE IN THE ARDENNES
## *The Bulge*

In the summer and fall of 1944, British and Americans fought their way across France, Belgium, and the Netherlands. By late autumn they had dug a toehold in Germany's Hürtgen Forest, and Soviet troops were closing in on the Germans from the east. In a final desperate attempt to stave off defeat, Hitler ordered his Panzers to break through the American lines in the Ardennes Forest of Belgium and Luxembourg, then push to the Belgian port of Antwerp and seize vitally needed fuel supplies. The Germans successfully concealed their buildup, and when they hurled twenty divisions into combat, on December 16, an American force of only five divisions stood against them. German tanks roared through the American lines on a fifty-mile front, bulging sixty miles into Allied territory. The Americans scrambled to regroup and stem the onrushing tide.

On the snowy afternoon of December 14, 1944, two days before the German assault in the Ardennes, Sgt. Ralph Neppel and the rest of his machine-gun squad set up a defensive position at the end of the main street of Birgel, Germany, a hamlet on the edge of the Hürtgen Forest. Before that time, Neppel's company had advanced steadily from the day it landed at Normandy on D-Day plus thirteen. The combat through the hedgerows and into Germany had been fierce, but nothing had prepared Neppel for what he was to endure that evening in Birgel. Near dusk, the crew heard the rumble of tanks entering the town. The sound of the grinding machinery came closer until a number of tanks emerged from the narrow side streets and turned toward the squad's position. German infantry followed the lead tank, using it as a shield.

Neppel waited until the Germans had advanced to within one hundred yards, then released a burst that killed several of the foot soldiers. The tank came to within thirty yards, then fired one cannon shot that blasted the Americans and sent the machine gun flying.

Neppel was thrown ten yards from the gun, his legs wounded terribly and one foot blown off. The other men were either dead or dying. He crawled on his elbows back to the gun. Its tripod had been knocked loose, so he cradled it in the crook of his arm and fired until he was too weak to lift it anymore, killing the remaining German infantrymen.

Without infantry cover, the Panzer was vulnerable to attack from bazookas or phosphorous grenades. The commander emerged from his tank and advanced on Neppel with his Luger pistol in hand. The officer fired, hitting Neppel in the helmet, and left him for dead. The helmet saved his life; Neppel's skull was creased but he was alive and conscious.

When Neppel again heard the rumbling of the tanks, he feared they would soon crush him under their tracks. Instead, they withdrew.

With rifles held for quick action, American infantrymen advance through the Hürtgen Forest in Germany.

American troops rescued Neppel and took him to a hospital, where he stayed six months. He had single-handedly turned back a Nazi armor attack but had lost both of his legs in the effort. When he heard that he was to receive the Medal of Honor his reaction was "to feel humble. You see so many die . . . then in the hospital you see triple amputees, guys who lost their eyesight . . . you feel there are so many more deserving that you shouldn't be taking the glory as an individual."

Private First Class Melvin "Bud" Biddle and the rest of his unit were in Reims, France, waiting to go home when the Germans launched their attack. Veterans of campaigns in Italy and in southern France, they had turned in their equipment and were passing the time listening to "Axis Sally," an English-speaking Nazi propagandist who played the latest hits from America while spouting misinformation in an attempt to demoralize the Allies. The troops were more amused than influenced by her show. That night, she announced, "The men of the 517th Parachute Infantry Regiment think you're going home . . . but you're not." This time, her information was correct.

The men of the 517th were issued new equipment, so new, in fact, that their rifles were still packed in Cosmoline grease, which the men had to clean off before they were boarded into trucks and driven to a crossroads in the area near the most advanced point of the German thrust into Belgium. The mission of the 517th was to clear the Germans—Panzer divisions, paratroops, and SS soldiers—out of three miles of territory between the towns of Soy and Hotton.

Private First Class Melvin "Bud" Biddle, the hawkeyed GI from Indiana.

Biddle, who had superb vision, was the lead scout for the 517th. On December 23, Biddle was ahead of his company as it crawled through thick underbrush toward railroad tracks leading out of Hotton. He crawled unseen to within ten feet of three German sentries. Firing with his M1 rifle, he wounded one man and killed a second. The third sentry fled, but not before Biddle shot him twice in the back. "I should have got him. He kept running and got to their machine guns and all hell broke loose."

Under heavy fire from several machine guns, Biddle stayed on point as his unit crawled to within range, lobbed grenades, and destroyed all but one of the guns. With his last grenade, Biddle blew up the remaining machine gun. Then he charged the surviving gunners, killing them all.

The next morning Biddle spotted a group of Germans dug in along a ridge. He ducked behind a small bank for cover but found that he could not properly maneuver in order to shoot. In basic training Biddle had learned to shoot from a sitting position, but at the time he had thought that there would be no way to use it in combat. Now, moving to a sitting stance, he shot fourteen men. He hit each one in the head, imagining that the helmets were the same as the targets he had aimed at in training. Although others in his unit later went to view the bodies, Biddle could not bring himself to look on the carnage he had wrought. His sharpshooting, however, had made it possible for his unit to secure the village.

American soldiers hunker down in the snow-covered Ardennes during the Battle of the Bulge in the winter of 1944–1945.

Biddle was wounded a few days later when a German 88mm artillery shell exploded against a building behind him. As he was returning to his unit from a hospital in London, another soldier asked him if he had heard about "that guy in the Bulge that shot all those people. My God, between Soy and Hotton it was littered with Germans. I think they're going to put that guy in for the Medal of Honor."

Biddle's outfit was just one of many units to be rushed to the Ardennes to relieve the embattled First Army. When General George S. Patton's Third Army rolled out of Lorraine, it left the Allied units in its wake vulnerable to attack. The Germans moved the 17th SS Panzer to the attack near Bitche, France, in an area where the 44th Division struggled to hang on.

Sergeant Charles MacGillivary was a Canadian national who joined the US Army in Boston, Massachusetts. He and the rest of Company I, 71st Regiment, had been taken off the line for Christmas dinner after they had held a key position during the initial German attacks of December 14–19. It was only their third respite from frontline combat in seven months of tough fighting across France. Soon, however Company I was summoned back to the front.

In the enemy attack, MacGillivary's squad was cut off from the others. On New Year's Day, 1945, the men found themselves trapped in a heavily wooded gully, surrounded by Germans, separated from their unit, and running out of food and ammunition. Four protected German machine guns held positions above them. Some of the men wanted to surrender, but MacGillivary pointed out that there was no one to surrender to other than the SS, and "we saw them leading prisoners in front of tanks . . . with their hands on their heads . . . and then we saw the prisoners fall. The SS troops were up on the machine guns shooting them."

MacGillivary took what grenades remained from his troops and then ordered the men to cover him with the few rounds of ammunition they had left. He inched close to the side of the bank, waited for his men to fire, and then scrambled out of the gully. MacGillivary's mission was two-fold: to knock out the machine guns facing the gully and to eliminate the infantry protecting them from the rear.

He lobbed his grenade at the first gun. When it detonated, he shot down the gunners with his .45-caliber Tommy gun, and then attacked the infantrymen with more grenades. When his submachine gun ran out of ammunition, MacGillivary retraced his steps to where he had seen abandoned haversacks and another submachine gun with ammunition clips. Under heavy fire, he returned to the machine-gun nests, remembering something he had learned in the hedgerows: "With automatic weapons you keep moving. You move towards them and the guy gets excited."

MacGillivary destroyed the remaining three nests in much the same manner as the first, using his last grenade on the fourth gun. He was just lifting his numbed hands out of the snow after the blast when he saw one of the wounded gunners crawl to the gun. MacGillivary emptied his submachine gun into the gunner, but the man brought the gun down on its swivel as he fell, and the fire scraped across MacGillivary's chest and carved a line down his left arm, cutting it off. "When you're hit by bullets it's like a burn . . . as if you've been hit with a poker. To cool it off . . . I kept jabbing it in the snow." MacGillivary's efforts froze his wound. "When they picked me up they picked up a red cake of ice [frozen to his severed arm]. I would have bled to death in the summer or in the South Pacific."

By January 29, 1945, the Germans had been pushed back to the line they had held before the Battle of the Bulge, but pockets of resistance still had to be eliminated. First Sergeant Leonard Funk and the men of his Company C, 508th Parachute Infantry, 82nd Airborne Division, discovered that the Germans, even in retreat, fought with ferocity. Company C had been decimated by the fighting in the preceding weeks. The executive officer of the company had been killed, so Funk, a veteran of the jumps on Normandy and Arnhem, had become acting executive officer as well as first sergeant.

That day it was snowing hard and was so cold that Funk had difficulty getting his Thompson submachine gun to work. "Everybody in my company had frostbitten feet . . . but there were no replacements, so we had to stick it out." Under heavy artillery fire, Funk led two columns into Holzheim, Belgium, taking prisoners along the way in furious house-to-house fighting.

First Sergeant Leonard Funk, whose speed with a submachine gun freed his unit from capture in Holzheim, Belgium, on January 29, 1945.

President Harry Truman presents the Medal of Honor to Sgt. Charles MacGillivary for bravery near Bitche, France, in a ceremony at the White House on August 23, 1945.

Funk could spare only four men to stay behind and guard eighty German prisoners. When the four guards saw shadowy figures moving toward them through the snowstorm, they assumed that a patrol from nearby Company B was coming in for a prearranged meeting. The soldiers were indeed from Company B, but they had been captured and were followed by Germans. Since all of the men on both sides were wearing white camouflage cover, the four Company C guards were unable to distinguish the Germans, who captured them and freed their German prisoners.

Sergeant Funk's men at the front had encountered an unexpected number of enemy soldiers, so Funk and his company clerk backtracked to alert the guards to be ready to move. He was so confident of the rear that he had shouldered his Tommy gun. His confidence soon dissipated. He later recounted that as he approached his guards, "a guy I'd never seen before in my life comes up to me speaking German." The officer pushed a submachine gun into Funk's stomach and demanded his surrender.

Funk realized that if he did not do something his command would be hit from the rear. In a lightning move, Funk sidestepped and got his own gun down. He still remembers the look of surprise on the man's face as he emptied his clip into the German officer. "It seemed like I had hollow bullets . . . I've never seen a man take so many in my life." Other Germans fired, and the company clerk, who was standing beside Funk, was killed. The sergeant reloaded and continued firing as men hit the ground and others sprinted toward nearby houses. During the chaos, the American prisoners seized weapons and began to fire as well. At the center of a firefight that killed twenty-one Germans and wounded many others stood Leonard Funk, unscratched and firing to the end. His Medal of Honor was presented to him on August 23, 1945, at the same ceremony honoring Ralph Neppel and Charles MacGillivary.

# THE END IN GERMANY
### Siegfried Line and Nuremberg

The deserate, failed gamble in the Ardennes cost Germany her lifeblood in men and materiel: more than 100,000 soldiers, as well as 1,600 airplanes, 700 tanks, and countless other vehicles. In January 1945, the Allies pushed the Germans back to the "Siegfried line" in western Germany, near the Rhine River. Allied Forces poured into Germany from the west while the Russians advanced from the east to within thirty miles of Berlin. The end of the Third Reich was at hand.

Many a frontline infantryman who lived through the European winter of 1944–1945 must remember feeling the way Master Sgt. Nick Oresko felt: "You're dirty and hungry and cold . . . you get so miserable and you feel so terrible you say, well, if I give my life and it helps win the war, so be it." Oresko, of Company C, 302nd Infantry, 94th Infantry Division, had been in what he later called "good combat," mostly patrolling and some minor firefights—until the Battle of the Bulge. His unit went on the offensive at the beginning of the year against both the Germans and the winter weather. On the evening of January 22, Oresko fell through the ice of a twelve-foot-deep water-filled tank trap during a battle. He was able to survive by holding his rifle like a chinning bar across

Men of the 83rd Infantry race through a German-held town in the Ardennes on January 15, 1945.

the hole in the ice, until his men arrived and pulled him out. He was soaked to the skin and slept on the ground that night in a uniform frozen down to the underwear.

Late the next afternoon, the flush of anticipated danger replaced the cold. Oresko's platoon was ordered to take and hold a German position near the Siegfried Line without benefit of covering artillery. Oresko had a terrible moment when he gave the order to "move out" and nobody stirred. A sergeant, Oresko said, has "to be ready to put [his] life on the line," so he stood up and started forward. The others followed. The Germans began dropping mortar shells behind Oresko but in front of his men. Cut off from the others, Oresko slowly groped forward while searching for cover. He moved close enough to the first of two machine guns to dismantle it with a well-aimed grenade, then charged forward and shot the gunners. "What do you do?" he said later. "I knew I was alone. . . . [I] looked for a place to hide."

Then the second machine gun opened up; a bullet tore a hole in Oresko's hip. "As I lay there, I could see . . . just over my head . . . the machine gun was spitting fire at my troops." Again he crawled forward, toward the second gun. When he realized he had lost his grenades, he crawled back again, retrieved them, and advanced once more. Alone in a no man's land, he tripped a booby trap; instead of injuring him, the explosion went over him.

When he reached the machine-gun bunker, he pulled the pin from a grenade, waited

Two American soldiers look down on a long row of "dragon's teeth," concrete devices to halt invading tanks at the Siegfried Line.

three seconds, threw it in the opening, and jumped in after the explosion. Oresko found three of the six men dead from the blast; he killed the others with his rifle, then lay bleeding among the bodies until his men came to carry him out.

While recovering from his wound, Oresko worked on limited duty in Le Havre, where he heard that he would be getting the Distinguished Service Cross for his action near the Siegfried Line. He assumed that he would soon be returning to combat. One day the officer in charge asked him, "How do you want to go home, by boat or by plane?" Oresko responded that he had not collected enough combat points to be rotated back to the States and the man replied, "You don't need them." Oresko knew at that moment that the DSC had been upgraded to the Medal of Honor.

The last deed earning the Medal of Honor in Europe was performed on April 18, 1945, by Lt. Michael Daly of Company A, 15th Infantry, 3rd Division. Daly, a twenty-year-old from Southport, Connecticut, had fought in every major battle from his days as private first class with the 18th Infantry on Omaha Beach to Nuremberg, where he fought with the 3rd Division. Already holding the Silver Star, the Purple Heart, and a battlefield commission, Daly "felt an obligation to protect [the surviving members of the company]. You do all the time. Maybe, in a way, more than normal, knowing the war was nearly over. "

President Truman congratulates Master Sgt. Nick Oresko on receiving the Medal of Honor.

Daly acted as the lead man for his troops as they fought toward the center of war-destroyed Nuremberg, once a showcase for the Reich. The city was contested from one pile of rubble to another, each pile a small fortress for hardened SS troops who ferociously resisted every inch of the American advance. For four days the Americans went about the bloody task of rooting them out.

April 18 was the second day of the attack. Daly was scouting a rail bridge that led into the city when a German machine gun on the other side of the bridge caught him and his men in the open. He charged forward, running to within fifty yards of the Germans before he opened fire with his carbine and killed the three gunners.

He again pushed ahead of his company, advancing on a house that contained a German antitank gun. In the words of one of his men, he was "taking his life in his hands and we all knew it." As he worked his way to the house, rifle fire kicked up the dust around him. With only his carbine, Daly killed all six Germans manning the antitank equipment.

Then, when he saw a longtime friend fall in the assault, Daly, in "hot blood," twice more led attacks on German machine-gun positions, each time moving to within point-blank range while directing the fire of his troops on the Germans. At one critical point, he seized a discarded M1, crawled forward to within ten yards of a German machine-gun nest, and killed the gunners, securing the position.

Daly was wounded badly in the face the following day. Once he recovered he was shipped home. Like so many medal recipients, Daly refused to see his award as a testament to individual heroism. "The medal is very important to me. . ." he later said, "to ensure the memory of those who died."

Captain Michael J. Daly, who led troops into the heart of Nuremberg, with his father, Col. Paul Daly, a much-decorated veteran of both world wars. Captain Daly received many honors, including two Purple Hearts and a Medal of Honor, for his service in World War II.

American tanks in the shattered city of Nuremberg.

## THE SILENT SERVICE

### *Submarines in the Pacific*

While US ground forces concentrated on defeating the Axis in Europe, war also raged half a world away. In the Pacific, the US submarine service spent the war years choking off resources vital to Japan's survival. At the outset of the war, problems plagued the submarine force—outmoded equipment, defective torpedoes, and excessively cautious commanders. During the war, new submarines were produced with the latest refinements in radar, data computers, and reliable torpedoes. Most important, though, were the bold young men who dared to take their boats deep into harm's way.

The submarines of the Pacific war were manned by a tightly knit band of volunteers who called themselves the "silent service" because their operations were cloaked in utmost secrecy.

Commander Howard Gilmore of the *Growler* was a legend among them. During a patrol in the South Pacific near Rabaul in February of 1943, Gilmore's sub closed on a small ship that he had been stalking on the surface, when the ship changed course and steamed toward the *Growler*. The two collided and the submarine sliced a hole amidships in the enemy vessel. Japanese machine gunners raked the bridge of the submarine, killing two men and wounding Gilmore and two others. Gilmore ordered the survivors to clear the bridge. Still topside, injured, he shouted to his executive officer "Take her down!" The exec obeyed, and Gilmore was last seen clutching the bridge as the Japanese continued to sweep the submarine with fire. The badly damaged *Growler* escaped and eventually struggled to Australia. Gilmore's Medal of Honor was the first ever awarded to a submariner.

The fate of Capt. John Cromwell of the *Sculpin* was only revealed at the war's end by men returning from Japanese prison camps. Cromwell led a submarine attack group off Truk Island in the central Pacific. He was the only man on patrol in possession of intelligence concerning top-secret, detailed plans for submarine warfare and fleet movements in the Pacific.

The *Sculpin* was discovered by Japanese destroyers, who rocked the submarine with a savage depth charge attack. The badly damaged boat initially sank deep below the surface. Cromwell ordered the *Sculpin* to the surface and commanded the crew to abandon ship. He stayed aboard as the crew escaped. Rather than face the possibility of revealing his secret information under torture or drugs, Cromwell chose to go down with his ship. His Medal of Honor citation reads, "His great moral courage in the face of certain death adds new luster to the traditions of the U.S. Navy."

One intrepid commander, Samuel Dealey of the *Harder*, sought out the destroyers protecting Japanese convoys with a special avidity. During one patrol, Dealey had already sunk

Mortally wounded Cdr. Howard Gilmore orders his sub, the *Growler*, to dive, leaving him and the bodies of two sailors topside. At top left is the sub's damaged nose.

The USS *Harder* helps a seaplane rescue a downed flier under fire from Japanese hidden in the trees of a Pacific island.

Commander Samuel Dealey, skipper of the *Harder*.

three destroyers and damaged two when, on the night of June 6, 1944, a bright moon exposed the *Harder* to two Japanese destroyer escorts. Dealey kept his boat on the surface, taunting the escorts, submerging only at the last moment. Then he fired stern torpedoes into one destroyer. The *Harder* escaped after enduring a severe attack by depth charges.

The next day, while at periscope depth, he invited the charge of two oncoming destroyers, holding fire until the ships had closed to within 650 yards. Dealey stuck his torpedoes directly into the bow of the onrushing lead ship, an extremely difficult and dangerous maneuver called "down-the-throat" firing. A fourth *Harder* torpedo hit the second destroyer. Dealey used the same maneuver and method of firing on June 10, this time passing the *Harder* directly under a destroyer as it erupted in a thunderous explosion. He came to be known as "Down-the-Throat" Dealey.

On the *Harder*'s next patrol, Dealey hunted as one of a three-boat wolf pack near Luzon. Frank Haylor, skipper of the *Hake*, one of the other boats in the pack, saw the *Harder* on August 23, when Dealey told him he was going after a particularly troublesome mine sweeper. A few hours later sonar reported concussions from at least fifteen depth charges. Dealey and the *Harder* were never heard from again. His Medal of Honor was presented to his widow.

Commander Richard H. O'Kane was a skipper cut from the same cloth as Gilmore, Cromwell, and Dealey. Fellow Medal of Honor recipient and submariner George Street called O'Kane "absolutely fearless." O'Kane proved to be the most successful submariner in the US Navy, sinking twenty-four ships in just nine months.

On the night of October 23, 1944, the *Tang* was patrolling the waters of the narrow, dangerous Formosa Strait. The radar operator reported what seemed to be an island where no island should be. The "island" proved to be a convoy including a transport, four enemy freighters, and numerous escorts. As the submarine maneuvered on the surface toward the Japanese ships, the radar screen showed a blip breaking away and moving in their direction. O'Kane made a wide arc and positioned the *Tang* in the spot the Japanese escort had vacated and began to "zig when they zigged." As soon as he was certain that he was dead ahead of the convoy, O'Kane turned his submarine so that it was pointing in the same direction as the convoy and allowed the Japanese ships to overtake him. Once he was between the two lines of ships, he fired from his bow on three of the leading ships.

A transport veered from its line and bore down on the *Tang*. O'Kane had no time to dive. Japanese gunners poured fire on the *Tang* from above. With less than one hundred yards between ships, O'Kane ordered "left full rudder," and the *Tang* pivoted into a turn and steamed straight down the side of the big ship, so nearly under it that the machine gunners could not lower the guns enough to score a hit. O'Kane prepared to dive but saw that the transport was about to collide with a Japanese freighter. He fired from the stern tubes, hitting the freighter. The night sky was ablaze.

The next night, O'Kane slipped into the front of another convoy. The *Tang* was sighted by destroyers, but O'Kane stayed on the surface long enough to hit a tanker and two transports. The enemy destroyers closed so fast that he had to escape. O'Kane waited an hour until it was safe to return to finish off the transport he had crippled. One torpedo hit the mark, but the second took a sharp turn, and, as the men on the bridge watched in horror, began to circle back toward the *Tang*. O'Kane called for emergency speed as the berserk torpedo porpoised in and out of the water on a direct line for the center of the boat. It hit the *Tang* with a "devastating detonation" that blew O'Kane and eight other men topside into the water. The sub immediately started to go down, and O'Kane watched helplessly as it sank—"like a pendulum might sink in a viscous fluid."

Thirteen men escaped through air locks and fought their way to the surface. Of the twenty-two men in the water, only O'Kane and eight others lived through the night. They were picked up by a Japanese patrol boat the next morning. O'Kane endured the remainder of the war in a secret POW camp at Ofuna, during which time the Japanese never released word of his capture to the Red Cross. His wife spent nearly a year without word of his fate. Because of fear of retaliation against O'Kane if he were alive, his Medal of Honor was not announced until his release.

Three more submarine commanders received the Medal of Honor during the war. Commander Eugene B. Fluckey of the *Barb* stalked a convoy until he found it anchored in fogged-in Namkwan Harbor, China. He sailed right into the center of it on the surface and fired torpedoes in all directions,

*Above*
Standing, at center, Cdr. Richard H. O'Kane of the USS *Tang*, with some of the fliers he rescued in the Pacific in April 1944.

*Right*
The battle flag of the USS *Barb* records its awesome toll on the enemy. Rising sun flags mark Japanese merchantmen sunk; sun with rays indicate warships sunk; hollowed-out suns of both kinds indicate ships damaged. The swastika represents a German cruiser sunk in the Atlantic in 1943. At top are citation ribbons, including the Medal of Honor (top center) earned by Cdr. Eugene B. Fluckey.

sinking several ships. Commander Lawson Ramage of the *Parche* received his medal for an attack similar to O'Kane's night attack off Formosa. On a patrol in Luzon Strait on July 31, 1944, Ramage located an enemy convoy. He kept his boat on the surface, attacking ships as the night exploded around him.

Lieutenant Commander George Street's Medal of Honor was the last given to a submariner in World War II. By the time of his action on April 14, 1945, the submarine service had been so effective that few of the remaining Japanese ships dared venture into the East China Sea. They preferred to dart in close to land from safe harbor to safe harbor. Street, of the *Tirante,* crept in close to shore in waters too shallow for a dive and slipped into a mined harbor on Quelpart Island off the coast of Korea. He avoided patrol boats and torpedoed an ammunition ship and two escorts as they lay at anchor.

Street and other daring skippers like him applied the final turns to the vise that crushed Japanese shipping. At the end of the war, the US submarine force hunted at will near the home islands of Japan. After Japan's surrender, Prime Minister Tōjō said that the US submarines had played a key role in defeating the Japanese.

# ISLAND FIGHTING

## *Iwo Jima*

By November of 1944, Marine island-hopping invasions had made possible an American air base on Saipan, an island 1,300 miles from Tokyo. From there, new B-29 Superfortresses could pound the Japanese in ever-increasing and more effective bombing raids. However, the B-29s needed shorter-range fighter escorts and an emergency landing area between Saipan and Japan. For that purpose, the island of Iwo Jima would have to be taken. Entrenched on Iwo were twenty-two thousand Japanese prepared to die in defense of the island. The job of taking the island was delegated to Marine combat infantrymen, who fought yard by bloody yard over thirty-six days.

Bedlam awaited the Marines who struggled ashore at Iwo Jima on D-Day, February 19, 1945. In the smoke and the noise of battle, those

Across the litter on Iwo Jima's black sands, Marines of the 4th Division shell Japanese positions cleverly concealed back from the beaches. Here, a gun pumps a stream of shells into Japanese positions inland on the tiny volcanic island.

fortunate enough to live through the first few moments thought only of digging for cover into the shifting black volcanic sand. Equipment and men in subsequent waves piled up behind the logjam on the beach.

One of the early casualties on Iwo was Sgt. John Basilone, killed by a mortar blast while he urged his crew to get off the killing ground of the beach. Iwo thus claimed the man who had received one of the Marine Corps's first Medals of Honor of World War II. Basilone led the defense that held off a nightlong *banzai* charge on Guadalcanal in 1942. After a much-publicized return to the United States, the veteran volunteered to return to combat—just in time for Iwo Jima.

Fire was so intense that first day that the 1st Battalion, 26th Marines, lost many of its sergeants and all its officers, except two second lieutenants and Capt. Robert Dunlap. Dunlap commanded Company C, 1st Battalion, 26th Marines, 5th Marine Division, part of a force ordered to storm across the narrow neck of land that connects Mount Suribachi at the western end of the island with the large expanse of flatter land to the east. He led his men out of the carnage on the beach and forward to the attack. Dunlap later said, "If I'm going to get men killed, I want them accomplishing something."

After advancing quickly up the neck of land, Dunlap and his men turned east, destroying Japanese fortifications as they went. Then they moved toward a large airfield on the eastern side of the island. With an open area of about four hundred yards of rolling hills in front of him, Dunlap could see that they had pierced the middle of a heavily defended area. Beyond the hills, he could make out a cliff face dotted with fortifications.

As Japanese artillery from the cliff began to pinpoint Company C's position, Dunlap watched a Japanese soldier stand up and walk calmly back toward the rear. This gave him an idea. Instructing his men not to shoot at the Japanese soldier, he rose and walked toward the enemy lines in just the same manner, hoping the Japanese would mistake him for one of their own. "My medal [citation] says I crawled. . . . There's no way to crawl [that distance] without getting killed, so I walked just like the Japanese."

The ruse worked. He mounted the top of a ridge nearly four hundred yards in front of his lines and looked out at the large guns hidden on the other side of the rise and in front of the cliff. Then "all of a sudden the Japs realized who I was. . . . I got back running and diving. I'd dive into a bomb crater . . . and then look for my next hole, [then] I'd zigzag, dive. The Japs were on me all the time."

His own men covered his retreat with a storm of fire. By now, the rest of the American advance had ground to a halt in the face of the enemy's intense artillery and mortar fire. Company C's flanks were unprotected, and the battalion commander ordered the men to fall back two hundred yards, flush with the line that marked the rest of the advance.

Dunlap remained at the front to act as a forward. Out front in a foxhole on the exposed hillside, he presented an inviting target to the Japanese. Runners from his company brought several field telephones to him, and Dunlap used them to call in coordinates for artillery fire. The Japanese hammered the hillside with mortar and artillery rounds, but Dunlap would not move. For forty-eight hours he directed both the Marine artillery and naval fire at the caves in the cliff face. By staying at his frontline vantage point, exposed to enemy gunfire, Dunlap made it possible for the bombardment to pinpoint and destroy Japanese resistance in his sector of the attack. Astoundingly, he walked down the hillside unwounded after two

Captain Robert Dunlap, who led his men off the beach at Iwo Jima.

Corpsmen patch up wounded Marines on Iwo Jima.

days of braving steady fire (although he was seriously wounded later in the battle). The reward for his vigil was the Medal of Honor.

As casualties mounted on Iwo, medical corpsmen found themselves in the hottest parts of the action. Pharmacist's Mate 1st Class Francis Pierce was already a veteran of the landings on Roi-Namur, Saipan, and Tinian. When he landed on Iwo, he knew what to expect but found the beach on Iwo was "hotter than hell."

The Pacific campaign was not fought according to any rules of war. The Japanese refused to honor the Geneva Convention code, which forbade firing on medics. "We didn't wear the Red Cross because those were just good targets," said Pierce. Pierce received the same training a Marine infantryman received in rifle, machine-gun, bayonet, and other combat skills; he had to apply it all to tend the wounded.

Pierce went after the fallen with Tommy gun in hand, saying it required "a firefight to get up to them and get them out." He reasoned that if he came at the Japanese shooting, they "would have to do some ducking too." He memorized every detail of the terrain in his three-company area of responsibility and marked an "X" on his map at every place where he had received fire. Using the map, he then plotted routes that would be relatively safe. He operated on the front lines for twenty-five days during one of the worst battles of the war without being wounded.

On March 15, Pierce and a group of corpsmen and stretcher-bearers were caught in a vicious crossfire while attempting to evacuate some wounded men. Two of his party were hit, but Pierce was able to lead the others back to an aid station while firing his Tommy gun to cover the litter bearers as they carried the wounded to safety. He then returned for the two wounded stretcher-bearers, who had remained under fire.

As Pierce worked on one of the wounded, a Japanese sniper fired from close range and hit the wounded man again. Pierce stood up to draw fire away from his patient, explaining later: "If I stood up, he'd be bound to make a motion. . . . I was a good shot." Pierce used the last of his ammunition to kill the sniper, then hoisted the wounded man on his shoulders and carried him two hundred feet back to his line. Pierce returned unarmed for the second wounded man and carried him to safety as Japanese fire swept the earth around him. Pierce said later that a bullet "sounds like a bullwhip . . . [if it is] real close. I heard a few that day."

By marking his map assiduously, Pierce identified an area where a particularly troublesome group of Japanese snipers was hiding. The next day, he led a patrol there. A furious firefight cleared the snipers out, but Pierce was shot in the left shoulder and wounded in the back and legs by shrapnel.

Pierce claimed that in all his actions he was just playing carefully calculated percentages, but he was never, as his Medal of Honor citation states, "completely fearless." He said that if he ever met a man who was completely fearless, "I want that man as far away as he can get because he's going to get me killed. One of the most exhilarating feelings is to know fear and be able to conquer it . . . to be scared to death yet be able to function."

Winning Iwo Jima meant that 2,251 damaged B-29s were able to use its airfields for emergency landings before the war's end. One flier who was saved by the conquest of Iwo Jima was US Army Air Corps Staff Sgt. Henry "Red" Erwin of Alabama. Erwin was flying his seventeenth bombing mission to Japan as a radioman of the B-29 *City of Los Angeles* when his ordeal began.

On April 12, 1945, *City of Los Angeles* was the pathfinder, the lead plane that marked the way for the rest of the bombers on the mission. It was the plane's task to circle about fifty miles from the coast and release phosphorous smoke bombs to guide the bombers that followed. They were dropped down a chute designed for the purpose. Approaching the coast on this mission, Erwin's plane was attacked unexpectedly by Japanese fighters. Just after Erwin dropped one of the bombs down a chute, it shot back up and hit him in the face. The device, spewing chemical flame, bounced at his feet. Temporarily blinded by the chemicals and "literally burning alive," Erwin groped for the white-hot bomb, cradled it between his forearm and his body, and began to make his way toward the pilot's window at the front of the aircraft.

The thirty-foot journey "seemed like an eternity" of unspeakable agony. His flight suit had burned off and his upper body was completely in flames by the time he felt his way past the navigator's table. The cockpit was now filled with noxious smoke and flaming phosphorus and the pilot could not see to control the plane, which was headed into a sickening dive. Erwin screamed for the copilot to open the window, then pitched his awful cargo into the sea. He fell to the floor as others extinguished the flames. Although burned in the face beyond recognition and charred over the upper half of his body, Erwin remained conscious. The pilot pulled the plane out of its dive, and Erwin heard him turn to the navigator and ask, "How far to Iwo Jima? How fast can we get to Iwo?" General Curtis LeMay hurried Erwin's Medal of Honor through channels and it was presented to him at his bedside on April 19, 1945. Erwin thought that they sped the presentation because they assumed he was dying. But Erwin would not give up on life. "I never thought I would die. I said, 'Lord, you showed me how to get that bomb out, you're surely not going to let me die now.'"

Erwin had to fight another battle with the same courage with which he had saved his plane: he endured the agony of forty-one major plastic surgery operations. Later, when he went to work for the US Veterans' Administration, he had to fight down nausea each time he smelled ether when he walked into a VA hospital. He continued to make the visits, however,

Pharmacist's Mate First Class Francis Pierce charted Japanese positions while tending wounded on Iwo Jima.

Army Air Corps Staff Sergeant Henry "Red" Erwin earned the Medal of Honor when he saved the plane he was on by throwing a burning phosphorous bomb out the window with his bare hands. Because he was critically wounded and thought not to be able to survive, he was presented the medal just days after the incident. He lived to be eighty years old.

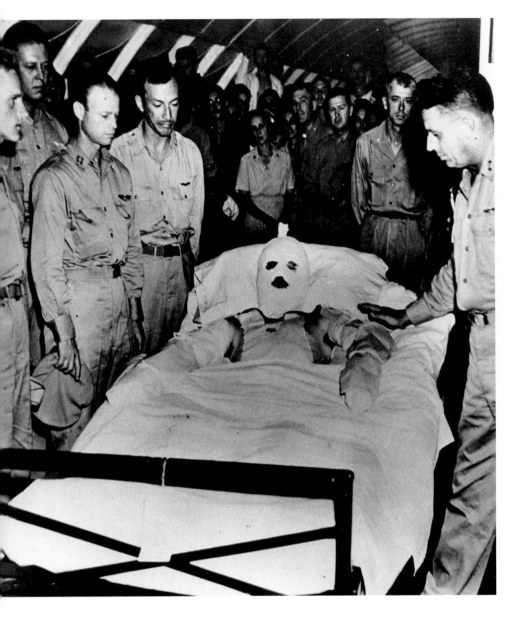

Erwin is given the Medal of Honor by Maj. Gen. Willis Hale (right) as the crewmen he saved look on.

because he felt a kinship with vets in the burn wards: "I knew the agony and pain they went through.... It's indescribable. If I live to be a hundred, I'll never forget it. The pain."

# ENDGAME IN THE PACIFIC
## *The Philippines Restored*

When he left the Philippines in 1942, Gen. Douglas MacArthur had vowed, "I shall return." There was some question whether the Allied stepping-stone to Japan would be Formosa or the Philippines, but when the Philippines was chosen, MacArthur returned in glory. The US Navy won the last decisive sea battle of the war while providing cover for the October 1944 invasion of Leyte Island. The Japanese military empire was in its death throes, but it would take ten more months and cost countless lives before it would finally die.

Curvature of the spine prevented John Sjogren from being accepted for service by his draft board in Rockford, Michigan. Sjogren always wanted to be in the infantry, so he kept trying. Friends from his hometown were fighting in the Pacific with Michigan's 32nd Infantry Division. Sjogren desperately wanted to join them and play "an actual part in winning this war."

He never did fight alongside his friends in the 32nd, but he persevered and was finally accepted for limited service in 1943. First assigned to serve as an M.P. in Camp McCoy, Wisconsin, he continually volunteered for infantry assignments and was finally sent to the 87th Division. While he was with the 87th in Mississippi, a call went out for volunteers for the Pacific-bound 40th Infantry. Sjogren volunteered once more. He was assigned to Company I, 160th Infantry, 40th Infantry Division.

Sjogren was wounded on Luzon as his unit fought to retake Clark Field. By the time he rejoined his company, it was on the island of Negros. The Americans pushed steadily inland until the Japanese halted the advance before a heavily fortified hill commanding a broad plain. The hill presented the Americans on Negros with the same problem Monte Cassino had presented their comrades in Italy: The enemy held the high ground in a nearly unassailable observation post. Two days of artillery and bombing from the air had done little to break down the Japanese resistance. The men of Company I were told that the hill was jeopardizing the success of the entire Negros operation and that it "had to be taken regardless of cost of life."

Sjogren's squad tackled the hill first. On the morning of May 23, 1945, Sjogren walked point for an entire battalion operation, leading an attack against what appeared to be an insurmountable obstacle. Sjogren knew "we were in for a rough day. No one was naive enough to believe there wasn't going to be considerable loss of life."

The squad struggled forward, pulling themselves up the nearly vertical slope by grasping tree trunks split by artillery fire. The Japanese pinned them down with fire from machine guns, mortars, and even from antiaircraft guns pointed downward. Sjogren saw his second-in-command take a machine-gun burst in the head. He realized they would all be dead if they stayed there. He ordered his men to pour fire on the fortifications as he went forward, loaded with grenades. "If they had hit me [it would have been] just like hitting a barrel of gasoline. I had grenades in every pocket."

Using the shattered trees, he made his way slowly, painfully up the slope. Somehow he dodged the automatic-weapons fire and reached the first level of fortifications. The men crawling behind him covered him by firing at the gun slits of the enemy fortifications, allowing Sjogren to crawl close enough to leap forward and drop grenades into the first bunkers. The machine-gun fire from them ceased, and the squad started firing on the next fortification. Again, Sjogren rushed up and dropped a grenade.

The attackers leapfrogged their way up the hill, but Sjogren had several close calls. At one of the bunkers the Japanese dropped grenades back out near Sjogren's feet, but he turned and flattened himself against the wall of the bunker and sustained only minor shrapnel wounds.

Farther on, a Japanese rifleman froze inexplicably after he had drawn a bead on Sjogren, allowing the sergeant to flip a grenade in his direction. Sjogren later burned his hand when he yanked a machine gun out of a bunker by its barrel, but he escaped without serious injury as the squad took the hill.

Years later, he still could not believe he survived: "We were taking fire from all directions. . . . [I]t just doesn't make any sense that we weren't all killed."

Sjogren's 40th Division was in the field on the Philippine island of Panay on August 6 when the B-29 *Enola Gay* dropped an atomic bomb on Hiroshima. Sixty percent of the city was destroyed in a single blast. Seventy-eight thousand people were killed. Three days later another bomb was dropped on Nagasaki. The atomic bombs destroyed the Japanese will to resist. The next day, August 10, they declared their intention to surrender. The formal signing came on September 2, 1945.

The 40th Division had been training for the impending invasion of the Japanese home islands, and Sjogren later discovered that the 40th was slated to go ashore a small island just off Honshu three days before D-Day. On his birthday, August 19, Sjogren was just leaving chapel services when he received a telegram saying that he would receive the Medal of Honor. With that he held a distinction that may be unparalleled in US history. He was a 4-F with a Medal of Honor.

Staff Sergeant John C. Sjogren, the former 4-F who led a battalion-sized attack on the Philippine island of Negros on May 23, 1945.

Nagasaki, Japan, under atomic bomb attack.

# ACES OVER THE PACIFIC

The usual measure of a fighter pilot's skill and daring is the number of enemy aircraft he shoots down. Many World War II fliers dreamed of breaking Capt. Eddie Rickenbacker's World War I record of twenty-six planes. A handful in the Pacific earned the Medal of Honor for their high tallies. Probably many died trying to equal or exceed those totals.

Many pilots, and the press, kept a running total of kills, and this put pressure on strong performers. Gregory "Pappy" Boyington, a Marine ace, recalled being hounded as he approached Rickenbacker's mark: "Everywhere I turned there was a correspondent waiting for me and asking the same old question, and it began to get on my nerves something terrific." Going into a dry spell after number twenty-five, and with only a few days left on his tour of duty, Boyington began to push himself for the record. He flew extra missions and took chances that he otherwise might not have taken. "I knew I couldn't stop," he wrote later. "Whether I died in the attempt made no difference." Boyington bagged number twenty-six on January 3, 1944, but was himself shot down and spent the rest of the war in a Japanese prison camp.

One unit especially known for competition was Marine Fighting Squadron 223, also known as the "Flying Fools." Two of its members, Majs. Robert Galer and John L. Smith, received Medals of Honor for their dogfights with the enemy. A third 223rd pilot, Capt. Marion E. Carl, was shot down, then drifted on a raft for several days until he was picked up by friendly island natives. Upon his return to the 223rd, the first thing Carl wanted to know was Smith's score. He then asked that Smith be grounded for five days, the time he had been lost at sea, to give Carl a chance to catch up. Carl eventually received the Navy Cross but not the Medal of Honor. He never did catch up to Smith's total of nineteen.

The flamboyant Marine pilots overshadowed their counterparts in the Navy. Of all the Navy fighter pilots who flew off carriers, only two were singled out for the Medal of Honor. The first was Lt. Edward H. "Butch" O'Hare, who received his medal for a single action in February 1942. During an attack on the carrier *Lexington* in the southwest Pacific, the twenty-seven-year-old pilot shot down five bombers, thus becoming the Navy's first ace. O'Hare was shot down and killed during a night battle off the Gilbert Islands on November 26, 1943; today the international airport in Chicago bears his name.

The other carrier pilot to receive the medal was Cdr. David McCampbell of the USS *Essex*, who in the course of the war downed thirty-four planes, a Navy record. McCampbell's highest totals were rung up during the "Marianas Turkey Shoot" of June 1944, when he shot down seven Japanese Zero fighters, and the Battle of the Philippines that October, when he scored nine in ninety minutes of fierce action. In all, McCampbell and his air group accounted for over six hundred enemy aircraft shot down and numerous ships damaged or sunk. Twenty-six of McCampbell's men qualified as aces.

The competition among some Army Air Corps pilots was also fierce. When Lt. Col. Neel E. Kearby arrived at the air base at New Guinea in June 1943, one of the first questions he asked his new commander was who had shot down the most planes and what was his total. The answer was Maj. Richard I. Bong, with eleven. Kearby spent the rest of his life trying to catch up to Bong. On March 4, 1944, the day he tied Bong at twenty-five, he was shot down and killed by three enemy fighters that had snuck up on him.

On April 12, 1944, Bong became the first American to shoot down twenty-seven planes. Rickenbacker had promised a case of scotch to the first Army pilot to break his record; he was deluged with offers to pay his end of the bargain. But Bong did not drink, so he gave the liquor to his wing mates and took the two cases of Coca-Cola sent by his commander, Gen. George C. Kenney. In December, Gen. Douglas MacArthur presented Bong with the Medal of Honor as the men of his squadron looked on. Setting aside his prepared speech, MacArthur grasped the young flier by the shoulders and said, "Major Richard Ira Bong, who has ruled the air from New Guinea to the Philippines, I now induct you into the society of the bravest of the brave, the wearers of the Congressional Medal of Honor of the United States."

*Army Air Corps Major Richard I. Bong was the first American to shoot down twenty-seven enemy planes.*

After Bong's fortieth kill, General Kenney began to fear for the safety of his top ace and ordered him grounded. Bong wanted to keep flying and aim for the fifty mark. One incident changed his outlook, though. As he and Kenney watched from the ground, a Japanese pilot bailed out without a parachute and plummeted some fifteen thousand feet, landing only about one hundred feet from the pair.

It was then that Bong, in Kenney's words, "found out that he was not shooting clay pigeons" and fully realized the stakes in the race of the aces. He was violently ill after the incident and became more amenable to being grounded. Dick Bong returned to the United States and was toasted as America's "Ace of Aces." Less than nine months later, on August 6, 1945, he was killed in a test plane crash. His total of forty kills became the record for World War II.

The same day, Lt. Gen. Jonathan Wainwright heard from his Japanese captors the news that the war was over. Wainwright was the man who had taken over the defense of the Philippines in March 1942 when President Roosevelt ordered General MacArthur to Australia. He spent three years and three months in Japanese custody after his defense and surrender of Bataan and Corregidor. Wainwright wrote that on August 19 a Japanese officer in the prison camp began an announcement this way: "By the order of the Emperor the war has now been amicably terminated."

Wainwright was flown to Yokohama to take part in "one of the great days of history"—September 2, 1945, the day of the surrender of Japan aboard the *Missouri*. An emaciated Wainwright was called forward by General MacArthur to accept the first of the fountain pens he used for the signing. For Wainwright the pen was a "wholly unexpected and very great gift." He also received another unexpected gift from President Truman: a promotion to four-star general along with an invitation to visit the White House.

Lieutenant General Jonathan Wainwright (foreground, second from left) salutes Gen. Douglas MacArthur during surrender ceremonies on September 2, 1945. Signing for the defeated Japanese are Foreign Minister Mamoru Shigemitsu (background, with cane) and Gen. Yoshijiro Umezu (beside Shigemitsu).

On September 19, 1945, Wainwright and Truman talked briefly in the president's office. The president then suggested a stroll in the garden because "some photographers want to get a picture of us together." Once in the Rose Garden, Truman led Wainwright to a battery of microphones. Wainwright wrote of the event that when the president stepped up and read a citation that included the words "above and beyond the call of duty," he "suddenly realized when I heard these magic words that this was the citation for the . . . Medal of Honor. . . . Nothing can supplant in my mind that afternoon in the garden of the White House."

On a gray, rainy day in Washington on August 23, 1945, the weather forced officials to move a Medal of Honor ceremony into the East Room. It was extremely crowded, even in that grand room, in large part because of the number of participants in the ceremony, the largest of its kind ever. President Truman presented twenty-eight Medals of Honor that day. Many of the awards had been delayed because the recipients, including Michael Daly, Ralph Neppel, and Charles MacGillivary, had been badly wounded.

The president stood rigidly at attention as the citations were read, then stepped forward to place a medal around the neck of each recipient in turn. Lieutenant Donald Rudolph, who had earned his medal in the Philippines, remembered, "My knees were knocking. [I was] just out of combat in the Pacific and all of a sudden [I was] in Washington." The president told Rudolph what he said to most of the men he honored: "I would rather have this medal than be president of the United States." In a short speech, Truman declared the men to be a "great cross-section of the United States. . . . These men love peace, but are able to adjust themselves to the necessity of war." As such, they were the living representatives of the kind of fighting man America had produced: the civilian soldier who defeated the warriors of the Axis. These men lived, but many others who earned the Medal of Honor in World War II died in action. In Ernie Pyle's words, "They died and thereby the rest of us can go on and on . . . [T]here is nothing we can do for the ones beneath the wooden crosses, except perhaps to pause and murmur, 'Thanks, pal.'"

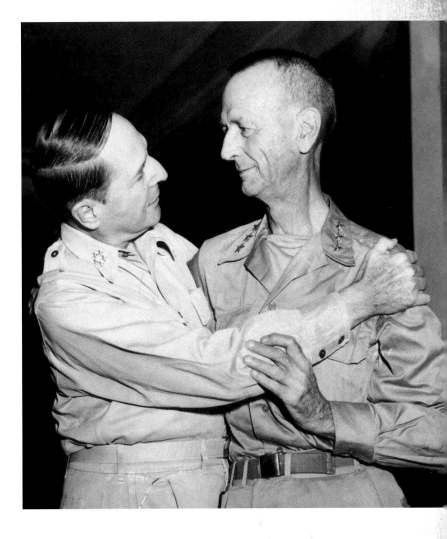

General MacArthur welcomes an emaciated Gen. Wainwright to freedom at Yokohama, August 31, 1945. Wainwright had spent over three years as a POW after his capture on Corregidor in 1942.

# CHAPTER SIX

# The Cold War

### Korea, 1950-1953
### Vietnam, 1954-1975

# Korea, Vietnam, and the Fight Against Communism

*Previous pages*
US Marines trudge along a snowy mountain pass during the bitter evacuation from the Chosin Reservoir to Hungnam in North Korea, November– December 1950.

THE GLOBAL CATACLYSM OF World War II gave way to a new struggle for supremacy between two great political blocs. Western capitalist countries led by the United States opposed Communist states led by the Soviet Union in a forty-five-year competition of ideologies, economic systems, and political and military power around the world.

The presence of nuclear weapons on both sides threatened mutual annihilation in direct warfare, and so as Europe became an uneasy front line between the blocs, military action took place elsewhere. Small countries in Asia, Latin America, and Africa were the site of proxy wars contending to extend their influence and instill their system of government. A "cold war" that was neither peace nor direct combat marked the stalemate among world powers.

The victory of Mao Zedong's Communist forces in China in 1948 worried those American leaders who believed that country after country would "fall like dominos" before the advancement of the Communist system. They determined to stop the spread of Soviet-style communism, nowhere more forcefully—or painfully—than in the small Asian countries of Korea and Vietnam. Despite its name, and ultimately its quiet resolution, the Cold War included some infernally hot conflicts. In places many Americans had barely heard of, servicemen were called on to fight, suffer, and sacrifice for their country.

Refugees and soldiers, including Americans and South Koreans, fill the railway station and plaza in Taejon, South Korea, before its fall to North Korean forces. Troops were being rushed north and refugees were fleeing south.

# The Korean War
## A "Police Action" in Name, a War in Reality

**J**UST BEFORE DAWN ON June 25, 1950, the small Asian peninsula of Korea erupted into war as 90,000 soldiers of the Communist *Inmin'gun*, the North Korean People's Army, swept across the border into South Korea (ROK). They met little organized resistance. The South Korean army, already badly outmanned, was caught by surprise; only one-sixth of its forces were on the border that morning. The rest raced north when they got word, but their defense was more suicide than battle as they confronted the heavily equipped the Inmin'gun's seven divisions one regiment at a time. Three days later, when the capital, Seoul, was overrun, the South Korean army had lost three-quarters of its original men.

For centuries, Korea had been a single nation. Only after the defeat of Japan in World War II and the occupation of Asia by the Soviet Union and the United States was it split into a Communist north and a Western-aligned south. Each side of the peninsula vowed it would someday reunite the country under its own form of government. Now, in June 1950, North Korean Premier Kim Il-Sung announced confidently that all of Korea would be in Communist hands by the end of the summer.

In Washington, President Harry S. Truman faced what he would call "my most important decision as President." Truman wrote, "If this was allowed to go unchallenged, it would mean a third World War, just as similar incidents had brought on the second World War."

Within a day of the invasion, Truman ordered Gen. Douglas MacArthur, commander of US forces in the western Pacific, to ship South Korea whatever material aid it needed. To emphasize his commitment, he dispatched the 7th Fleet to the area to join MacArthur's command. Washington, as well as MacArthur's Far East Command (FECOM) in Tokyo, was still confident that the North Koreans could be pushed back. "I can handle it with one arm tied behind my back," the general told a State Department delegation. But it was not long before the Inmin'gun's lightning march convinced the world otherwise. On June 26 (June 27 in Korea), Truman dispatched the US Navy and Air Force to the ROK's aid. The next night, one hour after the fall of Seoul, the United Nations Security Council passed a resolution, drafted by the US State Department and approved in advance by the president, calling on all members to help South Korea repel the attack. (The Soviet delegate boycotted the Security Council over a separate dispute, so he did not exercise his veto.)

On June 30, Truman granted MacArthur's request for US ground forces to stop the Communist tide. The first men were rushed in from occupation duty in Japan and were followed in swift succession by elements of the small post–World War II regular army, the reserves, and, in late autumn, the first draftees. Before the war was over, 5.5 million Americans would serve in Korea. More than one hundred thousand would return as casualties; thirty-five thousand would never return.

> Before the war was over, 5.5 million Americans would serve in Korea. More than one hundred thousand would return as casualties; thirty-five thousand would never return.

# ARCHIE VAN WINKLE

Marine Staff Sergeant Archie Van Winkle had already served almost three years of active duty as a gunner and mechanic in World War II. On November 2, 1950, serving as an infantry platoon sergeant near Sudong, Korea, he led a charge through heavy enemy fire. A bullet shattered his arm, and he was seriously wounded in the chest by a grenade. Bravely, he refused to be evacuated, and he continued to shout orders and encouragement to his men while lying on the ground, weak from loss of blood. His leadership helped his outnumbered platoon to repel the enemy attack. He earned a Medal of Honor for his actions.

Van Winkle spent his career as an officer in the Marine Corps and went on to serve as a commanding officer in the Vietnam War. In addition to the Medal of Honor, he earned the Distinguished Flying Cross, the Bronze Star, and the Purple Heart during his career.

*President Harry Truman presents the Medal of Honor to Staff Sergeant Van Winkle at the White House in 1952.*

Ultimately, twenty-one nations contributed troops or other direct assistance to the Republic of Korea. The United States took command under General MacArthur, providing over 90 percent of the foreign commitment, material and human.

At first, the Americans found themselves as helpless as their ROK allies before the North Korean tide. From their opening engagement a few miles south of Seoul, the US forces fell back steadily until they clung to a county-sized perimeter around the southeastern port city of Pusan. But Pusan was not Dunkirk. Along the 50-by-100-mile front, the Americans were able to fight the kind of war they had planned and trained for since World War I. With a clear and continuous battle line, connected by good roads, they could bring their superior fire-power and mechanization to bear to halt the Inmin'gun's "human wave" assaults. All August, the stretched and weakened North Koreans slammed futilely against the perimeter in a losing battle with time, while behind its lines the UN prepared a counterblow.

The landing of the Marines on September 15 at Inchon, 18 miles west of Seoul, proved to be one of the brilliant moments in American military history. MacArthur boldly struck the North Koreans hundreds of miles to their rear, trapping them inside South Korea, then crushed them in a giant pincer between the UN X Corps (Marines and infantry) moving south from Inchon and the rest of the Eighth Army heading north from Pusan. The Navy and Joint Chiefs of Staff had predicted failure, but the move was an almost unqualified success. On September 29, in front of hundreds of thousands of wildly cheering Koreans, MacArthur formally announced the restoration to the ROK of the seat of its government.

There the fighting might have ended. The aggressors had been turned back to their own borders. The UN had proved its mettle, and the status quo was preserved. But some twenty-five thousand North Korean soldiers had managed to escape north. In the exhilaration of near-triumph, the nature of the action changed dramatically. "Your military objective is the destruction of the North Korean Armed Forces," Truman cabled MacArthur. On October 1, the first South Korean troops crossed the 38th parallel into North Korea. The GIs were close behind. The UN General Assembly approved Truman's order at the end of the week.

As the UN force swept north, meeting little resistance, civilians and soldiers alike talked confidently of reuniting Korea by Christmas. The Eighth Army command ignored increasingly audible rumblings from China that it would tolerate no American presence on its border with Korea. Even reports of a Chinese buildup along the Yalu River were discounted by MacArthur. In case the Chinese did move against his forces, the general confidently told the president in mid-October, "There would be the greatest slaughter." MacArthur's prediction materialized, though in a way he had not envisioned.

The day after Thanksgiving, 180,000 Chinese troops attacked the Eighth Army on the northwest coast of Korea at the Chongchon River, wiping it out. Three days later, X Corps received similar treatment. At the Chosin Reservoir in northeastern Korea, 120,000 Chinese hit the Marines. There followed the longest retreat in US history. By early January, the Chinese had recaptured all of Korea to the 37th parallel, including Seoul. Then, tired and short on supplies, they stopped.

The scene was set for stalemate. On February 5, 1951, the UN forces launched a second counteroffensive and again pushed the Communists back. On March 18, Seoul changed hands for the fourth time in less than a year. By now, however, the leaders of the Western

There the fighting might have ended. The aggressors had been turned back to their own borders. The UN had proved its mettle, and the status quo was preserved.

President Truman decorates General MacArthur with his fifth Distinguished Service Medal on Wake Island, October 1950. Six months later he fired the general for insubordination.

world had lost their enthusiasm for reunification. The UN General Assembly, reversing its October position, called for a peaceful settlement between North and South Korea. On March 20, Truman notified MacArthur that he was preparing to announce his willingness to negotiate peace and that UN forces were not to advance beyond the 38th parallel. MacArthur replied by openly requesting freedom to strike at China. Each man sought to end the war, but their prescriptions offered no room for compromise. Moreover, the public argument had US allies, as well as its own citizens, growing jittery. Truman ordered MacArthur to be silent. MacArthur defied him by sending a letter, read on the floor of Congress, charging that "There is no substitute for victory." Faced with this repeated insubordination, on April 11 the president relieved MacArthur of his command. Though he arguably had little choice, Truman's action sapped much of the remaining public support for the already unpopular war.

During the war, Truman sought neither a declaration of war nor even the informal approval of Congress, avoiding that arm of government by refusing to classify the conflict as a war. "Police action" was the term the White House preferred. Nevertheless, it was a war—and one for which Americans were called upon to sacrifice their lives and dollars without really understanding why. The United States had not been attacked, and the principle of maintaining a balance of power between communism and Western democracy was difficult to defend in the face of military stalemate. The result was one of the least popular wars in American history. Six months after Truman committed American troops, 66 percent of Americans polled called for withdrawal from Korea. The president's own approval rating dropped to 23 percent, the lowest of his presidency. After Inchon, Americans had thought the war would be over in a few weeks. Instead, it lasted another two years, to be concluded only by an armistice.

The Korean conflict was fought more like wars of the nineteenth and early twentieth centuries than the modern technical war the Americans had trained for. In the first months, when UN forces faced a highly mobile, non-mechanized enemy in isolated actions over mountainous terrain, it resembled the Indian Wars of the American West. Later, when the war became a stalemate, it turned into the grinding trench warfare of World War I. Weapons also harkened to the past. Although air power and modern artillery played an important role, the brunt of the fighting was born by the rifle-wielding foot soldier. In Korea, a shrunken peacetime military found itself pitted against a foe at the peak of its power and motivation. That fact alone would take a shocking toll in American lives in the first weeks of war. The longstanding belief that the United States could not lose a war was to face in Korea its severest test.

# FIGHTING FOR TIME

*General William F. Dean*

The first commander of US ground forces in Korea was Maj. Gen. William F. Dean. For twenty days, Dean and his 24th Infantry Division fought a holding action against the North Koreans while other United Nations forces created a defensive perimeter around the southern port of Pusan. His commander, Lt. Gen. Walton Walker, credited Dean with saving South Korea. Dean countered: "Very few of the things I did could not have been done by any competent sergeant—and such a sergeant would have done some of them better."

At midnight of July 1, 1950, Maj. Gen. William F. Dean, the commander of the Japan-based 24th Infantry Division, received orders from Lt. Gen. Walton Walker, Eighth Army commander. Dean's division was to deploy across the Korea and Tsuchima Straits, and act as a delaying force against the advancing North Korean army while the United Nations organized its counterattack. The urgency of the situation, combined with mobilization and transportation problems, meant that the commitment would be made piecemeal. Two reinforced rifle companies, under Lt. Col. Charles B. Smith, would fly at once to Pusan and the rest of the division, spread out across southern Japan, would follow as best it could.

The first units of US Army ground forces, commanded by Gen. William Dean, arrive at a train station in South Korea.

Soldiers dig in and fire at Communist-led North Korean positions in September 1950.

Dean read the orders grimly. He knew the usual fate of regiments committed in bits and pieces against an advancing army. Dean was not optimistic about how long he could delay the North Koreans. But he was a tough commander and intended to give them a fight.

Piercing through the dense fog, an Air Force C-45 carried General Dean and his staff into Taejon, a key air and rail center in the middle of South Korea sixty miles south of the advancing North Korean army. Chaos confronted the Americans there. Tens of thousands of fleeing Koreans—civilians, national police, even soldiers—jammed the rain-drenched streets in a continuous southward wave. The scene at the US advance command post was only slightly less disordered. Communication lines were spotty or nonexistent.

On July 4, Dean ordered Task Force Smith to hold at Osan, between Seoul and Taejon. He sent the 34th Infantry to back it up at the strategically crucial Pyongtaek-Ansong Line, a narrow neck between the Yellow Sea and the rugged central mountain range. If they could stop the enemy anywhere north of Pusan, this seemed the likeliest spot.

With so small a force, Dean knew it was a long shot, but if the Americans could put some life back into the ROK resistance, it just might work.

Early the next day, thirty-three Russian-built T34 tanks, followed by two North Korean regiments, bore down on the 540 officers and men of Task Force Smith. The cool assuredness of the GIs—who had marched into this "police action" believing that the very sight of US soldiers would send the North Koreans scurrying back behind the border—melted away. In its place grew panic, as Americans fell to the fire of enemy rifles, grenades, and mortar shells. The six available rounds of outdated US artillery were ineffectual against the overwhelming tank force. Air support could not find its way through the low clouds. Communications broke down. There was not even enough small-arms ammunition.

Realizing there was no hope of hanging on, Colonel Smith called retreat. Within minutes it became an uncontrollable rout. In the driving rain, men poured down the hills in ones and twos. They abandoned their headgear, weapons, the dead, even the dozens of wounded who could not walk.

The rout did not stop at Osan. On July 6, after learning the fate of the task force, the commander of the 34th pulled his regiment back fifteen miles without engaging the enemy. Dean was furious at this news. He jumped into his jeep, raced to the 34th's command post, ordered the regiment back to Pyongtaek, and relieved the commander. But he knew this would not be enough.

Two days later, when General Walker flew into Taejon to find out how Dean's delaying action was faring, the two generals decided to drive up to the front to have a look. What they saw sickened them. The 34th had been told to hold at Chonan, halfway between Osan and Taejon, but the officers were having a difficult time keeping their troops on the line. Twice the new commander, Col. Robert Martin, had to go to the front to settle things down and induce the men to fight. The second time he was cut down while leading a bazooka assault against a group of tanks. Martin's death completely broke the regiment's spirit. As Dean and

Walker watched from a nearby hill, the Americans once more fled the front line.

Now the job would be doubly hard, for there was no good defensive line before Taejon. On July 16, two North Korean divisions, supported by some fifty tanks, broke through the main US line at the Kum River. Taejon was now less than fifteen miles away, defended only by the US 34th.

On July 19, the enemy reached the US line, thinly spread out three miles north of Taejon. The defenders were hopelessly outmatched. Against the Americans' assortment of light, outdated weaponry, the North Koreans delivered as heavy an artillery barrage as Dean had ever seen. It took extraordinary effort by the officers to keep the men from bolting, but they held. When the enemy threatened to break through, the division commander stood at the front with his men, directing tank fire. At day's end, the United States still held its position.

A .50-caliber machine-gun squad on Company E, 2nd Battalion, 7th Regiment, 1st Cavalry Division, fires on North Korean patrols along the north bank of the Naktong River, Korea, in August 1950.

When gunfire dwindled to sporadic sniping, Dean returned to his command post for a few hours' rest. Before dawn, though, the din of a major assault wrenched him awake. The Inmin'gun had broken through the line. At 6:30 a.m., the general heard that North Korean tanks had entered Taejon. For now, there were no decisions to make. The 34th's new commander was leading a fighting withdrawal. When the regiment reached Taejon, Dean would lead the retreat himself. But he had grown tired of sitting and waiting—especially when the enemy was at the gate. So, coining a term that would become famous among the men of the Eighth Army, he went "tank hunting."

Dean, his aide Lt. Arthur Clarke, and his Korean interpreter headed out into the streets of Taejon. Spotting a stalled T34 in the center of a once-busy intersection, the general commandeered the first artillery truck he could find and guided it into position. But the nervous gunner missed the tank with all five of his rounds. Cursing, Dean resumed the hunt. Not too far from two more idle tanks he found a soldier carrying a new-model 3.5-inch bazooka and a single round of ammunition. Dean grabbed the man, and the small party crept toward their prey. Suddenly, machine-gun fire from one of the turrets scattered over their heads. The bazooka party ran for cover. Again Dean led them on the attack. Maneuvering to within twenty feet of the street, he ordered the gunner to fire when they drew within range of the tank. But the bazooka man was too jittery and wasted his one round while the tanks were still well over three hundred feet away. Dean had to stand there helplessly as the giants trundled past. Overcome with rage, he emptied his pistol into the last one.

Private First Class Joseph R. Ouellette, who braved enemy fire to retrieve ammunition.

Now he was really angry. After calling in air strikes against the enemy tank force, Dean continued his hunt. This time he got lucky. A lone North Korean tank passed right by the regimental command post. Rounding up another bazooka man and an ammunition carrier, Dean's little army set out in hot pursuit, dodging and returning sniper fire all the way. They found the T34 parked on a bombed-out business street lined with crumbling two-story buildings. The first time they approached it, they were knocked back by a small-arms barrage. They tried another direction but again received fire. The third time Dean decided to stage the attack from inside one of the buildings, where they could strike at the tank from above.

Silently the Americans entered the rear of the building closest to the tank and climbed to the second floor. Dean and the gunner crawled to the window. The tank stood less than twelve feet away. Without speaking, Dean pointed where to aim. The bazooka fired—and this time scored a direct hit. The general had his tank.

It was now nearing dusk. At least fifteen enemy tanks lay dead in the streets. Dean's division had held back the North Koreans for the time Walker needed to deploy fresh troops. Dean gave the order to withdraw.

Shortly after 6:00 p.m., the convoy of Americans began to move out. Enemy fire grew heavier from all sides. It knocked out several of the lead trucks, blocking the division's planned exit route. Then North Korean rifle and machine-gun snipers lined up along the approach, blazing away at the stalled vehicles. Dean urgently looked for an alternate route, but word came that a large force of North Korean infantry was rapidly advancing on the city center. The convoy had no choice but to move.

The rest of the evening was a story of increasingly worse fortune for General Dean: ambushes, roadblocks, broken-down vehicles, lost weapons. By nightfall he found himself on foot, leading seventeen stray soldiers on a cross-country trek through North Korean lines. After guiding them across a river, up a ridge, and around a machine-gun nest, Dean relinquished the lead to help carry a badly wounded man. In the darkness and under order of silence, few noticed the general falling farther and farther back. Fewer still saw when he left to get the now-delirious man some water from a nearby stream. Nobody knew when he plunged down an embankment, cracked his head, and passed out.

Dean spent the next thirty-six days in the Korean hills trying to reach US lines. For most of this time he had no food and very little water. The fall had broken his shoulder and given him a concussion and severe stomach injuries. During his trek he would lose 80 pounds, dropping to an emaciated 130 on his six-foot frame. Still, Dean eluded capture a half-dozen times and managed to travel thirty-five miles south before being sold out by some Korean civilians on August 25. His ordeal was only beginning; for the next three years he would hold the bitter rank of POW.

A .30-caliber light machine-gun crew of the 5th RCT, 1st Cavalry Division, fires on Communist-led North Koreans as they push toward Taejon, Korea, in September 1950.

Dean's treatment at the hands of his captors was atypical. They kept him in total seclusion; he never saw another American nor even a Chinese. The first weeks were brutal. His guards stripped him and forced him to sit on the floor of an unheated room in freezing weather. His captors interrogated and propagandized him for days, allowing him no sleep and little food. Even though his wounds abscessed, he was refused treatment. Finally, unable to break his spirit, his chief interrogator threatened torture.

Dean was already concerned that his captivity gave the Communists a propaganda tool. Now he grew fearful that in his weakened condition he might reveal something under torture. He determined that his only way out was to kill himself, and he almost succeeded. Only a faulty bolt in the gun he stole from a sleeping guard prevented his death.

After that, his treatment improved. The North Koreans

did not want to lose so valuable a prize. They still kept him isolated and, for most of his captivity, refused even to let him stand up. But they made sure he was cared for adequately to keep him alive. The months stretched to three years. Finally, on September 4, 1953, a gaunt Dean ended his tour of duty in Korea at Freedom Village. He came home to receive the Medal of Honor for his intrepid stand at Taejon.

# VALOR IN A MOUNTAIN PASS

*The Chosin Reservoir*

While General Dean's 24th Division retreated down the Korean peninsula, thousands of American troops poured into a perimeter surrounding the port of Pusan. By August 31, 1950, UN troops outnumbered North Korean forces by almost two to one. The North Koreans, however, believed they could win the war if they struck the Pusan perimeter with all their remaining strength. Heroic American stands at the Naktong River and along the rest of the Pusan perimeter proved them wrong. The perimeter held and UN forces poured into southeast Korea.

On September 15, 1950, Gen. Douglas MacArthur's X Corps struck the enemy rear at Inchon Harbor, near the South Korean capital of Seoul. The brilliant maneuver shattered the North Korean offensive. Soon Seoul was liberated and X Corps and the Eighth Army headed north to end Communist rule over all Korea. The Eighth drove up the west coast to the Manchurian border, and X Corps approached from the east. Despite thinning supply lines and increasing evidence of impending Chinese intervention, MacArthur believed the war would soon be over. His error presaged one of the greatest defeats in US military history, when hundreds of thousands of Chinese "volunteers" crossed the border to confront MacArthur's armies. In the west, the Eighth Army was nearly destroyed. Only the tremendous fighting spirit and personal sacrifice of individual Marines saved X Corps from a similar fate in the east. As winter closed in, Marines and infantry fought a desperate retreat from the mountain-bound Chosin Reservoir to the Sea of Japan.

The UN advance to the north ended the day after Thanksgiving, when three hundred thousand Chinese Communist troops poured south from the Yalu River. Half of them defeated the Eighth Army forces on the western side of Korea. Three days later, at the Chosin Reservoir in eastern Korea, the rest of the Chinese hit the Marines and infantrymen of X Corps. They too retreated but fought all the way out, bringing their dead, wounded, and all their equipment with them.

The 5th and 7th Marine Regiments were caught halfway up the finger-shaped reservoir at Yudam-ni. The only route through the mountain range was along the forbidding Toktong Pass to Hagaru-ri and from there to Koto-ri and finally the port of Hungnam. Eight thousand Marines battled their way out of Yudam-ni. It was bitter cold on the mile-high pass, but the climate was less a concern than the terrain: Mountains closed in on either side of the dirt road, turning the Marines' escape route into a shooting gallery for the Chinese.

On November 28, Capt. William Barber, Company F, 2nd Battalion, 7th Marines, received orders to hold the Toktong Pass until the American Marines could escape from Yudam-ni. He positioned his 240-man company on a hill overlooking the highway and established a

General William Dean at a press conference at the Tokyo Army Hospital after his release at Panmunjom on September 4, 1953.

Christmastime in Korea. A soldier eats frozen beans one at a time on the road from Chosin. When photographer David Douglas Duncan asked this young man what he wanted for Christmas, he replied, "Give me tomorrow."

small but strong perimeter. It took the Marines hours of hacking away at the frozen earth to dig even shallow foxholes, but Barber made his men keep digging. His precautions were justified. That night a regiment of Chinese attacked. The company held, but took twenty-two casualties.

The next day Barber radioed regiment headquarters, telling of the attack and the approximate size of the opposing force. His colonel advised him to withdraw. But Barber contested the order. There were two reasons for his decision: his own wounded and the thousands of Marines still trapped in Yudam-ni.

The perimeter held through five days of grinding day-and-night fighting. When Company F marched off the hill and joined the tail end of the Marine retreat line, only seventy-two of its men were still on their feet. One of the casualties was Captain Barber himself, a bullet lodged in his groin. But they had left behind them over one thousand dead Chinese. More important, they had kept the pass clear for their comrades.

While the 5th and 7th Marines battled down the narrow mountain passage to Hagaru-ri, Captain Carl Sitter's Company G, 3rd Battalion, 1st Marines, fought its way up from Koto-ri. Sitter was guarding X Corps' command post on November 28 when he heard that the Chinese had captured the only road out of Hagaru-ri. The next morning, he was ordered to add his company to a task force under the command of Lt. Col. Douglas Drysdale of the British Royal Marine Corps. They were to re-open the highway and deliver needed supplies to Hagaru-ri.

At 9:00 a.m., Sitter's Marines, Drysdale's 41st Commandos, a US Army company, eight tanks, and a hundred supply trucks began the eleven-mile clearing operation. They faced fierce opposition. Every few hundred feet, enemy machine-gun and small-arms fire forced the column to halt until the UN troops could clear the nearby hill. At sunset, the convoy got started again through the hail of enemy bullets and mortar shells. One shell landed in the path of Sitter's jeep, sparing him but incinerating a box of cigars he had just received from home. That made him angrier than the loss of the jeep. When he saw his first sergeant drive by in a truck, Sitter jumped onto the running board and continued.

Again the lurching convoy came to a dead stop. Sitter ran forward to see what the trouble was and found that the front of the column had been halted by machine-gun fire. Drysdale was wounded. He told Sitter to take charge of getting the supplies to Hagaru-ri. The captain ordered the task force into a circle facing out ("like in the Western movies," he later said). When the Chinese charged, they fought them off in a pitched battle, then headed down the road once more.

Astonished Marines of the 5th and 7th Regiments, who hurled back a surprise onslaught by three Chinese Communist divisions, hear that they are to withdraw.

Marines escort the bodies of their fallen comrades to Hungnam. Determination to evacuate their dead characterized the spirit of the Marines during the march.

No sooner had the men begun to breathe easier, however, than dozens of Chinese emerged near the road and opened fire.

The task force groped its way through the black night, unsure of how far it had come and how many more miles it had yet to go to reach Hagaru-ri. Finally, the lead truck turned a corner and caught the welcome sight of lights a few miles ahead. "We've made it home," thought Sitter. No sooner had the men begun to breathe easier, however, than dozens of Chinese emerged near the road and opened fire. Five more trucks were lost before the UN force reached the perimeter. But the supplies that they brought—ammunition, blankets, food, and medicine—saved the lives of hundreds of hurt and exhausted Marines.

The men of Sitter's company were given only one night to rest on rock-hard ground in a snow-covered field, then went back to fighting. The new objective was East Hill, a point dominating the withdrawal route from Hagaru-ri. The Chinese had wrested the hill from a motley assortment of Army headquarters personnel the night of November 28. A few hours later, however, another hodgepodge of US servicemen had retaken part of it and were now barely holding on. Their commander was Maj. Reginald Myers, executive officer of the 3rd Battalion, 1st Marines.

When the Army force lost East Hill, the commander of the 3rd Battalion, Lt. Col. Thomas Ridge, had ordered Myers to grab all the men he could find to seize and hold the hill. This was not the usual line of work for a staff officer, nor for the twenty-five or so Marines he gathered up. They were, Myers said, "the cooks and the candlestick makers and the bakers and what-not," adding, "I'm sure that everybody was just absolutely frightened to death about the whole thing." Nevertheless, Myers put rifles in their hands and marched them to East Hill, adding anyone else he found along the way who seemed to have nothing better to do. By the time he reached the hill, he had between fifty and seventy-five Marines. To that force, he added approximately two hundred stray Army personnel (more cooks and bakers) whom he found milling around the base of the hill after being thrown off by the Chinese.

Myers asked if there were any non-coms or officers present. He designated those who raised their hands to lead ad hoc squads. Myers knew his greatest problem was morale. "I didn't know what to say to the men who had just been decisively beaten off the hill. I didn't know them—we were like foreigners. I was their commanding officer and they didn't even know my name." Swallowing hard, he ordered them to advance.

As the men climbed, they were shot at by hundreds of Chinese above them. Said Myers, "As you went up the hill, the bitter cold made every bullet sound like it was going through your eardrums. It would just be a whack, you know, and it made you feel like they were shooting at you instead of somebody else. So as we went up the hill, all of a sudden, everybody fell on their faces and we couldn't get them up. They just lay on the snow and didn't want to move." Only by running up and down the line, talking to the men, threatening them, kicking them, grabbing them by the collars, and hoisting them to their feet, could Myers keep the advance going.

Fortunately, the Chinese pulled back, thinking they were facing a powerful force. That allowed Myers's men to take the crest of the hill. They held it all the next day, despite heavy fire from a higher position. They also suffered heavy losses, although many of those lost in the fight were not casualties. "For every man that you had wounded, two or three people would jump up and grab that guy and take him down to the bottom of the hill and you wouldn't see those two or three people again." Myers called for a Marine guard to be posted at the bottom of the hill to send the strays back up, and even then, most stopped before they got halfway up the hill. By 6:00 p.m., Myers had only seventy-five troops. Ridge ordered him to pull back

The First Marine Regiment at Koto-ri, on the supply and withdrawal route of the beleaguered 5th and 7th Marines in the Chosin Reservoir area, had to repel repeated attacks by Chinese Communists. By counterattack and with the aid of close air support, which blasted the enemy with bullets, bombs, and napalm, the 1st Marines kept the lifeline open and operating.

to a reverse-slope defense. From there, those "ragtags" held off the enemy for another night, until Sitter's reinforced rifle company took over the position.

Sitter and his men, though exhausted from their trek from Koto-ri, attacked the hill with spirit and held it for four days. In hand-to-hand combat, the men of Sitter's staff were all so badly wounded that they had to be evacuated, but Sitter, himself wounded, stayed on his feet.

On December 3, Captain Sitter and ninety-six men walked off East Hill. The next day, the Marines from Yudam-ni reached Hagaru-ri. Without the efforts of Captain Barber, many of them would not have made it; without those of Sitter and Myers, many would have gone no farther. For their role in the Chosin escape, the three Marine officers would receive Medals of Honor. But on December 4, 1950, none was thinking of his own heroism. Their thoughts were on the courage of their comrades. Myers recalled:

> In the distance you could see the men wearily placing one foot in front of the other as they staggered down the road. . . . As they started to move within the perimeter, their heads came up, they straightened their shoulders, the wounded sat up in their stretchers. Uncontrolled cheers from the Hagaru-ri defenders spontaneously arose. . . . Tears uncontrolled were running down my cheek. I blew my nose and wiped my face. I wasn't alone.

# STALEMATE

## *Heartbreak Ridge*

By January 1951, the Communist counteroffensive in Korea had driven UN forces out of the North and deep into southern territory. MacArthur's forces fought their way back to the 38th parallel over the spring months, and in July, peace talks began. The conflict changed from a war of movement to a stagnant trench war. "Each day was like the last," a 2nd Division

Heartbreak Ridge lies shattered after a fierce battle. UN assaults on such ridges were common, even though the actual strategic significance of many of them was slight.

lieutenant wrote. "Fight, suffer, meet or escape death, sweat out the nights only to move out each new day to climb and battle up the endless hills."

It was the second year of the war, the fourth month of truce talks. No longer was there talk of victory. There were no more full-scale offensives. But the fighting—and dying—continued. General James Van Fleet, commander of the Eighth Army, called them "tidying up" operations, limited attacks designed to keep the UN line, and the men on it, taut. The first such limited engagement was the three-week battle for Bloody Ridge in central Korea. Even though UN forces pre-vailed, the fight produced over 2,700 UN casualties, most to the already brutalized 2nd Division. Only eight days after taking Bloody Ridge, the 2nd Division marched northward to more battle. Again the objective was an uninhabitable rock- and scrub-covered hill mass. It did not have a name, except for a series of Army numbers (Hills 894, 931, 605), until the men came to know it by a more meaningful label: Heartbreak Ridge.

Van Fleet planned the attack on Heartbreak Ridge to straighten the UN line and to keep the Inmin'gun off balance after its defeat at Bloody Ridge. Neither Eighth Army nor 2nd Division command thought it would be a very difficult mission. Heartbreak was occupied by a sizable force of North Koreans, but most were the soldiers whom the 2nd Division and attached units had just defeated. So confident was the division commander that he decided to commit only one regiment to the main assault force. What he did not know was that beneath the scrub trees covering the ridge, the enemy had built an elaborate system of connected bun-kers, impervious to air strikes and most artillery fire. Within those fortified chambers they had rebuilt and reinforced their units. The 2nd Division was about to face the North Korean army's main line of resistance.

On September 13, the 23rd Infantry Regiment and its attached French battalion approached the steep slope of Heartbreak's central peak. Before they had scaled even the foothills, they were knocked back by a flurry of mortar, machine-gun, and rifle fire from con-cealed bunkers above. The next day, they tried again. The hostile terrain prevented tanks from assisting the GIs, so the men moved up the ridge on their own. Slowly, they fought through the avalanche of bullets, taking out enemy bunkers one by one. By nightfall, they gained the crest. But the cruel, inching struggle up the hill had worn out the men. When the North Koreans attacked a few hours later, the Americans fell back. The next day they tried—and failed—again. And the next day.

By September 16, Heartbreak Ridge was a pockmarked mass of loose rocks and metal. Where once there grew thick underbrush, barely a bush survived. The North Koreans remained in control. All the United Nations could claim for its efforts was a piece of ridge line connecting two main hills. There, in a trio of perimeters, the 1st Battalion, 23rd Infantry, settled in for the night.

Private First Class Herbert K. Pililaau, Charlie Company, 1st Battalion, 23rd Infantry, was not the type of man people would have taken for a hero. Except for his tremendous strength and stamina—he was the top physically of his company in basic training—and his six-foot height, the native Hawaiian did not stand out in a crowd. He spoke little, did not smoke or drink, rarely socialized with the other men, and spent most of his spare time reading the Bible or writing his family. It surprised his platoon mates when he volunteered for the high-risk job of BAR gunner shortly after joining the 23rd in Korea that summer. Pililaau's explanation was characteristic: Someone had to do it. On September 17, 1951, Pililaau gave his comrades in Company C an even bigger surprise.

At 3:00 a.m., a battalion of North Koreans struck the company from a hill adjoining its ridge position. Charlie Company fought hard to hold on, but lack of ammunition finally forced its withdrawal to the back of the hill. Joined now by Company A, the men of Charlie prepared a countercharge, this time fixing bayonets and preparing for hand-to-hand fighting. Unfortunately, the enemy had plenty of ammunition.

The first American charge broke under the weight of heavy North Korean fire. The commander reorganized his men and sent them up again. Private Pililaau took the lead. In the dim light of early morning, the Americans forced the North Koreans back, regaining their perimeter and reaching the crest. But they had little time to rest. At midday, the enemy battalion burst up the hill, and the men of Company C once more found themselves fighting for their lives. The American resistance still suffered from lack of ammunition. Finally, the commander called retreat. Pililaau, behind his BAR, said he would cover. As his unit scrambled down the hill, Pililaau remained on top, firing his automatic at the onrushing enemy until he had exhausted his ammunition. Then he hit them with grenades. When those, too, were used up, he pulled out his trench knife and fought on.

From about six hundred feet down the ridge, Pililaau's company watched in awe. His squad leader recalls the last long minutes of the one-man battle:

> There was Herb standing up, fighting a lot of the enemy. It was hand-to-hand and just Herb against all of them. We all wanted to go back up to help him, but the captain said 'No.' We tried to help Herb by firing a few shots, but they didn't do any good. All of a sudden, they shot him and when he went down they bayoneted him. That was it.

Pililaau's courageous example put heart back into his tired unit. A half-hour after he fell, the Americans retook the ridge. There they found the body of the quiet private. Around it lay more than forty dead North Korean soldiers. For his valiant stand, Pililaau was awarded a posthumous Medal of Honor.

The battle for Heartbreak Ridge raged for several more weeks after the death of Private Pililaau. Eventually, though, the Eighth Army straightened the sag in its lines. While the peace talks dragged on for two more years, men like Pililaau were to fight and die for other uninhabitable ridges and nameless valleys. Victory or defeat, however, was out of their hands.

Private First Class Herbert K. Pililaau covered the withdrawal of his unit from Heartbreak Ridge on September 17, 1951.

# TO SAVE A LIFE
## Rescuers and Medics

Seven Navy men earned the Medal of Honor in the Korean War, though none was at sea during his medal-earning actions. The US Navy took control of the seas so early that the enemy never could launch a challenge. The Navy men singled out for their gallantry served on the land or in the skies. Five were medics attached to Marine units, one piloted a rescue helicopter, and the seventh flew a carrier fighter aircraft in support of both Army and Marine troops. Though all were armed for battle, all seven received the medal for their efforts to save lives.

On December 4, 1950, Lt. j.g. Thomas J. Hudner and three other F4U Corsair pilots from the carrier USS *Leyte* were flying an armed reconnaissance mission about fifteen miles north of the Chosin Reservoir. The Chinese had ambushed the Marines at Chosin nine days earlier. Hudner's flight group was covering the Marines' escape, looking for more Communist forces advancing from the north. Flying five hundred feet above the snow-covered mountains, they saw no sign of enemy troops. Perhaps they were down there; dressed in white for winter, Chinese soldiers could be hard to detect in the snow. But all seemed clear until Ensign Jesse Brown reported that he was losing power. "I think I may have been hit," he radioed. "I've lost my oil pressure and I'm going to have to go in."

Brown crash-landed in a clearing on a heavily wooded mountainside. The force of the impact mangled his plane. The engine broke off, and the fuselage twisted at a forty-five-degree angle near the cockpit. Tensely, Brown's flight mates circled overhead looking for a signal that he was alive. On the second pass, they saw Brown open his canopy and wave. But

A Vought F4U-4B Corsair of fighter squadron VF-113 Stingers flies over US ships at Inchon, Korea, in September 1950. The battleship USS *Missouri* is visible below the Corsair.

# LOOKING FOR A COMRADE

In July 2013, sixty-three years after the action that earned him the Medal of Honor, Tom Hudner returned to North Korea to search for Jesse Brown's remains. He recalled his trip for the revised edition of this book:

> We got clearance from the North Korean government to go over around the sixtieth anniversary of the war's end, what they call their glorious victory over the United States. I went with Adam Makos and his brother, Brian, writers who wanted to tell the story of Jesse and me.
>
> In Pyongyang we met with three senior North Korean army officers. They seemed to trust us, and we even made a type of friendship. We went from Pyongyang to the area of interest [where Jesse Brown's plane crashed] and checked into a nearby hotel.
>
> This was during the monsoon season, though, and when we woke the next morning, the rains had come so severely that nearby rivers were a raging torrent. Roads were wiped out and a couple of bridges were washed away. There was no way to get to the site.

Hudner's journey to find his comrade's remains was over, but a final bridge was crossed as he left North Korea.

> The three army officers held a dinner for us in Pyongyang the night before we left. They toasted us and everything was hunky dory. As we left the next day, Adam said, "Did you notice those guys had tears in their eyes when we were leaving?"

*Hudner and Adam Makos,* New York Times *best-selling author, meet with North Korean Army officers of the Panmunjom Commission, which handled the recovery of US MIAs.*

*Tom Hudner returns to North Korea sixty years after the end of the Korean War. Behind him is the Kumsusan Palace of the Sun in Pyongyang, where the embalmed bodies of Kim Il-Sung and Kim Jong-Il are held.*

*Hudner, seated between Chosin Marine veteran Dick Bonelli (right) and Adam Makos (left), during their final meeting with North Korean Army officers.*

Hudner, Brown's wingman, sensed something was wrong. Why, he wondered, did Brown not get out of the cockpit? His concern heightened when he saw a line of smoke wafting from the nose back toward the cockpit. At any moment, that smoke could turn to flame. Since Brown's plane faced into the wind, a fire in the front would rapidly engulf the trapped pilot. The flight leader called for a rescue copter, but Hudner, knowing it could be a half-hour before help arrived, informed his flight mates that he was going down.

Hudner, a graduate of Annapolis in 1946, had been with Fighter Squadron 32 since receiving his wings. One of the old hands he met when he joined the squadron was Jesse Brown, the Navy's first African American pilot. Hudner believed that Brown was special, an inspiration to all African Americans. More than that, the two pilots were friends. But, said Hudner later, he did not follow Brown into the Korean mountains for either of those reasons. He acted on the unspoken rule that a squadron looks out for its own: "If something happened to one of us, it wasn't 'OK, buddy. Somebody's got to go and you've gone.' You had that feeling of camaraderie and a team spirit that, by God, if there's anything that could be done, somebody was going to try to do it."

Hudner dropped his rockets and extra fuel tanks, put down his flaps, aimed his plane at the clearing next to Brown, "and made believe I was just making a carrier approach." His plane hit the mountainside hard and skidded across the snow, but it was a clean landing. Hudner's Corsair stopped only a few hundred feet from Brown's.

He leaped out of his plane and ran to the crash site. As he had feared, Brown was trapped. The fuselage had broken at the cockpit, pinning the pilot's leg at the knee. Brown was at that point suffering badly from the subfreezing cold. He had removed his helmet and then taken off his gloves to unbuckle his parachute. In the numbing cold he had dropped his gloves beyond reach. Now his hands were frozen solid. Hudner dashed back to his plane and grabbed a wool hat and scarf he kept for emergencies. He pulled the hat down over Brown's head and wrapped the scarf around his stiff hands. Then he wrestled hopelessly to pull him free.

The Corsair's cockpit was too high off the ground for Hudner to reach. He tried clambering up the plane's inverted gull wing, but his snow-covered soles slid off the icy metal. Finally, grasping the handholds in the fuselage side, he pulled himself to the top. Straddling the cockpit, he tried to reach down to grasp Brown but could not get a hold on him. Hudner ran back

An aerial photograph shows the plane Lieutenant Junior Grade Hudner crash-landed (top left) in an effort to assist Jesse Brown out of his downed plane (right).

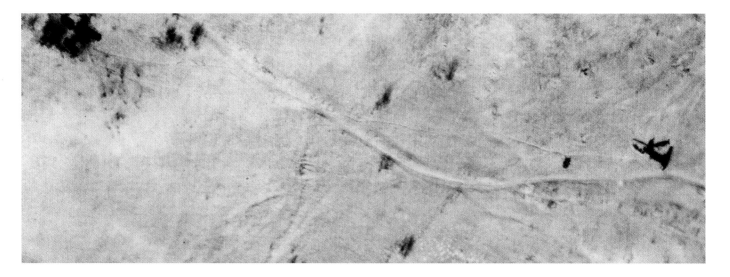

to his own plane and radioed for the helicopter to bring an ax and a fire extinguisher. Desperate to help his friend, Hudner piled handfuls of snow into the still-smoking nose.

Through all of this, Brown remained calm and alert. While waiting for rescue they talked a bit, but there was not a lot either could say. Hudner suspected that Brown had internal injuries from the crash, but the injured man gave no indication. "Never once did he say 'I hurt,'" Hudner recalled. "Just sort of a plea to get him out of there. But there was no panic in his voice."

After about another half-hour, Marine rescue helicopter pilot Lt. Charles Ward arrived and set his craft down on the slope. He brought out an ax and fire extinguisher and joined Hudner at Brown's plane. The situation looked ever more hopeless. The ax bounced like a toy hammer off the thick metal plate pressing against Brown's knee. The small fire extinguisher had no effect on the smoldering fire. And Brown was beginning to fade. His words became fewer, fainter. As the daylight began to dim, Ward reluctantly called Hudner aside. They had to get out before dusk, he said. His helicopter had no night-flying instruments, so to fly among the mountains at night could be fatal. "You can stay here if you want," he told Hudner, "but I can't see that either of us can do any good."

Hudner understood the sense of Ward's words. To remain would only doom all three men. The only way they could extricate Brown would be to cut off his pinned leg with an ax. Neither man was willing to do that, because they thought in Brown's present condition it would kill him. The single dim hope was to return to the base camp and round up some better metal-cutting equipment. Privately, though, they knew the injured man could not survive the wait.

Hudner told Brown he was going back for more help. Brown mumbled a last message for his wife. "He must have realized by that time that that was about it," Hudner later said sadly. "He couldn't move at all. And there were the two of us jumping in and out and not accomplishing a damn thing . . . One of the worst things when something has happened to you is the feeling that you're all alone. Just being with him to give him as much comfort as we could was worth the effort."

When Hudner returned to Brown for the last time, to say goodbye, he found him unconscious. If he felt any satisfaction, it was that they had stayed with his fellow pilot until the end.

Hudner and Ward climbed into the helicopter and took off, leaving Hudner's plane behind. At nightfall, they reached the Marine base where troops were straggling in from the tortuous trek down from the Chosin River valley. Hudner remained snowed in at the Marine base for three days. When he returned to the *Leyte*, the captain, Thomas Sisson, called him immediately to the bridge. He asked Hudner what had happened. Instead of reprimanding him for acting without orders, Sisson nominated Hudner for the Medal of Honor.

Thomas Hudner receives the Medal of Honor from President Truman, April 13, 1951.

# A CODE OF CONDUCT

As the USS *Leyte* prepared to pull out of Tokyo in January 1951, Lt. j.g. Tom Hudner was surprised to see among the crew of another carrier an old friend from his first days as a fighter pilot, Lt. j.g. John K. Koelsch. In a short conversation, Koelsch mentioned that he had become a helicopter rescue pilot. Then the two parted. Hudner embarked for the United States, where he would receive the Medal of Honor, Koelsch for a stint in Korea.

Rescue flying was much more than a job to Koelsch. He refused rotation to the United States at the end of his tour of duty; his conscience would not permit him to leave, he told a fellow officer, when others needed his help.

*Lieutenant Junior Grade John K. Koelsch, whose actions as a prisoner of war set the standard for future American POWs.*

In his off-duty hours, he tinkered with inventions that would make rescues safer and more successful. In the icy Korean winter, Koelsch came up with several devices to improve the operation of helicopters in cold weather. He also developed a widely used floating sling for pulling downed Airmen from the sea.

But Koelsch's greatest distinction would develop from his greatest trial. On July 3, 1951, he and a machinist's mate were shot down while trying to rescue a Marine pilot in the mountains. The three hid from enemy troops for three days, subsisting on one candy bar, two half-canteens of water, and a flask of brandy. Rescue aircraft combed the area, but no one spotted the downed Americans. On July 6, the three headed east to the sea, fifteen miles away, but were captured by a North Korean patrol in a fishing village on the coast. Wounded and sick from hunger and exposure, the Americans were paraded past villagers who showered them with taunts and abuse.

Koelsch's first concern was for his comrades. He demanded medical attention for the badly wounded pilot and better treatment for all three. When the guards ignored him, his protests grew louder. Finally the Airman was evacuated to a medical facility.

Later, Koelsch and the other American were taken to a prison camp. Though malnourished himself, Koelsch shared his meager rations with sick and injured prisoners. At the same time, he defied his captors by demanding proper treatment under the Geneva Convention guidelines for POWs. He refused to give any information beyond his name, rank, and serial number and resisted the daily brainwashing sessions.

John Koelsch's resolve enabled him to survive isolation and other mental abuse. His body was not as strong. On October 16, 1951, Lieutenant Koelsch died of malnutrition in prison. His perseverance inspired those imprisoned with him and earned him a posthumous Navy Medal of Honor. In addition, his actions were the basis for the Code of Conduct, the set of standards adopted in 1955 to guide all American prisoners of war.

Five other Medals of Honor in Korea went to Navy medics, all but one posthumously. By all odds, the man who lived to accept the honor from President Eisenhower, Hospital Corpsman 3rd Class William Charette, should not have made it either. In one day, the platoons he served lost three-quarters of their men. Though Charette remained out in the open the entire time tending the wounded in the hottest of battle, he somehow escaped with only surface wounds. His story is one of the most miraculous of the Korean War.

When Charette joined the Navy in 1951, he never expected to go to Korea. Only after he put in for hospital corpsman did he find out that medics served with the Marines. But after eighteen months of stateside duty, Charette requested assignment to the war zone. In January 1953 he joined the 2nd Battalion, 7th Marines, at the so-called Nevada complex north of Seoul. There the Marines fought the fiercest battles of the stalemated days of war.

On March 26, the Chinese overran the Marine outposts on Reno, Vegas, and Carson hills. On night maneuvers, Charette saw the flashes of artillery fire in the distance. The next day, he got word that his battalion was moving up to retake Vegas. The day broke sunny but cold as Charette's outfit headed to Vegas Outpost. As they neared the battleground, the soldiers' attention fixed on the horrors remaining from the previous night. The Marines, for all their reputation for getting out their wounded and dead, had been overwhelmed so quickly that they left the field strewn with men, dead and living. Corpses of Americans hung from the barbed wire surrounding the outpost. Men wounded hours earlier groaned for help. Charette broke from his platoon to treat the survivors, working his way slowly up the hillside of shattered men.

Throughout the day, moderate rifle and mortar fire peppered Vegas. The Chinese pulled back some, but they retained the crest of the hill. The Marines knew that after dark, the Chinese would counterattack with everything they had. It would be another long, bloody night. At dusk, the 1st Platoon, 2nd Battalion, assaulted the hill. Charette, now back with his own platoon, was waiting in reserve when an emergency call came in for a medic. Two of 1st Platoon's point men had been hit and needed attention badly. Their own corpsman was out of commission. Charette worked his way past the front lines to where the wounded men lay. By the time he reached them, it was dark.

Charette had just started treating the two Marines when the hill exploded in mortar and rifle fire. Worse for Charette and the five point men, the Chinese began rolling hand grenades down on them. In the dark, the guns and artillery shot wildly, but the grenades rolled right into the Americans' position. One burst near Charette, wounding him in the face and temporarily blinding and deafening him. Fortunately, his medical kit, blown completely off him, took the brunt of the blast. When his sight returned, Charette saw that he was the least injured of the group. Though now without medical supplies and hampered by darkness, he rushed to do what he could for the others. He had already given away his overcoat to a wounded man. Now, in the freezing night, he ripped up his clothes to make bandages and tourniquets.

As he bound the wounds of the Marine most badly mauled by shrapnel, Charette heard the man on the other side of him shout "grenade." The Navy corpsman threw himself over his patient to protect him from the blast. "I admire a man who can throw himself on a grenade," he said later. "I couldn't personally do that, because with grenades your chances of survival are fairly good if you can get some distance away. But this guy I was treating, I knew if he got hit any worse . . . and of course I did have a flak jacket on. So I just covered him." When the dust cleared, Charette resumed bandaging.

In the dark, the guns and artillery shot wildly, but the grenades rolled right into the Americans' position.

Hospital Corpsman Third Class William Charette (right) with President Dwight D. Eisenhower during Medal of Honor ceremonies on January 12, 1954. The other men receiving the medal are 1st Lt. Edward Schowalter Jr. (left) and Pfc. Ernest West.

After Charette had treated the point men, help arrived. First Platoon's leader, Sergeant Stagwell, led a small party up to the forward position to evacuate the wounded. They had taken the first injured man only a short distance, though, when they hit a snag. A mortar shell had caved in a portion of the trench they were using as cover. The only way to get the casualties past the logjam would be to bring them overland, directly through the enemy's line of fire. Charette leaped from the trench, lifted a man out, and carried him to a safe spot. Then he returned, straddled the trench, and picked up a second. He ran back and forth, lifting and carrying casualties through a cascade of bullets, until he had brought all the point men to safety. Then he sought more wounded.

Before the night was over, Charette had become the medic for all three platoons. The pace he kept was grueling, the conditions horrible. At one point he was working on injuries to his assistant platoon leader in darkness so complete he could barely see the wounds. A few moments later he stopped. Rigor mortis was setting in. The man was dead. But Charette saved many other lives that night. His actions inspired many men; when Sergeant Stagwell recommended him for the Medal of Honor, all three platoons in his battalion contributed testimony to support the recommendation.

Nine months later, after the armistice, Charette was still in Korea, working in a post-war MASH unit, when the chief surgeon brought him the news that he had been awarded the Medal of Honor. "I would have rather heard I was going home," he remembered of the moment, with a laugh. Still, he was clearly proud to receive another honor: In 1958, he was chosen to select the remains that would become the Unknown Soldier of World War II.

Many years later, when questioned about his actions on that hill in Korea, William Charette gave a prosaic reply: "What'd I do it for? The guys."

# Vietnam
## A Different Kind of War

**I**T WAS A WAR that few understood and many opposed. Born of Cold War power politics and a missionary zeal for democracy, the American effort in Vietnam ended in ambiguity and division. In 1965, after more than ten years of indirect opposition to the Communist forces of Ho Chi Minh, the United States stepped up its commitment of men and firepower to counter the threat to South Vietnam. With the American military deploying a vast amount of its nonnuclear resources against a smaller, scattered fighting force, it seemed the conflict would soon be over, the Communists quickly pounded into surrender. Eight years later, the United States had withdrawn; two years after that, North Vietnamese troops had captured Saigon, and North and South were reunited. In the eyes of many, Vietnam was the first war America lost.

American involvement in Indochina grew steadily from 1954, when France relinquished control of the region after more than eighty years of colonial rule. The French defeat by Ho's Viet Minh guerrillas at Dien Bien Phu that year led to the Geneva accord that partitioned North from South Vietnam, leaving Ho and his followers to establish a Communist government in the northern capital of Hanoi. For the Viet Minh who remained in the South, however, the struggle was not over, and the fight began for a reunified Vietnam. In the Mekong Delta and central highlands, clashes between the Army of the Republic of Vietnam (ARVN) and the Vietcong, as the Communist guerrillas came to be known, became bloodier.

In the United States, the growing Soviet influence in Europe after World War II and the fall of China to the forces of Mao Zedong lent urgency to the fight against communism. Given Ho Chi Minh's association with Mao and Stalin, the US foreign policy establishment considered him more a Communist than a nationalist and therefore a danger to freedom and democracy in Asia. During Dien Bien Phu, President Eisenhower had warned that "the loss of Indochina will cause the fall of Southeast Asia like a set of dominoes." The "domino theory," and the consequent commitment to the preservation of an anti-Communist government in South Vietnam, would haunt American foreign policy for the next twenty years.

Despite American aid, the South Vietnamese could not maintain a stable government, and ARVN forces could not get the upper hand against the Viet Cong, whose ranks had been bolstered by ever-larger numbers of North Vietnamese regulars since 1959. By the summer of 1964, ten years after Dien Bien Phu, Communist forces were firmly entrenched in the countryside, and government control of some areas was in name only. Ho's forces threatened to destroy the southern government and reunify Vietnam—unless the United States stepped up aid. President Johnson, who had inherited from Presidents Eisenhower and Kennedy the presence of US military advisors in South Vietnam, was pressed by various aides and military commanders to broaden the American military role in Southeast Asia.

The "domino theory," and the consequent commitment to the preservation of an anti-Communist government in South Vietnam, would haunt American foreign policy for the next twenty years.

The Gulf of Tonkin incident of August 1964 brought the country closer to such a commitment. On August 2, North Vietnamese gunboats fired upon a US Navy electronic surveillance ship, the USS *Maddox*, twelve miles off the coast of North Vietnam. Two days later, the *Maddox* was back in the Gulf of Tonkin, escorted by a destroyer, the USS *C. Turner Joy*. "The United States was not seeking to provoke another attack," wrote one historian, "but did not go out of its way to avoid one either. "

What happened in the Gulf of Tonkin on the night of August 4 remains unclear to this day. While the two American vessels reported that they were under attack, no enemy ships were sighted, and radar readings that stormy night were unreliable. Regardless, the White House insisted that a second attack had taken place, and the president ordered retaliatory air strikes against North Vietnamese naval bases and fuel depots. On August 7, both houses of Congress passed a resolution that allowed "the president, as commander-in-chief, to take all necessary measures to repel any armed attack against the forces of the United States and to prevent further aggression."

But Johnson did not take further action, at least not immediately. "We seek no wider war," he told crowds along the 1964 campaign trail. On the other hand, he realized a greater commitment might be necessary to shore up the weak ARVN defenses—and save lives.

UH-1D helicopters airlift members of the 2nd Battalion, 14th Infantry Regiment, from the Fihol Rubber Plantation to a new staging area during Operation Wahiawa, a search-and-destroy mission conducted by the 25th Infantry Division northeast of Cu Chi, Vietnam, May 16, 1966.

After a Viet Cong attack on an American base in Pleiku in February 1965 left eight dead, the president was ready to act. "We have kept our gun over the mantel and our shells in the cupboard for a long time now," he said to a wary Senator Mike Mansfield, "and what was the result? They are killing our men while they sleep in the night. I can't ask our American soldiers to fight with one hand tied behind their backs." Johnson ordered reprisal strikes against North Vietnam and a few days later approved Operation Rolling Thunder, the sustained bombing of the North. The bombing was to become one of the most pervasive, and controversial, American tactics in Southeast Asia.

Johnson's commander in Vietnam was still pessimistic about the success of a limited American effort. Predicting "a VC [Viet Cong] takeover of the country" if the president did not act further, Gen. William Westmoreland, backed by the Joint Chiefs of Staff, urged escalated bombing of North Vietnam and supply routes along the "Ho Chi Minh Trail" through Laos and Cambodia, as well as increased security for in-country air bases. To accomplish the latter, he requested two battalions of US Marines to defend the American base at Da Nang.

Despite misgivings among Johnson's staff, the president assented to the request. At dawn on March 8, 1965, two battalions of Marines splashed ashore at Da Nang and were met by smiling Vietnamese girls who draped garlands of flowers around their necks. It was an ironically tranquil beginning to a bitter and bloody eight-year task. By the end of 1965, there were over 184,000 US military personnel in Vietnam—eight times the numbers there in 1964. LBJ was firm: "We will stand in Vietnam."

The aim of American involvement in Southeast Asia seemed clear from the beginning: to assist the South Vietnamese in their struggle to defend themselves against Communist aggression, ensuring a stable, independent nation in the South. Support for the endeavor was widespread. A majority of Americans approved of the original deployment of troops in 1965, and thousands of men enlisted for their nation's latest war. One veteran remembered the prevailing sense of obligation: "Everybody told you that that was the thing to do." A Marine who was part of the original landing party recalled the optimistic mood of many of his countrymen: "America seemed omnipotent then: the country could still claim that it had never lost a war, and we believed that we were ordained to play cop to the Communists' robber and spread our own political faith throughout the world."

But playing cops and robbers with the Communists involved a fair amount of chasing. American forces soon expanded beyond their defensive posture and moved inland to engage the enemy in the jungles and paddies of the South. Traditional American infantry tactics called for the application of superior manpower and firepower, so American generals hoped to engineer clashes with large units of the North Vietnamese Army (NVA).

Large-scale battles were, however, rare in Vietnam. The Communists realized quickly that they could never match the mammoth US war machine. Instead, guerrillas operated in small cadres, relying on stealth and mobility to fight. In order to survive against a stronger foe, they struck selectively, ambushing and harassing the enemy. Ho Chi Minh's analogy for the struggle against the French rang true for the Communist fight against the Americans a decade later. Comparing the guerrilla to a tiger and the stronger enemy to an elephant, Ho said, "If the tiger ever pauses, the elephant will impale him on his mighty tusks. But the tiger will not pause, and the elephant will die of exhaustion and loss of blood."

The bombing was to become one of the most pervasive, and controversial, American tactics in Southeast Asia.

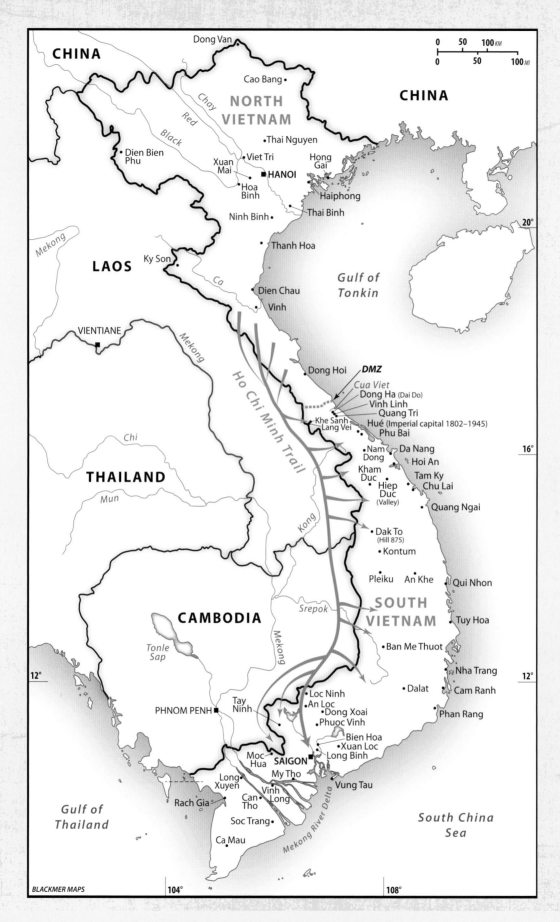

CHINA

Dong Van

Cao Bang

**NORTH VIETNAM**

Chay

Red

Black

Thai Nguyen

Dien Bien Phu

Viet Tri

Xuan Mai

Hong Gai

HANOI

Hoa Binh

Haiphong

Ninh Binh

Thai Binh

Mekong

**LAOS**

Ky Son

Ca

Thanh Hoa

*Gulf of Tonkin*

Dien Chau

Vinh

VIENTIANE

Mekong

Dong Hoi

*DMZ*

*Cua Viet*

Dong Ha (Dai Do)

Vinh Linh

Quang Tri

Khe Sanh

Lang Vei

Hué (Imperial capital 1802–1945)

Phu Bai

Chi

Ho Chi Minh Trail

Nam Dong

Da Nang

Hoi An

Kham Duc

Tam Ky

Chu Lai

**THAILAND**

Hiep Duc (Valley)

Mun

Quang Ngai

Kong

Dak To (Hill 875)

Kontum

Pleiku

An Khe

Qui Nhon

**CAMBODIA**

Srepok

**SOUTH VIETNAM**

Tuy Hoa

Tonle Sap

Ban Me Thuot

Mekong

Nha Trang

Cam Ranh

Dalat

Loc Ninh

An Loc

Dong Xoai

Phuoc Vinh

Phan Rang

PHNOM PENH

Tay Ninh

Bien Hoa

Xuan Loc

Long Binh

Moc Hua

SAIGON

Vung Tau

Long Xuyen

My Tho

Vinh Long

*Gulf of Thailand*

Rach Gia

Can Tho

*South China Sea*

Soc Trang

Ca Mau

*Mekong River Delta*

CHINA

20°

16°

12°

12°

The guerrillas' elusiveness eventually forced American tactics to include counterinsurgency and guerrilla fighting, although large "search and destroy" sweeps remained common. Vietnam was a war without fronts; the enemy was not across the trenches, he was usually underfoot, or hiding in the countryside. The average infantryman in Vietnam spent much of his time sloshing through swamps and jungles or trudging through elephant grass on patrols in search of the enemy. When American forces encountered VC or NVA troops, they often called in air or artillery strikes to flush them out of the dense undergrowth. One officer explained the standard operating procedure for many commanders when engaging the enemy: "Blow the hell out of him and police up." While this tactic often saved American lives, it usually drove the Communists from the battlefield, either into vast tunnel complexes in nearby villages or to sanctuaries in Laos and Cambodia. US forces rarely occupied remote areas for any length of time; after the enemy had been forced out, the Americans usually moved on to the next area, often allowing the Communists to reoccupy their old territory until the next US patrol.

A more subtle battle with the Communists took place in Vietnamese villages, where both sides vied for control of the "hearts and minds" of the peasants. Subscribing to Mao's aphorism that "the people are the ocean in which the guerrilla swims," the VC elicited the support and material assistance of the people, often with notable success. As a result, many populated areas were Communist-controlled, despite American and ARVN pacification programs. Describing one region particularly sympathetic to the VC, one soldier said, "We owned them in the daytime and the VC owned them at night. . . . We stayed the hell out of the villages at night." The questionable loyalty of the population led American soldiers to wonder sometimes just who the enemy was. The same villager who welcomed them by day may have ambushed them by night. Homemade booby traps were common: Americans entering a village would frequently trip a rudimentary grenade or step onto "punji" stakes.

Complicating the American task was the inexorable intertwining of military strategy and political goals that frustrated many military men. Commanders were exasperated by the limits imposed on them by their government. Washington occasionally halted the bombing of North Vietnam and the Ho Chi Minh Trail as a peace gesture, despite requests that it be continued in order to wear down the enemy and to protect American troops.

Although the Communists used Laos and Cambodia as sanctuaries, American units were forbidden to go in and rout them. General Westmoreland continually expressed frustration at not being allowed to take the war to the enemy wherever he was, but President Johnson, fearful of provoking China into entering the conflict, as had happened in Korea, was determined to have Vietnam remain a "limited war." American forces would respect international boundaries, even though their enemy did not. Incursions into Laos and Cambodia later in the war had little effect on enemy activity; for the American command, they were too little, too late.

# THE OUTPOSTS
## *Fighting in the Highlands*

The remote jungles and highlands of Vietnam were the battlefield of the Viet Cong. To monitor enemy presence in these areas, the American military command established Special Forces camps, manned by "Green Berets" trained in counterinsurgency guerrilla fighting

One officer explained the standard operating procedure for many commanders when engaging the enemy: "Blow the hell out of him and police up."

*Opposite*
After the Marine landing at Da Nang in 1965, the American presence in South Vietnam expanded to remote areas in hopes of eliminating the Communist guerrillas, who were aided by supply lines along the Ho Chi Minh Trail. Large battles in I Corps and the central highlands were followed by the enemy's 1968 Tet Offensive, which caused the United States to reconsider its commitment to the war. After gradual American disengagement, the weak South Vietnamese army could not hold back advancing Communist forces. Saigon fell in April 1975.

and in working with local militia. When these camps came under attack, as they often did, commanders faced a tough choice: Either defend the outpost against a frequently stronger force or evacuate, temporarily conceding the area to the enemy.

On July 5, 1964, many of the twelve Green Berets manning the camp at Nam Dong were convinced that their post was about to be attacked. Nam Dong's location in the central highlands of South Vietnam, only fifteen miles from Laos, invited constant probing by VC and NVA troops infiltrating the border. In the past two days, patrols had encountered evidence of a greater enemy presence, including the bodies of two murdered village chiefs. Also, a recent scuffle between the South Vietnamese troops and the Montagnard natives of the highlands had fragmented the force, and this infighting had probably come to the attention of the enemy. By the night of the fifth, the mood was one of jittery anticipation: One American wrote his wife, "All hell is going to break loose here before the night is over."

Early the next morning, Capt. Roger H. C. Donlon was finishing his patrol of the American sector of the camp. A native of New York State, Donlon had enlisted in the Army in 1958 after two years in the Air Force and one year at West Point. Now, after training at the Army's Special Forces school at Fort Bragg, he was commander of Detachment A-726 at Nam Dong, numbering over three hundred men, mostly South Vietnamese and Montagnards. Donlon also expected an attack that night, but as he walked around the camp at 2:25 a.m., all was quiet, leading him to think that perhaps he had been wrong.

Moments later, Captain Donlon's worst fears were confirmed. An enemy mortar round whistled into the camp, destroying the mess hall Donlon was about to enter. Another shell hit the command post, setting it on fire. Small-arms fire and explosions erupted in the darkness around the camp.

A nearby mortar explosion knocked Donlon to the ground. Pulling himself up, he scrambled to a mortar pit, grabbed a flare gun, and fired, only to hear the shell fizzle out in the darkness. He moved to the next emplacement for more rounds.

In the light of another flare, Donlon saw three VC sappers—guerrillas wired with explosives—lurking near the gate. He set his AR15 rifle on semi-automatic and squeezed off six rounds, then threw a hand grenade, killing all three of the raiders.

As Donlon ran for the next pit, a grenade exploded near him, driving shrapnel into his left arm and stomach. Despite his wounds, he visited

Captain Roger Donlon stands in the pit where he was wounded by a mortar blast during a Viet Cong attack on the Special Forces camp at Nam Dong on July 6, 1964.

three additional emplacements, helping his men direct fire at guerrillas trying to scale or blast through the fence. He was hit again by fragments from at least three mortar blasts, which wounded his leg and side. Bleeding heavily now, Donlon made for another pit, where he and three other Americans continued firing. The pit was, in Donlon's words, "a hellhole." The VC had overrun part of the outer sector of the camp and threatened to breach the inner American perimeter. Grenades were now coming over the fence five or six at a time.

As the onslaught continued, the four men prepared to evacuate the bunker. Donlon fired cover as two men fled, but the third, Master Sgt. Gabriel Alamo, was too badly wounded to move. Donlon started to pull Alamo up the steps of the pit just as a mortar round landed at the top of the stairs in front of the captain's face. Donlon remembered screaming as he took the brunt of the explosion. "*I am going to die*, I thought. The screaming . . . was the wail of death."

Donlon did not die, but he was badly hurt, bleeding from wounds to the left shoulder, head, and stomach. He checked Alamo, but the sergeant had been killed by the blast. Donlon ran over to some Montagnards and tended their wounds, tearing his T-shirt for bandages and using one of his socks as a tourniquet. Ordering the men to cover him, he scuttled over to another bunker, bent over by the pain of his stomach wounds. After getting a report on the defense of the camp, he was hit again by shrapnel but did not stop for treatment, instead directing his men in the darkness.

An American flareship arrived at 4:00 a.m., but the enemy persisted. From the dark jungle a voice called in Vietnamese and then in English. "Lay down your weapons!" the voice said. "We are going to annihilate your camp! You will all be killed!" But Captain Donlon and the defenders of Nam Dong held out. By daylight, what was left of the enemy force, later estimated at over eight hundred, had retreated, leaving over fifty of their dead. Captain Donlon was directing the treatment and evacuation of the wounded, including, finally, himself. By the end of the year, Donlon had recovered from his wounds and was called to the White House to receive the first Medal of Honor for the Vietnam War.

The Special Forces camp at Kham Duc, like its counterpart at Nam Dong, was tucked away in the central highlands, ten miles from the Laotian border. After the fall of Camp Lang Vei during the Tet Offensive in February 1968, Kham Duc was the only observation camp remaining in I Corps, the northernmost military district in South Vietnam and the scene of some of the heaviest fighting. In the spring of 1968, intelligence reports indicated an enemy buildup in the area, and a nearby forward operating post was overrun on May 10. When Kham

Roger Donlon serves as the grand marshal for the El Paso, Texas, Loyalty Day Parade on May 2, 1967.

Roger Donlon receives the first Medal of Honor for the Vietnam War from President Lyndon Johnson on December 5, 1964.

Lieutenant Colonel Joe M. Jackson, a Korean War veteran and former U-2 pilot, earned the Medal of Honor piloting a cargo plane in the rescue of a combat control team at Kham Duc air base.

Duc came under heavy mortar attack on the 10th and 11th, General Westmoreland ordered it evacuated the next day.

As the sun came up on the 12th—Mother's Day—a heavy fog hung over the camp, obscuring enemy movements in the surrounding hills. An Army CH-47 helicopter and two Air Force C-130 Hercules cargo ships tried to land and take off with personnel, but all were disabled by enemy fire. One C-130 burst into flames at the end of the runway, killing the crew and over 150 Vietnamese civilians. Finally a C-130 was able to land and take off with passengers, but as it left, its pilot warned other aircraft: "For God's sake stay out of Kham Duc. It belongs to Charlie."

At three that afternoon, an Air Force C-123 Provider cargo plane took off from Da Nang, bound for Kham Duc. At the controls was Lt. Col. Joe M. Jackson, a twenty-seven-year veteran who had flown 107 combat missions in Korea. In 1967, Jackson received orders to go to Vietnam to fly transport planes, although, in his words, "my bag was really fighter planes." The C-123 was a "pretty big clumsy old airplane," Jackson remembered, "very slow, but very strong."

Jackson and his three-man crew reached the Kham Duc area at about 3:30 p.m., just as a plane was about to take off with the last of the men on the ground aboard. At that point, flames had engulfed the camp, and enemy shells still rained down from the hills. As the last C-130 pilot to leave the ground announced that he had picked up the remaining personnel, the airborne commander ordered the fighters circling overhead to descend and destroy the camp.

Just then the C-130 broke in. "Negative! Negative! Three men are still on the ground!" The combat control team, in charge of directing the evacuation, was still at the base, unaware that the evacuation was complete. As they searched the camp for anyone who had been left behind, they realized that they were the only ones left.

Meanwhile, above the camp, the airborne commander asked the next aircraft in line to try to land on the airstrip to pick up the men. Lieutenant Colonel Alfred Jeanotte guided his C-123 down over the hills and onto the debris-covered runway, cutting his speed as he and his crew looked for the three men. Enemy fire intensified, however, so Jeanotte accelerated for takeoff—too late to see the men jump from a ditch and try to signal him. As Jeanotte took off, several pilots overhead spotted the team. When the commander asked for a volunteer to go in for another try, Jackson and his copilot, Maj. Jesse Campbell, realized that they were in the best position to land. While Campbell radioed, "Roger, going in," Jackson started the descent from nine thousand feet.

The approach was more like that of a jet fighter than a "big clumsy old air-plane." The C-123 dove at a rate of almost four thousand feet per minute—nearly eight times the standard drop for a normal cargo planes landing. At four thousand feet, the C-123 came under heavy fire that followed it down onto the runway.

Jackson realized that if he reversed his propellers to stop the aircraft, he would shut off the two auxiliary engines he needed for a quick escape. Instead, he simply jammed on the brakes, and the C-123 skidded halfway down the six-thousand-foot runway. Campbell spotted the three men in a ditch beside the runway, but debris prevented Jackson from taxiing any closer to them. As the C-123 turned to take off the way it came in, the three men jumped from the culvert and ran for the plane, under fire from enemy gun positions farther down the runway. They jumped into the open cargo door at the rear, the loadmaster shouted, "All on board!" and Jackson prepared to take off down the runway.

In one of the few known photographs of a Medal of Honor action, Jackson turns his C-123 on the runway of the Kham Duc base under heavy fire as three men left on the ground run to the plane. This photo was taken by another American pilot circling overhead.

Just then Campbell shouted, "Look out!" From the edge of the runway came a 122mm rocket, fired from just outside the perimeter. The two watched as the shell skidded along the asphalt, broke in half, and stopped only about thirty feet from the plane. It did not explode. Jackson taxied around the shell and applied full power, taking off under heavy fire from the hills on either side. The plane had been on the ground at Kham Duc for less than a minute. Upon landing at Da Nang, Jackson and Campbell inspected the plane and were amazed to discover that it had not been hit by enemy bullets. "I will never understand that," said Jackson.

Later that day, Joe Jackson wrote a Mother's Day letter to his wife. "I had an extremely exciting mission today," he said. "I can't describe it to you in a letter but one of these days I'll tell you all about it." Eight months later, on January 16, 1969, Rosie Jackson heard the rest of the story as President Johnson hung the Air Force Medal of Honor around her husband's neck.

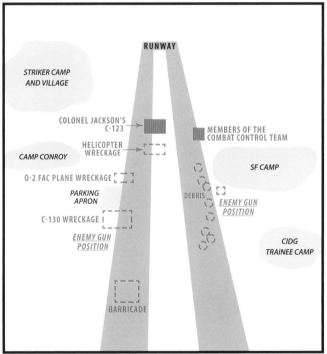

This diagram of the photograph at top indicates the positions of the wreckage on the runway that prevented a full landing and of the two enemy guns.

Captain Jay Vargas led a company of Marines in a two-day battle with enemy soldiers in the village of Dai Do. Though he was wounded three times, he carried several other injured men to safety.

Captain James E. Livingston, shown here in recent years, also received the Medal of Honor for bravery at Dai Do. Even after his wounds made it impossible for him to walk, Livingston continued to lead his company in the battle.

# JUNGLE WAR
## *Fighting in a Graveyard*

Combat can be a solitary action. The soldier fighting in the field is concerned not so much with the movement of divisions and regiments as with a more immediate, personal goal: staying alive. While thousands of men may march in a single battle, each fights not for the glory of nations but for his own world—his personal survival and that of those closest to him.

Many of the acts of valor in Vietnam reflected this individual aspect of war. While these incidents may not have been part of some grand offensive or victory, they typify a more personal triumph of men in the isolated forests and jungles of Southeast Asia.

Jay Vargas had never seen a Medal of Honor recipient in person until he was a twenty-five-year-old second lieutenant with the 3rd Marine Division in Okinawa in 1964. Absent-mindedly walking into the office of Brig. Gen. Raymond G. Davis, a Korea Medal of Honor recipient, Vargas was flabbergasted to see Davis talking to four other men—Reginald Myers, Carl Sitter, William Barber, and Louis Wilson—all wearing the distinctive blue ribbon of the medal. He sheepishly excused himself, but Davis asked him to stay, and the young officer spent some time with the group. Reporting back to his commander, Vargas almost forgot the message he was to deliver; all he could say was that he had just met five Medal of Honor men.

Four years later, on the morning of May 1, 1968, Capt. Jay Vargas and his unit, Company G of the 2nd Battalion, 4th Marines, floated down the Cua Viet River in tank-bearing boats. The objective was the village of Dai Do, nine miles south of the demilitarized zone (DMZ), the border between North and South Vietnam, where two Marine companies had been battered by a North Vietnamese regiment. Pulling ashore two miles southeast of the village, Vargas and his men, with Bravo Company on the left flank, set out across almost half a mile of rice fields toward Dai Do. For the next two days, they would be involved in a bloody seesaw battle for control of the village.

Company G came under heavy fire almost as soon as it hit the shore. As the Americans swept across the open fields, NVA soldiers popped up from hidden "spider holes" and poured AK-47 fire on them. Nearby, Bravo Company lost most of its officers in the fire. An inexperienced second lieutenant assumed command, then got on the radio and started babbling hysterically, talking of pulling his men back.

Vargas realized that Bravo's withdrawal could decimate his own company, so he got on the radio and calmed the lieutenant down. Then he continued the attack by bringing up his reserve platoon to help. Soon the Marines had taken Dai Do and had pushed the NVA into another village a few miles away, where they were battered by American gunships.

Eventually, however, the enemy counterattacked and pushed the Marines to the other side of Dai Do. Vargas and sixty men took cover in a graveyard, pulling bodies from freshly dug graves to improvise foxholes. The enemy threatened from all sides as the Marines drew a perimeter. When night fell, Vargas ordered his men to stay down and shoot at anything that moved above them.

AC-130 gunships circled overhead, and American artillery shells, some fired from Navy ships offshore, landed within 160 feet of the men of Company G. Throughout the night, several American commanders, even General Westmoreland, spoke to Vargas on the radio, offering encouragement. "It was almost as if the World Series had started and they didn't have a ticket," Vargas recalled. "And all they could do was listen on the radio." Years later, Vargas met one of the admirals who had spoken to him on that occasion; the admiral told him that he and his fellow officers had doubted that any of the Marines would last the night.

At sunrise on May 2, the men were still in the graveyard, and Vargas, as he recounted later, "decided that I'd had enough." Hooking up with Echo Company, commanded by Capt. James E. Livingston, Vargas launched a counterattack through Dai Do and once more cleared out the enemy. In the aftermath of ground fighting and air strikes, recalled Vargas, the village "almost looked like the moon," with bomb craters, denuded trees, and leveled shacks. Scores of North Vietnamese bodies lay in the streets.

No sooner had the Marines relaxed than the enemy reversed and counterattacked yet again. Vargas and his men were low on ammunition, so they grabbed anything that could be used as a weapon and fought the enemy hand-to-hand. Vargas was wounded by shrapnel for the third time in as many days: One piece lodged between his skull and scalp; another split his lip, making it difficult for him to speak.

The 2nd Battalion commander joined Vargas and his men in a trench in the village. As artillery fire edged closer, an NVA soldier fired into the ditch, killing three men and wounding the commander. Vargas hoisted the colonel onto his back and, armed with only a .45-caliber pistol, made his way through a nearby paddy. On the way, an enemy soldier raised his rifle to fire at the two men. Vargas stumbled and his pistol discharged; the bullet ricocheted off a wall and struck the enemy soldier in the stomach. "He was more surprised than I was," Vargas remembered.

That afternoon, Captain Vargas brought at least six men back for medical attention, fighting his way to his men each time and killing eight enemy soldiers at close range. By the night of the 2nd, reinforcements had arrived and the enemy was routed, with over eight hundred dead. Seventy-two Marines were killed, hundreds wounded. Said Vargas, "I don't know why I didn't get killed."

Both Jay Vargas and James Livingston (who led Company E against enemy emplacements despite shrapnel wounds) were awarded the Medal of Honor for this battle. The men were told to bring their families to Washington for the presentation at the White House on May 14, 1970.

A few months before the ceremony, Vargas's mother, an Italian immigrant widely respected in her Arizona community, died suddenly. Grieved by the loss, Vargas had a unique request: He asked that the name of his mother, Maria Teresa Sandini Vargas, be engraved on the back of his medal instead of his own. President Nixon was touched by the sentiment and granted the request. So the name on the medal, and the name entered onto the Medal of Honor rolls, is "M. Sando Vargas," a tribute not only to a Marine's valor in Vietnam, but also a son's love for his mother.

US Marines in the decimated village of Dai Do after heavy fighting between North Vietnamese and American troops, May 1968.

A member of the 173rd Airborne Brigade crouches beside the body of a dead comrade and equipment left by the wounded at the height of the battle on Hill 875. US Army paratroopers then began a final assault up the bloody slopes of Hill 875.

# HILL 875

## *The Battle for Dak To*

In November 1967, one of the few large battles of the war pitted American troops against a well-entrenched North Vietnamese force near Dak To in the central highlands beside the Laotian and Cambodian borders. After two weeks of fighting, American and ARVN troops got the upper hand, and the NVA began to retreat to its sanctuaries across the border, leapfrogging over its fortifications to slow down its pursuers. But the Communists were determined to make one last stand inside the border and on November 19 began a furious battle less than four miles from Cambodia. Like many others in the war, it was a battle for a remote hill known to most only by its height in meters: 875.

On the morning of November 19, 1967, US Army paratroopers were poised to push the North Vietnamese over the border into Cambodia. The NVA was still dug in on the summit of Hill 875, despite American bombs and artillery that had reduced much of the heavy foliage to twigs and branches. At 9:45 a.m., after American planes peppered the hill with fire, Companies C and D of the 2nd Battalion, 503rd Infantry, 173rd Airborne Brigade, started up the steep north side of 875. Taking up the rear was Alpha Company, on the lookout for NVA attacks from the forest below. Despite the bare trees and scattered bamboo, the Americans knew that the enemy still had plenty of places to hide.

Contact was not long in coming. Within forty-five minutes, the two lead companies came under rifle and grenade fire from above. Alpha Company, about three hundred feet downhill, braced for an assault from below.

Taking up the rear of Company A was a four-man squad led by Specialist Fourth Class James Kelley. Just after 2:00, the four heard rustling in the brush below. Holding his fire until the enemy got close, Pfc. Carlos Lozada, a twenty-one-year-old native of Puerto Rico, gripped his M60 machine gun and waited.

Suddenly enemy fire broke out on the left. Lozada yelled, "Here they come, Kelley!" and started firing down the hill at a group of about fifteen regulars advancing toward him. Several fell, but others continued to press up the slope. Kelley ordered the other three to fall back, and Lozada carried his machine gun to a log and continued firing in long sweeps. Kelley shot an enemy soldier at close range, but then his M16 jammed. To cover him, Lozada jumped up from his cover and into the trail, holding the twenty-four-pound M60 at his hip as he fired at the advancing enemy.

Kelley cleared his rifle and started firing downhill. Lozada ran out of ammunition, so he retreated up the trail behind another member of the squad. An instant later an enemy bullet

Private First Class Carlos Lozada earned the medal for his bravery in singlehandedly withstanding a furious assault by enemy North Vietnamese and providing cover in efforts to protect his entire company.

A wounded paratrooper is given plasma in the heat of battle on Hill 875.

Father Charles Watters was one of three chaplains awarded the Medal of Honor for valor during the Vietnam War; two medals were posthumous, including Watters's.

struck him in the head, knocking him into his comrade. Lozada was mortally wounded, but Kelley and the others carried him uphill as they fired at the enemy and dropped grenades on the trail. By the time they had rejoined the rest of the men farther up the hill, the NVA were swarming up the side of 875. The three companies were surrounded by close to three hundred North Vietnamese, firing from bunkers and tunnels amid the bamboo.

As the afternoon wore on, the three companies consolidated their perimeters. Enemy rifle and rocket fire fell all around them. American fighters dropped bombs and strafed NVA positions just outside the 2nd Battalion lines. At the center of the perimeter a combined command post was established where the scores of wounded were brought for treatment.

One of those assisting was Maj. Charles J. Watters, a Roman Catholic priest from New Jersey, one of the 173rd's chaplains. In the months before Dak To, Father Watters had been a comfort for many of the weary men of the 173rd. One soldier had told Watters of his brother, who had just been drafted. He spoke of his fear that his brother might be killed. "I said, 'If it's got to happen, let it happen to me.'" Watters replied, "Let it happen to me, then, son."

On the morning of the 19th, Charlie Watters had celebrated mass with the men of the 2nd Battalion before they started up Hill 875. Several hours later, he was braving enemy fire to care for the wounded and dying. When a wounded soldier had frozen in shock before the NVA, Father Watters ran out to pull him to safety. Six times he went beyond the perimeter to retrieve wounded men, braving heavy enemy fire. In the late afternoon, with so many men lying wounded in the hot sun, Father Watters continued to perform his duties, assisting the medics and administering last rites while fighters pounded enemy positions on the hill.

Just before 7:00 p.m., dusk fell over the area. From out of the west flew an American fighter, about to strike an enemy position. One of its 750-pound bombs fell short of its target, however, and landed directly on the center of the Charlie Company command post. At least forty-two men were killed, including the entire company command group. Killed instantly was Father Watters, a victim of "friendly fire."

*Above*
Chaplain Charles Watters of New Jersey holds Easter services in a jungle clearing in War Zone C on March 26, 1967.

*Right*
Paratroopers of the 173rd Airborne Brigade honor their comrades killed on Hill 875 at their base camp near the airstrip at Dak To. Among their fallen comrades, survivors spoke most frequently about Father Charles Watters and Pfc. Carlos Lozada.

Four days later, Hill 875 fell to the 173rd paratroopers. It was Thanksgiving Day; in the afternoon, helicopters flew in turkey dinners, which the men ate amid the ruins of a costly battle. The two battalions that had fought for Hill 875 had lost 158 men, with another 402 wounded. North Vietnamese dead from the fighting around Dak To exceeded 1,600. General Westmoreland, stating that the Communists were seeking a headline victory, called Dak To "the beginning of a great defeat for the enemy."

Private First Class Carlos Lozada and Maj. Charles J. Watters were later awarded the Medal of Honor posthumously for their actions on Hill 875. Father Watters was one of seven chaplains who have received the medal, three of whom were decorated for service in Vietnam. His uncle, John J. Doran, had received the medal sixty-eight years earlier during the Spanish-American War for helping cut the enemy cables in Cienfuegos Harbor, Cuba.

# THREE WEEKS AT HUE
## *The Tet Offensive*

Dak To and the other "border battles" of 1967 were only a dress rehearsal for things to come. Despite optimistic public pronouncements, General Westmoreland and other American commanders expected a bold Communist offensive sometime in early 1968, probably after Tet, the Vietnamese New Year, at the end of January. Instead, the enemy attacked in the middle of Tet, catching many American and ARVN troops off guard. Over eighty thousand Viet Cong and North Vietnamese troops emerged from the countryside to attack more than one hundred South Vietnamese cities, towns, and military installations. Although the Communists were not able to hold any towns and suffered tremendous casualties, the Tet Offensive struck a fatal blow to American resolve to continue the war.

At 3:40 on the morning of January 31, 1968, a savage rain of mortar shells and rockets began to pour down out of the early morning fog over Hue, fifty miles south of the DMZ. Like scores of other cities and towns all across South Vietnam, the ancient imperial capital was under Communist attack. The Tet Offensive, the enemy's attempt to take the war to the streets of the South, had begun.

Over the next several hours, five battalions of North Vietnamese regulars swarmed into the city, meeting little resistance as they swept along both banks of the Perfume River. Outnumbered ARVN troops quickly called for help. Two companies of US Marines moved from Phu Bai, eight miles to the south, but were unsuccessful in their first attempts to breach the Citadel, the sacred palace of mandarin rulers of traditional Vietnam. By late morning, the gold, blue, and red flag of the National Liberation Front, the formal Viet Cong organization, flew over Hue.

Chief Warrant Officer Fred Ferguson in a UH-1 Iroquois "Huey" helicopter. On the first day of the Tet Offensive Ferguson flew into Hue to rescue five men.

To the south of the Citadel, across the Perfume, the enemy seized houses and controlled entire streets, threatening the US advisory compound. At 10:00 a.m., an American Huey helicopter was shot down near the base, but the crew escaped to the compound under heavy fire. Five choppers tried to touch down to retrieve the men, some of whom were wounded, but were driven off by withering enemy fire. By noon, all South Vietnamese and American aircraft were advised to stay clear of Hue.

At a base near Phu Bai, at least one Huey pilot was preparing to ignore that advice. Chief Warrant Officer Fred Ferguson, whose flight service with the 227th Aviation Battalion ran the gamut from carrying troops to jungle landing zones to shipping supplies to isolated outposts, had been following the plight of the downed crew on his radio. He decided to try to get into the compound. "If I was there, I'd want someone to get me out," Ferguson said later. "It was my duty, my job, to get them out."

After takeoff, Ferguson radioed the besieged crew that he was going to attempt a rescue. Flying parallel to the Perfume River and covered by volunteers in three other gunships, he made his approach through enemy mortar rounds and bullets. The chopper took several hits, scattering shrapnel in the cabin.

The only area in the compound where Ferguson had any chance of landing was a small space between one of the buildings and a flagpole. With only a few meters of clearance on either side for the overhead rotor, Ferguson touched down. The downed crew jumped on board as mortar shells slammed into the ground around them. The last of the five men climbed safely aboard, but just then a mortar round exploded near the tail, wounding the crew chief and causing the craft to shudder violently. When Ferguson saw that all were aboard, he applied full power, and the Huey rose slowly.

Just as the chopper got off the ground, a mortar shell landed on the patch of ground where the ship had been. The explosion spun the aircraft around, but Ferguson regained control and continued his ascent, passing within 160 feet of the enemy. The three ships covering for him were shot down and his own gunners ran out of ammunition, but the chopper limped back to Phu Bai. "The helicopter was coming apart," Ferguson remembered. "It was shaking so bad, I couldn't read the instruments." But the Huey made it back with the five men Ferguson had rescued.

In the first week of February, it became apparent that the enemy intended to hold Hue as long as they could. Eight to ten NVA battalions controlled the city, and efforts to dislodge them met with little success. By February 3, four days into the fight, a thousand Marines had arrived in Hue, but they had seized only three blocks. They took on the enemy house-by-house, combat the likes of which had not been seen by Americans since the battle for Seoul in Korea seventeen years earlier.

Sergeant Alfredo Gonzalez was a platoon leader in Alpha Company of the 1st Battalion, 1st Marines, 1st Marine Division, the first unit deployed to Hue on the morning of January 31. After a battle with snipers along Highway 1 south of the city, Gonzalez and the rest of the company climbed aboard five tanks and slowly crossed the Perfume to the Citadel, where they came under immediate attack. A rocket-propelled grenade knocked the Marines off the lead vehicle. Sergeant Gonzalez leaped from his tank, ran down the fire-swept street, and carried one of the men to safety, but was wounded by a fragmentation grenade.

Moving down the street, the men came under attack from a machine gun fired by a guerrilla hidden in a house. Gonzalez led his men to a low wall, then ran up to the window of the

"If I was there, I'd want someone to get me out," Ferguson said later. "It was my duty, my job, to get them out."

house and lobbed in a few grenades, silencing the gun. During the fighting, the Alpha commander was wounded and evacuated, making Gonzalez commander.

The Marines of Company A remained in the thick of the fighting over the next few days. On February 3, Gonzalez was wounded again in street fighting but refused evacuation. The next day, the men were again pinned down by rocket and small-arms fire. Gonzalez picked up single-shot M72 light antitank weapons from the dead and wounded as he moved down the street, firing at enemy positions in the houses and on the rooftops. During this exchange, he was cut down by a burst of enemy machine-gun fire. Sergeant Gonzalez died after five days of fighting in the streets of Hue.

As the Marines continued their push through Hue, the Army moved to cut the supply lines that had allowed the enemy to hold the city. Elements of the 1st Cavalry Division (Airmobile) and the 101st Airborne Division took up positions west of the city and pushed through villages and rice fields toward the Citadel. By February 21, the combined force was about to break through.

In the early afternoon of the 21st, Delta Company of the 2nd Battalion, 501st Infantry, 101st Airborne Division, was approaching a river west of the city when Communist troops fired upon the men from the opposite shore. One squad leader, Sgt. Joe R. Hooper, led eight men across the river. After killing several enemy soldiers, they set up a machine-gun position in the nearby woods. Two grenades exploded nearby, wounding Hooper in the leg and groin, but he went back and led more men into the woods.

Sergeant Alfredo Gonzalez, Company A, 1st Battalion, 1st Marines, was killed in the fight to retake Hue.

Amid rubble and smoke from a napalm strike, US Marines advance up the outer wall of the Citadel at Hue.

Sergeant Joe R. Hooper of the 101st Airborne Division was one of the most decorated soldiers of the Vietnam War.

Staff Sergeant Clifford Sims gave his life to save his comrades battling in the fields west of Hue.

There the fighting intensified. Hooper destroyed five enemy positions and wrestled with several enemy troops, killing one officer with his bayonet. Although bleeding badly, he continued to lead the assault into the woods. Inside the small forest, another squad leader, Staff Sgt. Clifford C. Sims, led his unit against an enemy force that had pinned down another platoon. Moving forward to hook up with another group, the men came upon a burning enemy ammunition shack. Exploding ordnance injured two men almost immediately. Sims moved the rest of his men back, knowing that the rest of the ammunition could blow any time.

On the move again, Sims and his men were advancing through the woods when they suddenly heard a distinctive click: the sound of a trip wire activating a booby trap. Within seconds the charge would explode, killing or wounding many of Sims's men. Shouting a warning to his men, Sims threw himself on the charge and was killed instantly by the blast. Saved by their squad leader, the men pressed on through the woods.

When the battle was over, all but 8 of the 190 Americans in Delta Company had been killed or wounded. Nonetheless, the Americans had overrun a North Vietnamese radio complex that had been relaying messages to Hue. Isolated from their supply and communication lines, the NVA lost control of the Citadel two days later, and the South Vietnamese flag once again went up over the city.

For their actions during the battle at Hue, Fred Ferguson, Alfredo Gonzalez, Joe Hooper, and Clifford Sims later received the Medal of Honor. Despite an unwritten rule prohibiting Medal of Honor recipients from serving again in combat, Joe Hooper returned to Vietnam to serve once more with the 101st Airborne.

The Tet Offensive began the period of the heaviest fighting of the war. After the setbacks suffered during the offensive, North Vietnamese regulars beefed up the depleted ranks of Viet Cong battalions. In subsequent engagements, American forces faced a better-equipped, more professional enemy force. With the escalation of the fighting also came a rise in the number of incidents for which the Medal of Honor was later awarded. Fifty-eight medals were awarded for actions during 1968, more than in any other year of the war.

# DUSTOFF
### *Rescue from Above*

Helicopter evacuation of the wounded was first practiced in Korea, but it came of age in Vietnam. Flying the UH-1 Iroquois, better known as the Huey, American pilots went unarmed into combat areas, loaded on casualties, and took off for field hospitals, often under heavy enemy fire. Such an operation carried the code name "dustoff," after the call sign of an early medevac pilot. To the wounded man in the field, the call sign meant rescue.

Michael J. Novosel was a twenty-two-year-old bomber pilot at the end of World War II. Joining the Army Air Corps ten months before Pearl Harbor, he was eager to see action overseas but spent most of the war as a flight instructor in Texas. In mid-1945, Novosel at last flew a few bombing missions over Japan. In the last days of the war, he also dropped supplies to American POWs in Japanese camps. When Gen. Douglas MacArthur accepted the Japanese surrender on the deck of the USS *Missouri* on September 2, 1945, Lieutenant Novosel piloted one of the B-29s that passed overhead.

Nineteen years later, Novosel, by then a lieutenant colonel in the Air Force Reserve, took a leave of absence from his job as a commercial airline pilot and asked to be returned to active duty and assigned to Vietnam. "I had skills my country needed," he later explained. After being told that the Air Force already had enough officers and that he was too old at forty-two, Novosel enlisted in the Army as a warrant officer, a substantial reduction in rank. Because he did not require extensive training, Novosel recalled, "I came to the Army quite cheap." Neither age nor size (he barely met the five-foot, four-inch minimum height for pilots) deterred him: "Given enough cushions," he joked, "I could fly anything."

In a year of duty in Vietnam, Novosel flew medical evacuation helicopters, ferrying more than two thousand soldiers and civilians from the battlefield to local hospitals. It was a gratifying experience: He remembered thinking, "For the first time, I'm involved in a war and I'm not hurting anybody." After his tour, he was set to go back to his airline, but his discharge physical found that he had glaucoma, disqualifying him from further commercial flying. So Novosel re-enlisted in the Army, where he was able to fly after agreeing to take medication four times a day. By the beginning of October 1969, he was flying Hueys again, this time near the Cambodian border west of Saigon.

At 4:00 p.m. on October 2, Novosel and his three-man crew had been on various dustoff missions for about seven hours when an urgent, highest-priority call came over the radio. A South Vietnamese strike force had been pinned down by the enemy on the border since early morning and now needed immediate medical evacuation. Novosel's Huey, given the call sign "Dustoff 88," headed for the battle area, flying through heavy thunderstorms before coming upon the thick elephant grass of the Plain of Reeds.

A command and control pilot flying overhead told Novosel that three ARVN companies now lay scattered and demoralized below. Hovering over the high grass, Novosel and his crew searched for any wounded men hiding in the growth, but the "friendlies" were unwilling to signal the chopper, fearing exposure to enemy fire. When small-arms fire intensified, Novosel backed off, radioing to the command and control helicopter, "They're most unfriendly down there."

Knowing that there might be men in the high grass, Novosel circled the area, a standard signal to the men below to prepare for evacuation. As he flew clockwise, enemy automatic weapons spit fire from every direction. "I never heard so much enemy fire before," Novosel's veteran crew chief said later, remembering enemy gun flashes "all around us."

One man stood up in the waist-high grass and started running toward the chopper. Novosel dropped to about one meter off the ground, still moving forward to evade fire. The ARVN soldier reached the ship and was pulled aboard by the crew chief and medic. "All of a sudden," Novosel recalled, "we started seeing others all over," waving to the helicopter or running after it as enemy bullets flew around them. Each was pulled in by the crewmen and shoved to the floor. After nine or ten men had been loaded, Novosel headed for his base at Moc Hoa. There he refueled and headed back for more pickups. He rescued a second load, refueled, and then headed back a third time as dusk began to fall. While Air Force jets strafed the area, Novosel flew over a group of soldiers, leading them away from deep irrigation ditches to shallower water.

He was about to head back with his third load when he saw a wounded soldier lying in front of an enemy bunker. Novosel turned his craft around, warned his men to stay down,

In two tours of duty in Vietnam, Chief Warrant Officer Michael Novosel evacuated more than 5,500 wounded men.

and gingerly backed toward the bunker. This tactic would allow for a quick getaway and also put the tail between the passengers and enemy bullets. The chopper reached the man, and the crew chief grabbed him to pull him aboard.

At that moment, an enemy soldier jumped up from the grass in front of the Huey and fired directly at Novosel. An AK-47 round shattered the Plexiglas windshield, sending fragments into his leg and hand. Novosel momentarily lost control of the aircraft, then regained it. The wounded soldier slipped from the crew chief's grasp but held onto the skid of the aircraft as it gained altitude. He was pulled into the helicopter sixty feet off the ground. With another load of wounded, Dustoff 88 headed back to Moc Hoa. In all, Novosel had carried twenty-nine men out of the Plain of Reeds.

Novosel knew that the events of those three hours went "beyond a regular mission. You know when you go a little bit further than you're supposed to." Discounting his own actions, he recommended his three crewmembers for the Silver Star. But as he found out later, his men recommended him for a higher award. On June 15, 1971, President Nixon presented the Medal of Honor to Chief Warrant Officer Michael Novosel as his son, Michael Junior, who served with his father as a dustoff pilot, looked on. (The two Novosels were the only father-son flying team of the war, evacuating more than eight thousand wounded men.) On March 1, 1985, Mike Novosel Sr., the last World War II Army aviator on active duty, retired after forty-four years of military service.

A medevac helicopter, similar to what Chief Warrant Officer Novosel flew in Vietnam, takes off to pick up an injured member of the 101st Airborne Division near the demilitarized zone.

*Opposite*
In Vietnam scenes like this were common: almost nine hundred thousand wounded soldiers and civilians were evacuated by helicopter to field hospitals.

When Novosel was awarded his Army "Master Aviator" badge, it was pinned on by Maj. Patrick Henry Brady, who had been a dustoff pilot since 1964. Brady acquired a reputation as an especially good foul weather flier, able to operate in even "zero-zero" conditions, when rain or fog allowed only minimum visibility in both distance and altitude.

Such were the conditions in the mountains near Chu Lai on the morning of January 6, 1968. After a firefight in the area known as "Death Valley," two ARVN soldiers lay badly wounded on the valley floor. A thick ground fog made it seem unlikely they would be evacuated. Early that morning, Major Brady, the most experienced pilot in the 54th Medical Detachment and the one who flew most of the "weather missions," took off to try to reach the wounded men.

*Right*
Major Patrick Brady in a medevac helicopter.

*Far right*
In addition to the Medal of Honor, Patrick Brady received the Distinguished Flying Cross for heroism and extraordinary achievement in aerial flight in Vietnam on June 21, 1964. Pictured here, Col. William A. Hamrick congratulates Brady on November 28, 1964, upon receiving the Distinguished Flying Cross.

Patrick Henry Brady earned a reputation as an excellent foul-weather dustoff pilot in Vietnam.

The fog was several hundred feet deep, so Brady used a technique he had perfected on previous missions in fog. Tilting his UH-1H sideways, he used the chopper's rotor to blow away some of the mist. He found a trail on the valley floor and followed it, staying at an angle to cut through the stubborn murkiness and also to avoid presenting a clear target for the enemy. "The VC couldn't see me, so I was pretty secure," Brady remembered. "The trick was just flying sideways in that ground fog." Hugging the treetops, Brady came upon a small clearing near the ARVN troops and touched down. His crew helped the wounded aboard and "Dustoff 55" took off through the mist and headed for the hospital at Chu Lai.

On the way to the base, Brady received another call to fly to the Hiep Duc Valley to the north, after dropping off his patients. A hilltop firebase had come under attack overnight, and now at least sixty men of the 198th Light Infantry Brigade lay wounded on the hillside and in the valley below the firebase. Two other aircraft had been shot down trying to reach the men in the fog, and enemy troops were within 160 feet of the Americans.

Descending through the fog from the firebase, the helicopter passed over the heads of a group of North Vietnamese regulars, but disappeared too fast to draw any fire. On the valley floor, recalled Brady, "there was a hell of a fight going on." Flying through occasional enemy fire, he landed at the pickup site, where his crewmen took on twelve wounded. The Huey rose straight up through the fog and returned to the firebase to the cheers of the waiting men. After explaining the rescue procedure to the other pilots, Brady led four ships down into the mist, but the pilots all panicked and turned back. So Dustoff 55 went down alone three more times, carrying out thirty-nine men.

In subsequent missions that day, Pat Brady rescued soldiers from two more locations, including a minefield. It was well after dark when he ended his day's work. He had evacuated fifty-one men, using three helicopters, but he considered January 6, 1968, "a series of rather routine missions. I had a lot worse days." Still, Major Brady's actions on that particular day impressed more than one eyewitness, and he was recommended for the Medal of Honor, which he received at the White House on October 9, 1969. Brady remained in the Army after the war to become a brigadier general in 1985.

# AIRBORNE VALOR
## *The War in the Skies*

Some Americans in Vietnam only saw the jungle from the air. In fast-moving aircraft they took to the skies, operating hundreds, even thousands of feet above the humid plains and jungles of Vietnam, striking military and industrial targets in North Vietnam and supporting American and ARVN ground troops in the South. Many fliers were career military men, experienced veterans of Korea and World War II. Some were recruits fresh out of flight school. All fought a war of modern machines, flying faster and controlling weapons more lethal and accurate than ever before.

The largest concentration of antiaircraft guns ever assembled guarded the area around Hanoi. The defensive arsenal ranged from small hand-sighted machine guns to radar-guided surface-to-air missiles. Every day, American pilots dodged heavy fire in raids against North Vietnam. Every flier faced being shot down and killed or taken prisoner. Many never came back.

Part of the American air arsenal was the F-105 Thunderchief fighter-bomber, or "Thud." Although primarily used as a conventional bomber, it could be equipped with radar detection and jamming equipment for use as a "Wild Weasel" for attack missions against SAM (surface-to-air missile) sites and to protect strike-force bombers. For Air Force Maj. Leo K. Thorsness, one Wild Weasel mission turned into a hair-raising dogfight and rescue attempt.

On April 19, 1967, Thorsness and his backseater, Capt. Harry Johnson, who tended to the navigation and target equipment, were part of a four-aircraft team attacking the defenses at the Xuan Mai army base, about forty miles southwest of Hanoi. A few miles southeast of the base, the Wild Weasel's radar picked up a SAM site ahead. Maneuvering into position, Thorsness launched a Shrike missile with a device that homed in on the SAM's radar. Seconds

An F-105F Thunderchief similar to the one used by Maj. Leo Thorsness to engage enemy MiGs over North Vietnam on April 19, 1967.

Leo Thorsness is released by the North Vietnamese in Hanoi, March 4, 1973. Thorsness had learned from a fellow prisoner that he was to be awarded the Medal of Honor.

later the blip disappeared from the screen, indicating the SAM site had been destroyed.

Turning north, Thorsness headed for another SAM site with his wingman, Capt. Tom Madison. Thorsness dove toward the emplacement, releasing a cluster bomb at eight thousand feet, then dropped another three thousand feet in time to see the site explode. Unsure of the location of additional SAM sites, Thorsness and Madison stayed close to the ground, on the lookout for more.

But with increased visibility came greater danger. Ground fire erupted around the two Wild Weasels, and soon Madison radioed that he had been hit. Thorsness ordered him to head for the nearby hills and ditch the craft if necessary, then listened for a radio signal in case Madison and his backseater, Capt. Tom Sterling, ejected. Seconds later, a high-pitched beep told him that the two men had bailed out.

Thorsness, now the only Wild Weasel pilot in the area, headed for the descending parachutes of his fellow fliers. Suddenly an enemy MiG-17 appeared at nine o'clock. "I wasn't sure whether he was going to attack the parachutes," Thorsness recalled later, "so I said, 'Why not?' and took off after him." No sooner had he pulled up for a shot at the enemy plane than Johnson's voice crackled in his headphones: "Leo, we've got MiGs on our ass!" Thorsness hit the front MiG with his second 20mm cannon burst, then switched on his afterburner to outrun the pursuers. After he had lost them, he rendezvoused with an airborne tanker over Laos and refueled while a convoy of choppers and small planes was dispatched to pick up Madison and Sterling. Thorsness and Johnson headed back to Xuan Mai as darkness fell to provide cover for the rescue team, even though they were low on ammunition.

As Thorsness briefed the pilots from the rescue team by radio, he spotted three MiGs ahead. Johnson warned him of four more closing on the rear. He turned the aircraft toward the mountains, twisting through valleys and around peaks; at least one MiG crashed in the hills as Thorsness outran his pursuers. Again low on fuel and now out of ammunition, Thorsness headed for the remaining MiGs to divert them from the rescue craft. At last, more F-105s arrived on the scene, and Thorsness and Johnson headed back to their base in Thailand. (Despite the efforts of Thorsness and the other pilots, the MiGs made the rescue of Sterling and Madison impossible. The two men spent the next six years in a North Vietnamese prison.)

Nearing a tanker on the way back, Thorsness received an urgent call from another pilot who was also low on fuel. He directed the tanker to the other plane and headed for base, hoping that his fuel would hold out. "With just seventy miles to go, I pulled the power back to idle and we just glided in," he said. "We were indicating 'empty' when the runway came up in front of us, and we landed a little long."

Eleven days later, on another Wild Weasel mission, Thorsness and Johnson were shot down and taken prisoner by North Vietnam. Not until after his release in 1973 was Lt. Col. Thorsness presented with the Air Force Medal of Honor by President Nixon for his actions on that April day six years earlier.

Thorsness earned the Medal of Honor for fighting enemy MiGs while assisting in the rescue of downed crew members.

Airborne acts of valor were not limited to pilots and officers. Although Air Force Medals of Honor were usually given for actions carried out while flying a plane or helicopter, one medal was awarded for quick thinking and courage on the part of a gunship crewman that saved the lives of his fellow fliers.

At 8:00 p.m. on February 24, 1969, an Air Force AC-47 gunship took off from Bien Hoa airfield near Saigon on a scheduled patrol around the capital. Nicknamed "Puff the Magic Dragon," AC-47s were equipped with three rapid-firing 7.62mm miniguns and magnesium illumination flares to provide light for ground troops below or to highlight a target. Because of its use in nighttime actions, the AC-47 had acquired the call sign "Spooky."

One of "Spooky 71's" eight-man crew that night was twenty-three-year-old Airman 1st Class John L. Levitow,

President Richard Nixon awards the Medal of Honor to Leo Thorsness in 1973 as his family looks on.

who had been transferred to Vietnam the previous July. Levitow was filling in for a sick friend that night. As gunship loadmaster, his job was to set the timing and ignition controls on each flare before it was dropped underneath a parachute. Levitow would adjust the three-foot-long, twenty-seven-pound cylinder, then pass it to Sgt. Ellis Owen, the gunner, who would pull the lanyard, which triggered the flare's time-delay firing mechanism, and drop the flare out the open cargo door at the command of the pilot.

Four hours after takeoff, Spooky 71 had just finished firing on enemy positions outside of Bien Hoa when it received a request for illumination near Long Binh, the large military complex just north of Saigon. Pilot Maj. Ken Carpenter turned toward Long Binh and the flashes of enemy mortars. Amid enemy shelling, Owen began dropping illumination rounds.

Suddenly the gunship was jarred by a tremendous blast. An enemy 82mm shell had struck the right wing and exploded inside the frame, rocking the entire plane. A three-foot hole was blown in the side of the aircraft, sending shrapnel flying across the cabin.

Four crewmen, including Levitow, were knocked off their feet. As Owen fell to the floor, he inadvertently pulled the lanyard from one flare. The cylinder rolled across the cabin, fully charged. In ten seconds, the parachute canister would explode, and another ten seconds later the magnesium would ignite, causing a blast of heat reaching four thousand degrees Fahrenheit.

John Levitow had taken over forty shrapnel wounds in his right leg and hip, a sensation that he later recalled "felt like a two-by-four had been struck against my side." He pulled himself up and helped one of the more severely wounded men to the front of the plane. Then he turned around and saw the live flare lying between the number one gun and some ammunition cans.

"From that point," Levitow said later, "I don't remember anything. My mind went blank." As the wounded men watched, Levitow moved to the back of the plane and fell on the flare. He slowly and painfully dragged himself toward the open cargo door, his wounds leaving a trail of blood. Though he almost lost consciousness, Levitow finally reached the door and shoved out the armed flare. Moments later it exploded with a brilliant white flash.

Spooky 71, with a hole in its wing caused by a blast from an enemy shell.

Levitow remembered being conscious as the plane landed at Bien Hoa and being loaded onto a medical chopper still wearing his radio headset. Major Carpenter pieced together what had happened by studying the trail of blood on the cabin floor and recommended Levitow for the nation's highest decoration, saying that he had "never seen such a courageous act performed under such adverse circumstances."

When John Levitow received the Medal of Honor on May 14, 1970, he became the only enlisted man and the youngest to receive the Air Force award during the war. Asked what made him risk his life to get rid of that flare, Levitow chuckled and said, "Temporary insanity."

# HELL HOLE
## *Prisoners of War*

For most American soldiers, one of the greatest fears was being captured by the enemy. One put it simply: "I'd rather die." Seven hundred and sixty-six men were taken prisoner by the North Vietnamese and Viet Cong, most of them Air Force and Navy Airmen shot down over the North. Because the United States never declared war on North Vietnam, the Communists refused to honor the Geneva guidelines regarding POWs. Instead, they withheld mail, tortured them to the brink of death, and constantly tried to force them to confess to being war criminals against the people of Vietnam. Throughout this ordeal, most of the men resisted, surreptitiously organizing and communicating to bond together to follow the Prisoners' Code of Conduct.

The stars were shining brightly overhead as US Air Force Major George "Bud" Day crawled out of his tiny underground cell, unseen by his North Vietnamese guard. It was Friday night, September 1, 1967. Shot down near Vinh Linh just five days before, Day, a forty-two-year-old veteran of both World War II and Korea, had been beaten several times, then placed in an underground bunker, stripped to his shorts with hands and feet bound. He had worked his way out of his knots and escaped from his cell. Now he prepared to navigate by the stars to reach South Vietnam, some thirty miles away.

Day was barely fit to travel. His arm had been broken in three places during the ejection from his F-100 Supersabre fighter, and his sprained left knee was now swollen from his having been hung upside down for several hours by his captors. Limping through the mud, his right arm totally encased in a crude cast, Day set out for freedom.

Slogging through the paddies, feeling with every step the terrible pain of his injuries, Day could see the moving lights of his pursuers behind him. When he reached solid ground, he

American gunships, like this AC-47 Spooky, were armed with machine guns, tracer bullets, and flares for nighttime operations. They provided spectacular displays of concentrated firepower in the skies over South Vietnam.

Captain James Stockdale as a prisoner of war at Hoa Lo Prison, February 1973.

cut his feet running on sharp rocks strewn over land that had been devastated by American bombs and artillery. During the next few days he survived on berries, one bael fruit, and two frogs, swallowed live.

Day had stopped to rest when an American rocket or shell landed right near him, tossing him up in the air, wounding him in the right leg, and rupturing his sinuses and eardrums. With virtually no equilibrium and vomiting profusely, Day lay in the brush "like a sick animal" for several days. When he was able to rise he limped south and came upon a sight over which he had flown many times. It was the Ben Hai River, the boundary between North and South Vietnam in the DMZ.

Sleeping near the edge of the river, trying to muster the strength to cross, Day once again came under a barrage of American artillery. His ears and nose started bleeding and he lost his sense of direction. At last he got his bearings and floated across the Ben Hai, clinging to a bamboo log.

Although he was now in South Vietnam, Day knew that there was still a very good chance that he would run into North Vietnamese, so he carefully concealed his movements. He came upon enemy units but was able to evade them.

Finally, over one week after his escape, Day thought that salvation had come when an American scout plane passed overhead. He tried to signal the aircraft, but the pilot did not see him. Later Day tried to flag down two Marine helicopters, but once again he was not seen. After these two missed chances, Day said later, "I could have cried."

Freedom continued to tantalize him. Hearing more helicopters and artillery guns, Day knew that he was near a Marine camp but wondered if he had the strength to go farther. Down to almost one hundred pounds, his arm mangled under the wet, broken cast, his legs throbbing, Day was "almost at the end of my tether. If I was going to make it, it was going to have to be today or tomorrow."

As he headed toward the American base, Day was startled to hear excited shouting and turned to see two teenage Vietnamese boys running toward him. Realizing from their AK-47s that they were the enemy, he jumped into the bushes just as two rounds cut into his hand and thigh. Soon the youths were upon him. One of them cocked his rifle and kicked Day as he lay on the ground. His twelve-day bid for freedom was over. He was taken back to the camp he had escaped, and then on to Hanoi's Hoa Lo prison, the central jail for prisoners of war.

Built by the French at the end of the nineteenth century, Hoa Lo (Vietnamese for "hot furnace," also known as "Hell Hole") stood in downtown Hanoi, a few miles from the residence of Ho Chi Minh. Surrounded by five-meter walls topped with broken glass and barbed wire, the camp held approximately 150 men in three sectors given names by the Americans: "New Guy Village," "Heartbreak Hotel," and "Las Vegas." Although many prisoners were moved to various prisons around Hanoi, a substantial number spent some time at "The Hanoi Hilton."

As in past wars, American prisoners were obligated to follow the orders of senior commanders in the camp, just as they would in normal military situations. The senior officer at Hoa Lo was Capt. James Bond Stockdale, a Navy pilot shot down in September 1965 (and the cousin of Robert Dunlap, a World War II Medal of Honor recipient). By means of the "tap code," which allowed Americans to communicate from cell to cell, Stockdale established a command chain, issuing orders to resist North Vietnamese efforts to extract "confessions" or use the prisoners for other propaganda purposes.

Stockdale had a special reason to be concerned about being used for propaganda statements. On August 4, 1964, Stockdale had flown one of three jets supporting the *Maddox* and the *C. Turner Joy* in the Gulf of Tonkin. The vessels radioed that they were coming under attack from North Vietnamese boats that night, but after searching the stormy waters and not seeing any enemy ships, Stockdale became convinced that the Gulf of Tonkin incident, the "enemy attack" that caused Congress and many Americans to support President Johnson's handling of the war, was nothing but "a Chinese fire drill."

After being shot down, Jim Stockdale lived in fear that the North Vietnamese would somehow discover that he possessed "the most damaging information a North Vietnamese torturer could possibly extract from an American prisoner." Every torture session, every statement he was asked to sign, brought new anxieties: "When was the Tonkin Gulf shoe to fall? How in God's name was I going to handle it?"

At the beginning of September 1969, a torture session pushed Stockdale to the limits of his resistance. After his guard had left, Stockdale, as he later recounted, thought quickly. "I've got to go on the offensive. . . . I have to stop that interrogation. I have to stop the *flow*. If it costs, it costs."

Once released, when the Pentagon lifted the restrictions that kept POWs from describing conditions in Communist prison camps, Col. Robinson Risner and four other POWs described the tortures they endured while in North Vietnamese prison camps. Left to right: Col. Fred V. Cherry; Col. Risner, who was deputy commander of all American POWs; Col. Norman Gaddis; and Lt. Col. John Dramosi.

Americans were given cellmates later in the war, when their captors allowed photographers into the camps.

Moving to a window, he broke the glass with the heel of his hand, grabbed one of the large pieces, and sat down in the center of the room. He quickly chopped at his wrists with the shard, causing blood to ooze all over his arms and onto the floor. Wringing his hand to increase the flow of blood, Stockdale collapsed on the floor as his jailers returned.

Stockdale's wounds were bandaged, and he was not tortured the next day. When one of his jailers told him that he would be moved out of the torture room, Stockdale realized that his bold action had worked. The North Vietnamese never asked Stockdale about the Gulf of Tonkin incident.

As Stockdale, Day, and the other Americans continued to follow the code of conduct for prisoners, conditions improved slightly at the camps. In the early 1970s, the North Vietnamese realized that the Americans might soon be released; as a result, beatings occurred less often, and many prisoners who had been in solitary confinement were allowed roommates. In turn, the prisoners became more daring in their expressions of solidarity. In February 1971, some inmates of Hoa Lo gathered quietly for a religious service, forbidden by camp rules. After the guards burst in and broke up the gathering, Day started singing "The Star Spangled Banner," and Stockdale and the other Americans quickly joined in. One by one, the other prison buildings broke out in song. Stockdale wrote later that although he was punished for the episode, it was exhilarating: "Our minds were now free, and we knew it."

On January 27, 1973, the Paris Accords were signed, and the American combat role in the Vietnam War came to an end. Over the next two months, 473 Americans walked across the tarmac of Hanoi's Gia Lam Airport to waiting Air Force C-141s—and freedom. As they took off, they left behind a nightmare that for some had dragged on for eight years.

Day, Stockdale, and Capt. Lance P. Sijan, an Air Force pilot who died in captivity, were recommended by their fellow prisoners for the Medal of Honor for their conduct as POWs. On March 4, 1976, Day, Stockdale, and Sijan's family were presented medals by President Gerald Ford.

James Stockdale's public story might have ended there, but his heroism was brought to light twice more: In 1992, presidential candidate Ross Perot asked him to join the Reform Party ticket as candidate for vice president (he famously introduced himself in the televised debate, "Who am I? Why am I here?") And in 2002, business management guru Jim Collins coined "The Stockdale Paradox" based on Stockdale's resolution in captivity. The Stockdale Paradox states that those who survive difficult circumstances are the ones who confront the most brutal facts of their current situation, while still maintaining faith they will prevail.

Rear Admiral James Stockdale receives the Medal of Honor from President Gerald Ford.

## CONCLUDING THE WAR

As the war wore on, the American public showed signs of exhaustion. While US forces had the upper hand in the vast majority of actions against the enemy, the Communist Tet Offensive in 1968 shattered the illusion that an American victory was in sight. The generation that had been told that fighting the war was "the thing to do" questioned the conflict in much greater numbers. Popular opposition continued to climb: By March 1968, polls showed a majority of Americans had come to believe that US involvement in Vietnam was a mistake. Later that month, President Johnson opened the door for a negotiated settlement, denying Westmoreland's request for more than two hundred thousand additional troops and announcing that he would not seek reelection.

Johnson's successor, Richard Nixon, began to reduce American participation in the fighting. He pushed "Vietnamization," an ultimately futile process that was supposed to shore up ARVN forces to continue the fight alone. To Nixon, however, withdrawal did not necessarily mean weakness: The fury of the Christmas 1972 bombing of North Vietnam indicated that "Peace with Honor" included a clear exhibition of American might.

The Paris Accords signed in January 1973 and the North Vietnamese conquest of the South two years later made many Americans wonder what the country had been doing in Vietnam in the first place. But after fifty-eight thousand American deaths, billions of dollars, and twenty years, the answer to such a question was still not evident. The war had split America in two. It took nearly a decade for the wounds to start to heal.

# CHAPTER SEVEN

# New Enemies, New Conflicts

## 1990–Present

# A New World Order

**O**N SEPTEMBER 11, 1990, President George H. W. Bush addressed a joint session of Congress on the looming prospect of war in the Middle East. Two months before, Iraq's dictator Saddam Hussein had invaded the tiny oil-rich kingdom of Kuwait, which sits at the head of the Persian Gulf. Hussein stood poised to invade Saudi Arabia and control oil resources that fed the world's largest economies.

Bush and his advisors had witnessed the collapse of the Soviet Union in the previous two years and managed the end of the Cold War with steady, calm diplomacy. For a brief time, some scholars spoke of "the end of history," as capitalist democracy spread through Eastern Europe. The Soviet Union devolved into a "Commonwealth of Independent States," in fact nine separate, often quarrelling nations. As Russia turned inward to consolidate its changes, America remained as the world's only true superpower. Domestic concerns moved to the fore, and the defense buildup begun under President Ronald Reagan slowed. Politicians spoke of a "peace dividend" that would move America's time, money, and attention to problems at home, because the threat everyone feared—another great land war in Europe—effectively disappeared with the fall of the Berlin Wall.

On that September night in 1990, Bush called on the United States and its allies to achieve "a victory over tyranny and savage aggression," and named the coming age with a memorable phrase:

"For two centuries, we've done the hard work of freedom. . . . What is at stake is a big idea—a *New World Order*—where diverse nations are drawn together in common cause to achieve the universal aspirations of mankind."

Eleven years later to the day, a different President Bush addressed a nation shaken to its core by the most deadly attack on its soil since the Civil War. Although American military men and women had continued the fight against tyranny and savage aggression in the intervening decade, what George W. Bush called "the very worst of human nature" arose like a many-headed hydra around the world, this time in the form of the terrorist attacks of September 11, 2001.

*Previous pages*
Iraqi tanks destroyed by coalition forces in the liberation of Kuwait are gathered near Ali al-Salem military airfield in Northern Kuwait. The military equipment left in working condition is rumored to be used now for target practice by the Kuwaiti armed forces.

New York City firefighters walk through the rubble at the World Trade Center, the skeletal remains of the Twin Towers behind them. On the morning of September 11, 2001, two hijacked planes were crashed into the Twin Towers in Manhattan, killing nearly three thousand people, including hundreds of firefighters involved in rescue operations.

# A DIFFERENT ENEMY

The elder Bush was correct that a new world was emerging, but it was more complex, dangerous, and disordered that anyone imagined. In the next decade, American soldiers, sailors, and Airmen fought in numerous undeclared wars in the world's trouble spots. Instead of leading a bloc of democracies against a single opponent, the United States acted as a de facto global police force, trying in fits and starts to impose order where its economic, political, or humanitarian interests were threatened.

In the Gulf War to liberate Kuwait, the American military demonstrated its unmatched ability to enforce international will (and America demonstrated its political ability to shape that will). George H. W. Bush and his Secretary of State James A. Baker united a broad coalition of nations, including fellow Arab states, to force Hussein back.

An aerial bombardment of Iraqi targets in Kuwait and Iraq commenced in January. Within days, Secretary of Defense Dick Cheney commented that, Scud missiles and five hundred thousand troops notwithstanding, Hussein could not "change the basic course of the war." General Colin Powell, the Chairman of the Joint Chiefs, previewed the war plan: "Our strategy to go after this army is very, very simple. First we're going to cut it off, and then we're going to kill it." The ground war, a vast armored flanking maneuver commanded by Gen. Norman Schwarzkopf, ejected the Iraqi military from Kuwait in one hundred hours. Its stated objective met, the military did not press on to conquer Iraq. Saddam Hussein remained in control of his country. America had demonstrated both overwhelming power and political/military restraint.

US Navy F-14A Tomcat in flight over burning Kuwaiti oil wells set ablaze by retreating Iraqi forces during the Gulf War, 1991.

Politically, the triumph of Western-style democracy over Soviet-style communism meant liberation for a number of countries, particularly in Eastern Europe. Actual democracy and individual freedom was still a dream for most of the world's people. China's government wiped out a nascent democracy movement at Tiananmen Square in 1989. Many former Soviet republics languished under new dictatorships or were split by ethnic rivalries. In Africa, sectarian and tribal warfare led to horrors like the 1994 genocide in Rwanda, in which up to a million people were killed. For much of the 1990s, remnants of the former Yugoslavia warred among each other. Dictatorships and narco-states from Pakistan to Panama suppressed their populations and made trouble for the West.

In such a world, the rationale for American military action became complex and at times inconsistent. The United States and the rest of the world stood by in impotent witness to the horrors of

Names of the 248 people killed in the 1998 bombing of the US embassy are seen on the memorial wall in Nairobi, Kenya. The Cooperative Bank building, which was also damaged in the August 7, 1998, truck bomb attacks aimed at US embassies in Kenya, is reflected on the memorial wall.

Rwanda, but American air power twice halted wars in the former Yugoslavia. The first President Bush conducted an illegal invasion of Panama to bring its drug-dealing dictator Manuel Noriega to an American court of law. President Bill Clinton supported a military-humanitarian mission he inherited from Bush in Somalia but withdrew American troops after a sharp battle against militia in the streets of Mogadishu, a fight in which two soldiers earned the Medal of Honor.

Most worrisome to American military and political leaders was the rise of "non-state actors." These were not countries but elusive organizations united by grievance against the West, sectarian divides, and ancient rivalries. The 1,400-year-old schism between Shiite and Sunni factions of Islam fueled the rise of such groups in the Persian Gulf, where Iraq and Iran had fought a bloody eight-year war in the 1980s. Afghanistan, which had driven out Soviet occupiers after ten years, devolved into its traditional state of warring factions until the Islamic fundamentalist Taliban took over the country in 1996. The anti-Western Taliban provided a home base for the most effective and sophisticated non-state actor, a terrorist organization calling itself Al-Qaeda ("the base").

Al-Qaeda was founded by Osama bin Laden, a wealthy Saudi Arabian who viewed America's presence in Saudi Arabia during the Gulf War as an abomination against his religion. Over a decade, he and his associates carried out attacks on American targets around the world. In 1993, Al-Qaeda operative Ramzi Yousef detonated a truck filled with explosives in a parking garage beneath the World Trade Center in New York, an attack that killed six and wounded more than a thousand. Al-Qaeda associates bombed embassies in Kenya and Tanzania in 1998; in 2000 a suicide bomber killed seventeen American sailors on the guided-missile destroyer USS *Cole*.

Investigations of the *Cole* bombing showed that certain hostile governments, such as those in Sudan and Afghanistan, helped Al-Qaeda with safe haven, money, and material support. The United States responded with sanctions and occasional cruise missile strikes but did not engage in full-scale warfare until the attacks of September 11, 2001.

## THE FOREVER WAR

Almost three thousand people died in the 9/11 attacks on the World Trade Center in New York, on the Pentagon in Virginia, and in the foiled airliner attack that ended with a crash near Shanksville, Pennsylvania. The attacks were quickly tied to Al-Qaeda and its home base in Afghanistan. By early October, American and allied air forces bombed both Al-Qaeda and Taliban targets, and within a few weeks, the combined operations of allied military and an Afghan militia called the Northern Alliance had driven the Taliban from the capital, Kabul. On December 9, the Taliban evacuated its last Afghan redoubt in the city of Kandahar, its leaders escaping into the mountains of Pakistan. Later that month, Osama bin Laden escaped into Pakistan after a battle with Afghan militia in the mountains of Tora Bora.

Although bin Laden and Taliban leader Mullah Omar had quit the country, and an interim government friendly to the West had taken control of the capital, Afghanistan remained, as it had been for centuries, a land of warring factions, tribal loyalties and rivalries, and shifting battlegrounds. Soldiers, sailors, and Airmen of the United States and its allies began a long series of operations meant to root out Taliban and Al-Qaeda fighters from their strongholds. With few set-piece battles, devilishly difficult terrain, and a weak and corrupt central government as its host, military operations became smaller, if no less deadly. America's Special Forces, CIA-associated fighters, and regular units trained Afghans to take over the war and looked forward to a final withdrawal. It would not come for more than twelve years, making Afghanistan the longest war in American history.

In the meantime, the younger President Bush and his advisors turned their attention elsewhere.

Following the 9/11 attacks, Bush used the term "War on Terrorism" to describe a new political and military stance. The US military, law enforcement, and intelligence apparatuses would all pursue non-state actors who directed terrorist attacks at Americans and their allies. Terrorist attacks continued sporadically around the world, usually in the form of bombs against civilians in marketplaces, on transportation and infrastructure targets—anywhere large numbers of people gathered. Some groups were associated with a radical vision of Islam, some with a specific political or social grievance. All used terror as a tactic, and in a time of easily concealed weapons and worldwide communications, individual terrorists and their organizations had no central location. The "War on Terror" was a long struggle against diverse enemies, not war as the world had come to think of it, as national armies clashing in battle. There would be no surrender documents to sign, and no event that marked the end of conflict. The War on Terror was a forever war.

Pictured is the damage sustained by the USS *Cole* after a suspected terrorist bomb exploded during a refueling operation in Yemen on October 12, 2000.

# Peacekeepers at War
## Mogadishu 1993

**W**HEN SOMALIA'S MILITARY LEADER Mohamed Siad Barre was overthrown in a coup in January 1991, few Americans took notice. The event was similar to so many other troubles in post-colonial Africa. Occupying the horn of Africa, Somalia had strategic positioning near sea routes to the Suez Canal and Persian Gulf but otherwise seemed a dry and miserable home of periodic droughts and constant feuding. Fighting continued among the coalition that overthrew Siad Barre, destroying farmland and causing widespread hunger by late 1991. Three hundred thousand Somalis starved to death in a year. The world responded with food aid, but 80 percent of it was stolen by militias who bartered food for weapons and influence. The United Nations humanitarian mission requested help, and in December 1992, departing President George H. W. Bush deployed twenty-five thousand US troops to secure delivery of help in Operation Restore Hope. Bush hoped the troops would return in time for the inauguration of President-elect Bill Clinton one month later, but Somalia proved difficult to leave.

Clinton drew down the American presence as UN soldiers from Pakistan, Malaysia, and other countries took over the mission. After six months, 1,200 American soldiers remained, but then a string of militia killings—of Pakistani and Italian soldiers, Western journalists, and American troops—caused the United Nations and then the United States to pursue the arrest of Mohamed Farrah Aidid, a warlord who led an alliance of warlords called the Somali National Alliance. Clinton approved the deployment to Mogadishu of four hundred US Army Rangers and Delta Force commandos, as well as sixteen helicopters of the 160th Special Operations Aviation Regiment, Navy SEALs, and Air Force personnel from the 24th Special Tactics Squadron. Led by Maj. Gen. William F. Garrison, Task Force Rangers arrived on August 22 with the mission to find and arrest Aidid and his senior commanders.

### INTO THE MAZE

Task Force Rangers scored some quick arrests of Aidid sympathizers and operators but also suffered embarrassments such as the inadvertent arrest of UN personnel. A US helicopter (not part of the task force) was downed by a militia rocket propelled grenade (RPG) near Mogadishu, killing three crew members. Mogadishu itself was a frustrating hunting ground; a sprawling grid of narrow streets and alleyways filled with civilians, various militia members, and an inexhaustible supply of small arms. It was an easy place in which to hide and a difficult place in which to hunt. Aidid remained at large and in power.

On October 3, the task force received intelligence that top Aidid commanders would meet in a building near the Olympic Hotel, a central city landmark. Garrison ordered the

> Mogadishu itself was a frustrating hunting ground; a sprawling grid of narrow streets and alleyways filled with civilians, various militia members, and an inexhaustible supply of small arms.

A US soldier patrols a Mogadishu street during Operation Restore Hope.

push-off of Operation Gothic Serpent, an intricate land-air operation to capture them. Task Force Ranger soldiers flew into Mogadishu in UH-60 Black Hawk helicopters. AH-1 Cobra and MH-6 Little Bird gunships provided extra firepower from the air with Gatling-type miniguns and TOW antitank missiles. Delta Force snipers prepared to shoot from the air or ground at enemy soldiers in the tight urban setting. An infantry convoy drove from the American outpost at Mogadishu airport toward the suspected gathering in Humvees and trucks, intending to pick up prisoners after their arrest. American weaponry was light and the plan called for a quick in-and-out strike.

The initial shock attack on the building almost went according to plan. Rangers and commandos dropped by ropes from Black Hawks. Gunships pounded the building as civilians fled the area. As Rangers set up a protective perimeter, Delta Forces entered the building and took twenty-four Somalis prisoner. Aidid was nowhere to be found, however, and following the attack, Somali militia from all over the city ran toward the site. The sound of AK-47 fire and RPGs echoed in streets and alleys.

A few blocks away, an RPG struck an American Black Hawk *Super Six One* in the tail. The explosion disabled the aircraft and it plunged to the ground. The pilots, Chief Warrant Officers Cliff Wolcott and Donovan Briley, were killed, but crew survived the crash. Chief Warrant Officers Keith Jones and Karl Maier, pilots of Little Bird *Star Four One*, flew to the crash site to rescue survivors. Air Force Tech. Sgt. Tim Wilkinson and Delta Force medic

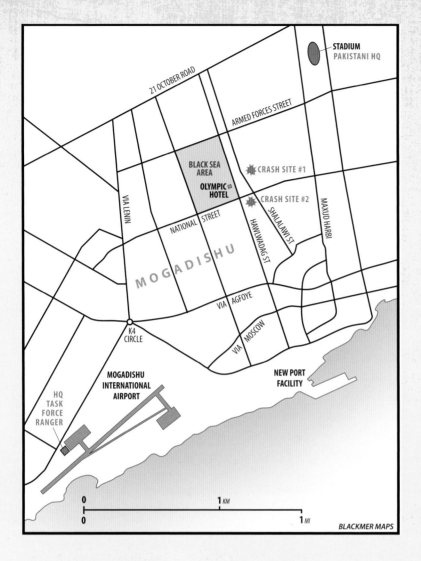

A map of Mogadishu in 1993, showing the crash sites of the two Black Hawk helicopters.

Sergeant Bob Mabry arrived on foot, and with crash survivor Delta Force sniper Sgt. James McMahon and crew member Staff Sgt. Daniel Busch, they struggled to free the living and the dead under fire. A team of Rangers set out from the original target building to the crash site.

A mile southwest of *Super Six One*, Chief Warrant Officer Mike Durant flew Black Hawk *Super Six Four* in support of the Rangers and Deltas he had dropped off at the arrest site. A nearby pilot saw Durant's tail rotor hit by an RPG, but the chopper stayed flying and *Super Six Four* turned back toward the airport. Suddenly the tail rotor assembly disintegrated, and the Black Hawk spun down toward the street. At the last moment its spin slowed, and the craft banged down to a level rest four blocks south of the Olympic Hotel. A mob of militia and civilians quickly gathered near the craft. Severely injured in the crash and surrounded by hostile Somali fighters, Durant and his three-man crew seemed doomed.

Above the hulk of *Super Six Four*, the Black Hawk *Super Six Two* circled, and three Delta Force sergeants, all snipers, tried to suppress the growing crowd of armed and unarmed Somalis with their sniper rifles. The helicopter took small arms fire from below, but pilot Mike Goffena eluded a killing strike and Master Sgt. Gary Gordon, Sgt. 1st Class Randy Shughart, and Sgt. 1st Class Brad Hollings fought back from the doorways of the Black Hawk, singling out Somalis who held RPGs. Americans in nearby Little Birds also tried to push back the mob with fire from above.

The crew would have to be evacuated by men on the ground, and a rescue team unit was dispatched from the arrest site but quickly ran into fire. The crew of *Super Six Two* determined that the Rangers would arrive too late, and requested permission to insert their Delta snipers to protect survivors. A crewman was injured and Hollings took over his door-mounted minigun. That left Shughart and Gordon. Goffena dropped his Black Hawk low and the two sergeants jumped out and then ran to crash site two.

Gordon and Shughart lifted Durant, whose leg was broken, from the cockpit and set him, armed with a machine pistol, in what shelter they could find. They set a perimeter with the wounded crew, shooting at the mob that receded and then advanced like a tide. *Super Six Two* continued to swoop and attack militia fighters until it too was struck by an RPG and limped off to land in friendly territory, with a severely wounded Brad Hollings bleeding by his gun.

Hostile Somalis kept coming, over walls, through shanties, near the helicopter. Gordon and the crew were killed by intense gunfire. Shughart brought another weapon to Durant,

Somalis observe the wreckage of a US helicopter in a Mogadishu
street after it was shot down during a battle with Somali fighters.

Master Sergeant Gary Gordon (top) and Sgt. 1st Class Randall Shughart (above), who died trying to protect the crew of their Black Hawk helicopter in Mogadishu.

US soldiers return fire at snipers from behind a wall outside the compound of Somali warlord Mohamed Farrah Aidid in Mogadishu. Somali supporters of Aidid shot down two US helicopters and damaged others, leading to the heroic actions of Master Sergeant Gordon and Sergeant First Class Shughart.

signaled on a radio for help, and disappeared around the Black Hawk. Durant did not see him alive again.

Somali fighters surrounded Durant before the rescue team arrived. They carried him away alive, and then paraded the bodies of the crew and the Delta Force soldiers into the streets of Mogadishu. He was held by Aidid's militia and released to the Red Cross eleven days later.

For their attempt to protect the crew of *Super Six Four*, Master Sgt. Gary Gordon and Sgt. 1st Class Randy Shughart were awarded the Medal of Honor posthumously on May 23, 1994. President Clinton presented the medals to their widows.

For seventeen hours, the battle of Mogadishu raged beyond the crash sites. Two convoys set out, first to collect prisoners, and then to relieve and rescue units that were pinned down. The convoys were horribly shot up in the narrow streets, and the mission inflicted terrible harm on Somali militia and civilians. In all, eighteen Americans and one Malaysian soldier were killed; an estimated one thousand Somalis died. Although the mission was technically a success, capturing Aidid's militia leaders, images of American dead and the seeming futility of such combat in a humanitarian mission turned public opinion against an American presence in Somalia. President Clinton withdrew US forces from Mogadishu in March 1994. Aidid was killed two years later and Somalia remained a weak, failed state for years. In the days following the battle, the bodies of American dead were returned slowly, all of them mutilated by enraged crowds. Randy Shughart's was the last to come home.

# Iraq

I N AUGUST 2002, DICK CHENEY, now vice president, spoke to the 103rd convention of the Veterans of Foreign Wars. Much of the speech described a threat the Bush Administration perceived from Saddam Hussein of Iraq, who had remained in power after the 1991 Gulf War. The president and his advisors indicated that Hussein had revived a program to produce weapons of mass destruction, including chemical, biological, and nuclear weapons. They believed a decade of sanctions had not worked, and called for Hussein to open his programs to international inspection or face unspecified consequences. Over seven months, their drumbeat for war against Iraq grew louder as they conflated the War on Terror with the threat they perceived from the country of Iraq.

On March 20, 2003, America and its allies struck the Iraqi capital of Baghdad from the air, and launched a multi-pronged ground assault from the south. Iraqi units fell quickly, and by April 9, the United States occupied Baghdad as the Iraqi government melted away. On May 1, President Bush appeared beneath a giant MISSION ACCOMPLISHED banner on the deck of the USS *Abraham Lincoln* and declared an end to major combat operations, saying the conquest of Iraq was "one victory in a war on terror that began on September 11, 2001, and still goes on." On the same day, Defense Secretary Donald Rumsfeld told reporters in Kabul that "major combat operations" in Afghanistan were over.

The fighting was not over for thousands of American and allied military personnel in either country. Having punched the hornets' nests, the United States remained to fight in lands riven by rivalries, power grabs, and score-settling that its leaders barely understood. The military learned, adapted, changed tactics, and persevered. Hard-won military victories translated into political settlement fitfully, and public support for both wars waned. But during years of frustration there were also signs of progress. Elections took place in both countries; the West spent billions on reconstruction. Active combat troops left Iraq in December 2011 and American troops were scheduled to leave Afghanistan in 2014.

In large battles like Fallujah and Helmand, American and allied arms prevailed against militia. In small, sharp engagements like Ramadi or Kumar, Americans fought bravely and well. Thousands of Americans died and tens of thousands were wounded. (The number of Afghans and Iraqis dead in all the fighting will never be fully known, but most estimates place it well over one hundred thousand, and as in all wars they were mostly civilians.) A few warriors, singled out by circumstance and their actions, earned the distinction conferred by the Medal of Honor.

Third Infantry Division tanks attack in Iraq.

# OPERATION IRAQI FREEDOM

President George W. Bush talked about the War in Iraq in terms reminiscent of the earlier Gulf War: America and its allies would enforce the will of an international community as expressed in UN resolutions. The proximate cause of war was Saddam Hussein's resistance to UN weapons inspections, who searched Iraq for signs of weapons of mass destruction. In the second war with Hussein, Bush earned less military and political support than his father had received in 1990, and so the burden of fighting fell mostly to American soldiers, sailors, Marines, and Airmen.

Army and Marine units moved with unprecedented speed across the desert landscape of southern Iraq in a giant two-pronged attack up the Tigris and Euphrates rivers. In two days, Bravo Company of the 11th Engineer Battalion sped 300 kilometers (186 miles) up the west side of the Euphrates River with the rest of the 3rd Infantry Division. After intense fighting against the Iraqi Republican Guards' elite Medina Division, the 3rd crossed the river at the town of Musayyib and advanced north toward Baghdad, the capital. Its objective was to capture the Baghdad airport, where the Marines and Army would link up from the south and southwest.

Sergeant First Class Paul Ray Smith led a platoon of engineers in Bravo Company. The thirty-three-year-old had been in the Army for almost fourteen years, and had served in the Gulf War and in the peacekeeping missions of the 1990s in Bosnia and Kosovo. On April 4, after a full night of travel, Smith's 2nd Platoon was ordered to establish a blocking position on the eastern side of the airport, where the big road from Baghdad came in. Combat engineers build things, and Bravo Company quickly built serpentine berms across the thoroughfare to block enemy forces. Platoon leader 2nd Lt. Brian Borkowski left Smith in charge of the platoon when he left on a reconnaissance mission with the company commander. A short time later, the platoon was tasked with building a temporary holding pen for enemy prisoners of war.

Smith chose an enclosed courtyard nearby for the holding area, and Sgt. Joshua Dean drove an opening in the courtyard wall with an Armored Combat Earthmover (ACE). Posting guards, Smith supervised the work until his men spotted thirty to fifty Iraqi soldiers approaching with small arms and RPGs. Smith set up a skirmish line and called for Bradley Fighting Vehicles and Armored Personnel Carriers (APC).

The Iraqis, now numbering one hundred, took a nearby tower and fought hard. Sergeant Smith led the Bradley outside the courtyard and fought back with machine guns, grenades, rifles, and anti-tank weapons. An APC entered the courtyard but was crippled by an Iraqi RPG. The crew evacuated the immobile vehicle, and Iraqi mortar fire threw back another APC. Realizing that the .50-caliber machine gun on the crippled APC was still working, Smith climbed into the commander's hatch, bringing along Pvt. Michael Seaman to feed him ammunition. Ordering Seaman to back the slowly moving vehicle into position, Smith fired on the attacking Iraqis, expending more than three hundred rounds before he was mortally wounded.

Sergeant First Class Paul Ray Smith died helping to defeat Iraqi fighters and capture Baghdad Airport.

US Marines from the 1st Battalion, Charlie Company, cover each other with assault rifles as they prepare to enter one of Saddam Hussein's palaces.

The Iraqis were defeated, the airport was secured, and the next day, the 3rd Infantry Division drove an armored column through southwestern Baghdad toward the Marines. For his bravery in the face of fire, Sgt. 1st Class Paul Ray Smith received the Medal of Honor, which President Bush presented to his widow on April 4, 2005.

# VICTORY WITHOUT PEACE

Baghdad fell, the Iraqi military crumbled, the statues came down, and Saddam Hussein went into hiding. His notorious sons were cornered and killed. President Bush declared major combat operations over and mission accomplished. The United Nations arrived to help with the reconstruction effort. Money was pledged, political reconciliation promised.

And then pretty much everything went wrong. There were no weapons of mass destruction. Large caches of weapons disappeared, along with antique treasures from the museums. The sectarian and tribal divisions that had simmered under the boot of Hussein's secular Baathist regime first boiled over, and then exploded. Across Iraq, militias and terrorist cells attacked occupying US and British soldiers, international aid workers, and each other. A suicide truck bomber killed the United Nations' respected envoy, Sergio Vieira de Mello, on August 19, 2003. The armed forces of the United States, still fighting in Afghanistan, faced an indeterminate occupation and rebuilding of a restive, angry, fractured society.

For three years, military commanders got a few things right and many things wrong. At Abu Ghraib and other prisons, poorly trained soldiers (many called up from National Guard units) committed such appalling blunders and humiliations that the occupation seemed to manufacture resentful insurgents. By October 2005, more than three thousand insurgent attacks a day were taking place in Iraq. Entire provinces were described as under the control of insurgents by military and civilian authorities alike. Cities like Ramadi, in Anbar Province, were taken, lost, and taken again, sometimes in house-by-house fighting. Here the connection between Iraq and terrorism was finally and firmly established, as Abu Musab al Zarqawi's

Al-Qaeda in Iraq fought US Marines in a long struggle called the second battle of Ramadi, a turning point in the war.

A few commanders, such as Gen. David Petraeus, Col. Sean McFarland, and Col. H. R. McMaster, rewrote the book (figuratively and later, literally) on counterinsurgency operations. In insurgent-held cities like Ramadi, Fallujah, and Tal Afar, they engaged the trust of tribal leaders and the respect of civilians. They minimized American presence in places where they could train and put forward Iraqi forces. Within the military chain of command, their results broke through a political mindset of denial. By 2006, the occupation and rebuilding mission had turned a corner, but there was much fighting left to do.

# SACRIFICE IN THE STREETS

Master-at-Arms Michael A. Monsoor (above) and Pfc. Ross A. McGinnis (below) both jumped on grenades in heroic efforts to save the lives of their fellow soldiers.

Master-at-Arms Michael A. Monsoor was a Navy SEAL, described by his commander as "the toughest member of my platoon." He earned the Silver Star, the military's third-highest honor, for rescuing a teammate under fire in Ramadi on May 9, 2006. He was a big man, carrying his SEAL team's MK-48 machine gun with a heavy load of 7.62mm ammunition.

Ramadi's insurgents gave ground slowly, and unlike the early assaults across the desert, American fighting forces rarely found clear ground on which to fight. As a communications specialist, Monsoor spent time in sniper positions on rooftops and behind walls, calling in supporting fire on insurgent positions. Through the infernal desert summer, the SEALs and Marines hunted insurgents, who hunted them in return. They made progress under the command of Col. Sean McFarland, and by September the tide seemed to shift in favor of the Americans. McFarland planned Operation Kentucky Jumper, an operation involving both American and Iraqi soldiers, to clear southern Ramadi. The operation kicked off on September 29, 2006.

Monsoor soon found himself on another rooftop, wedged with his machine gun between two SEAL snipers in a small hiding site as they guarded an expected attack route from insurgents. As the three scanned the streets for enemy activity, a hand grenade from an unseen assailant dropped into the position, striking Monsoor in the chest and rolling to the deck. Monsoor leaped up yelling, "Grenade!" and then, realizing there was no escape for his teammates from the cramped space, threw himself on the weapon a moment before it exploded, mortally wounding him.

President Bush presented the Medal of Honor to Michael Monsoor's parents on April 8, 2008, and on May 23, 2013, the second ship of the new *Zumwalt* class of Navy destroyers was christened *Michael Monsoor*.

The SEAL was not the last to earn a Medal of Honor in Iraq. Ten weeks later and eighty miles to the west, Pfc. Ross A. McGinnis manned a .50-caliber machine gun in a Humvee patrolling the Adamiyah neighborhood of Baghdad, a hotbed of insurgent attacks. His unit, C Company, 1st Battalion, 26th Infantry Regiment, had lost men to snipers and the preferred weapon of the insurgency, the Improvised Explosive Device (IED). On December 4, 2006, Private McGinnis rode facing backward in the last of a six-vehicle patrol, covering the rear. As they turned a corner, an insurgent threw a grenade from a rooftop at the Humvee. Private McGinnis tried to deflect the explosive, but it landed inside the vehicle. It was a situation for

# AN HONOR POSTPONED

Over the last twenty-five years, the Medal of Honor has been awarded to seventy-two individuals in retrospect, long after the action that earned them, most of them posthumously. Most went to soldiers of the World War II era onward, but some reached even farther back in time.

President Barack Obama awarded the Medal of Honor to soldiers who served in World War II, Korea, and Vietnam. Most recently, in a ceremony held in March 2014, Obama presented medals to twenty-four veterans—the three living recipients all in attendance—many of whom had been passed over for the honor, it is believed, because they were Hispanic, Jewish, or African American.

President George W. Bush, looking back to the Civil War era, awarded the medal in 2001 to African American Cpl. Andrew Jackson Smith of the 55th Massachusetts Voluntary Infantry for valor at the battle of Honey Hill, South Carolina, in 1864. In that same ceremony, the medal was awarded to Lt. Col. (later President) Theodore Roosevelt for valor during the Spanish-American War.

President Bill Clinton awarded the Medal of Honor to twenty-nine African American, Asian American, and Pacific Islander World War II veterans who had not been recognized in their time due to racial prejudice. Among the recipients was Hawaii Sen. Daniel Inouye. President George H. W. Bush awarded the medal to Freddie Stowers, an African American, for action during World War I on the belief that he was overlooked due to racial prejudice.

In 1989, the US Army restored medals to five scouts from the Indian Campaigns (including Buffalo Bill Cody) whose medals had been rescinded in the purge of 1917 because of their civilian status. Upon reinstatement, civilian doctor Mary Walker's Medal of Honor restoration in 1977 was cited as precedent.

which he had been trained. According to Maj. Michael Baka, commander of C Company, "The machine gunner [is] supposed to announce the grenade, give a fair amount of time for people in the vehicle to react, and then he's supposed to save himself," by jumping from the Humvee to the street.

McGinnis did announce, "Grenade!" but then immediately slid down and laid his back on top of it. The grenade exploded under Private McGinnis, killing him instantly and wounding, but not killing, his buddies in the cab of the vehicle. All of them survived.

McGinnis received a Silver Star as an interim award while Baka's recommendation for the Medal of Honor was considered up the chain of command. On June 2, 2008, President George W. Bush declared that Ross A. McGinnis would receive the nation's highest honor.

# Afghanistan

**O**PERATION ENDURING FREEDOM BEGAN with quick gains. Less than a month after 9/11, the US military launched a bombing campaign against the Taliban regime ruling Afghanistan. Britain, Australia, Canada, France, and Germany (and later, other NATO members) joined in support. A thousand US Special Forces troops coordinated with the militia of the Afghan Northern Alliance, fighters from Afghan tribal groups, and other opponents of the Taliban in a quick assault on Kabul. Although Osama Bin Laden and top Taliban leaders escaped at Tora Bora, it looked like Afghanistan would no longer serve as a base for anti-Western terror operations.

In March 2002, a large ground assault called Operation Anaconda pitched elements of America's 10th Mountain Division, 101st Airborne, and Special Forces against Taliban and Al-Qaeda fighters. Although an estimated two to three hundred of the enemy were killed, many escaped into Pakistan. Anaconda highlighted the difficulty of fighting an elusive, dispersed enemy in some of the worst fighting terrain in the world. Cognizant of the ten-year Soviet quagmire in Afghanistan, and turning their attention to Iraq, policy and military authorities determined not to become a large-scale occupier in the country that had been called "the graveyard of empires."

President Bush and later President Obama pursued a "decapitation" strategy, aiming to kill or capture leaders of anti-US groups. From the drone strikes that killed operatives in Afghanistan, to the killing of Osama bin Laden by SEAL Team Six in 2011, to missions by Army "Night Stalker" units, they took a steady toll on terrorist leadership.

In August 2003, NATO took over formal command of forces in Afghanistan, which over time morphed into the International Security Assistance Force (ISAF). As of August 2013, forty-nine nations contributed troops to the ISAF, with eighty-seven thousand military men and women, of which sixty thousand were Americans. They planned to supply combat support to the Afghan armed forces until the end of 2014.

From 2002 to 2014, there were two essential questions: How to find and destroy anti-US terrorists inside the country, and how to leave a stable Afghanistan behind, so that it would not again harbor America's enemies. As months and years went by, the questions became intertwined. NATO's presence in the country inspired recruitment of insurgents, many of them radically anti-Western; and pursuing those insurgents involved more fighting and destruction, delaying a withdrawal. Complicating matters was the diversion of military resources to Iraq, and the unsavory, often corrupt government of Hamid Karzai, elected leader of Afghanistan and allied with the West, but a troublesome and occasionally fickle friend. Afghan political power was not modeled on Western liberal democracy, but on long-standing traditions of alliance, tribal loyalty, and deeply felt religious and cultural identity. The two essential questions of American involvement became a Gordian knot of military and policy decisions.

In these shifting circumstances, American soldiers, Airmen, Marines, and sailors fought engagements with the tactics of anti-insurgency and counterterrorism, not set-piece battles. As in Iraq, they adjusted, adapted, and changed with the terrain and the local political situation. They manned outposts and flew missions in remote mountain valleys. They trained Afghan forces. And they fought and were wounded and died performing, as the traditional language of the Medal of Honor Citation says, "above and beyond the call of duty."

# THE WORST DAY

After Operation Anaconda, much of the fighting in Afghanistan focused on attempts to find and kill Taliban and Al-Qaeda leadership in their remote strongholds. The landlocked, mountainous terrain forced small teams to fight at high altitudes, frequently above ten thousand feet, in temperatures and thin air that compounded the brutal physical demands of combat.

Into one of these mountain hideouts, in the Hindu Kush, four Navy SEALs sought Ahmad Shah, a.k.a. Muhammad Ismail, leader of a guerrilla group called the "Mountain Tigers." It was June 28, 2005, three and a half years into the war.

They ran into trouble on a mountainside; fifty guerrilla fighters launched an attack from three sides. The SEALs fought back as they retreated down the mountain, seeking cover in a ravine. Within forty-five minutes, each of the Americans was wounded. Seeking open ground to radio for help, Gunner's Mate 2nd Class (SEAL) Danny Dietz was shot, a bullet shattering his thumb. Lieutenant Michael P. Murphy (SEAL), the mission commander, then moved into the open, shooting and calling on his radio for a Quick Reaction Force (QRF) to come in fast. He took several gunshot wounds as he called in the SEALs' position, and then returned to cover.

The SEALs might have heard the MH-47 Chinook helicopter approach. On board were eight additional SEALs and eight Army Night Stalker operators, all elite fighters trained in fast reaction. The Chinook is a big, fast bird, but lightly armored; in its haste to come to the aid of Murphy and his men, Chief Warrant Officers Chris J. Scherkenbach and Corey J. Goodnature piloted the helicopter ahead of its heavily armed escort. As they approached the firefight, an RPG struck the Chinook, killing all aboard.

The fight continued on the ground, but three of the SEALs, including Murphy, Dietz, and Sonar Technician 2nd Class (SEAL) Matthew Axelson were killed. Hospital Corpsman 2nd Class (SEAL) Marcus Luttrell was thrown from a ridge by an RPG explosion and escaped capture until he was found and hidden by sympathetic Afghans. He was rescued on July 2.

With the loss of the SEALs and their rescuers, June 28 marked the single worst day of the war to date for American forces. For his courage in exposing himself to fire despite his wounds, and continuing to lead his men against overwhelming odds, Navy Lt. Michael P. Murphy was posthumously awarded the Medal of Honor by President George W. Bush on October 22, 2007.

Lieutenant Michael Murphy was killed trying to save his fellow SEALs while fighting in Afghanistan.

# BATTLE ON THE BORDER

Afghanistan's Kunar Province borders Pakistan, 155 miles east of Kabul. It is a region of farms terraced with rock walls, with the sharp mountain ranges of the Hindu Kush marking the border. In a six-hour engagement near the Kunar village of Ganjgal, two Americans earned the Medal of Honor on September 8, 2009. Their actions came with consequences that reached beyond the battlefield in the following years—proof that in battle, almost nothing is simple, certain, or clear.

Captain William D. Swenson and Cpl. Dakota Meyer entered the terraced valley near Ganjgal with eleven Marine and Army personnel as embedded advisors to thirty Afghan Border Police and sixty Afghan Army troops. A reporter from the McClatchy newspaper group accompanied the soldiers in the early morning mission. Near the village, insurgents tipped off to the patrol caught the soldiers in a crossfire at about 6:00 a.m. Two groups of Americans and Afghans were trapped behind terrace walls. Three Marines and a Navy Corpsman in the vanguard made it to a courtyard at the village outskirts but were also trapped. Major Kevin Williams, Swenson, and others radioed repeatedly for help, but US gunships didn't show up for ninety minutes. In the meantime, the soldiers returned fire against sixty well-armed insurgents. RPGs, mortar shells, and automatic weapons fire killed several American and Afghan soldiers.

Captain Swenson called for suppression fire and smoke to cover the withdrawal of the lead elements, but they were unable to withdraw. Marines, soldiers, and Afghan friendlies took fire, and the wounded list grew. Swenson's NCO, Sgt. 1st Class Kenneth Westbrook, was struck in the face and chest and lay exposed as the surrounding enemy poured in fire. Swenson raced fifty yards across open ground to aid Westbrook, joined by Capt. Ademola Fabayo. Insurgents called for them to surrender, but they answered with grenades and bullets.

Westbrook was severely wounded; Swenson and Fabayo carried him to a medevac site as armed scout helicopters arrived to give support. A Black Hawk chopper landed to evacuate Westbrook, and an onboard camera captured one of the most poignant pictures of the war: Swenson bending over to kiss his friend on the head and murmur that he would be all right (Westbrook was able to evacuate to his family in the United States but died of his wounds a few weeks later).

Then Swenson and Fabayo jumped into an unarmored Afghan pickup and returned to the battle site to rescue the wounded and locate the missing Marines. At the same time, Marine Staff Sgt. Juan Rodriguez-Chaves and Meyer arrived from a rear vehicle staging area, also to retrieve wounded. They gathered the wounded and the dead in several trips, bringing them to a casualty collection point while Swenson radioed air support, searching for the Marines.

Swenson and others created a convoy of armored vehicles and returned to the kill zone, still searching for the Marines. As they evacuated Afghan soldiers, a helicopter spotted the Marines in a forward position, tried to land, but was repelled by heavy fire. Swenson, Fabayo, Rodriguez-Chavez, and Meyer drove with Afghan soldiers once more into the killing grounds, finally locating the three Marines and Navy Corpsman in a deep ditch, all killed while trying to treat the wounds of Afghan casualties. In the last act of a grim engagement, Meyer and Swenson loaded the bodies into a Humvee, covered by the others, and the tiny convoy withdrew.

Capt. William D. Swenson is awarded the Medal of Honor on October 15, 2013, at the White House. Swenson (above) and Cpl. Dakota Meyer (top) both earned the Medal of Honor for their heroics in helping wounded comrades in a lengthy battle against Afghan insurgents in the Ganjgal Valley on September 8, 2009.

# BATTLE IN THE GANJGAL VALLEY

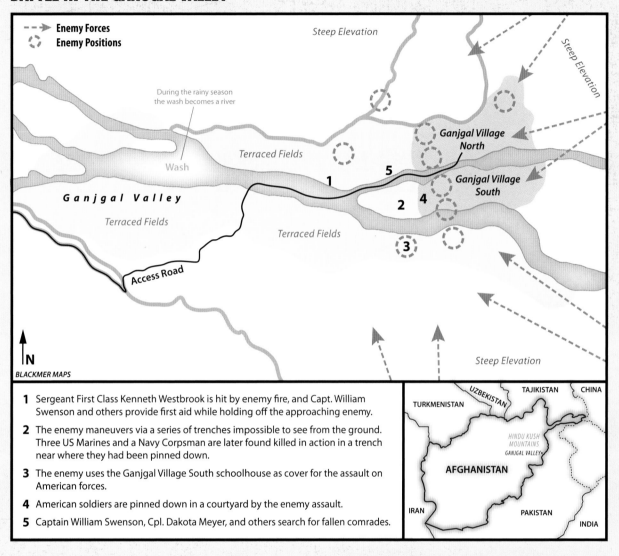

**Enemy Forces**
**Enemy Positions**

Steep Elevation

Steep Elevation

During the rainy season the wash becomes a river

Terraced Fields

Wash

Ganjgal Village North

*Ganjgal Valley*

Terraced Fields

Terraced Fields

Ganjgal Village South

Access Road

N

BLACKMER MAPS

Steep Elevation

1 Sergeant First Class Kenneth Westbrook is hit by enemy fire, and Capt. William Swenson and others provide first aid while holding off the approaching enemy.

2 The enemy maneuvers via a series of trenches impossible to see from the ground. Three US Marines and a Navy Corpsman are later found killed in action in a trench near where they had been pinned down.

3 The enemy uses the Ganjgal Village South schoolhouse as cover for the assault on American forces.

4 American soldiers are pinned down in a courtyard by the enemy assault.

5 Captain William Swenson, Cpl. Dakota Meyer, and others search for fallen comrades.

TURKMENISTAN  UZBEKISTAN  TAJIKISTAN  CHINA

*HINDU KUSH MOUNTAINS*
*GANJGAL VALLEY*

**AFGHANISTAN**

IRAN  PAKISTAN  INDIA

Corporal (now Sergeant) Dakota Meyer was awarded the Medal of Honor for "daring initiative and bold fighting" at the White House in September 2011. President Barack Obama placed a Medal of Honor around Capt. William Swenson's neck on October 15, 2013. The fog of war, however, swirled around more than the combat in which they distinguished themselves. Certain sequences and events in Meyer's narrative were questioned by McClatchy investigative reporting. Swenson's public criticism of the Army's delay in providing supporting fire early in the battle caused a stir. His Medal of Honor nomination process took two years longer than Meyer's. The Army later said his nomination packet was lost in a computer system for nineteen months.

## FIGHTING FOR FRIENDS ABROAD AND AT HOME

Ty Michael Carter brought his courage home and fought for his friends with words as well as weapons.

Staff Sergeant Carter was stationed with fifty-two comrades of B Troop, 3rd Squadron of the 61st Cavalry Regiment in Combat Outpost (COP) Keating, at the bottom of a valley in Nuristan Province, northeast of Kabul. Look at a map of Nuristan and you'll find only mountains and valleys—perfect terrain for guerrilla warfare, a place where fighters can get close without detection. In addition, the sparsely populated region was, in the official term, "ambivalent" about coalition forces in their homeland. Beginning at 6:00 a.m. on October 3, 2009, more than three hundred anti-coalition fighters got close enough to COP Keating to kill eight soldiers and wound twenty-five, more than half the company.

Enemy fire from above the base and behind mountainous cover rained down. The Americans fought back with machine guns and rifles, but the surprise raid had caught several positions lightly supplied. Emerging from his barracks, Carter saw an imperiled position where three soldiers fought from a Humvee with three different firearms. They were running out of ammo.

Carter grabbed bags of M240 ammunition and M4 clips and sprinted a hundred yards through heavy fire across open ground to the Humvee. When he realized that a .50-caliber machine gun mounted on the vehicle was also running low, he returned to the ammo depot

Staff Sergeant Ty Michael Carter conducts overwatch outside Combat Outpost Keating, Afghanistan. Carter received the Medal of Honor for his heroic actions keeping his fellow soldiers supplied with ammunition and rescuing a comrade during a battle with insurgents.

through a storm of fire, retrieved more supplies, and ran the deadly gauntlet a third time.

The fighting continued for hours. At one point insurgents breached the outpost, but Carter, Sgt. Bradley Larson, and other soldiers drove them back. Carter kept finding and supplying ammunition in the midst of battle, at one point delinking rounds from an M240 drum to feed their rifles for more accurate fire.

Specialist Stephan L. Mace lay wounded thirty yards from Carter's position, pleading for help. Carter told Larson he would rescue Mace, and Larson replied, "You're no good to Mace if you're dead." Nevertheless, Ty Carter ran through small-arms fire to Mace, applied a tourniquet to a terrible leg wound, and then lugged him back to the relative safety of the Humvee. Then he and Larson strapped Mace to a litter and carried him to the company aid station, near barracks where the Americans who were still living had drawn a perimeter.

In the following hours, Carter turned from sprinter to sniper, preserving ammunition and covering teams of soldiers who recovered the wounded and the fallen as attack helicop-

Carter receives the Medal of Honor from President Barack Obama at the White House on August 26, 2013.

ters blunted the attack, and the fighting raged on. After twelve hours, COP Keating was reinforced when a QRF battled its way to the outpost.

Carter and Larson, and many of their comrades, acted heroically in combat at COP Keating, and Carter was honored on August 26, 2013, as President Barack Obama conferred the Medal of Honor on him. But there was one more chapter to the story.

On his return from the war zone, Ty Carter suffered the terrible price of post-traumatic stress disorder (PTSD), like so many of his comrades. What had been euphemistically called "combat fatigue" in earlier wars is now recognized as a pernicious and sometimes deadly condition. A long tradition of silent shame, however, had prevented frontline soldiers from discussing it much. Carter decided to go public about his symptoms with dramatic statements. "I lost some of my hearing in that fight," Carter said, "but I'll hear the voice of Mace, and his pleas for help, for the rest of my life." Safe at home, Carter still put himself on the line to call attention to his comrades, not just in arms, but also in suffering and recovery from PTSD.

President Obama cited his courage as he addressed those silently suffering: "Look at this soldier," he said. "Look at this warrior. He's as tough as they come, and if he can find the courage and the strength to not only seek help but also to speak out about it, to take care of himself and to stay strong, then so can you."

And at the ceremony in which he received the Medal of Honor, Ty Carter said to Americans, "Know that a soldier suffering from post-traumatic stress is one of the most passionate, dedicated men or women you'll ever meet," he said. "Know that they are not damaged. They are simply burdened with living what others did not."

Staff Sergeant Ty Carter risked his life on the battlefield for a reason. He risked his pride and public image at home for the same reason—to save his comrades-in-arms.

It is a battle worth fighting.

# Register of Recipients

As of June 2014

KEY

**KEY**

| | |
|---|---|
| * | posthumous award |
| + | double recipient (earned in different conflicts) |
| # | double recipient (earned in same conflict) |
| ^ | double recipient (awarded the Army Medal of Honor for same action) |
| 1 | first recipient (awarded on March 25, 1863) |
| 2 | only female recipient |
| 3 | earliest action (occurred February 13–14, 1861) |
| 4 | served under the name John Lafferty in Civil War |
| 5 | served under the name Charles F. Hoffman at time of action |
| 6 | received the Army version of the Medal of Honor |
| 7 | awarded the Medal of Honor for action during the Six-Day War |

| Name | | | Rank at Time of Action | Place of Action |
|---|---|---|---|---|
| **The Civil War, 1861–1865** | | | | |
| **Army** | | | | |
| Adams | James | F. | Private | Ninevah, Virginia |
| Adams | John | G. B. | Second Lieutenant | Fredericksburg, Virginia |
| Alber | Frederick | | Private | Spotsylvania, Virginia |
| Albert | Christian | | Private | Vicksburg, Mississippi |
| Allen | Abner | P. | Corporal | Petersburg, Virginia |
| Allen | James | | Private | South Mountain, Maryland |
| Allen | Nathaniel | M. | Corporal | Gettysburg, Pennsylvania |
| Ames | Adelbert | | First Lieutenant | Bull Run, Virginia |
| Ammerman | Robert | W. | Private | Spotsylvania, Virginia |
| Anderson | Bruce | | Private | Fort Fisher, North Carolina |
| Anderson | Charles | W. | Private | Waynesboro, Virginia |
| Anderson | Everett | W. | Sergeant | Crosby's Creek, Tennessee |
| Anderson | Frederick | C. | Private | Weldon Railroad, Virginia |
| Anderson | Marion | T. | Captain | Nashville, Tennessee |
| Anderson | Peter | T. | Private | Bentonville, North Carolina |
| Anderson | Thomas | | Corporal | Appomattox Station, Virginia |
| Apple | Andrew | O. | Corporal | Petersburg, Virginia |
| Appleton | William | H. | First Lieutenant | Petersburg, Virginia |
| Archer | James | W. | First Lieutenant/Adjutant | Corinth, Mississippi |
| * Archer | Lester | | Sergeant | Fort Harrison, Virginia |
| Archinal | William | J. | Corporal | Vicksburg, Mississippi |
| Armstrong | Clinton | L. | Private | Vicksburg, Mississippi |
| Arnold | Abraham | K. | Captain | Davenport Bridge, Virginia |
| Avery | William | B. | Second Lieutenant | Tranter's Creek, North Carolina |
| Ayers | David | | Sergeant | Vicksburg, Mississippi |
| Ayers | John | G. K. | Private | Vicksburg, Mississippi |
| Babcock | William | J. | Sergeant | Petersburg, Virginia |
| * Bacon | Elijah | W. | Private | Gettysburg, Pennsylvania |
| Baird | Absalom | | Brigadier General | Jonesboro, Georgia |
| + Baldwin | Frank | D. | Captain | Peach Tree Creek, Georgia |
| Ballen | Frederick | A. | Private | Vicksburg, Mississippi |
| Banks | George | L. | Sergeant | Missionary Ridge, Tennessee |
| Barber | James | A. | Corporal | Petersburg, Virginia |
| Barker | Nathaniel | C. | Sergeant | Spotsylvania, Virginia |
| Barnes | William | H. | Private | Chapin's Farm, Virginia |
| Barnum | Henry | A. | Colonel | Chattanooga, Tennessee |
| Barrell | Charles | L. | First Lieutenant | Near Camden, South Carolina |
| Barrick | Jesse | T. | Corporal | Duck River, Tennessee |
| Barringer | William | H. | Private | Vicksburg, Mississippi |
| Barry | Augustus | | Sergeant Major | Tennessee and Georgia |
| Batchelder | Richard | N. | Lieutenant Colonel/ Chief Quartermaster | Catlett and Fairfax Stations, Virginia |
| Bates | Delavan | | Colonel | Cemetery Hill, Petersburg, Virginia |
| Bates | Norman | F. | Sergeant | Columbus, Georgia |
| Baybutt | Philip | | Private | Luray, Virginia |
| Beatty | Alexander | M. | Captain | Cold Harbor, Virginia |
| Beaty | Powhatan | | First Sergeant | Chapin's Farm, Virginia |
| Beaufort | Jean | J. | Corporal | Port Hudson, Louisiana |

| Name | | | Rank at Time of Action | Place of Action |
|---|---|---|---|---|
| Beaumont | Eugene | B. | Major/Asst. Adj. Gen. | Harpeth River, Tennessee; Selma, Alabama |
| Bebb | Edward | J. | Private | Columbus, Georgia |
| Beckwith | Wallace | A. | Private | Fredericksburg, Virginia |
| Beddows | Richard | | Private | Spotsylvania, Virginia |
| Beebe | William | S. | First Lieutenant | Cane River Crossing, Louisiana |
| Beech | John | P. | Sergeant | Spotsylvania Courthouse, Virginia |
| * Begley | Terrence | | Sergeant | Cold Harbor, Virginia |
| Belcher | Thomas | | Private | Chapin's Farm, Virginia |
| Bell | James | B. | Sergeant | Missionary Ridge, Tennessee |
| Benedict | George | G. | Second Lieutenant | Gettysburg, Pennsylvania |
| Benjamin | John | F. | Corporal | Deatonsville (Sailor's Creek), Virginia |
| Benjamin | Samuel | N. | First Lieutenant | Bull Run to Spotsylvania, Virginia |
| Bennett | Orrin | | Private | Deatonsville (Sailor's Creek), Virginia |
| Bennett | Orson | W. | First Lieutenant | Honey Hill, South Carolina |
| Bensinger | William | | Private | Georgia |
| Benyaurd | William | H. H. | First Lieutenant, Engineers | Five Forks, Virginia |
| Betts | Charles | M. | Lieutenant Colonel | Greensboro, North Carolina |
| Beyer | Hillary | | Second Lieutenant | Antietam, Maryland |
| Bickford | Henry | H. | Corporal | Waynesboro, Virginia |
| Bickford | Matthew | | Corporal | Vicksburg, Mississippi |
| Bieger | Charles | | Private | Ivy Farm, Mississippi |
| Bingham | Henry | H. | Captain | Wilderness Campaign |
| Birdsall | Horatio | L. | Sergeant | Columbus, Georgia |
| Bishop | Francis | A. | Private | Spotsylvania, Virginia |
| Black | John | C. | Lieutenant Colonel | Prairie Grove, Arkansas |
| Black | William | P. | Captain | Pea Ridge, Arkansas |
| Blackmar | Wilmon | W. | Lieutenant | Five Forks, Virginia |
| Blackwood | William | R. D. | Surgeon | Petersburg, Virginia |
| Blasdel | Thomas | A. | Private | Vicksburg, Mississippi |
| Blickensderfer | Milton | | Corporal | Petersburg, Virginia |
| Bliss | George | N. | Captain | Waynesboro, Virginia |
| Bliss | Zenas | R. | Colonel | Fredericksburg, Virginia |
| Blodgett | Wells | H. | First Lieutenant | Newtonia, Missouri |
| Blucher | Charles | | Corporal | Fort Harrison, Virginia |
| Blunt | John | W. | First Lieutenant | Cedar Creek, Virginia |
| Boehm | Peter | M. | Second Lieutenant | Dinwiddie Courthouse, Virginia |
| Bonebrake | Henry | G. | First Lieutenant | Five Forks, Virginia |
| Bonnaffon Jr. | Sylvester | | First Lieutenant | Boydton Plank Road, Virginia |
| Boody | Robert | M. | Sergeant | Williamsburg and Chancellorsville, Virginia |
| Boon | Hugh | P. | Captain | Deatonsville (Sailor's Creek), Virginia |
| Boss | Orlando | P. | Corporal | Cold Harbor, Virginia |
| Bouquet | Nicholas | S. | Private | Wilson's Creek, Missouri |
| Bourke | John | G. | Private | Stone River, Tennessee |
| Boury | Richard | | Sergeant | Charlottesville, Virginia |
| Boutwell | John | W. | Private | Petersburg, Virginia |
| Bowen | Chester | B. | Corporal | Winchester, Virginia |
| Bowen | Emmer | | Private | Vicksburg, Mississippi |
| Box | Thomas | J. | Captain | Resaca, Georgia |
| Boynton | Henry | V. | Lieutenant Colonel | Missionary Ridge, Tennessee |
| Bradley | Thomas | W. | Sergeant | Chancellorsville, Virginia |
| Brady | James | | Private | Chapin's Farm, Virginia |
| Brandle | Joseph | E. | Private | Lenoire, Tennessee |
| Brannigan | Felix | | Private | Chancellorsville, Virginia |
| Brant Jr. | William | | Lieutenant | Petersburg, Virginia |
| Bras | Edgar | A. | Sergeant | Spanish Fort, Alabama |
| Brest | Lewis | F. | Private | Deatonsville (Sailor's Creek), Virginia |
| Brewer | William | J. | Private | Appomattox Campaign, Virginia |
| Breyer | Charles | | Sergeant | Rappahannock Station, Virginia |
| Briggs | Elijah | A. | Corporal | Petersburg, Virginia |
| Bringle | Andrew | | Corporal | Deatonsville (Sailor's Creek), Virginia |
| Bronner | August | F. | Private | White Oak Swamp, Virginia |
| Bronson | James | H. | First Sergeant | Chapin's Farm, Virginia |
| Brosnan | John | | Sergeant | Petersburg, Virginia |
| Brouse | Charles | W. | Captain | Missionary Ridge, Tennessee |

| Name | | | Rank at Time of Action | Place of Action |
|---|---|---|---|---|
| Brown | Charles | E. | Sergeant | Weldon Railroad, Virginia |
| Brown | Henri | L. | Sergeant | Wilderness Campaign, Virginia |
| Brown | Jeremiah | Z. | Captain | Petersburg, Virginia |
| Brown | John | | First Sergeant | Vicksburg, Mississippi |
| Brown | John | H. | Captain | Franklin, Tennessee |
| Brown | Robert | B. | Private | Missionary Ridge, Tennessee |
| Brown | Uriah | H. | Private | Vicksburg, Mississippi |
| Brown | Wilson | W. | Private | Georgia |
| Brown Jr. | Edward | | Corporal | Fredericksburg and Salem Heights, Virginia |
| * Brown Jr. | Morris | | Captain | Gettysburg, Pennsylvania |
| Brownell | Francis | E. | Private | Alexandria, Virginia |
| Bruner | Louis | J. | Private | Walker's Ford, Tennessee |
| Brush | George | W. | Second Lieutenant | Ashepoo River, South Carolina |
| Bruton | Christopher | C. | Captain | Waynesboro, Virginia |
| Bryant | Andrew | S. | Sergeant | New Bern, North Carolina |
| * Buchanan | George | A. | Private | Chapin's Farm, Virginia |
| Buck | Frederick | C. | Corporal | Chapin's Farm, Virginia |
| Buckingham | David | E. | First Lieutenant | Rowanty Creek, Virginia |
| Buckles | Abram | J. | Sergeant | Wilderness Campaign, Virginia |
| * Buckley | Denis | | Private | Peach Tree Creek, Georgia |
| Buckley | John | C. | Sergeant | Vicksburg, Mississippi |
| Bucklyn | John | K. | First Lieutenant | Chancellorsville, Virginia |
| Buffington | John | C. | Sergeant | Petersburg, Virginia |
| Buffum | Robert | | Private | Georgia |
| Buhrman | Henry | G. | Private | Vicksburg, Mississippi |
| Bumgarner | William | | Sergeant | Petersburg, Virginia |
| Burbank | James | H. | Sergeant | Blackwater River, Virginia |
| Burger | Joseph | | Private | Nolensville, Tennessee |
| Burk | E. | Michael | Private | Spotsylvania, Virginia |
| Burk | Thomas | | Sergeant | Wilderness Campaign, Virginia |
| Burke | Daniel | W. | First Sergeant | Shepherdstown Ford, West Virginia |
| Burke | Thomas | M. | Private | Hanover Courthouse, Virginia |
| Burns | James | M. | Sergeant | New Market, Virginia |
| Burritt | William | W. | Private | Vicksburg, Mississippi |
| Butterfield | Daniel | A. | Brigadier General | Gaines's Mill, Virginia |
| Butterfield | Franklin | G. | First Lieutenant | Salem Heights, Virginia |
| Cadwallader | Abel | G. | Corporal | Hatcher's Run and Dabney's Mill, Virginia |
| Cadwell | Luman | L. | Sergeant | Alabama Bayou, Louisiana |
| Caldwell | Daniel | G. | Sergeant | Hatcher's Run, Virginia |
| Calkin | Ivers | S. | First Sergeant | Deatonsville (Sailor's Creek), Virginia |
| Callahan | John | H. | Private | Fort Blakely, Alabama |
| Camp | Carlton | N. | Private | Petersburg, Virginia |
| Campbell | James | A. | Private | Woodstock and Amelia Courthouse, Virginia |
| Campbell | William | | Private | Vicksburg, Mississippi |
| Capehart | Charles | E. | Major | Monterey Mountain, Pennsylvania |
| Capehart | Henry | | Colonel | Greenbrier River, West Virginia |
| * Capron Jr. | Horace | | Sergeant | Chickahominy and Ashland, Virginia |
| * Carey | Hugh | | Sergeant | Gettysburg, Pennsylvania |
| Carey | James | L. | Sergeant | Appomattox Courthouse, Virginia |
| Carlisle | Casper | R. | Private | Gettysburg, Pennsylvania |
| Carman | Warren | | Private | Waynesboro, Virginia |
| Carmin | Isaac | H. | Corporal | Vicksburg, Mississippi |
| Carney | William | H. | Sergeant | Fort Wagner, South Carolina |
| Carr | Eugene | A. | Colonel | Pea Ridge, Arkansas |
| Carr | Franklin | | Corporal | Nashville, Tennessee |
| Carson | William | J. | Musician | Chickamauga, Georgia |
| Cart | Jacob | | Private | Fredericksburg, Virginia |
| Carter | John | J. | Second Lieutenant | Antietam, Maryland |
| Carter | Joseph | F. | Captain | Fort Stedman, Virginia |
| Caruana | Orlando | E. | Private | New Bern, North Carolina; South Mountain, Maryland |
| Casey | David | P. | Private | Cold Harbor, Virginia |
| Casey | Henry | | Private | Vicksburg, Mississippi |
| Catlin | Isaac | S. | Colonel | Petersburg, Virginia |
| Cayer | Ovila | | Sergeant | Weldon Railroad, Virginia |
| Chamberlain | Joshua | L. | Colonel | Gettysburg, Pennsylvania |
| Chamberlain | Orville | T. | Second Lieutenant | Chickamauga, Georgia |
| Chambers | Joseph | B. | Private | Petersburg, Virginia |
| Chandler | Henry | F. | Sergeant | Petersburg, Virginia |
| Chandler | Stephen | E. | Quartermaster Sergeant | Amelia Springs, Virginia |
| Chapin | Alaric | B. | Private | Fort Fisher, North Carolina |
| Chapman | John | | Private | Deatonsville (Sailor's Creek), Virginia |
| Chase | John | F. | Private | Chancellorsville, Virginia |
| Child | Benjamin | H. | Corporal | Antietam, Maryland |
| Chisman | William | W. | Private | Vicksburg, Mississippi |
| Christiancy | James | I. | First Lieutenant | Hawe's Shop, Virginia |
| Churchill | Samuel | J. | Corporal | Nashville, Tennessee |
| Cilley | Clinton | A. | Captain | Chickamauga, Georgia |
| Clancy | James | T. | Sergeant | Vaughn Road, Virginia |
| Clapp | Albert | A. | First Sergeant | Deatonsville (Sailor's Creek), Virginia |
| Clark | Charles | A. | Lieutenant/Adjutant | Brooks Ford, Virginia |
| Clark | Harrison | | Corporal | Gettysburg, Pennsylvania |
| Clark | James | G. | Private | Petersburg, Virginia |
| Clark | John | W. | First Lt./Reg. Qtrmaster | Near Warrenton, Virginia |
| Clark | William | A. | Corporal | Nolensville, Tennessee |
| Clarke | Dayton | P. | Captain | Spotsylvania, Virginia |
| Clausen | Charles | H. | First Lieutenant | Spotsylvania, Virginia |
| Clay | Cecil | | Captain | Fort Harrison, Virginia |
| Cleveland | Charles | F. | Private | Antietam, Maryland |
| Clopp | John | E. | Private | Gettysburg, Pennsylvania |
| Clute | George | W. | Corporal | Bentonville, North Carolina |
| Coates | Jefferson | | Sergeant | Gettysburg, Pennsylvania |
| Cockley | David | L. | First Lieutenant | Waynesboro, Georgia |
| Coey | James | | Major | Hatcher's Run, Virginia |
| Coffey | Robert | J. | Sergeant | Bank's Ford, Virginia |
| Cohn | Abraham | | Sergeant Major | Wilderness Campaign and at the mine, Petersburg, Virginia |
| Colby | Carlos | W. | Sergeant | Vicksburg, Mississippi |
| Cole | Gabriel | | Corporal | Winchester, Virginia |
| Collins | Harrison | | Corporal | Richland Creek, Tennessee |
| Collins Sr. | Thomas | D. | Sergeant | Resaca, Georgia |
| Collis | Charles | H. T. | Colonel | Fredericksburg, Virginia |
| Colwell | Oliver | | First Lieutenant | Nashville, Tennessee |
| Compson | Hartwell | B. | Major | Waynesboro, Virginia |
| Conaway | John | W. | Private | Vicksburg, Mississippi |
| Conboy | Martin | | First Sergeant | Williamsburg, Virginia |
| Connell | Trustrim | | Corporal | Deatonsville (Sailor's Creek), Virginia |
| Conner | Richard | | Private | Bull Run, Virginia |
| Connors | James | | Private | Fisher's Hill, Virginia |
| Cook | John | | Bugler | Antietam, Maryland |
| Cook | John | H. | Sergeant | Pleasant Hill, Louisiana |
| Cooke | Walter | H. | Captain | Bull Run, Virginia |
| Copp | Charles | D. | Second Lieutenant | Fredericksburg, Virginia |
| Corcoran | John | | Private | Petersburg, Virginia |
| Corliss | George | W. | Captain | Cedar Mountain, Virginia |
| Corliss | Stephen | P. | First Lieutenant | South Side Railroad, Virginia |
| Corson | Joseph | K. | Assistant Surgeon | Near Bristoe Station, Virginia |
| Cosgriff | Richard | H. | Private | Columbus, Georgia |
| Cosgrove | Thomas | | Private | Drewry's Bluff, Virginia |
| Coughlin | John | | Lieutenant Colonel | Swift Creek, Virginia |
| Cox | Robert | M. | Corporal | Vicksburg, Mississippi |
| Coyne | John | N. | Sergeant | Williamsburg, Virginia |
| Cranston | William | W. | Private | Chancellorsville, Virginia |
| Creed | John | | Private | Fisher's Hill, Virginia |
| Crocker | Henry | H. | Captain | Cedar Creek, Virginia |
| Crocker | Ulric | L. | Private | Cedar Creek, Virginia |
| Croft | James | E. | Private | Allatoona, Georgia |
| Crosier | William | H. H. | Sergeant | Peach Tree Creek, Georgia |
| Cross | James | E. | Corporal | Blackburn's Ford, Virginia |

| Name | | | Rank at Time of Action | Place of Action |
|---|---|---|---|---|
| Crowley | Michael | | Private | Waynesboro, Virginia |
| Cullen | Thomas | | Corporal | Bristoe Station, Virginia |
| Cummings | Amos | J. | Sergeant Major | Salem Heights, Virginia |
| Cumpston | James | M. | Private | Shenandoah Valley Campaign, Virginia |
| Cunningham | Francis | M. | First Sergeant | Deatonsville (Sailor's Creek), Virginia |
| Cunningham | James | S. | Private | Vicksburg, Mississippi |
| Curran | Richard | J. | Assistant Surgeon | Antietam, Maryland |
| Curtis | John | C. | Sergeant Major | Baton Rouge, Louisiana |
| Curtis | Josiah | M. | Second Lieutenant | Petersburg, Virginia |
| Curtis | Newton | M. | Brigadier General | Fort Fisher, North Carolina |
| # Custer | Thomas | W. | Second Lieutenant | Namozine Church and Sailor's Creek, Virginia |
| Cutcheon | Byron | M. | Major | Horseshoe Bend, Kentucky |
| Cutts | James | M. | Captain | Wilderness Campaign, Spotsylvania, and Petersburg, Virginia |
| Darrough | John | S. | Sergeant | Eastport, Mississippi |
| Davidsizer | John | A. | Sergeant | Paine's Crossroads, Virginia |
| Davidson | Andrew | | Assistant Surgeon | Vicksburg, Mississippi |
| Davidson | Andrew | | First Lieutenant | Petersburg at the mine, Virginia |
| Davis | Charles | C. | Major | Shelbyville, Tennessee |
| Davis | Freeman | | Sergeant | Missionary Ridge, Tennessee |
| Davis | George | E. | First Lieutenant | Monocacy, Maryland |
| Davis | Harry | C. | Private | Atlanta, Georgia |
| Davis | John | | Private | Culloden, Georgia |
| Davis | Joseph | | Corporal | Franklin, Tennessee |
| Davis | Martin | K. | Sergeant | Vicksburg, Mississippi |
| Davis | Thomas | | Private | Deatonsville (Sailor's Creek), Virginia |
| Day | Charles | | Private | Hatcher's Run, Virginia |
| Day | David | F. | Private | Vicksburg, Mississippi |
| Deane | John | M. | Major | Fort Stedman, Virginia |
| DeCastro | Joseph | H. | Corporal | Gettysburg, Pennsylvania |
| DeLacey | Patrick | | First Sergeant | Wilderness Campaign, Virginia |
| DeLand | Frederick | N. | Private | Port Hudson, Louisiana |
| Delaney | John | C. | Sergeant | Danby's Mill, Virginia |
| DeLavie | Hiram | A. | Sergeant | Five Forks, Virginia |
| DePuy | Charles | H. | First Sergeant | Petersburg, Virginia |
| DeWitt | Richard | W. | Corporal | Vicksburg, Mississippi |
| Di Cesnola | Louis | P. | Colonel | Aldie, Virginia |
| Dickey | William | D. | Captain | Petersburg, Virginia |
| Dickie | David | | Sergeant | Vicksburg, Mississippi |
| Dilger | Hubert | | Captain | Chancellorsville, Virginia |
| Dillon | Michael | A. | Private | Williamsburg and Oak Grove, Virginia |
| Dockum | Warren | C. | Private | Deatonsville (Sailor's Creek), Virginia |
| Dodd | Robert | F. | Private | Petersburg, Virginia |
| Dodds | Edward | E. | Sergeant | Ashby's Gap, Virginia |
| Dolloff | Charles | W. | Corporal | Petersburg, Virginia |
| Donaldson | John | P. | Sergeant | Appomattox Courthouse, Virginia |
| Donoghue | Timothy | | Private | Fredericksburg, Virginia |
| Doody | Patrick | H. | Corporal | Cold Harbor, Virginia |
| Dore | George | H. | Sergeant | Gettysburg, Pennsylvania |
| Dorley | August | | Private | Mount Pleasant, Alabama |
| Dorsey | Daniel | A. | Corporal | Georgia |
| Dorsey | Decatur | | Sergeant | Petersburg, Virginia |
| Dougall | Allan | H. | First Lt./ Adjutant | Bentonville, North Carolina |
| Dougherty | Michael | | Private | Jefferson, Virginia |
| Dow | George | P. | Sergeant | Near Richmond, Virginia |
| Downey | William | | Private | Ashepoo River, South Carolina |
| Downs | Henry | W. | Sergeant | Winchester, Virginia |
| Drake | James | M. | Second Lieutenant | Bermuda Hundred, Virginia |
| Drury | James | | Sergeant | Weldon Railroad, Virginia |
| Du Pont | Henry | A. | Captain | Cedar Creek, Virginia |
| Duffey | John | | Private | Ashepoo River, South Carolina |
| Dunlavy | James | | Private | Osage, Kansas |
| Dunne | James | | Corporal | Vicksburg, Mississippi |
| Durham | James | R. | Second Lieutenant | Winchester, Virginia |
| Durham | John | S. | Sergeant | Perryville, Kentucky |
| Eckes | John | N. | Private | Vicksburg, Mississippi |
| Eddy | Samuel | E. | Private | Deatonville (Sailor's Creek), Virginia |
| Edgerton | Nathan | H. | First Lt./ Adjutant | Chapin's Farm, Virginia |
| Edwards | David | | Private | Five Forks, Virginia |
| Elliott | Alexander | | Sergeant | Paine's Crossroads, Virginia |
| Elliott | Russell | C. | Sergeant | Natchitoches, Louisiana |
| Ellis | Horace | | Private | Weldon Railroad, Virginia |
| Ellis | William | | First Sergeant | Dardanelles, Arkansas |
| Ellsworth | Thomas | F. | Captain | Honey Hill, South Carolina |
| Elson | James | M. | Sergeant | Vicksburg, Mississippi |
| Embler | Andrew | H. | Captain | Boydton Plank Road, Virginia |
| Enderlin | Richard | | Musician | Gettysburg, Pennsylvania |
| Engle | James | E. | Sergeant | Bermuda Hundred, Virginia |
| English | Edmund | | First Sergeant | Wilderness Campaign, Virginia |
| Ennis | Charles | D. | Private | Petersburg, Virginia |
| Estes | Lewellyn | G. | Capt./Asst. Adj. Gen. | Flint River, Georgia |
| Evans | Coron | D. | Private | Deatonsville (Sailor's Creek), Virginia |
| Evans | Ira | H. | Captain | Hatcher's Run, Virginia |
| Evans | James | R. | Private | Wilderness Campaign, Virginia |
| Evans | Thomas | | Private | Piedmont, Virginia |
| Everson | Adelbert | | Private | Five Forks, Virginia |
| Ewing | John | C. | Private | Petersburg, Virginia |
| Falconer | John | A. | Corporal | Fort Sanders, Knoxville, Tennessee |
| Fall | Charles | S. | Sergeant | Spotsylvania Courthouse, Virginia |
| Fallon | Thomas | T. | Private | Williamsburg and Fair Oaks, Virginia; Big Shanty, Georgia |
| * Falls | Benjamin | F. | Color Sergeant | Gettysburg, Pennsylvania |
| Fanning | Nicholas | | Private | Selma, Alabama |
| Farnsworth | Herbert | E. | Sergeant Major | Trevilian Station, Virginia |
| Farquhar | John | M. | Sergeant Major | Stone River, Tennessee |
| Fasnacht | Charles | H. | Sergeant | Spotsylvania, Virginia |
| Fassett | John | B. | Captain | Gettysburg, Pennsylvania |
| Fernald | Albert | E. | First Lieutenant | Five Forks, Virginia |
| Ferrier | Daniel | T. | Sergeant | Varnell's Station, Georgia |
| Ferris | Eugene | W. | First Lt./ Adjutant | Berryville, Virginia |
| Fesq | Frank | E. | Private | Petersburg, Virginia |
| Finkenbiner | Henry | S. | Private | Dingle's Mill, South Carolina |
| Fisher | John | H. | First Lieutenant | Vicksburg, Mississippi |
| Fisher | Joseph | | Corporal | Petersburg, Virginia |
| Flanagan | Augustin | D. | Sergeant | Chapin's Farm, Virginia |
| Flannigan | James | | Private | Nolensville, Tennessee |
| Fleetwood | Christian | A. | Sergeant Major | Chapin's Farm, Virginia |
| Flynn | Christopher | | Corporal | Gettysburg, Pennsylvania |
| Flynn | James | E. | Sergeant | Vicksburg, Mississippi |
| Follett | Joseph | L. | Sergeant | New Madrid, Missouri; Stone River, Tennessee |
| Force | Manning | F. | Brigadier General | Atlanta, Georgia |
| Ford | George | W. | First Lieutenant | Deatonsville (Sailor's Creek), Virginia |
| Forman | Alexander | A. | Corporal | Fair Oaks, Virginia |
| Fout | Frederick | W. | Second Lieutenant | Near Harpers Ferry, West Virginia |
| Fox | Henry | | Sergeant | Near Jackson, Tennessee |
| Fox | Henry | M. | Sergeant | Winchester, Virginia |
| Fox | Nicholas | | Private | Port Hudson, Louisiana |
| Fox | William | R. | Private | Petersburg, Virginia |
| Frantz | Joseph | | Private | Vicksburg, Mississippi |
| Fraser | William | W. | Private | Vicksburg, Mississippi |
| Freeman | Archibald | | Private | Spotsylvania, Virginia |
| Freeman | Henry | B. | First Lieutenant | Stone River, Tennessee |
| Freeman | William | H. | Private | Fort Fisher, North Carolina |
| French | Samuel | S. | Private | Fair Oaks, Virginia |
| Frey | Franz | | Corporal | Vicksburg, Mississippi |
| Frick | Jacob | G. | Colonel | Fredericksburg and Chancellorsville, Virginia |
| Frizzell | Henry | F. | Private | Vicksburg, Mississippi |
| Fuger | Frederick | W. | Sergeant | Gettysburg, Pennsylvania |
| Funk | West | | Major | Appomattox Courthouse, Virginia |

| Name | | | Rank at Time of Action | Place of Action |
|---|---|---|---|---|
| Furman | Chester | S. | Corporal | Gettysburg, Pennsylvania |
| Furness | Frank | | Captain | Trevilian Station, Virginia |
| Gage | Richard | J. | Private | Elk River, Tennessee |
| Galloway | George | N. | Private | Alsops Farm, Virginia |
| Galloway | John | | Commissary Sergeant | Farmville, Virginia |
| Gardiner | James | | Private | Chapin's Farm, Virginia |
| Gardner | Charles | N. | Private | Five Forks, Virginia |
| Gardner | Robert | J. | Sergeant | Petersburg, Virginia |
| Garrett | William | | Sergeant | Nashville, Tennessee |
| * Gasson | Richard | | Sergeant | Chapin's Farm, Virginia |
| Gaunt | John | C. | Private | Franklin, Tennessee |
| Gause | Isaac | | Corporal | Near Berryville, Virginia |
| Gaylord | Levi | B. | Sergeant | Fort Stedman, Virginia |
| Gere | Thomas | P. | First Lt./Adjutant | Nashville, Tennessee |
| Geschwind | Nicholas | | Captain | Vicksburg, Mississippi |
| Gibbs | Wesley | | Sergeant | Petersburg, Virginia |
| Gifford | Benjamin | | Private | Deatonsville (Sailor's Creek), Virginia |
| Gifford | David | L. | Private | Ashepoo River, South Carolina |
| Gillespie Jr. | George | L. | First Lieutenant | Near Bethesda Church, Virginia |
| Gilligan | Edward | L. | First Sergeant | Gettysburg, Pennsylvania |
| Gilmore | John | C. | Major | Salem Heights, Virginia |
| Ginley | Patrick | J. | Private | Ream's Station, Virginia |
| Gion | Joseph | | Private | Chancellorsville, Virginia |
| Godley | Leonidas | M. | First Sergeant | Vicksburg, Mississippi |
| Goettel | Philip | | Private | Ringgold, Georgia |
| Goheen | Charles | A. | First Sergeant | Waynesboro, Virginia |
| Goldsbery | Andrew | E. | Private | Vicksburg, Mississippi |
| Goodall | Francis | H. | First Sergeant | Fredericksburg, Virginia |
| Goodman | William | E. | First Lieutenant | Chancellorsville, Virginia |
| Goodrich | Edwin | | First Lieutenant | Near Cedar Creek, Virginia |
| Gould | Charles | G. | Captain | Petersburg, Virginia |
| Gould | Newton | T. | Private | Vicksburg, Mississippi |
| Gouraud | George | E. | Captain/Aide-de-Camp | Honey Hill, South Carolina |
| Grace | Peter | | Sergeant | Wilderness Campaign, Virginia |
| Graham | Thomas | N. | Second Lieutenant | Missionary Ridge, Tennessee |
| Grant | Gabriel | | Surgeon | Fair Oaks, Virginia |
| Grant | Lewis | A. | Colonel | Salem Heights, Virginia |
| Graul | William | L. | Corporal | Fort Harrison, Virginia |
| Gray | John | | Private | Port Republic, Virginia |
| Gray | Robert | A. | Sergeant | Drewry's Bluff, Virginia |
| Grebe | M. R. | William | Captain | Jonesboro, Georgia |
| Green | George | | Corporal | Missionary Ridge, Tennessee |
| Greenawalt | Abraham | | Private | Franklin, Tennessee |
| Greene | Oliver | D. | Major/Asst. Adj. Gen. | Antietam, Maryland |
| Gregg | Joseph | O. | Private | Near the Richmond and Petersburg Railway, Virginia |
| Greig | Theodore | W. | Second Lieutenant | Antietam, Maryland |
| Gresser | Ignatz | | Corporal | Antietam, Maryland |
| Gribben | James | H. | First Lieutenant | Deatonsville (Sailor's Creek), Virginia |
| Grimshaw | Samuel | | Private | Atlanta, Georgia |
| Grindlay | James | G. | Colonel | Five Forks, Virginia |
| Grueb | George | M. | Private | Chapin's Farm, Virginia |
| Guerin | Fitz | W. | Private | Grand Gulf, Mississippi |
| Guinn | Thomas | | Private | Vicksburg, Mississippi |
| Gwynne | Nathaniel | M. | Private | Petersburg, Virginia |
| Hack | John | | Private | Vicksburg, Mississippi |
| Hack | Lester | G. | Sergeant | Petersburg, Virginia |
| Hadley | Cornelius | M. | Sergeant | Knoxville, Tennessee |
| Hadley | Osgood | T. | Corporal | Near Pegram House, Virginia |
| Hagerty | Asel | | Private | Deatonsville (Sailor's Creek), Virginia |
| Haight | John | H. | Sergeant | Williamsburg, Bristol Station, and Manassas, Virginia |
| Haight | Sidney | | Corporal | Petersburg, Virginia |
| Hall | Francis | B. | Chaplain | Salem Heights, Virginia |
| Hall | Henry | S. | Second Lt./Capt. | Gaines's Mill and Rappahannock Station, Virginia |
| Hall | Newton | H. | Corporal | Franklin, Tennessee |

| Name | | | Rank at Time of Action | Place of Action |
|---|---|---|---|---|
| Hallock | Nathan | M. | Private | Bristoe Station, Virginia |
| Hammel | Henry | A. | Sergeant | Grand Gulf, Mississippi |
| Haney | Milton | L. | Regimental Chaplain | Atlanta, Georgia |
| Hanford | Edward | R. | Private | Woodstock, Virginia |
| Hanks | Joseph | | Private | Vicksburg, Mississippi |
| Hanna | Marcus | A. | Sergeant | Port Hudson, Louisiana |
| Hanna | Milton | | Corporal | Nolensville, Tennessee |
| Hanscom | Moses | C. | Corporal | Bristoe Station, Virginia |
| Hapeman | Douglas | | Lieutenant Colonel | Peach Tree Creek, Georgia |
| Harbourne | John | H. | Private | Petersburg, Virginia |
| * Hardenbergh | Henry | M. | Private | Deep Run, Virginia |
| Haring | Abram | P. | First Lieutenant | Bachelor's Creek, North Carolina |
| Harmon | Amzi | D. | Corporal | Petersburg, Virginia |
| Harrington | Ephraim | W. | Sergeant | Fredericksburg, Virginia |
| Harris | George | W. | Private | Spotsylvania, Virginia |
| Harris | James | H. | Sergeant | New Market Heights, Virginia |
| Harris | Moses | | First Lieutenant | Smithfield, Virginia |
| Harris | Sampson | | Private | Vicksburg, Mississippi |
| Hart | John | W. | Sergeant | Gettysburg, Pennsylvania |
| Hart | William | E. | Private | Shenandoah Valley, Virginia |
| Hartranft | John | F. | Colonel | Bull Run, Virginia |
| Harvey | Harry | | Corporal | Waynesboro, Virginia |
| Haskell | Frank | W. | Sergeant Major | Fair Oaks, Virginia |
| Haskell | Marcus | M. | Sergeant | Antietam, Maryland |
| Hastings | Smith | H. | Captain | Newby's Crossroads, Virginia |
| Hatch | John | P. | Brigadier General | South Mountain, Maryland |
| Havron | John | H. | Sergeant | Petersburg, Virginia |
| Hawkins | Gardner | C. | First Lieutenant | Petersburg, Virginia |
| Hawkins | Martin | J. | Corporal | Georgia |
| Hawkins | Thomas | R. | Sergeant Major | Chapin's Farm, Virginia |
| Hawthorne | Harris | S. | Corporal | Deatonsville (Sailor's Creek), Virginia |
| Haynes | Asbury | F. | Corporal | Deatonsville (Sailor's Creek), Virginia |
| Hays | John | H. | Private | Columbus, Georgia |
| Healey | George | W. | Private | Newman, Georgia |
| Hedges | Joseph | S. | First Lieutenant | Near Harpeth River, Tennessee |
| Heermance | William | L. | Captain | Chancellorsville, Virginia |
| Heller | Henry | | Sergeant | Chancellorsville, Virginia |
| Helms | David | H. | Private | Vicksburg, Mississippi |
| Henry | Guy | V. | Colonel | Cold Harbor, Virginia |
| Henry | James | | Sergeant | Vicksburg, Mississippi |
| Henry | William | W. | Colonel | Cedar Creek, Virginia |
| Herington | Pitt | B. | Private | Near Kenesaw Mountain, Georgia |
| Herron | Francis | J. | Lieutenant Colonel | Pea Ridge, Arkansas |
| Hesseltine | Francis | S. | Lieutenant Colonel | Matagorda Bay, Texas |
| Hibson | Joseph | C. | Private | Near Fort Wagner, South Carolina |
| Hickey | Dennis | W. | Sergeant | Stony Creek Bridge, Virginia |
| Hickok | Nathan | E. | Corporal | Chapin's Farm, Virginia |
| Higby | Charles | | Private | Appomattox Campaign, Virginia |
| Higgins | Thomas | J. | Sergeant | Vicksburg, Mississippi |
| Highland | Patrick | | Corporal | Petersburg, Virginia |
| Hill | Edward | | Captain | Cold Harbor, Virginia |
| Hill | Henry | | Corporal | Wilderness Campaign, Virginia |
| Hill | James | | First Lieutenant | Champion Hill, Mississippi |
| * Hill | James | S. | Sergeant | Petersburg, Virginia |
| Hilliker | Benjamin | F. | Musician | Mechanicsburg, Mississippi |
| Hills | William | G. | Private | North Fork, Virginia |
| * Hilton | Alfred | B. | Sergeant | Chapin's Farm, Virginia |
| Hincks | William | B. | Sergeant Major | Gettysburg, Pennsylvania |
| Hodges | Addison | J. | Private | Vicksburg, Mississippi |
| Hoffman | Henry | | Corporal | Deatonsville (Sailor's Creek), Virginia |
| Hoffman | Thomas | W. | Captain | Petersburg, Virginia |
| Hogan | Franklin | | Corporal | Petersburg, Virginia |
| Hogarty | William | P. | Private | Antietam, Maryland; Fredericksburg, Virginia |
| Holcomb | Daniel | I. | Private | Brentwood Hills, Tennessee |

| Name | | | Rank at Time of Action | Place of Action |
|---|---|---|---|---|
| Holehouse | James | | Private | Marye's Heights, Virginia |
| Holland | Lemuel | F. | Corporal | Elk River, Tennessee |
| Holland | Milton | M. | Sergeant Major | Chapin's Farm, Virginia |
| Holmes | Lovilo | N. | First Sergeant | Nolensville, Tennessee |
| Holmes | William | T. | Private | Deatonsville (Sailor's Creek), Virginia |
| Holton | Charles | M. | First Sergeant | Falling Waters, Virginia |
| Holton | Edward | A. | First Sergeant | Lee's Mills, Virginia |
| Homan | Conrad | | Color Sergeant | Near Petersburg, Virginia |
| Hooker | George | W. | First Lieutenant | South Mountain, Maryland |
| Hooper | William | B. | Corporal | Chamberlain's Creek, Virginia |
| Hopkins | Charles | F. | Corporal | Gaines's Mill, Virginia |
| Horan | Thomas | | Sergeant | Gettysburg, Pennsylvania |
| Horne | Samuel | B. | Captain | Fort Harrison, Virginia |
| Horsfall | William | H. | Drummer | Corinth, Mississippi |
| Hottenstine | Solomon | J. | Private | Petersburg and Norfolk Railroad, Virginia |
| Hough | Ira | | Private | Cedar Creek, Virginia |
| Houghton | Charles | H. | Captain | Petersburg, Virginia |
| Houghton | George | L. | Private | Elk River, Tennessee |
| Houlton | William | M. | Commissary Sergeant | Deatonsville (Sailor's Creek), Virginia |
| Howard | Henderson | C. | Corporal | Glendale, Virginia |
| Howard | Hiram | R. | Private | Missionary Ridge, Tennessee |
| Howard | James | | Sergeant | Near Petersburg (Battery Gregg), Virginia |
| Howard | Oliver | O. | Brigadier General | Fair Oaks, Virginia |
| Howard | Squire | E. | First Sergeant | Bayou Teche, Louisiana |
| Howe | Orion | P. | Musician | Vicksburg, Mississippi |
| Howe | William | H. | Sergeant | Fort Stedman, Virginia |
| Hubbell | William | S. | Captain | Fort Harrison, Virginia |
| Hudson | Aaron | R. | Private | Culloden, Georgia |
| Hughes | Oliver | | Corporal | Town Creek, North Carolina |
| Hughey | John | P. | Corporal | Deatonsville (Sailor's Creek), Virginia |
| Huidekoper | Henry | S. | Lieutenant Colonel | Gettysburg, Pennsylvania |
| Hunt | Louis | T. | Private | Vicksburg, Mississippi |
| Hunter | Charles | A. | Sergeant | Petersburg, Virginia |
| Hunterson | John | C. | Private | On the Peninsula, Virginia |
| Hyatt | Theodore | | First Sergeant | Vicksburg, Mississippi |
| Hyde | Thomas | W. | Major | Antietam, Maryland |
| Hymer | Samuel | | Captain | Buzzard's Roost Gap, Georgia |
| Ilgenfritz | Charles | H. | Sergeant | Fort Sedgwick, Virginia |
| Immell | Lorenzo | D. | Corporal | Wilson's Creek, Missouri |
| Ingalls | Lewis | J. | Private | Boutte Station, Louisiana |
| Inscho | Leonidas | H. | Corporal | South Mountain, Maryland |
| Irsch | Francis | | Captain | Gettysburg, Pennsylvania |
| Irwin | Patrick | | First Sergeant | Jonesboro, Georgia |
| Jackson | Frederick | R. | First Sergeant | James Island, South Carolina |
| Jacobson | Eugene | P. | Sergeant Major | Chancellorsville, Virginia |
| James | Isaac | | Private | Petersburg, Virginia |
| James | Miles | | Corporal | Chapin's Farm, Virginia |
| Jamieson | Walter | | First Sergeant | Petersburg and Fort Harrison, Virginia |
| Jardine | James | | Sergeant | Vicksburg, Mississippi |
| Jellison | Benjamin | H. | Sergeant | Gettysburg, Pennsylvania |
| Jennings | James | T. | Private | Weldon Railroad, Virginia |
| Jewett | Erastus | W. | First Lieutenant | Newport Barracks, North Carolina |
| John | William | F. | Private | Vicksburg, Mississippi |
| Johndro | Franklin | | Private | Chapin's Farm, Virginia |
| Johns | Elisha | | Corporal | Vicksburg, Mississippi |
| Johns | Henry | T. | Private | Port Hudson, Louisiana |
| Johnson | Andrew | | Private | Vicksburg, Mississippi |
| Johnson | Follett | | Corporal | New Hope Church, Georgia |
| Johnson | John | | Private | Fredericksburg, Virginia |
| Johnson | Joseph | E. | First Lieutenant | Fort Harrison, Virginia |
| Johnson | Ruel | M. | Major | Chattanooga, Tennessee |
| Johnson | Samuel | | Private | Antietam, Maryland |
| Johnson | Wallace | W. | Sergeant | Gettysburg, Pennsylvania |
| Johnston | David | H. | Private | Vicksburg, Mississippi |
| Johnston | William | | Musician | Seven Day Battle and on the Peninsula Campaign, Virginia |
| Jones | David | | Private | Vicksburg, Mississippi |
| * Jones | William | | First Sergeant | Spotsylvania, Virginia |
| Jordan | Absalom | | Corporal | Deatonsville (Sailor's Creek), Virginia |
| Josselyn | Simeon | T. | First Lieutenant | Missionary Ridge, Tennessee |
| Judge | Francis | W. | First Sergeant | Fort Sanders, Knoxville, Tennessee |
| Kaiser | John | | First Sergeant | Richmond, Virginia |
| Kaltenbach | Luther | | Corporal | Nashville, Tennessee |
| Kane | John | | Corporal | Petersburg, Virginia |
| Kappesser | Peter | | Private | Lookout Mountain, Tennessee |
| Karpeles | Leopold | | Sergeant | Wilderness Campaign, Virginia |
| Kauss | August | | Corporal | Five Forks, Virginia |
| Keele | Joseph | | Sergeant Major | North Anna River, Virginia |
| Keen | Joseph | S. | Sergeant | Near the Chattahoochee River, Georgia |
| Keene | Joseph | | Private | Fredericksburg, Virginia |
| Kelley | Andrew | J. | Private | Knoxville, Tennessee |
| Kelley | George | V. | Captain | Franklin, Tennessee |
| Kelley | Leverett | M. | Sergeant | Missionary Ridge, Tennessee |
| Kelly | Alexander | | First Sergeant | Chapin's Farm, Virginia |
| Kelly | Daniel | A. | Sergeant | Waynesboro, Virginia |
| Kelly | Thomas | | Private | Front Royal, Virginia |
| Kemp | Joseph | B. | First Sergeant | Wilderness Campaign, Virginia |
| Kendall | William | W. | First Sergeant | Black River Bridge, Mississippi |
| Kennedy | John | | Private | Trevilian Station, Virginia |
| Kenyon | John | S. | Sergeant | Trenton, North Carolina |
| Kenyon | Samuel | P. | Private | Deatonsville (Sailor's Creek), Virginia |
| Keough | John | | Corporal | Deatonsville (Sailor's Creek), Virginia |
| Kephart | James | | Private | Vicksburg, Mississippi |
| Kerr | Thomas | R. | Captain | Moorfield, West Virginia |
| Kiggins | John | | Sergeant | Lookout Mountain, Tennessee |
| Kimball | Joseph | | Private | Deatonsville (Sailor's Creek), Virginia |
| Kindig | John | M. | Corporal | Spotsylvania, Virginia |
| King | Horatio | C. | Major/Quartermaster | Near Dinwiddie Courthouse, Virginia |
| King Jr. | Rufus | | First Lieutenant | White Oak Swamp Bridge, Virginia |
| Kinsey | John | | Corporal | Spotsylvania, Virginia |
| Kirby | Dennis | T. | Major | Vicksburg, Mississippi |
| Kirk | Jonathan | C. | Captain | North Anna River, Virginia |
| Kline | Harry | | Private | Deatonsville (Sailor's Creek), Virginia |
| Kloth | Charles | H. | Private | Vicksburg, Mississippi |
| Knight | Charles | H. | Corporal | Petersburg, Virginia |
| Knight | William | J. | Private | Georgia |
| Knowles | Abiather | J. | Private | Bull Run, Virginia |
| Knox | Edward | M. | Second Lieutenant | Gettysburg, Pennsylvania |
| Koogle | Jacob | | First Lieutenant | Five Forks, Virginia |
| Kountz | John | S. | Musician | Missionary Ridge, Tennessee |
| Kramer | Theodore | L. | Private | Chapin's Farm, Virginia |
| Kretsinger | George | | Private | Vicksburg, Mississippi |
| Kuder | Andrew | | Second Lieutenant | Waynesboro, Virginia |
| Kuder | Jeremiah | | Lieutenant | Jonesboro, Georgia |
| Labill | Joseph | S. | Private | Vicksburg, Mississippi |
| Ladd | George | | Private | Waynesboro, Virginia |
| * Laing | William | | Sergeant | Chapin's Farm, Virginia |
| Landis | James | P. | Chief Bugler | Paine's Crossroads, Virginia |
| Lane | Morgan | D. | Private | Jetersville, Virginia |
| Lanfare | Aaron | S. | First Lieutenant | Deatonsville (Sailor's Creek), Virginia |
| Langbein | Johann | C. J. | Musician | Camden, North Carolina |
| Larimer | Smith | | Corporal | Deatonsville (Sailor's Creek), Virginia |
| Larrabee | James | W. | Corporal | Vicksburg, Mississippi |
| Lawson | Gaines | | First Sergeant | Minville, Tennessee |
| Lawton | Henry | W. | Captain | Atlanta, Georgia |
| Leonard | Edwin | | Sergeant | Near Petersburg, Virginia |
| Leonard | William | E. | Private | Deep Bottom, Virginia |
| Leslie | Frank | | Private | Front Royal, Virginia |
| Levy | Benjamin | B. | Private | Glendale, Virginia |

| Name | | | Rank at Time of Action | Place of Action |
| --- | --- | --- | --- | --- |
| Lewis | Dewitt | C. | Captain | Secessionville, South Carolina |
| Lewis | Henry | | Corporal | Vicksburg, Mississippi |
| Lewis | Samuel | E. | Corporal | Petersburg, Virginia |
| Libaire | Adolph | | Captain | Antietam, Maryland |
| Lilley | John | | Private | Petersburg, Virginia |
| Little | Henry | F. W. | Sergeant | Near Richmond, Virginia |
| Littlefield | George | H. | Corporal | Fort Fisher, North Carolina |
| Livingston | Josiah | O. | First Lt./Adjutant | Newport Barracks, North Carolina |
| Locke | Lewis | | Private | Paine's Crossroads, Virginia |
| Lonergan | John | | Captain | Gettysburg, Pennsylvania |
| Longshore | William | H. | Private | Vicksburg, Mississippi |
| Lonsway | Joseph | | Private | Murfrees Station, Virginia |
| Lord | William | | Musician | Drewry's Bluff, Virginia |
| Lorish | Andrew | J. | Commissary Sergeant | Winchester, Virginia |
| Love | George | M. | Colonel | Cedar Creek, Virginia |
| Lovering | George | M. | First Sergeant | Port Hudson, Louisiana |
| Lower | Cyrus | B. | Private | Wilderness Campaign, Virginia |
| Lower | Robert | A. | Private | Vicksburg, Mississippi |
| Loyd | George | A. | Private | Petersburg, Virginia |
| Lucas | George | W. | Private | Benton, Arkansas |
| Luce | Moses | A. | Sergeant | Laurel Hill, Virginia |
| Ludgate | William | | Captain | Farmville, Virginia |
| Ludwig | Carl | | Private | Petersburg, Virginia |
| Lunt | Alphonso | M. | Sergeant | Opequan Creek, Virginia |
| Lutes | Franklin | W. | Corporal | Petersburg, Virginia |
| Luther | James | H. | Private | Fredericksburg, Virginia |
| Luty | Gotlieb | | Corporal | Chancellorsville, Virginia |
| Lyman | Joel | H. | Quartermaster Sergeant | Winchester, Virginia |
| Lyon | Frederick | A. | Corporal | Cedar Creek, Virginia |
| MacArthur Jr. | Arthur | | First Lt./Adjutant | Missionary Ridge, Tennessee |
| Madden | Michael | | Private | Mason's Island, Maryland |
| Madison | James | | Sergeant | Waynesboro, Virginia |
| Magee | William | | Drummer | Murfreesboro, Tennessee |
| Mahoney | Jeremiah | | First Sergeant | Fort Sanders, Knoxville, Tennessee |
| Mandy | Harry | J. | First Sergeant | Front Royal, Virginia |
| Mangam | Richard | C. | Private | Hatcher's Run, Virginia |
| Manning | Joseph | S. | Private | Fort Sanders, Knoxville, Tennessee |
| Marland | William | | First Lieutenant | Grand Coteau, Louisiana |
| Marquette | Charles | D. | Sergeant | Petersburg, Virginia |
| Marsh | Albert | | Sergeant | Spotsylvania, Virginia |
| Marsh | Charles | H. | Private | Back Creek Valley, West Virginia |
| Marsh | George | | Sergeant | Elk River, Tennessee |
| Martin | Sylvester | H. | Lieutenant | Weldon Railroad, Virginia |
| Mason | Elihu | H. | Sergeant | Georgia |
| Mathews | William | H. | First Sergeant | Petersburg, Virginia |
| Matthews | John | C. | Corporal | Petersburg, Virginia |
| Matthews | Milton | | Private | Petersburg, Virginia |
| Mattingly | Henry | B. | Private | Jonesboro, Georgia |
| Mattocks | Charles | P. | Colonel | Deatonsville (Sailor's Creek), Virginia |
| Maxham | Lowell | M. | Corporal | Fredericksburg, Virginia |
| May | William | C. | Private | Nashville, Tennessee |
| Mayberry | John | B. | Private | Gettysburg, Pennsylvania |
| Mayes | William | B. | Private | Near Kenesaw Mountain, Georgia |
| Maynard | George | H. | Private | Fredericksburg, Virginia |
| McAdams | Peter | | Corporal | Salem Heights, Virginia |
| McAwee | Benjamin | F. | Sergeant | Petersburg, Virginia |
| McAnally | Charles | | Second Lieutenant | Spotsylvania, Virginia |
| McCammon | William | W. | First Lieutenant | Corinth, Mississippi |
| McCarren | Bernard | | Private | Gettysburg, Pennsylvania |
| McCauslin | Joseph | | Private | Petersburg, Virginia |
| McCleary | Charles | E. | First Lieutenant | Nashville, Tennessee |
| McClelland | James | M. | Private | Vicksburg, Mississippi |
| McConnell | Samuel | | Captain | Fort Blakely, Alabama |
| McCornack | Andrew | | Private | Vicksburg, Mississippi |
| McDonald | George | E. | Private | Fort Stedman, Virginia |
| McDonald | John | W. | Private | Pittsburg Landing, Tennessee |
| McElhinny | Samuel | O. | Private | Deatonsville (Sailor's Creek), Virginia |
| McEnroe | Patrick | H. | Sergeant | Winchester, Virginia |
| McFall | Daniel | R. | Sergeant | Spotsylvania, Virginia |
| McGinn | Edward | | Private | Vicksburg, Mississippi |
| McGonagle | Wilson | | Private | Vicksburg, Mississippi |
| McGonnigle | Andrew | J. | Capt./Asst. Quartermaster | Cedar Creek, Virginia |
| McGough | Owen | | Corporal | Bull Run, Virginia |
| McGraw | Thomas | | Sergeant | Petersburg, Virginia |
| McGuire | Patrick | | Private | Vicksburg, Mississippi |
| McHale | Alexander | U. | Corporal | Spotsylvania Courthouse, Virginia |
| McKay | Charles | W. | Sergeant | Dug Gap, Georgia |
| McKee | George | | Color Sergeant | Petersburg, Virginia |
| McKeen | Nineveh | S. | First Lieutenant | Stone River and Liberty Gap, Tennessee |
| McKeever | Michael | | Private | Burnt Ordinary, Virginia |
| McKown | Nathaniel | A. | Sergeant | Chapin's Farm, Virginia |
| McMahon | Martin | T. | Captain/Aide-de-Camp | White Oak Swamp, Virginia |
| McMillen | Francis | M. | Sergeant | Petersburg, Virginia |
| * McVeane | John | P. | Corporal | Fredericksburg Heights, Virginia |
| McWhorter | Walter | F. | Commissary Sergeant | Deatonsville (Sailor's Creek), Virginia |
| Meach | George | E. | Farrier | Winchester, Virginia |
| Meagher | Thomas | | First Sergeant | Chapin's Farm, Virginia |
| Mears | George | W. | Sergeant | Gettysburg, Pennsylvania |
| Menter | John | W. | Sergeant | Deatonsville (Sailor's Creek), Virginia |
| Merriam | Henry | C. | Lieutenant Colonel | Fort Blakely, Alabama |
| Merrifield | James | K. | Corporal | Franklin, Tennessee |
| Merrill | Augustus | | Captain | Petersburg, Virginia |
| Merrill | George | | Private | Fort Fisher, North Carolina |
| Merritt | John | G. | Sergeant | Bull Run, Virginia |
| Meyer | Henry | C. | Captain | Petersburg, Virginia |
| Miles | Nelson | A. | Colonel | Chancellorsville, Virginia |
| Miller | Frank | | Private | Deatonsville (Sailor's Creek), Virginia |
| Miller | Henry | A. | Captain | Fort Blakely, Alabama |
| Miller | Jacob | C. | Private | Vicksburg, Mississippi |
| Miller | James | P. | Private | Selma, Alabama |
| Miller | John | | Private | Waynesboro, Virginia |
| Miller | John | G. | Corporal | Gettysburg, Pennsylvania |
| Miller | William | E. | Captain | Gettysburg, Pennsylvania |
| Mills | Frank | W. | Sergeant | Sandy Cross Roads, North Carolina |
| Mindil | George | W. | Captain | Williamsburg, Virginia |
| Mitchell | Alexander | H. | First Lieutenant | Spotsylvania, Virginia |
| Mitchell | Theodore | | Private | Petersburg, Virginia |
| Moffitt | John | H. | Corporal | Gaines's Mill, Virginia |
| Molbone | Archibald | | Sergeant | Petersburg, Virginia |
| Monaghan | Patrick | H. | Corporal | Petersburg, Virginia |
| Moore | Daniel | B. | Corporal | Fort Blakely, Alabama |
| Moore | George | G. | Private | Fisher's Hill, Virginia |
| Moore | Wilbur | F. | Private | Nashville, Tennessee |
| Morey | Delano | | Private | McDowell, Virginia |
| Morford | Jerome | | Private | Vicksburg, Mississippi |
| * Morgan | Lewis | | Private | Spotsylvania, Virginia |
| Morgan | Richard | H. | Corporal | Columbus, Georgia |
| Morrill | Walter | G. | Captain | Rappahannock Station, Virginia |
| Morris | William | P. | Sergeant | Deatonsville (Sailor's Creek), Virginia |
| Morrison | Francis | | Private | Bermuda Hundred, Virginia |
| Morse | Benjamin | | Private | Spotsylvania, Virginia |
| Morse | Charles | E. | Sergeant | Wilderness Campaign, Virginia |
| Mostoller | John | W. | Private | Lynchburg, Virginia |
| Mulholland | St. Clair | A. | Major | Chancellorsville, Virginia |
| Mundell | Walter | L. | Corporal | Deatonsville (Sailor's Creek), Virginia |
| Munsell | Harvey | M. | Sergeant | Gettysburg, Pennsylvania |
| Murphy | Charles | J. | First Lt./Quartermaster | Bull Run, Virginia |
| Murphy | Daniel | J. | Sergeant | Hatcher's Run, Virginia |

| Name | | | Rank at Time of Action | Place of Action |
|---|---|---|---|---|
| Murphy | Dennis | J. F. | Sergeant | Corinth, Mississippi |
| Murphy | James | T. | Private | Petersburg, Virginia |
| Murphy | John | P. | Private | Antietam, Maryland |
| Murphy | Michael | C. | Lieutenant Colonel | North Anna River, Virginia |
| Murphy | Robinson | B. | Musician | Atlanta, Georgia |
| Murphy | Thomas | | Corporal | Chapin's Farm, Virginia |
| Murphy | Thomas | C. | Corporal | Vicksburg, Mississippi |
| Murphy | Thomas | J. | First Sergeant | Five Forks, Virginia |
| Myers | George | S. | Private | Chickamauga, Georgia |
| Myers | William | H. | Private | Appomattox Courthouse, Virginia |
| Nash | Henry | H. | Corporal | Vicksburg, Mississippi |
| Neahr | Zachariah | C. | Private | Fort Fisher, North Carolina |
| Neville | Edwin | M. | Captain | Deatonsville (Sailor's Creek), Virginia |
| Newman | Marcellus | J. | Private | Resaca, Georgia |
| Newman | William | H. | Lieutenant | Amelia Springs, Virginia |
| Nichols | Henry | C. | Captain | Fort Blakely, Alabama |
| Niven | Robert | | Second Lieutenant | Waynesboro, Virginia |
| Nolan | John | J. | Sergeant | Georgia Landing, Louisiana |
| Noll | Conrad | | Sergeant | Spotsylvania, Virginia |
| North | Jasper | N. | Private | Vicksburg, Mississippi |
| Norton | Elliott | M. | Second Lieutenant | Deatonsville (Sailor's Creek), Virginia |
| Norton | John | R. | Second Lieutenant | Deatonsville (Sailor's Creek), Virginia |
| Norton | Llewellyn | P. | Sergeant | Deatonsville (Sailor's Creek), Virginia |
| Noyes | William | W. | Private | Spotsylvania, Virginia |
| Nutting | Lee | | Captain | Todd's Tavern, Virginia |
| O'Beirne | James | R. | Captain | Fair Oaks, Virginia |
| O'Brien | Henry | D. | Corporal | Gettysburg, Pennsylvania |
| O'Brien | Peter | | Private | Waynesboro, Virginia |
| O'Connor | Albert | | Sergeant | Gravelly Run, Virginia |
| O'Donnor | Timothy | | Private | Near Malvern, Virginia |
| O'Dea | John | | Private | Vicksburg, Mississippi |
| O'Donnell | Menomen | | First Lieutenant | Vicksburg, Mississippi; Fort DeRussy, Louisiana |
| O'Neill | Stephen | | Corporal | Chancellorsville, Virginia |
| Oliver | Charles | | Sergeant | Petersburg, Virginia |
| Oliver | Paul | A. | Captain | Resaca, Georgia |
| Opel | John | N. | Private | Wilderness Campaign, Virginia |
| Orbansky | David | | Private | Shiloh, Tennessee; Vicksburg, Mississippi |
| Orr | Charles | A. | Private | Hatcher's Run, Virginia |
| Orr | Robert | L. | Major | Petersburg, Virginia |
| Orth | Jacob | G. | Corporal | Antietam, Maryland |
| Osborne | William | H. | Private | Malvern Hill, Virginia |
| Oss | Albert | | Private | Chancellorsville, Virginia |
| Overturf | Jacob | H. | Private | Vicksburg, Mississippi |
| Packard | Loron | F. | Private | Raccoon Ford, Virginia |
| Palmer | George | H. | Musician | Lexington, Missouri |
| Palmer | John | G. | Corporal | Fredericksburg, Virginia |
| Palmer | William | J. | Colonel | Red Hill, Alabama |
| Parker | Thomas | | Corporal | Petersburg and Deatonsville (Sailor's Creek), Virginia |
| Parks | Henry | J. | Private | Cedar Creek, Virginia |
| Parks | James | W. | Corporal | Nashville, Tennessee |
| ¹ Parrott | Jacob | | Private | Georgia |
| Parsons | Joel | | Private | Vicksburg, Mississippi |
| Patterson | John | H. | First Lieutenant | Wilderness Campaign, Virginia |
| Patterson | John | T. | Principal Musician | Winchester, Virginia |
| Paul | William | H. | Private | Antietam, Maryland |
| Pay | Byron | E. | Private | Nolensville, Tennessee |
| Payne | Irvin | C. | Corporal | Deatonsville (Sailor's Creek), Virginia |
| Payne | Thomas | H. L. | First Lieutenant | Fort Blakely, Alabama |
| Pearsall | Platt | | Corporal | Vicksburg, Mississippi |
| Pearson | Alfred | L. | Colonel | Lewis's Farm, Virginia |
| Peck | Cassius | | Private | Near Blackburn's Ford, West Virginia |
| Peck | Theodore | S. | First Lieutenant | Newport Barracks, North Carolina |
| Peirsol | James | K. | Sergeant | Paine's Crossroads, Virginia |
| Pennypacker | Galusha | | Colonel | Fort Fisher, North Carolina |

| Name | | | Rank at Time of Action | Place of Action |
|---|---|---|---|---|
| Pentzer | Patrick | H. | Captain | Fort Blakely, Alabama |
| Pesch | Joseph | M. | Private | Grand Gulf, Mississippi |
| Peters | Henry | C. | Private | Vicksburg, Mississippi |
| Petty | Philip | | Sergeant | Fredericksburg, Virginia |
| Phelps | Charles | E. | Colonel | Laurel Hill, Virginia |
| Phillips | Josiah | | Private | Sutherland Station, Virginia |
| Phisterer | Frederick | | First Lieutenant | Stone River, Tennessee |
| Pickle | Alonzo | H. | Sergeant | Deep Bottom, Virginia |
| Pike | Edward | M. | First Sergeant | Cache River, Arkansas |
| Pingree | Samuel | E. | Captain | Lee's Mills, Virginia |
| Pinkham | Charles | H. | Sergeant Major | Fort Stedman, Virginia |
| Pinn | Robert | A. | First Sergeant | Chapin's Farm, Virginia |
| Pipes | James | M. | Captain | Gettysburg, Pennsylvania; Ream's Station, Virginia |
| Pitman | George | J. | Sergeant | Deatonsville (Sailor's Creek), Virginia |
| Pittinger | William | | Sergeant | Georgia |
| Plant | Henry | E. | Corporal | Bentonville, North Carolina |
| Platt | George | C. | Private | Fairfield, Pennsylvania |
| Plimley | William | | First Lieutenant | Hatcher's Run, Virginia |
| Plowman | George | H. | Sergeant Major | Petersburg, Virginia |
| Plunkett | Thomas | | Sergeant | Fredericksburg, Virginia |
| Pond | George | F. | Private | Drywood, Kansas |
| Pond | James | B. | First Lieutenant | Baxter Springs, Kansas |
| Porter | Ambrose | | Commissary Sergeant | Tallahatchie River, Mississippi |
| Porter | Horace | | Captain | Chickamauga, Georgia |
| Porter | John | R. | Private | Georgia |
| Porter | William | | Sergeant | Deatonsville (Sailor's Creek), Virginia |
| Post | Philip | S. | Colonel | Nashville, Tennessee |
| Postles | James | P. | Captain | Gettysburg, Pennsylvania |
| Potter | George | W. | Private | Petersburg, Virginia |
| Potter | Norman | F. | First Sergeant | Lookout Mountain, Tennessee |
| Powell | William | H. | Major | Sinking Creek, Virginia |
| Power | Albert | | Private | Pea Ridge, Arkansas |
| Powers | Wesley | J. | Corporal | Oostanaula River, Georgia |
| Prentice | Joseph | R. | Private | Stone River, Tennessee |
| Preston | Noble | D. | First Lt./Commissary | Trevilian Station, Virginia |
| Purcell | Hiram | W. | Sergeant | Fair Oaks, Virginia |
| Purman | James | J. | Lieutenant | Gettysburg, Pennsylvania |
| Putnam | Edgar | P. | Sergeant | Crumps Creek, Virginia |
| Putnam | Winthrop | D. | Corporal | Vicksburg, Mississippi |
| Quay | Matthew | S. | Colonel | Fredericksburg, Virginia |
| Quinlan | James | | Major | Savage Station, Virginia |
| Rafferty | Peter | F. | Private | Malvern Hill, Virginia |
| Rand | Charles | F. | Private | Blackburn's Ford, Virginia |
| Ranney | George | E. | Assistant Surgeon | Resaca, Georgia |
| Ranney | Myron | H. | Private | Bull Run, Virginia |
| Ransbottom | Alfred | | First Sergeant | Franklin, Tennessee |
| Ratcliff | Edward | | First Sergeant | Chapin's Farm, Virginia |
| Raub | Jacob | F. | Assistant Surgeon | Hatcher's Run, Virginia |
| Raymond | William | H. | Corporal | Gettysburg, Pennsylvania |
| Read | Morton | A. | First Lieutenant | Appomattox Station, Virginia |
| Rebmann | George | F. | Sergeant | Fort Blakely, Alabama |
| Reddick | William | H. H. | Corporal | Georgia |
| Reed | Axel | H. | Sergeant | Chickamauga, Georgia; Missionary Ridge, Tennessee |
| Reed | Charles | W. | Bugler | Gettysburg, Pennsylvania |
| Reed | George | W. | Private | Weldon Railroad, Virginia |
| Reed | William | | Private | Vicksburg, Mississippi |
| Reeder | Charles | A. | Private | Battery Gregg, Virginia |
| Reid | Robert | A. | Private | Petersburg, Virginia |
| Reigle | Daniel | P. | Corporal | Cedar Creek, Virginia |
| Reisinger | James | M. | Corporal | Gettysburg, Pennsylvania |
| Renninger | Louis | | Corporal | Vicksburg, Mississippi |
| Reynolds | George | | Private | Winchester, Virginia |
| Rhodes | Julius | D. | Private | Thoroughfare Gap and Bull Run, Virginia |
| Rhodes | Sylvester | D. | Sergeant | Fisher's Hill, Virginia |

| Last | First | M. | Rank at Time of Action | Place of Action |
| --- | --- | --- | --- | --- |
| Rice | Edmund | | Major | Gettysburg, Pennsylvania |
| Rich | Carlos | H. | First Sergeant | Wilderness Campaign, Virginia |
| Richardson | William | R. | Private | Deatonsville (Sailor's Creek), Virginia |
| Richey | William | E. | Corporal | Chickamauga, Georgia |
| * Richmond | James | | Private | Gettysburg, Pennsylvania |
| Ricksecker | John | H. | Private | Franklin, Tennessee |
| Riddell | Rudolph | R. | Lieutenant | Deatonsville (Sailor's Creek), Virginia |
| Riley | Thomas | | Private | Fort Blakely, Alabama |
| Ripley | William | Y. W. | Lieutenant Colonel | Malvern Hill, Virginia |
| Robbins | Augustus | J. | Second Lieutenant | Spotsylvania, Virginia |
| Roberts | Otis | O. | Sergeant | Rappahannock Station, Virginia |
| Robertson | Robert | S. | First Lieutenant | Corbin's Bridge, Virginia |
| * Robertson | Samuel | | Private | Georgia |
| Robie | George | F. | Sergeant | Richmond, Virginia |
| Robinson | Elbridge | | Private | Winchester, Virginia |
| Robinson | James | H. | Private | Brownsville Station, Arkansas |
| Robinson | John | C. | Brigadier General | Laurel Hill, Virginia |
| Robinson | John | H. | Private | Gettysburg, Pennsylvania |
| Robinson | Thomas | | Private | Spotsylvania, Virginia |
| Rock | Frederick | | Private | Vicksburg, Mississippi |
| Rockefeller | Charles | M. | Lieutenant | Fort Blakely, Alabama |
| Rodenbough | Theophilus | F. | Captain | Trevilian Station, Virginia |
| Rohm | Ferdinand | F. | Chief Bugler | Ream's Station, Virginia |
| Rood | Oliver | P. | Private | Gettysburg, Pennsylvania |
| Roosevelt | George | W. | First Sergeant | Bull Run, Virginia; Gettysburg, Pennsylvania |
| * Ross | Marion | A. | Sergeant Major | Georgia |
| Rossbach | Valentine | | Sergeant | Spotsylvania, Virginia |
| Rought | Stephen | | Sergeant | Wilderness Campaign, Virginia |
| Rounds | Lewis | A. | Private | Spotsylvania, Virginia |
| Roush | James | L. | Corporal | Gettysburg, Pennsylvania |
| Rowand Jr. | Archibald | H. | Private | Virginia |
| Rowe | Henry | W. | Private | Petersburg, Virginia |
| Rundle | Charles | W. | Private | Vicksburg, Mississippi |
| Russell | Charles | L. | Corporal | Spotsylvania, Virginia |
| Russell | Milton | F. | Captain | Stone River, Tennessee |
| Rutherford | John | T. | First Lieutenant | Yellow Tavern and Hanovertown, Virginia |
| Rutter | James | M. | Sergeant | Gettysburg, Pennsylvania |
| Ryan | Peter | J. | Private | Winchester, Virginia |
| Sacriste | Louis | J. | First Lieutenant | Chancellorsville and Auburn, Virginia |
| Sagelhurst | John | C. | Sergeant | Hatcher's Run, Virginia |
| Sancrainte | Charles | F. | Private | Atlanta, Georgia |
| Sands | William | | First Sergeant | Dabney's Mill, Virginia |
| Sanford | Jacob | | Private | Vicksburg, Mississippi |
| Sargent | Jackson | G. | Sergeant | Petersburg, Virginia |
| Sartwell | Henry | | Sergeant | Chancellorsville, Virginia |
| Savacool | Edwin | F. | Captain | Deatonsville (Sailor's Creek), Virginia |
| Saxton Jr. | Rufus | | Brigadier General | Harpers Ferry, West Virginia |
| Scanlan | Patrick | | Private | Ashepoo River, South Carolina |
| Scheibner | Martin | E. | Private | Mine Run, Virginia |
| Schenck | Benjamin | W. | Private | Vicksburg, Mississippi |
| Schiller | John | | Private | Chapin's Farm, Virginia |
| Schlachter | Philipp | | Private | Spotsylvania, Virginia |
| Schmal | George | W. | Blacksmith | Paine's Crossroads, Virginia |
| Schmauch | Andrew | | Private | Vicksburg, Mississippi |
| Schmidt | Conrad | | First Sergeant | Winchester, Virginia |
| Schmidt | William | | Private | Missionary Ridge, Tennessee |
| Schneider | George | | Sergeant | Petersburg, Virginia |
| Schnell | Christian | | Corporal | Vicksburg, Mississippi |
| Schofield | John | M. | Major | Wilson's Creek, Missouri |
| Schoonmaker | James | M. | Colonel | Winchester, Virginia |
| Schorn | Charles | | Chief Bugler | Appomattox, Virginia |
| Schubert | Martin | | Private | Fredericksburg, Virginia |
| Schwan | Theodore | | First Lieutenant | Peebles Farm, Virginia |
| Schwenk | Martin | | Sergeant | Millerstown, Pennsylvania |
| Scofield | David | H. | Quartermaster Sergeant | Cedar Creek, Virginia |
| Scott | Alexander | | Corporal | Monocacy, Maryland |
| * Scott | John | M. | Sergeant | Georgia |
| Scott | John | W. | Captain | Five Forks, Virginia |
| Scott | Julian | A. | Drummer | Lee's Mill, Virginia |
| Seaman | Elisha | B. | Private | Chancellorsville, Virginia |
| Sears | Cyrus | | First Lieutenant | Iuka, Mississippi |
| Seaver | Thomas | O. | Colonel | Spotsylvania Courthouse, Virginia |
| Seitzinger | James | M. | Private | Cold Harbor, Virginia |
| Sellers | Alfred | J. | Major | Gettysburg, Pennsylvania |
| * Seston | Charles | H. | Sergeant | Winchester, Virginia |
| Sewell | William | J. | Colonel | Chancellorsville, Virginia |
| Shafter | William | R. | First Lieutenant | Fair Oaks, Virginia |
| Shahan | Emisire | | Corporal | Deatonsville (Sailor's Creek), Virginia |
| Shaler | Alexander | | Colonel | Marye's Heights, Virginia |
| Shambaugh | Charles | | Corporal | Charles City Crossroads, Virginia |
| Shanes | John | | Private | Carter's Farm, Virginia |
| Shapland | John | | Private | Elk River, Tennessee |
| Shea | Joseph | H. | Private | Chapin's Farm, Virginia |
| Shellenberger | John | | Corporal | Deep Run, Virginia |
| Shepard | Irwin | | Corporal | Knoxville, Tennessee |
| Shepherd | William | | Private | Deatonsville (Sailor's Creek), Virginia |
| Sherman | Marshall | | Private | Gettysburg, Pennsylvania |
| Shiel | John | | Corporal | Fredericksburg, Virginia |
| Shields | Bernard | | Private | Appomattox, Virginia |
| Shilling | John | | First Sergeant | Weldon Railroad, Virginia |
| Shipley | Robert | F. | First Sergeant | Five Forks, Virginia |
| Shoemaker | Levi | | Sergeant | Nineveh, Virginia |
| Shopp | George | J. | Private | Five Forks, Virginia |
| Shubert | Frank | | Sergeant | Petersburg, Virginia |
| Sickles | Daniel | E. | Major General | Gettysburg, Pennsylvania |
| Sickles | William | H. | Sergeant | Gravelly Run, Virginia |
| Sidman | George | D. | Private | Gaines's Mill, Virginia |
| Simmons | John | | Private | Deatonsville (Sailor's Creek), Virginia |
| Simmons | William | T. | First Lieutenant | Nashville, Tennessee |
| Simonds | William | E. | Sergeant Major | Irish Bend, Louisiana |
| Simons | Charles | J. | Sergeant | Petersburg, Virginia |
| Skellie | Ebenezer | | Corporal | Chapin's Farm, Virginia |
| Sladen | Joseph | A. | Private | Resaca, Georgia |
| Slagle | Oscar | | Private | Elk River, Tennessee |
| * Slavens | Samuel | | Private | Georgia |
| Sloan | Andrew | J. | Private | Nashville, Tennessee |
| Slusher | Henry | C. | Private | Near Moorefield, West Virginia |
| Smalley | Reuben | | Private | Vicksburg, Mississippi |
| Smalley | Reuben | S. | Private | Elk River, Tennessee |
| Smith | Alonzo | | Sergeant | Hatcher's Run, Virginia |
| * Smith | Andrew | J. | Corporal | Honey Hill, South Carolina |
| Smith | Charles | H. | Colonel | St. Mary's Church, Virginia |
| Smith | David | L. | Sergeant | Warwick Courthouse, Virginia |
| Smith | Francis | M. | First Lt./Adjutant | Dabney's Mill, Virginia |
| Smith | Henry | I. | First Lieutenant | Black River, North Carolina |
| Smith | James | | Private | Georgia |
| Smith | Joseph | S. | Lieutenant Colonel | Hatcher's Run, Virginia |
| Smith | Otis | W. | Private | Nashville, Tennessee |
| Smith | Richard | | Private | Weldon Railroad, Virginia |
| Smith | Samuel | R. | Captain | Rowanty Creek, Virginia |
| Smith | Thaddeus | S. | Corporal | Gettysburg, Pennsylvania |
| Smith | Wilson | | Corporal | Washington, North Carolina |
| Snedden | James | | Musician | Piedmont, Virginia |
| Southard | David | | Sergeant | Deatonsville (Sailor's Creek), Virginia |
| Sova | Joseph | E. | Saddler | Appomattox Campaign, Virginia |
| Sowers | Michael | A. | Private | Stony Creek Station, Virginia |
| Spalding | Edward | B. | Sergeant | Pittsburg Landing, Tennessee |
| Sperry | William | J. | Major | Petersburg, Virginia |

| Name | | | Rank at Time of Action | Place of Action |
|---|---|---|---|---|
| Spillane | Timothy | | Private | Hatcher's Run, Virginia |
| Sprague | Benona | | Corporal | Vicksburg, Mississippi |
| * Sprague | John | W. | Colonel | Decatur, Georgia |
| Spurling | Andrew | B. | Lieutenant Colonel | Evergreen, Alabama |
| Stacey | Charles | | Private | Gettysburg, Pennsylvania |
| Stahel | Julius | H. | Major General | Piedmont, Virginia |
| Stanley | David | S. | Major General | Franklin, Tennessee |
| Starkins | John | H. | Sergeant | Campbell Station, Tennessee |
| Steele | John | W. | Major/Aide-de-Camp | Spring Hill, Tennessee |
| Steinmetz | William | | Private | Vicksburg, Mississippi |
| Stephens | William | G. | Private | Vicksburg, Mississippi |
| Sterling | John | T. | Private | Winchester, Virginia |
| Stevens | Hazard | | Capt./Asst. Adj. Gen. | Fort Huger, Virginia |
| Stewart | George | W. | First Sergeant | Paine's Crossroads, Virginia |
| Stewart | Joseph | | Private | Five Forks, Virginia |
| Stickels | Joseph | | Sergeant | Fort Blakely, Alabama |
| Stockman | George | H. | First Lieutenant | Vicksburg, Mississippi |
| Stokes | George | | Private | Nashville, Tennessee |
| Stolz | Frank | | Private | Vicksburg, Mississippi |
| Storey | John | H. R. | Sergeant | Dallas, Georgia |
| * Strausburgh | Bernard | A. | First Sergeant | Petersburg, Virginia |
| Streile | Christian | | Private | Paine's Crossroads, Virginia |
| Strong | James | N. | Sergeant | Port Hudson, Louisiana |
| Sturgeon | James | K. | Private | Kenesaw Mountain, Georgia |
| Summers | James | C. | Private | Vicksburg, Mississippi |
| Surles | William | H. | Private | Perryville, Kentucky |
| Swan | Charles | A. | Private | Selma, Alabama |
| Swap | Jacob | E. | Private | Wilderness Campaign, Virginia |
| Swayne | Wager | | Lieutenant Colonel | Corinth, Mississippi |
| Sweatt | Joseph | S. G. | Private | Carrsville, Virginia |
| Sweeney | James | | Private | Cedar Creek, Virginia |
| Swegheimer | Jacob | | Private | Vicksburg, Mississippi |
| Swift | Frederic | W. | Lieutenant Colonel | Lenoire Station, Tennessee |
| Swift | Harlan | J. | Second Lieutenant | Petersburg, Virginia |
| Sype | Peter | | Private | Vicksburg, Mississippi |
| Tabor | William | L. S. | Private | Port Hudson, Louisiana |
| Taggart | Charles | A. | Private | Deatonsville (Sailor's Creek), Virginia |
| Tanner | Charles | B. | Second Lieutenant | Antietam, Maryland |
| Taylor | Anthony | | First Lieutenant | Chickamauga, Georgia |
| Taylor | Forrester | L. | Captain | Chancellorsville, Virginia |
| Taylor | Henry | H. | Sergeant | Vicksburg, Mississippi |
| Taylor | Joseph | | Private | Weldon Railroad, Virginia |
| Taylor | Richard | | Private | Cedar Creek, Virginia |
| Taylor | William | | Sergeant/Second Lieutenant | Front Royal and Weldon Railroad, Virginia |
| Terry | John | D. | Sergeant | New Bern, North Carolina |
| Thackrah | Benjamin | | Private | Near Fort Gates, Florida |
| Thatcher | Charles | M. | Private | Petersburg, Virginia |
| Thaxter | Sidney | W. | Major | Hatcher's Run, Virginia |
| Thomas | Hampton | S. | Major | Amelia Springs, Virginia |
| Thomas | Stephen | | Colonel | Cedar Creek, Virginia |
| Thompkins | George | W. | Corporal | Petersburg, Virginia |
| Thompson | Allen | | Private | White Oak Road, Virginia |
| Thompson | Charles | A. | Sergeant | Spotsylvania, Virginia |
| Thompson | Freeman | C. | Corporal | Petersburg, Virginia |
| Thompson | James | B. | Sergeant | Gettysburg, Pennsylvania |
| Thompson | James | G. | Private | White Oak Road, Virginia |
| Thompson | James | H. | Surgeon | New Bern, North Carolina |
| Thompson | John | J. | Corporal | Hatcher's Run, Virginia |
| Thompson | Thomas | W. | Sergeant | Chancellorsville, Virginia |
| * Thompson | William | P. | Sergeant | Wilderness Campaign, Virginia |
| Thomson | Clifford | | First Lieutenant | Chancellorsville, Virginia |
| Thorn | Walter | | Second Lieutenant | Dutch Gap Canal, Virginia |
| Tibbets | Andrew | W. | Private | Columbus, Georgia |
| Tilton | William | | Sergeant | Richmond Campaign, Virginia |
| Tinkham | Eugene | M. | Corporal | Cold Harbor, Virginia |
| Titus | Charles | | Sergeant | Deatonsville (Sailor's Creek), Virginia |
| Toban | James | W. | Sergeant | Aiken, South Carolina |
| Tobie Jr. | Edward | P. | Sergeant Major | Appomattox Campaign, Virginia |
| Tobin | John | M. | First Lt./Adjutant | Malvern Hill, Virginia |
| Toffey | John | J. | First Lieutenant | Chattanooga, Tennessee |
| Tompkins | Aaron | B. | Sergeant | Deatonsville (Sailor's Creek), Virginia |
| Tompkins | Charles | H. | First Lieutenant | Fairfax, Virginia |
| Toohey | Thomas | | Sergeant | Franklin, Tennessee |
| Toomer | William | | Sergeant | Vicksburg, Mississippi |
| Torgler | Ernest | R. | Sergeant | Ezra Chapel, Georgia |
| Tozier | Andrew | J. | Sergeant | Gettysburg, Pennsylvania |
| Tracy | Amasa | S. | Lieutenant Colonel | Cedar Creek, Virginia |
| Tracy | Benjamin | F. | Colonel | Wilderness Campaign, Virginia |
| Tracy | Charles | H. | Sergeant | Spotsylvania and Petersburg, Virginia |
| Tracy | William | G. | Second Lieutenant | Chancellorsville, Virginia |
| Traynor | Andrew | | Corporal | Mason's Hill, Virginia |
| Treat | Howell | B. | Sergeant | Buzzard's Roost, Georgia |
| Tremain | Henry | E. | Major/Aide-de-Camp | Resaca, Georgia |
| Tribe | John | | Private | Waterloo Bridge, Virginia |
| Trogden | Howell | G. | Private | Vicksburg, Mississippi |
| Truell | Edwin | M. | Private | Near Atlanta, Georgia |
| Tucker | Allen | | Sergeant | Petersburg, Virginia |
| Tucker | Jacob | R. | Corporal | Petersburg, Virginia |
| Tweedale | John | | Private | Stone River, Tennessee |
| Twombly | Voltare | P. | Corporal | Fort Donelson, Tennessee |
| Tyrrell | George | W. | Corporal | Resaca, Georgia |
| Uhrl | George | | Sergeant | White Oak Swamp Bridge, Virginia |
| Urell | Michael | E. | Private | Bristoe Station, Virginia |
| Vale | John | | Private | Nolensville, Tennessee |
| Van Matre | Joseph | | Private | Petersburg, Virginia |
| Van Winkle | Edward | | Corporal | Chapin's Farm, Virginia |
| Vance | Wilson | J. | Private | Stone River, Tennessee |
| Vanderslice | John | M. | Private | Hatcher's Run, Virginia |
| Veal | Charles | | Private | Chapin's Farm, Virginia |
| Veale | Moses | | Captain | Wauhatchie, Tennessee |
| Veazey | Wheelock | G. | Colonel | Gettysburg, Pennsylvania |
| Vernay | James | D. | Second Lieutenant | Vicksburg, Mississippi |
| Vifquain | Victor | | Lieutenant Colonel | Fort Blakely, Alabama |
| Von Vegesack | Ernest | | Major/Aide-de-Camp | Gaines's Mill, Virginia |
| Wageman | John | H. | Private | Petersburg, Virginia |
| Wagner | John | W. | Corporal | Vicksburg, Mississippi |
| Wainwright | John | | First Lieutenant | Fort Fisher, North Carolina |
| Walker | James | C. | Private | Missionary Ridge, Tennessee |
| 2 Walker | Mary | E. | Contract Surgeon (Civilian) | Battle of Bull Run, Chattanooga, Tenn., etc. |
| Wall | Jerry | C. | Private | Gettysburg, Pennsylvania |
| Waller | Francis | A. | Corporal | Gettysburg, Pennsylvania |
| Walling | William | H. | Captain | Fort Fisher, North Carolina |
| Walsh | John | | Corporal | Cedar Creek, Virginia |
| Walton | George | W. | Private | Fort Hell, Petersburg, Virginia |
| Wambsgan | Martin | | Private | Cedar Creek, Virginia |
| Ward | Nelson | W. | Private | Staunton River Bridge, Virginia |
| Ward | Thomas | J. | Private | Vicksburg, Mississippi |
| Ward | William | H. | Captain | Vicksburg, Mississippi |
| Warden | John | | Corporal | Vicksburg, Mississippi |
| Warfel | Henry | C. | Private | Paine's Crossroads, Virginia |
| Warren | Francis | E. | Corporal | Port Hudson, Louisiana |
| Webb | Alexander | S. | Brigadier General | Gettysburg, Pennsylvania |
| Webb | James | W. | Private | Bull Run, Virginia |
| Webber | Alason | P. | Musician | Kenesaw Mountain, Georgia |
| Weeks | John | H. | Private | Spotsylvania, Virginia |
| Weir | Henry | C. | Capt./Asst. Adj.Gen. | St. Mary's Church, Virginia |
| Welch | George | W. | Private | Nashville, Tennessee |
| Welch | Richard | | Corporal | Petersburg, Virginia |

| Name | | | Rank at Time of Action | Place of Action |
|---|---|---|---|---|
| Welch | Stephen | | Sergeant | Dug Gap, Georgia |
| * Wells | Henry | S. | Private | Chapin's Farm, Virginia |
| Wells | Thomas | M. | Chief Bugler | Cedar Creek, Virginia |
| Wells | William | | Major | Gettysburg, Pennsylvania |
| Welsh | Edward | | Private | Vicksburg, Mississippi |
| Welsh | James | | Private | Petersburg, Virginia |
| Westerhold | William | | Sergeant | Spotsylvania, Virginia |
| Weston | John | F. | Major | Wetumpka, Alabama |
| Wheaton | Loyd | | Lieutenant Colonel | Fort Blakely, Alabama |
| Wheeler | Daniel | D. | First Lieutenant | Salem Heights, Virginia |
| Wheeler | Henry | W. | Private | Bull Run, Virginia |
| Wherry | William | M. | First Lieutenant | Wilson's Creek, Missouri |
| Whitaker | Edward | W. | Captain | Ream's Station, Virginia |
| White | Adam | | Corporal | Hatcher's Run, Virginia |
| White | John | H. | Private | Rappahannock Station, Virginia |
| White | Patrick | H. | Captain | Vicksburg, Mississippi |
| Whitehead | John | M. | Chaplain | Stone River, Tennessee |
| Whitman | Frank | M. | Private | Antietam, Maryland |
| Whitmore | John | W. | Private | Fort Blakely, Alabama |
| Whitney | William | G. | Sergeant | Chickamauga, Georgia |
| Whittier | Edward | N. | First Lieutenant | Fisher's Hill, Virginia |
| Widick | Andrew | J. | Private | Vicksburg, Mississippi |
| Wilcox | William | H. | Sergeant | Spotsylvania, Virginia |
| Wiley | James | | Sergeant | Gettysburg, Pennsylvania |
| Wilhelm | George | | Captain | Champion Hill or Baker's Creek, Mississippi |
| Wilkins | Leander | A. | Sergeant | Petersburg, Virginia |
| Willcox | Orlando | B. | Colonel | Bull Run, Virginia |
| Williams | Elwood | N. | Private | Shiloh, Tennessee |
| Williams | George | C. | Quartermaster Sergeant | Gaines's Mill, Virginia |
| Williams | Leroy | | Sergeant | Cold Harbor, Virginia |
| Williams | William | H. | Private | Peach Tree Creek, Georgia |
| Williamson | James | A. | Colonel | Chickasaw Bayou, Mississippi |
| Williston | Edward | B. | First Lieutenant | Trevilian Station, Virginia |
| Wilson | Charles | E. | Sergeant | Deatonsville (Sailor's Creek), Virginia |
| Wilson | Christopher | W. | Private | Spotsylvania, Virginia |
| Wilson | Francis | A. | Corporal | Petersburg, Virginia |
| Wilson | John | | Sergeant | Chamberlain's Creek, Virginia |
| Wilson | John | A. | Private | Georgia |
| Wilson | John | M. | First Lieutenant | Malvern Hill, Virginia |
| Winegar | William | W. | First Lieutenant | Five Forks, Virginia |
| Wisner | Lewis | S. | First Lieutenant | Spotsylvania, Virginia |
| Withington | William | H. | Captain | Bull Run, Virginia |
| Wollam | John | | Private | Georgia |
| Wood | Henry | C. | First Lieutenant | Wilson's Creek, Missouri |
| Wood | Mark | | Private | Georgia |
| Wood | Richard | H. | Captain | Vicksburg, Mississippi |
| Woodall | William | H. | Scout | Deatonsville (Sailor's Creek), Virginia |
| Woodbury | Eri | D. | Sergeant | Cedar Creek, Virginia |
| Woodruff | Alonzo | | Sergeant | Hatcher's Run, Virginia |
| Woodruff | Carle | A. | First Lieutenant | Newby's Crossroads, Virginia |
| Woods | Daniel | A. | Private | Deatonsville (Sailor's Creek), Virginia |
| Woodward | Evan | M. | First Lieutenant/Adjutant | Fredericksburg, Virginia |
| Wortick | Joseph | | Private | Vicksburg, Mississippi |
| Wray | William | J. | Sergeant | Fort Stevens, Washington, D.C. |
| Wright | Albert | D. | Captain | Petersburg, Virginia |
| Wright | Robert | | Private | Chapel House Farm, Virginia |
| Wright | Samuel | | Corporal | Nolensville, Tennessee |
| Wright | Samuel | C. | Private | Antietam, Maryland |
| Yeager | Jacob | F. | Private | Buzzard's Roost, Georgia |
| Young | Andrew | J. | Sergeant | Paine's Crossroads, Virginia |
| Young | Benjamin | F. | Corporal | Petersburg, Virginia |
| Young | Calvary | M. | Sergeant | Osage, Kansas |
| Young | James | M. | Private | Wilderness Campaign, Virginia |
| Younker | John | L. | Private | Cedar Mountain, Virginia |

| Name | | | Rank at Time of Action | Place of Action |
|---|---|---|---|---|
| **Marines** | | | | |
| Binder | Richard | | Sergeant | Fort Fisher, North Carolina |
| Denig | John | H. | Sergeant | Mobile Bay, Alabama |
| Fry | Isaac | N. | Orderly Sergeant | Fort Fisher, North Carolina |
| Hudson | Michael | | Sergeant | Mobile Bay, Alabama |
| Mackie | John | F. | Corporal | Fort Darling at Drewry's Bluff, Virginia |
| Martin | James | | Sergeant | Mobile Bay, Alabama |
| Miller | Andrew | | Sergeant | Mobile Bay, Alabama |
| Nugent | Christopher | | Orderly Sergeant | Crystal River, Florida |
| Oviatt | Miles | M. | Corporal | Mobile Bay, Alabama |
| Rannahan | John | | Corporal | Fort Fisher, North Carolina |
| Roantree | James | S. | Sergeant | Mobile Bay, Alabama |
| Shivers | John | | Private | Fort Fisher, North Carolina |
| Smith | Willard | M. | Corporal | Mobile Bay, Alabama |
| Sprowle | David | | Orderly Sergeant | Mobile Bay, Alabama |
| Thompson | Henry | A. | Private | Fort Fisher, North Carolina |
| Tomlin | Andrew | J. | Corporal | Fort Fisher, North Carolina |
| Vaughn | Pinkerton | R. | Sergeant | Port Hudson, Louisiana |
| **Navy** | | | | |
| Aheam | Michael | | Paymaster's Steward | Off Cherbourg, France |
| Anderson | Robert | N. | Quartermaster | Charleston, South Carolina |
| Angling | John | | Cabin Boy | Fort Fisher and Wilmington, North Carolina |
| Arther | Matthew | | Signal Quartermaster | Forts Henry and Donelson, Tennessee |
| Asten | Charles | | Quarter Gunner | Red River, Louisiana |
| Atkinson | Thomas | E. | Yeoman | Mobile Bay, Alabama |
| Avery | James | | Seaman | Mobile Bay, Alabama |
| Baker | Charles | | Quarter Gunner | Mobile Bay, Alabama |
| Baldwin | Charles | H. | Coal Heaver | Roanoke River, North Carolina |
| Barnum | James | | Boatswain's Mate | Fort Fisher, North Carolina |
| Barter | Gurdon | H. | Landsman | Fort Fisher, North Carolina |
| Barton | Thomas | | Seaman | Franklin, Virginia |
| Bass | David | L. | Seaman | Fort Fisher, North Carolina |
| Bazaar | Philip | | Ordinary Seaman | Fort Fisher, North Carolina |
| Bell | George | H. | Captain of the Afterguard | Galveston Bay, Texas |
| Betham | Asa | | Coxswain | Fort Fisher and Wilmington, North Carolina |
| Bibber | Charles | J. | Gunner's Mate | Fort Fisher, North Carolina |
| Bickford | John | F. | Captain of the Top | Off Cherbourg, France |
| Blagheen | William | | Ship's Cook | Fort Morgan, Mobile Bay, Alabama |
| Blair | Robert | M. | Boatswain's Mate | Fort Fisher and Wilmington, North Carolina |
| Blake | Robert | | Contraband | Off Legareville, Stono River, John's Island, South Carolina |
| Bois | Frank | | Quartermaster | Vicksburg, Mississippi |
| Bond | William | S. | Boatswain's Mate | Off Cherbourg, France |
| Bourne | Thomas | | Seaman/Gun Captain | Forts Jackson and St. Philip, Louisiana |
| Bowman | Edward | R. | Quartermaster | Fort Fisher, North Carolina |
| Bradley | Amos | | Landsman | Fort Jackson and St. Philip, Louisiana |
| Bradley | Charles | | Boatswain's Mate | Fort Hindman, Arkansas |
| Brazell | John | | Quartermaster | Mobile Bay, Alabama |
| Breen | John | | Boatswain's Mate | Franklin, Virginia |
| Brennan | Christopher | | Seaman | Forts Jackson and St. Philip and New Orleans, Louisiana |
| Brinn | Andrew | | Seaman | Port Hudson, Louisiana |
| Brown | James | | Quartermaster | Fort DeRussy, Red River, Louisiana |
| Brown | John | | Captain of the Forecastle | Mobile Bay, Alabama |
| Brown | Robert | | Captain of the Top | Fort Morgan, Mobile Bay, Alabama |
| Brown | William | H. | Landsman | Fort Morgan, Mobile Bay, Alabama |
| Brown | Wilson | | Landsman | Fort Morgan, Mobile Bay, Alabama |
| Brownell | William | P. | Coxswain | Great Gulf Bay and Vicksburg, Mississippi |
| Brutsche | Henry | | Landsman | Plymouth, North Carolina |
| Buck | James | | Quartermaster | Forts Jackson and St. Philip, Louisiana |
| Burns | John | M. | Seaman | Fort Morgan, Mobile Bay, Alabama |
| Burton | Albert | | Seaman | Fort Fisher, North Carolina |
| Butts | George | | Gunner's Mate | Red River, Louisiana |
| Byrnes | James | | Boatswain's Mate | Fort Hindman, Arkansas |
| Campbell | William | | Boatswain's Mate | Fort Fisher, North Carolina |

| Name | | | Rank at Time of Action | Place of Action |
|---|---|---|---|---|
| Carr | William | M. | Master-at-Arms | Mobile Bay, Alabama |
| Cassidy | Michael | | Landsman | Mobile Bay, Alabama |
| Chandler | James | B. | Coxswain | Mobile Bay, Alabama |
| Chaput | Louis | G. | Landsman | Mobile Bay, Alabama |
| Clifford | Robert | T. | Master-at-Arms | New Topsail Inlet, off Wilmington, North Carolina |
| Colbert | Patrick | | Coxswain | Plymouth, North Carolina |
| Conlan | Dennis | | Seaman | Fort Fisher, North Carolina |
| Connor | Thomas | | Ordinary Seaman | Fort Fisher, North Carolina |
| Connor | William | C. | Boatswain's Mate | Off Wilmington, Delaware |
| + Cooper | John | | Coxswain | Mobile Bay, Alabama |
| Corcoran | Thomas | E. | Landsman | Vicksburg, Mississippi |
| Cotton | Peter | | Ordinary Seaman | Yazoo River, Mississippi |
| Crawford | Alexander | | Fireman | Roanoke River, North Carolina |
| Cripps | Thomas | H. | Quartermaster | Mobile Bay, Alabama |
| Cronin | Cornelius | | Chief Quartermaster | Mobile Bay; New Orleans; below Vicksburg |
| Davis | John | | Quarter Gunner | Off Elizabeth City, North Carolina |
| Davis | Samuel | W. | Ordinary Seaman | Mobile Bay, Alabama |
| Deakin | Charles | | Boatswain's Mate | Mobile Bay, Alabama |
| Dempster | John | | Coxswain | Fort Fisher, North Carolina |
| Denning | Lorenzo | | Landsman | Plymouth, North Carolina |
| Dennis | Richard | | Boatswain's Mate | Mobile Bay, Alabama |
| Densmore | William | | Chief Boatswain's Mate | Mobile Bay, Alabama |
| Diggins | Bartholomew | | Ordinary Seaman | Mobile Bay, Alabama |
| Ditzenback | John | | Quartermaster | Near Nashville, Tennessee |
| Donnelly | John | C. | Ordinary Seaman | Mobile Bay, Alabama |
| Doolen | William | | Coal Heaver | Mobile Bay, Alabama |
| Dorman | John | H. | Seaman | Fort Henry, Tennessee; Vicksburg, Mississippi |
| Dougherty | Patrick | | Landsman | Fort Morgan, Mobile Bay, Alabama |
| Dow | Henry | | Boatswain's Mate | Vicksburg, Mississippi |
| Duncan | Adam | | Boatswain's Mate | Mobile Bay, Alabama |
| Duncan | James | K. L. | Ordinary Seaman | Near Harrisonburg, Louisiana |
| Dunn | William | | Quartermaster | Fort Fisher, North Carolina |
| Dunphy | Richard | D. | Coal Heaver | Mobile Bay, Alabama |
| Edwards | John | | Captain of the Top | Mobile Bay, Alabama |
| English | Thomas | | Signal Quartermaster | Fort Fisher, North Carolina |
| Erickson | John | P. | Captain of the Forecastle | Forts Fisher and Wilmington, North Carolina |
| Farley | William | | Boatswain's Mate | Off Legareville, John's Island, Stono River, South Carolina |
| Farrell | Edward | | Quartermaster | Forts Jackson and St. Philip, Louisiana |
| Ferrell | John | H. | Pilot (Civilian) | Bells Mills, Cumberland River, Nashville, Tennessee |
| Fitzpatrick | Thomas | | Coxswain | Mobile Bay, Alabama |
| Flood | Thomas | S. | Boy | Forts Jackson and St. Philip, Louisiana |
| Foy | Charles | H. | Signal Quartermaster | Fort Fisher and the Federal Point Batteries, North Carolina |
| Franks | William | J. | Seaman | Off Yazoo City, Mississippi |
| Freeman | Martin | | First Class Pilot (Civilian) | Mobile Bay, Alabama |
| Frisbee | John | B. | Gunner's Mate | Forts Jackson and St. Philip and New Orleans, Louisiana |
| Gardner | William | | Seaman | Mobile Bay, Alabama |
| Garrison | James | R. | Coal Heaver | Mobile Bay, Alabama |
| Garvin | William | | Captain of the Forecastle | Fort Fisher, North Carolina |
| George | Daniel | G. | Ordinary Seaman | Plymouth, North Carolina |
| Gile | Frank | S. | Landsman | Charleston Harbor, South Carolina |
| Graham | Robert | | Landsman | Plymouth, North Carolina |
| Greene | John | | Captain of the Forecastle | Forts Jackson and St. Philip, Louisiana |
| Griffiths | John | | Captain of the Forecastle | Fort Fisher, North Carolina |
| Griswold | Luke | M. | Ordinary Seaman | Off Cape Hatteras, North Carolina |
| Haffee | Edmund | | Quarter Gunner | Fort Fisher, North Carolina |
| Haley | James | | Captain of the Forecastle | Off Cherbourg, France |
| Halstead | William | W. | Coxswain | Mobile Bay, Alabama |
| Ham | Mark | G. | Carpenter's Mate | Off Cherbourg, France |
| Hamilton | Hugh | | Coxswain | Mobile Bay, Alabama |
| Hamilton | Richard | | Coal Heaver | Plymouth, North Carolina |
| Hamilton | Thomas | W. | Quartermaster | Vicksburg, Mississippi |
| Hand | Allexander | | Quartermaster | Near Hamilton, Roanoke River, North Carolina |
| Harcourt | Thomas | | Ordinary Seaman | Fort Fisher, North Carolina |
| Harding | Thomas | | Captain of the Forecastle | Beaufort, North Carolina |
| Harley | Bernard | | Ordinary Seaman | Plymouth, North Carolina |
| Harrington | Daniel | C. | Landsman | Near Brunswick, Georgia |
| Harris | John | | Captain of the Forecastle | Mobile Bay, Alabama |
| Harrison | George | H. | Seaman | Off Cherbourg, France |
| Hathaway | Edward | W. | Seaman | Near Vicksburg, Mississippi |
| Hawkins | Charles | | Seaman | Fort Fisher, North Carolina |
| Hayden | Joseph | B. | Quartermaster | Fort Fisher, North Carolina |
| Hayes | John | | Coxswain | Off Cherbourg, France |
| Hayes | Thomas | | Coxswain | Mobile Bay, Alabama |
| Hickman | John | S. | Second Class Fireman | Port Hudson, Louisiana |
| Hinnegan | William | | Second Class Fireman | Fort Fisher, North Carolina |
| Hollat | George | | Third Class Boy | Forts Jackson and St. Philip, Louisiana |
| Horton | James | | Gunner's Mate | Off Port Royal, South Carolina |
| Horton | Lewis | A. | Seaman | Off Cape Hatteras, North Carolina |
| Houghton | Edward | J. | Ordinary Seaman | Plymouth, North Carolina |
| Howard | Martin | | Landsman | Plymouth, North Carolina |
| Howard | Peter | | Boatswain's Mate | Port Hudson, Louisiana |
| Huskey | Michael | | Fireman | Deer Creek Expedition, Mississippi |
| Hyland | John | | Seaman | Red River, Louisiana |
| Irlam | Joseph | | Seaman | Mobile Bay, Alabama |
| Irving | John | | Coxswain | Mobile Bay, Alabama |
| Irving | Thomas | | Coxswain | Charleston Harbor, South Carolina |
| Irwin | Nicholas | | Seaman | Mobile Bay, Alabama |
| James | John | H. | Captain of the Top | Mobile Bay, Alabama |
| Jenkins | Thomas | | Seaman | Vicksburg, Mississippi |
| Johnson | Henry | | Seaman | Mobile Bay, Alabama |
| Johnston | William | P. | Landsman | Harrisonburg, Louisiana |
| Jones | Andrew | | Chief Boatswain's Mate | Mobile Bay, Alabama |
| Jones | John | | Landsman | Off Cape Hatteras, North Carolina |
| Jones | John | E. | Quartermaster | Mobile Bay, Alabama |
| Jones | Thomas | | Coxswain | Fort Fisher, North Carolina |
| Jones | William | | Captain of the Top | Mobile Bay, Alabama |
| Jordan | Robert | | Coxswain | Nansemond River, Virginia |
| Jordan | Thomas | H. | Quartermaster | Mobile Bay, Alabama |
| Kane | Thomas | | Captain of the Hold | Fort Fisher, North Carolina |
| Kelley | John | | Second Class Fireman | Roanoke River, North Carolina |
| Kendrick | Thomas | | Coxswain | Mobile Bay, Alabama |
| Kenna | Barnett | | Quartermaster | Mobile Bay, Alabama |
| Kenyon | Charles | W. | Fireman | Drewry's Bluff, James River, Virginia |
| King | Robert | H. | Landsman | Plymouth, North Carolina |
| Kinnaird | Samuel | W. | Landsman | Mobile Bay, Alabama |
| + Lafferty | John | | Fireman | Roanoke River, North Carolina |
| Laffey | Bartlett | | Seaman | Off Yazoo City, Mississippi |
| Lakin | Daniel | | Seaman | Franklin, Virginia |
| Lann | John | S. | Landsman | St. Marks, Florida |
| Lawson | John | H. | Landsman | Mobile Bay, Alabama |
| Lear | Nicholas | | Quartermaster | Fort Fisher, North Carolina |
| Lee | James | H. | Seaman | Off Cherbourg, France |
| Leland | George | W. | Gunner's Mate | Charleston Harbor, South Carolina |
| Leon | Pierre | | Captain of the Forecastle | Yazoo River, Mississippi |
| Lloyd | Benjamin | | Coal Heaver | Roanoke River, North Carolina |
| Lloyd | John | W. | Coxswain | Roanoke River, North Carolina |
| Logan | Hugh | | Captain of the Afterguard | Off Cape Hatteras, North Carolina |
| Lyons | Thomas | G. | Seaman | Forts Jackson and St. Philip, Louisiana |
| Machon | James | | Boy | Mobile Bay, Alabama |
| Mack | Alexander | | Captain of the Top | Mobile Bay, Alabama |
| Mack | John | | Seaman | St. Marks, Florida |
| Madden | William | | Coal Heaver | Mobile Bay, Alabama |
| Martin | Edward | S. | Quartermaster | Mobile Bay, Alabama |
| Martin | William | | Seaman | Forts Jackson and St. Philip, Louisiana |
| Martin | William | | Boatswain's Mate | Haines Bluff, Yazoo River, Mississippi |
| McClelland | Matthew | | First Class Fireman | Port Hudson, Louisiana |
| McCormick | Michael | | Boatswain's Mate | Red River, Louisiana |
| * McCullock | Adam | | Seaman | Mobile Bay, Alabama |

| Name | | | Rank at Time of Action | Place of Action |
|---|---|---|---|---|
| McDonald | John | | Boatswain's Mate | Yazoo River Expedition, Mississippi |
| McFarland | John | C. | Captain of the Forecastle | Mobile Bay, Alabama |
| McGowan | John | | Quartermaster | Forts Jackson and St. Philip, Louisiana |
| McHugh | Martin | | Seaman | Vicksburg, Mississippi |
| McIntosh | James | | Captain of the Top | Mobile Bay, Alabama |
| McKnight | William | | Coxswain | Forts Jackson and St. Philip, Louisiana |
| McLeod | James | | Captain of the Foretop | Forts Jackson and St. Philip and New Orleans, Louisiana |
| McWilliams | George | W. | Landsman | Fort Fisher and Wilmington, North Carolina |
| Melville | Charles | | Ordinary Seaman | Mobile Bay, Alabama |
| Mifflin | James | | Engineer's Cook | Mobile Bay, Alabama |
| Miller | James | | Quartermaster | Off Legareville, John's Island, Stono River, South Carolina |
| Milliken | Daniel | | Quarter Gunner | Fort Fisher, North Carolina |
| Mills | Charles | | Seaman | Fort Fisher, North Carolina |
| Molloy | Hugh | | Ordinary Seaman | Near Harrisonburg, Louisiana |
| Montgomery | Robert | W. | Captain of the Afterguard | Fort Fisher, North Carolina |
| Moore | Charles | | Seaman | Off Cherbourg, France |
| Moore | Charles | | Landsman | Off Legareville, John's Island, Stono River, South Carolina |
| Moore | George | | Seaman | Off Cape Hatteras, North Carolina |
| Moore | William | | Boatswain's Mate | Haines Bluff, Yazoo River, Mississippi |
| Morgan | James | H. | Captain of the Top | Mobile Bay, Alabama |
| Morrison | John | G. | Coxswain | Yazoo River, Mississippi |
| Morton | Charles | W. | Boatswain's Mate | Yazoo River Expedition, Mississippi |
| + Mullen | Patrick | | Boatswain's Mate | Mattox Creek, Virginia |
| Murphy | Patrick | | Boatswain's Mate | Mobile Bay, Alabama |
| Naylor | David | J. | Landsman | Mobile Bay, Alabama |
| Neil | John | | Quarter Gunner | Fort Fisher, North Carolina |
| Newland | William | D. | Ordinary Seaman | Mobile Bay, Alabama |
| Nibbe | John | H. | Quartermaster | Yazoo River, Mississippi |
| Nichols | William | | Quartermaster | Mobile Bay, Alabama |
| Noble | Daniel | | Landsman | Mobile Bay, Alabama |
| O'Brien | Oliver | A. | Coxswain | Sullivan's Island Channel, South Carolina |
| O'Connell | Thomas | | Coal Heaver | Mobile Bay, Alabama |
| O'Donoghue | Timothy | | Seaman | Red River, Louisiana |
| Ortega | John | | Seaman | Off the coast, Georgia |
| Parker | William | | Captain of the Afterguard | Forts Jackson and St. Philip and New Orleans, Louisiana |
| Parks | George | | Captain of the Forecastle | Fort Morgan, Mobile Bay, Alabama |
| Pease | Joachim | | Seaman | Off Cherbourg, France |
| Peck | Oscar | E. | Second Class Boy | Forts Jackson and St. Philip, Louisiana |
| Pelham | William | | Landsman | Mobile Bay, Alabama |
| Perry | Thomas | | Boatswain's Mate | Off Cherbourg, France |
| Peterson | Alfred | | Seaman | Franklin, Virginia |
| Phinney | William | | Boatswain's Mate | Fort Morgan, Mobile Bay, Alabama |
| Poole | William | B. | Quartermaster | Off Cherbourg, France |
| Prance | George | | Captain of the Main Top | Fort Fisher, North Carolina |
| Preston | John | | Landsman | Fort Morgan, Mobile Bay, Alabama |
| Price | Edward | | Coxswain | Fort Morgan, Mobile Bay, Alabama |
| Province | George | | Ordinary Seaman | Fort Fisher, North Carolina |
| Pyne | George | | Seaman | St. Marks, Florida |
| Read | Charles | | Ordinary Seaman | St. Marks, Florida |
| Read | Charles | A. | Coxswain | Off Cherbourg, France |
| Read | George | E. | Seaman | Off Cherbourg, France |
| Regan | Jeremiah | | Quartermaster | Drewry's Bluff, Virginia |
| Rice | Charles | | Coal Heaver | Fort Fisher, North Carolina |
| Richards | Louis | | Quartermaster | Forts Jackson and St. Philip and New Orleans, Louisiana |
| Ringold | Edward | | Coxswain | Pocataligo, South Carolina |
| Roberts | James | | Seaman | Fort Fisher, North Carolina |
| Robinson | Alexander | | Boatswain's Mate | Off Wilmington, North Carolina |
| Robinson | Charles | | Boatswain's Mate | Yazoo River, Mississippi |
| Rountry | John | | First Class Fireman | Off Port Royal, South Carolina |
| Rush | John | | First Class Fireman | Port Hudson, Louisiana |
| Sanderson | Aaron | | Landsman | Mattox Creek, Virginia |
| Saunders | James | | Quartermaster | Off Cherbourg, France |
| Savage | Auzella | | Ordinary Seaman | Fort Fisher, North Carolina |
| Schutt | George | | Coxswain | St. Marks, Florida |

| Name | | | Rank at Time of Action | Place of Action |
|---|---|---|---|---|
| Seanor | James | | Master-at-Arms | Fort Morgan, Mobile Bay, Alabama |
| Seward | Richard | H. | Paymaster's Steward | Ship Island Sound, Louisiana |
| Sharp | Hendrick | | Seaman | Fort Mogan, Mobile Bay, Alabama |
| Shepard | Louis | C. | Ordinary Seaman | Fort Fisher, North Carolina |
| Sheridan | James | | Quartermaster | Mobile Bay, Alabama |
| Shipman | William | | Coxswain | Fort Fisher, North Carolina |
| Shutes | Henry | | Captain of the Forecastle | New Orleans, Louisiana; Fort McAllister, Georgia |
| Simkins | Lebbeus | | Coxswain | Mobile Bay, Alabama |
| Smith | Charles | H. | Coxswain | Off Cape Hatteras, North Carolina |
| Smith | Edwin | | Ordinary Seaman | Franklin, Virginia |
| Smith | James | | Captain of the Forecastle | Mobile Bay, Alabama |
| Smith | John | | Captain of the Forecastle | Fort Morgan, Mobile Bay, Alabama |
| Smith | John | | Second Captain of the Top | Fort Morgan, Mobile Bay, Alabama |
| Smith | Oloff | | Coxswain | Fort Morgan, Mobile Bay, Alabama |
| Smith | Thomas | | Seaman | St. Marks, Florida |
| Smith | Walter | B. | Ordinary Seaman | Fort Morgan, Mobile Bay, Alabama |
| Smith | William | | Quartermaster | Off Cherbourg, France |
| Stanley | William | A. | Shell Man | Fort Morgan, Mobile Bay, Alabama |
| Sterling | James | E. | Coal Heaver | Fort Morgan, Mobile Bay, Alabama |
| Stevens | Daniel | D. | Quartermaster | Fort Fisher, North Carolina |
| Stoddard | James | | Seaman | Off Yazoo City, Mississippi |
| Stout | Richard | | Landsman | Stono River, South Carolina |
| Strahan | Robert | | Captain of the Top | Off Cherbourg, France |
| Sullivan | James | | Ordinary Seaman | Fort Fisher, North Carolina |
| Sullivan | John | | Seaman | Wilmington, North Carolina |
| Sullivan | Timothy | | Coxswain | Arkansas, Tennessee, and Mississippi |
| Summers | Robert | | Chief Quartermaster | Fort Fisher, North Carolina |
| Swanson | John | | Seaman | Fort Fisher, North Carolina |
| Swatton | Edward | | Seaman | Fort Fisher, North Carolina |
| Swearer | Benjamin | | Seaman | Fort Clark, off Baltimore Inlet, Maryland |
| Talbott | William | | Captain of the Forecastle | Arkansas Post (Fort Hindman), Arkansas |
| Tallentine | James | | Quarter Gunner | Plymouth, North Carolina |
| Taylor | George | | Armorer | Mobile Bay, Alabama |
| Taylor | Thomas | | Coxswain | Mobile Bay, Alabama |
| Taylor | William | G. | Captain of the Forecastle | Fort Fisher, North Carolina |
| Thielberg | Henry | | Seaman | Nansemond River, Virginia |
| Thompson | William | | Signal Quartermaster | Hilton Head, South Carolina |
| Todd | Samuel | | Quartermaster | Fort Morgan, Mobile Bay, Alabama |
| Tripp | Othniel | | Chief Boatswain's Mate | Fort Fisher, North Carolina |
| Truett | Alexander | H. | Coxswain | Fort Morgan, Mobile Bay, Alabama |
| Vantine | Joseph | E. | First Class Fireman | Port Hudson, Louisiana |
| Verney | James | W. | Chief Quartermaster | Fort Fisher and Wilmington, North Carolina |
| Wagg | Maurice | | Coxswain | Off Cape Hatteras, North Carolina |
| Ward | James | | Quarter Gunner | Fort Morgan, Mobile Bay, Alabama |
| Warren | David | | Coxswain | Wilmington, North Carolina |
| Webster | Henry | S. | Landsman | Fort Fisher, North Carolina |
| Weeks | Charles | H. | Captain of the Foretop | Off Port Royal, South Carolina |
| Wells | William | | Quartermaster | Fort Morgan, Mobile Bay, Alabama |
| White | Joseph | | Coxswain | Fort Fisher, North Carolina |
| Whitfield | Daniel | | Quartermaster | Fort Morgan, Mobile Bay, Alabama |
| Wilcox | Franklin | L. | Ordinary Seaman | Fort Fisher, North Carolina |
| Wilkes | Henry | | Landsman | Plymouth, North Carolina |
| Wilkes | Perry | | Pilot | Red River, Louisiana |
| Williams | Anthony | | Sailmaker's Mate | Fort Fisher and Wilmington, North Carolina |
| Williams | Augustus | | Seaman | Fort Fisher, North Carolina |
| Williams | John | | Captain of the Main Top | Matthias Point, Virginia |
| Williams | John | | Seaman | Franklin, Virginia |
| Williams | Peter | | Seaman | Hampton Roads, Virginia |
| Williams | Robert | | Signal Quartermaster | Drumgould's Bluff, Mississippi |
| Williams | William | | Landsman | Charleston Harbor, South Carolina |
| Williams II | John | | Boatswain's Mate | Hilton Head, South Carolina |
| Willis | Richard | | Coxswain | Fort Fisher, North Carolina |
| Wood | Robert | B. | Coxswain | Nansemond River, Virginia |
| Woods | Samuel | | Seaman | Nansemond River, Virginia |

| Name | Rank at Time of Action | Place of Action |
| --- | --- | --- |
| Woon John | Boatswain's Mate | Grand Gulf, Mississippi River, Mississippi |
| Woram Charles B. | Seaman | Mobile Bay, Alabama |
| Wright Edward | Quartermaster | Forts St. Philip and Jackson and New Orleans, Louisiana |
| Wright William | Yeoman | Wilmington, North Carolina |
| Young Edward B. | Coxswain | Mobile Bay, Alabama |
| Young Horatio N. | Seaman | Charleston Harbor, South Carolina |
| Young William | Boatswain's Mate | Forts St. Philip and Jackson and New Orleans, Louisiana |

## The Indian Campaigns, 1861–1898

### Army

| Name | Rank at Time of Action | Place of Action |
| --- | --- | --- |
| Albee George E. | First Lieutenant | Brazos River, Texas |
| Alchesay William | Sergeant | Apache Campaigns |
| Allen William | First Sergeant | Turret Mountain, Arizona Territory |
| Anderson James | Private | Wichita River, Texas |
| Aston Edgar R. | Private | San Carlos, Arizona Territory |
| Austin William G. | Sergeant | Wounded Knee Creek, South Dakota |
| Ayers James F. | Private | Sappa Creek, Kansas |
| Babcock John B. | First Lieutenant | Spring Creek, Nebraska |
| Bailey James E. | Sergeant | Apache Campaigns |
| Baird George W. | First Lt./Adjutant | Bear Paw Mountain, Montana |
| Baker John | Musician | Cedar Creek, Montana |
| + Baldwin Frank D. | First Lieutenant | McClellan's Creek, Texas |
| Bancroft Neil | Private | Little Big Horn, Montana |
| Barnes Will C. | Private First Class | Arizona Territory |
| Barrett Richard | First Sergeant | Sycamore Canyon, Arizona Territory |
| Beauford Clay | First Sergeant | Apache Campaigns |
| Bell James | Private | Big Horn, Montana |
| Bergendahl Frederick | Private | Staked Plains, Texas |
| Bertram Heinrich | Corporal | Arizona Territory |
| Bessey Charles A. | Corporal | Elkhorn Creek, Wyoming |
| Bishop Daniel | Sergeant | Turret Mountain, Arizona Territory |
| Blair James | First Sergeant | Apache Campaigns |
| Blanquet | Indian Scout | Apache Campaigns |
| Bowden Samuel | Corporal | Wichita River, Texas |
| Bowman Alonzo | Sergeant | Cibecue Creek, Arizona Territory |
| Boyne Thomas | Sergeant | Cuchillo Negro River and Mimbres Mountains, New Mex. |
| Bradbury Sanford | First Sergeant | Hell Canyon, Arizona Territory |
| Branagan Edward | Private | Red River, Texas |
| * Brant Abram B. | Private | Little Big Horn, Montana |
| * Bratling Frank | Corporal | Fort Selden, New Mexico |
| Brett Lloyd M. | Second Lieutenant | O'Fallon's Creek, Montana |
| Brogan James | Sergeant | Simon Valley, Arizona Territory |
| Brophy James | Private | Arizona Territory |
| Brown Benjamin | Sergeant | Arizona Territory |
| Brown James | Sergeant | Davidson Canyon, Arizona Territory |
| Brown Lorenzo D. | Private | Big Hole, Montana |
| Bryan William C. | Hospital Steward | Powder River, Wyoming |
| Burkard Oscar R. | Private | Leech Lake, Minnesota |
| Burke Patrick J. | Farrier | Arizona Territory |
| Burke Richard | Private | Cedar Creek, Montana |
| Burnett George R. | Second Lieutenant | Cuchillo Negro Mountains, New Mexico |
| Butler Edmond T. | Captain | Wolf Mountain, Montana |
| Byrne Denis | Sergeant | Cedar Creek, Montana |
| Cable Joseph A. | Private | Cedar Creek, Montana |
| Callen Thomas J. | Private | Little Big Horn, Montana |
| Calvert James S. | Private | Cedar Creek, Montana |
| Canfield Heth | Private | Little Blue, Nebraska |
| Carpenter Louis H. | Captain | Kansas and Colorado |
| Carr John | Private | Chiricahua Mountains, Arizona Territory |
| Carroll Thomas | Private | Arizona Territory |
| Carter George | Private | Arizona Territory |
| Carter Mason | First Lieutenant | Bear Paw Mountain, Montana |
| Carter Robert G. | Second Lieutenant | Brazos River, Texas |
| Carter William H. | First Lieutenant | Cibecue, Arizona Territory |
| Casey James S. | Captain | Wolf Mountain, Montana |
| Chapman Amos | Scout (Civilian) | Washita River, Texas |
| Cheever Jr. Benjamin H. | First Lieutenant | White River, South Dakota |
| Chiquito | Scout | Arizona Territory |
| Clancy John E. | Musician | Wounded Knee Creek, South Dakota |
| Clark Wilfred | Private | Big Hole, Montana; Camas Meadows, Idaho |
| Clarke Powhatan H. | Second Lieutenant | Pinito Mountains, Sonora, Mexico |
| Co-Rux-Te-Chod-Ish (Mad Bear) | Sergeant | Republican River, Kansas |
| Cody William F. | Guide (Civilian) | Loupe Fork of the Platte River, Nebraska |
| Comfort John W. | Corporal | Staked Plains, Texas |
| Connor John | Corporal | Wichita River, Texas |
| Coonrod Aquilla | Sergeant | Cedar Creek, Montana |
| Corcoran Michael | Corporal | Agua Fria River, Arizona Territory |
| Craig Samuel H. | Sergeant | Santa Cruz Mountains, Mexico |
| Crandall Charles | Private | Arizona Territory |
| Crist John | Sergeant | Arizona Territory |
| Criswell Benjamin C. | Sergeant | Little Bighorn River, Montana |
| Cruse Thomas | Second Lieutenant | Big Dry Fork (Chevelon's Fork), Arizona Territory |
| Cubberly William G. | Private | San Carlos, Arizona Territory |
| Cunningham Charles | Corporal | Little Bighorn River, Montana |
| Daily Charles | Private | Arizona Territory |
| Daniels James T. | Sergeant | Arizona Territory |
| Dawson Michael | Trumpeter | Sappa Creek, Kansas |
| Day Matthias W. | Second Lieutenant | Las Animas Canyon, New Mexico |
| Day William L. | First Sergeant | Apache Campaigns |
| * De Armond William | Sergeant | Upper Washita, Texas |
| Deary George | Sergeant | Apache Creek, Arizona Territory |
| Deetline Frederick | Private | Little Big Horn, Montana |
| Denny John | Sergeant | Las Animas Canyon, New Mexico |
| Dickens Charles H. | Corporal | Chiricahua Mountains, Arizona Territory |
| Dixon William | Scout (Civilian) | Washita River, Texas |
| Dodge Francis S. | Captain | White River Agency, Colorado |
| Donahue John L. | Private | Chiricahua Mountains, Arizona Territory |
| Donavan Cornelius | Sergeant | Agua Fria River, Arizona Territory |
| Donelly John S. | Private | Cedar Creek, Montana |
| Dougherty William | Blacksmith | Arizona Territory |
| Dowling James | Corporal | Arizona Territory |
| Dozier James B. | Guide (Civilian) | Wichita River, Texas |
| Edwards William D. | First Sergeant | Big Hole, Montana |
| Eldridge George H. | Sergeant | Wichita River, Texas |
| Elsatsoosu | Corporal | Apache Campaigns |
| Elwood Edwin L. | Private | Chiricahua Mountains, Arizona Territory |
| Emmet Robert T. | Second Lieutenant | Las Animas Canyon, New Mexico |
| Evans William | Private | Big Horn, Montana |
| Factor Pompey | Private | Pecos River, Texas |
| Falcott Henry | Sergeant | Arizona Territory |
| Farren Daniel | Private | Arizona Territory |
| Feaster Mosheim | Private | Wounded Knee Creek, South Dakota |
| Fegan James | Sergeant | Plum Creek, Kansas |
| Ferrari George | Corporal | Red Creek, Arizona Territory |
| Fichter Hermann E. | Private | Whetstone Mountains, Arizona Territory |
| Foley John H. | Sergeant | Loupe Fork of the Platte River, Nebraska |
| Folly William H. | Private | Arizona Territory |
| Foran Nicholas | Private | Arizona Territory |
| Forsyth Thomas H. | First Sergeant | Powder River, Wyoming |
| Foster William | Sergeant | Red River, Texas |
| Freemeyer Christopher | Private | Cedar Creek, Montana |
| Gardiner Peter W. | Private | Sappa Creek, Kansas |
| Gardner Charles | Private | Arizona Territory |
| Garland Harry | Corporal | Little Muddy Creek, Montana; Camas Meadows, Idaho |
| Garlington Ernest A. | First Lieutenant | Wounded Knee Creek, South Dakota |
| Gates George | Bugler | Picacho Mountain, Arizona Territory |
| Gay Thomas H. | Private | Arizona Territory |
| Geiger George | Sergeant | Little Bighorn River, Montana |

| Name | | | Rank at Time of Action | Place of Action |
|---|---|---|---|---|
| Georgian | John | | Private | Chiricahua Mountains, Arizona Territory |
| * Given | John | J. | Corporal | Wichita River, Texas |
| Glavinski | Albert | | Blacksmith | Powder River, Montana |
| Glover | Thaddeus | B. | Sergeant | Mizpah and Pumpkin Creek, Montana |
| Glynn | Michael | | Private | Whetstone Mountains, Arizona Territory |
| Godfrey | Edward | S. | Captain | Bear Paw Mountain, Montana |
| Golden | Patrick | | First Sergeant | Arizona Territory |
| Goldin | Theodore | W. B. | Private | Little Big Horn, Montana |
| Goodman | David | | Private | Lyry Creek, Arizona Territory |
| Grant | George | | Sergeant | Fort Phil Kearny to Fort C. F. Smith, Dakota Territory |
| Greaves | Clinton | | Corporal | Florida Mountains, New Mexico |
| Green | Francis | C. | Sergeant | Arizona Territory |
| Green | John | | Major | Lava Beds, California |
| Gresham | John | C. | First Lieutenant | Wounded Knee Creek, South Dakota |
| Grimes | Edward | P. | Sergeant | Milk River, Colorado |
| Gunther | Jacob | | Corporal | Arizona Territory |
| Haddoo | John | | Corporal | Cedar Creek, Montana |
| Hall | John | | Private | Arizona Territory |
| Hall | William | P. | First Lieutenant | Near Camp, White River, Colorado |
| Hamilton | Frank | | Private | Agua Fria River, Arizona Territory |
| Hamilton | Mathew | H. | Private | Wounded Knee Creek, South Dakota |
| Hanley | Richard | P. | Sergeant | Little Bighorn River, Montana |
| Harding | Mosher | A. | Blacksmith | Chiricahua Mountains, Arizona Territory |
| Harrington | John | | Private | Washita River, Texas |
| Harris | Charles | D. | Sergeant | Red Creek, Arizona Territory |
| Harris | David | W. | Private | Little Bighorn River, Montana |
| Harris | William | H. | Private | Little Bighorn River, Montana |
| Hartzog | Joshua | B. | Private | Wounded Knee Creek, South Dakota |
| Haupt | Paul | | Corporal | Hell Canyon, Arizona Territory |
| Hawthorne | Harry | L. | Second Lieutenant | Wounded Knee Creek, South Dakota |
| Hay | Fred | S. | Sergeant | Upper Wichita River, Texas |
| Heartery | Richard | | Private | Cibecue, Arizona Territory |
| Heise | Clamor | | Private | Arizona Territory |
| Herron | Leander | T. | Corporal | Fort Dodge, Kansas |
| Heyl | Charles | P. H. | Second Lieutenant | Fort Hartsuff, Nebraska |
| Higgins | Thomas | P. | Private | Arizona Territory |
| Hill | Frank | E. | Sergeant | Date Creek, Arizona Territory |
| Hill | James | M. | First Sergeant | Turret Mountain, Arizona Territory |
| Hillock | Marvin | C. | Private | Wounded Knee Creek, South Dakota |
| Himmelsback | Michael | | Private | Little Blue, Nebraska |
| Hinemann | Lehmann | | Sergeant | Arizona Territory |
| Hobday | George | | Private | Wounded Knee Creek, South Dakota |
| # Hogan | Henry | | Private | Cedar Creek and Bear Paw Mountain, Montana |
| Holden | Henry | | Private | Little Bighorn River, Montana |
| Holland | David | | Corporal | Cedar Creek, Montana |
| * Hooker | George | | Private | Tonto Creek, Arizona Territory |
| Hoover | Samuel | | Bugler | Santa Maria Mountains, Arizona Territory |
| Hornaday | Elisha | S. | Private | Sappa Creek, Kansas |
| Howze | Robert | L. | Second Lieutenant | White River, South Dakota |
| Hubbard | Thomas | H. | Private | Little Blue, Nebraska |
| Huff | James | W. | Private | Arizona Territory |
| Huggins | Eli | L. | Captain | O'Fallon's Creek, Montana |
| Humphrey | Charles | F. | First Lieutenant | Clearwater, Idaho |
| Hunt | Frederick | D. | Private | Cedar Creek, Montana |
| Hutchinson | Rufus | D. | Sergeant | Little Bighorn River, Montana |
| Hyde | Henry | J. | Sergeant | Arizona Territory |
| 3 Irwin | Bernard | J. D. | Assistant Surgeon | Apache Pass, Arizona Territory |
| Jackson | James | | Captain | Camas Meadows, Idaho |
| James | John | | Corporal | Upper Washita River, Texas |
| Jarvis | Frederick | | Sergeant | Chiricahua Mountains, Arizona Territory |
| Jetter | Bernhard | | Sergeant | Sioux Campaign, South Dakota |
| Jim | | | Sergeant | Arizona Territory |
| Johnson | Henry | | Sergeant | Milk River, Colorado |
| Johnston | Edward | | Corporal | Cedar Creek, Montana |

| Name | | | Rank at Time of Action | Place of Action |
|---|---|---|---|---|
| Jones | William | H. | Farrier | Little Muddy Creek, Montana |
| Jordan | George | | Sergeant | Fort Tularosa and Carrizo Canyon, New Mexico |
| Kay | John | | Private | Arizona Territory |
| Keating | Daniel | | Corporal | Wichita River, Texas |
| Keenan | Bartholomew T. | | Trumpeter | Chiricahua Mountains, Arizona Territory |
| Keenan | John | | Private | Arizona Territory |
| Kelley | Charles | | Private | Chiricahua Mountains, Arizona Territory |
| Kelly | John | J. H. | Corporal | Upper Wichita River, Texas |
| Kelly | Thomas | | Private | Upper Wichita River, Texas |
| Kelsay | | | Scout | Arizona Territory |
| * Kennedy | Philip | | Private | Cedar Creek, Montana |
| Kerr | John | B. | Captain | White River, South Dakota |
| Kerrigan | Thomas | | Sergeant | Wichita River, Texas |
| Kilmartin | John | | Private | Whetstone Mountains, Arizona Territory |
| Kirk | John | | First Sergeant | Wichita River, Texas |
| Kirkwood | John | A. | Sergeant | Slim Buttes, Dakota Territory |
| Kitchen | George | K. | Sergeant | Upper Wichita River, Texas |
| Knaak | Albert | | Private | Arizona Territory |
| Knight | Joseph | F. | Sergeant | White River, South Dakota |
| Knox | John | W. | Sergeant | Upper Wichita River, Texas |
| Koelpin | William | | Sergeant | Upper Wichita River, Texas |
| Kosoha | | | Scout | Arizona Territory |
| * Kreher | Wendelin | | First Sergeant | Cedar Creek, Montana |
| Kyle | John | | Corporal | Republican River, Kansas |
| Larkin | David | | Farrier | Red River, Texas |
| Lawrence | James | | Private | Arizona Territory |
| Lawton | John | S. | Sergeant | Milk River, Colorado |
| Lenihan | James | | Private | Clear Creek, Arizona Territory |
| Leonard | Patrick | J. | Sergeant | Little Blue, Nebraska |
| Leonard | Patrick | T. | Corporal | Fort Hartsuff (Grace Creek), Nebraska |
| Leonard | William | | Private | Muddy Creek, Montana |
| Lewis | William | B. | Sergeant | Bluff Station, Wyoming |
| Little | Thomas | | Bugler | Arizona Territory |
| Lloyd | George | | Sergeant | Wounded Knee Creek, South Dakota |
| Lohnes | Frank | W. | Private | Gilman's Ranch, Nebraska |
| Long | Oscar | F. | Second Lieutenant | Bear Paw Mountain, Montana |
| Lowthers | James | | Private | Sappa Creek, Kansas |
| Lytle | Leonidas | S. | Sergeant | Fort Selden, New Mexico |
| Lytton | Jeptha | L. | Corporal | Fort Hartsuff, Nebraska |
| Machol | | | Private | Arizona Territory |
| Mahers | Herbert | | Private | Seneca Mountain, Arizona Territory |
| Mahoney | Gregory | | Private | Red River, Texas |
| Martin | Patrick | | Sergeant | Castle Dome and Santa Maria Mts., Az. Terr. |
| Matthews | David | A. | Corporal | Arizona Territory |
| Maus | Marion | P. | First Lieutenant | Rio Aros, Sierra Madre Mountains, Mexico |
| May | John | | Sergeant | Wichita River, Texas |
| Mays | Isaiah | | Corporal | Cedar Springs, Arizona Territory |
| McBride | Bernard | | Private | Arizona Territory |
| McBryar | William | | Sergeant | Arizona Territory |
| McCabe | William | | Private | Red River, Texas |
| * McCann | Bernard | | Private | Cedar Creek, Montana |
| McCarthy | Michael | | First Sergeant | White Bird Canyon, Idaho |
| McClernand | Edward | J. | Second Lieutenant | Bear Paw Mountain, Montana |
| McCormick | Michael | P. | Private | Cedar Creek, Montana |
| McDonald | Franklin | M. | Private | Fort Griffin, Texas |
| McDonald | James | | Corporal | Arizona Territory |
| McDonald | Robert | | First Lieutenant | Wolf Mountain, Montana |
| McGann | Michael | A. | First Sergeant | Rosebud River, Montana |
| McGar | Owen | | Private | Cedar Creek, Montana |
| McHugh | John | | Private | Cedar Creek, Montana |
| McKinley | Daniel | | Private | Arizona Territory |
| McLennon | John | | Musician | Big Hole, Montana |
| McLoughlin | Michael | | Sergeant | Cedar Creek, Montana |
| * McMasters | Henry | A. | Corporal | Red River, Texas |

| Name | | | Rank at Time of Action | Place of Action |
|---|---|---|---|---|
| McMillian | Albert | W. | Sergeant | Wounded Knee Creek, South Dakota |
| McNally | James | | First Sergeant | Arizona Territory |
| McNamara | William | | First Sergeant | Red River, Texas |
| McPhelan | Robert | | Sergeant | Cedar Creek, Montana |
| McVeagh | Charles | H. | Private | Arizona Territory |
| Meaher | Nicholas | | Corporal | Chiricahua Mountains, Arizona Territory |
| Mechlin | Henry | W. B. | Blacksmith | Little Big Horn, Montana |
| Merrill | John | M. | Sergeant | Milk River, Colorado |
| Miller | Daniel | H. | Private | Whetstone Mountains, Arizona Territory |
| Miller | George | | Corporal | Cedar Creek, Montana |
| Miller | George | W. | Private | Arizona Territory |
| Mitchell | John | | First Sergeant | Upper Washita, Texas |
| Mitchell | John | J. | Corporal | Hell Canyon, Arizona Territory |
| Montrose | Charles | H. | Private | Cedar Creek, Montana |
| Moquin | George | | Corporal | Milk River, Colorado |
| Moran | John | | Private | Seneca Mountain, Arizona Territory |
| Morgan | George | H. | Second Lieutenant | Big Dry Fork, Arizona Territory |
| Moriarity | John | | Sergeant | Arizona Territory |
| Morris | James | L. | First Sergeant | Fort Selden, New Mexico |
| Morris | William | W. | Corporal | Upper Washita, Texas |
| Mott | John | | Sergeant | Whetstone Mountains, Arizona Territory |
| Moylan | Myles | | Captain | Bear Paw Mountain, Montana |
| Murphy | Edward | | Private | Chiricahua Mountains, Arizona Territory |
| Murphy | Edward | F. | Corporal | Milk River, Colorado |
| Murphy | Jeremiah | J. | Private | Powder River, Montana |
| Murphy | Philip | | Corporal | Seneca Mountain, Arizona Territory |
| Murphy | Thomas | | Corporal | Seneca Mountain, Arizona Territory |
| Murray | Thomas | | Sergeant | Little Big Horn, Montana |
| Myers | Fred | | Sergeant | White River, South Dakota |
| Nannasaddie | | | Scout | Arizona Territory |
| Nantaje | | | Scout | Arizona Territory |
| Neal | Solon | D. | Private | Wichita River, Texas |
| Neder | Adam | | Corporal | Sioux Campaign |
| Neilon | Frederick | S. | Sergeant | Upper Washita, Texas |
| Newman | Henry | | First Sergeant | Whetstone Mountains, Arizona Territory |
| Nihill | John | | Private | Whetstone Mountains, Arizona Territory |
| Nolan | Richard | J. | Farrier | White Clay Creek, South Dakota |
| O'Callaghan | John | | Sergeant | Arizona Territory |
| O'Neill | William | | Corporal | Red River, Texas |
| O'Regan | Michael | | Private | Arizona Territory |
| O'Sullivan | John | F. | Private | Staked Plains, Texas |
| Oliver | Francis | | First Sergeant | Chiricahua Mountains, Arizona Territory |
| Orr | Moses | | Private | Apache Campaigns |
| Osborne | William | | Sergeant | Apache Campaigns |
| Paine | Adam | | Private | Canyon Blanco Tributary of the Red River, Texas |
| Parnell | William | R. | First Lieutenant | White Bird Canyon, Idaho |
| Payne | Isaac | | Trumpeter | Pecos River, Texas |
| Pengally | Edward | | Private | Chiricahua Mountains, Arizona Territory |
| Pennsyl | Josiah | | Sergeant | Upper Washita, Texas |
| Phife | Lewis | | Sergeant | Arizona Territory |
| Philipsen | Wilhelm | O. | Blacksmith | Milk Creek, Colorado |
| Phillips | Samuel | D. | Private | Muddy Creek, Montana |
| Phoenix | Edwin | | Corporal | Red River, Texas |
| Platten | Frederick | | Sergeant | Sappa Creek, Kansas |
| Poppe | John | A. | Sergeant | Milk River, Colorado |
| Porter | Samuel | | Farrier | Wichita River, Texas |
| Powers | Thomas | | Corporal | Chiricahua Mountains, Arizona Territory |
| Pratt | James | N. | Blacksmith | Red River, Texas |
| Pym | James | | Private | Little Bighorn River, Montana |
| Raerick | John | | Private | Lyry Creek, Arizona Territory |
| Ragnar | Theodore | | First Sergeant | White Clay Creek, South Dakota |
| Rankin | William | | Private | Red River, Texas |
| Reed | James | C. | Private | Arizona Territory |
| Richman | Samuel | | Private | Arizona Territory |

| Name | | | Rank at Time of Action | Place of Action |
|---|---|---|---|---|
| Roach | Hampton | M. | Corporal | Milk River, Colorado |
| Robbins | Marcus | M. | Private | Sappa Creek, Kansas |
| Robinson | Joseph | | First Sergeant | Rosebud River, Montana |
| Roche | David | | First Sergeant | Cedar Creek, Montana |
| Rodenburg | Henry | | Private | Cedar Creek, Montana |
| Rogan | Patrick | | Sergeant | Big Hole, Montana |
| Romeyn | Henry | | First Lieutenant | Bear Paw Mountain, Montana |
| Rooney | Edward | | Private | Cedar Creek, Montana |
| Roth | Peter | P. | Private | Washita River, Texas |
| Rowalt | John | F. | Private | Lyry Creek, Arizona Territory |
| Rowdy | | | Sergeant | Arizona Territory |
| Roy | Stanislaus | | Sergeant | Little Big Horn, Montana |
| Russell | James | | Private | Chiricahua Mountains, Arizona Territory |
| Ryan | David | | Private | Cedar Creek, Montana |
| Ryan | Denis | | First Sergeant | Gageby Creek, Indian Territory |
| Sale | Albert | | Private | Santa Maria River, Arizona Territory |
| Schnitzer | John | P. | Wagoner | Horseshoe Canyon, New Mexico |
| Schou | Julius | A. | Corporal | Sioux Campaign |
| Schroeter | Charles | | Private | Chiricahua Mountains, Arizona Territory |
| Scott | George | D. | Private | Little Big Horn, Montana |
| Scott | Robert | B. | Private | Chiricahua Mountains, Arizona Territory |
| Seward | Griffin | | Wagoner | Chiricahua Mountains, Arizona Territory |
| Shaffer | William | | Private | Arizona Territory |
| Sharpless | Edward | C. | Corporal | Upper Washita River, Texas |
| Shaw | Thomas | | Sergeant | Carrizo Canyon, New Mexico |
| Sheerin | John | | Blacksmith | Fort Selden, New Mexico |
| Sheppard | Charles | | Private | Cedar Creek, etc., Montana |
| Shingle | John | H. | First Sergeant | Rosebud River, Montana |
| Skinner | John | O. | Contract Surgeon (Civilian) | Lava Beds, California |
| Smith | Andrew | J. | Sergeant | Chiricahua Mountains, Arizona Territory |
| Smith | Charles | E. | Corporal | Wichita River, Texas |
| Smith | Cornelius | C. | First Sergeant | White River, South Dakota |
| * Smith | George | W. | Private | Washita River, Texas |
| Smith | Otto | | Private | Arizona Territory |
| Smith | Robert | | Private | Slim Buttes, Dakota Territory |
| Smith | Theodore | F. | Private | Chiricahua Mountains, Arizona Territory |
| Smith | Thomas | | Private | Chiricahua Mountains, Arizona Territory |
| Smith | Thomas | J. | Private | Chiricahua Mountains, Arizona Territory |
| Smith | William | | Private | Chiricahua Mountains, Arizona Territory |
| Smith | William | H. | Private | Chiricahua Mountains, Arizona Territory |
| Snow | Elmer | A. | Trumpeter | Rosebud Creek, Montana |
| Spence | Orizoba | | Private | Chiricahua Mountains, Arizona Territory |
| Springer | George | | Private | Chiricahua Mountains, Arizona Territory |
| Stance | Emanuel | | Sergeant | Kickapoo Springs, Texas |
| Stanley | Eben | | Private | Turret Mountain, Arizona Territory |
| Stanley | Edward | | Corporal | Seneca Mountain, Arizona Territory |
| Stauffer | Rudolph | | First Sergeant | Camp Hualpai, Arizona Territory |
| Steiner | Christian | | Saddler | Chiricahua Mountains, Arizona Territory |
| * Stivers | Thomas | W. | Private | Little Big Horn, Montana |
| Stewart | Benjamin | F. | Private | Bighorn River, Montana |
| Stickoffer | Julius | H. | Saddler | Cienaga Springs, Utah |
| Stokes | Alonzo | | First Sergeant | Wichita River, Texas |
| Strayer | William | H. | Private | Loupe Fork of the Platte River, Nebraska |
| Strivson | Benoni | | Private | Arizona Territory |
| Sullivan | Thomas | | Private | Wounded Knee Creek, South Dakota |
| Sullivan | Thomas | | Private | Chiricahua Mountains, Arizona Territory |
| Sumner | James | | Private | Chiricahua Mountains, Arizona Territory |
| Sutherland | John | A. | Corporal | Arizona Territory |
| * Taylor | Bernard | | Sergeant | Sunset Pass, Arizona Territory |
| Taylor | Charles | | First Sergeant | Big Dry Wash, Arizona Territory |
| Taylor | Wilbur | N. | Corporal | Arizona Territory |
| Tea | Richard | L. | Sergeant | Sappa Creek, Kansas |
| Thomas | Charles | L. | Sergeant | Powder River Expedition, Dakota Territory |
| Thompson | George | W. | Private | Little Blue, Nebraska |

| Name | | | Rank at Time of Action | Place of Action |
|---|---|---|---|---|
| Thompson | John | | Sergeant | Chiricahua Mountains, Arizona Territory |
| Thompson | Peter | | Private | Little Big Horn, Montana |
| Tilton | Henry | R. | Major and Surgeon | Bear Paw Mountain, Montana |
| Tolan | Frank | | Private | Little Big Horn, Montana |
| Toy | Frederick | E. | First Sergeant | Wounded Knee Creek, South Dakota |
| Tracy | John | | Private | Chiricahua Mountains, Arizona Territory |
| Trautman | Jacob | | First Sergeant | Wounded Knee Creek, South Dakota |
| Turpin | James | H. | First Sergeant | Arizona Territory |
| Varnum | Charles | A. | Captain | White Clay Creek, South Dakota |
| Veuve | Ernest | | Farrier | Staked Plains, Texas |
| Voit | Otto | E. | Saddler | Little Big Horn, Montana |
| Vokes | Leroy | H. | First Sergeant | Loupe Fork of the Platte River, Nebraska |
| Von Medem | Rudolph | | Sergeant | Apache Campaigns |
| Walker | Allen | | Private | Texas |
| Walker | John | | Private | Red Creek, Arizona Territory |
| Wallace | William | | Sergeant | Cedar Creek, Montana |
| Walley | Augustus | | Private | Cuchillo Negro Mountains, New Mexico |
| Ward | Charles | H. | Private | Chiricahua Mountains, Arizona Territory |
| Ward | James | | Sergeant | Wounded Knee Creek, South Dakota |
| Ward | John | | Sergeant | Pecos River, Texas |
| Warrington | Lewis | | First Lieutenant | Muchague Valley, Texas |
| Watson | James | C. | Corporal | Wichita River, Texas |
| Watson | Joseph | | Private | Picacho Mountain, Arizona Territory |
| Weaher | Andrew | J. | Private | Arizona Territory |
| Weinert | Paul | H. | Corporal | Wounded Knee Creek, South Dakota |
| Weiss | Enoch | R. | Private | Chiricahua Mountains, Arizona Territory |
| Welch | Charles | H. | Sergeant | Little Big Horn, Montana |
| Welch | Michael | | Sergeant | Wichita River, Texas |
| West | Frank | | First Lieutenant | Big Dry Wash, Arizona Territory |
| Whitehead | Patton | G. | Private | Cedar Creek, Montana |
| Widmer | Jacob | | First Sergeant | Milk River, Colorado |
| Wilder | Wilber | E. | First Lieutenant | Horseshoe Canyon, New Mexico |
| Wilkens | Henry | | First Sergeant | Little Muddy Creek, Montana; Camas Meadows, Idaho |
| Williams | Moses | | First Sergeant | Foothills of the Cuchillo Negro Mountains, New Mexico |
| Wills | Henry | | Private | Fort Selden, New Mexico |
| Wilson | Benjamin | | Private | Wichita River, Texas |
| Wilson | Charles | | Corporal | Cedar Creek, Montana |
| Wilson | Milden | H. | Sergeant | Big Hole, Montana |
| # Wilson | William | | Sergeant | Colorado Valley and Red River, Texas |
| Wilson | William | O. | Corporal | Sioux Campaign |
| Windolph | Charles | | Private | Little Big Horn, Montana |
| Windus | Claron | | Bugler | Wichita River, Texas |
| Winterbottom | William | | Sergeant | Wichita River, Texas |
| Witcome | Joseph | | Private | Arizona Territory |
| Wood | Leonard | | Assistant Surgeon | Arizona Territory |
| Woodall | Zachariah | | Sergeant | Washita River, Texas |
| Woods | Brent | | Sergeant | New Mexico |
| Wortman | George | G. | Sergeant | Arizona Territory |
| Yount | John | P. | Private | Whetstone Mountains, Arizona Territory |
| Ziegner | Herman | | Private | Wounded Knee Creek and White Clay Creek, South Dakota |

## The Wars of American Expansion, 1871–1933

### Korea, 1871

*All actions took place at Korean forts.*

#### Marines

| Brown | Charles | Corporal |
|---|---|---|
| Coleman | John | Private |
| Dougherty | James | Private |
| McNamara | Michael | Private |
| Owens | Michael | Private |
| Purvis | Hugh | Private |

| Name | | | Rank at Time of Action | Place of Action |
|---|---|---|---|---|
| **Navy** | | | | |
| Andrews | John | | Ordinary Seaman | |
| Franklin | Frederick | H. | Quartermaster | |
| Grace | Patrick | H. | Chief Quartermaster | |
| Hayden | Cyrus | | Carpenter | |
| Lukes | William | F. | Landsman | |
| McKenzie | Alexander | | Boatswain's Mate | |
| Merton | James | F. | Landsman | |
| Rogers | Samuel | F. | Quartermaster | |
| Troy | William | | Ordinary Seaman | |

### The Spanish-American War, 1898

*Actions took place In Cuba unless otherwise noted.*

#### Army

| Baker Jr. | Edward | L. | Sergeant Major | Santiago |
|---|---|---|---|---|
| Bell | Dennis | | Private | Tayabacoa |
| Berg | George | F. | Private | El Caney |
| Brookin | Oscar | | Private | El Caney |
| Buzzard | Ulysses | G. | Private | El Caney |
| Cantrell | Charles | P. | Private | Santiago |
| Church | James | R. | Assistant Surgeon | Las Guasimas |
| Cummins | Andrew | J. | Sergeant | Santiago |
| Deswan | John | F. | Private | Santiago |
| Doherty | Thomas | M. | Corporal | Santiago de Cuba |
| Fournia | Frank | O. | Private | Santiago |
| Graves | Thomas | J. | Private | El Caney |
| Hardaway | Benjamin | F. | First Lieutenant | El Caney |
| Heard | John | W. | First Lieutenant | Mouth of Manimani River, west of Bahia Honda |
| Keller | William | G. | Private | Santiago de Cuba |
| Kelly | Thomas | | Private | Santiago de Cuba |
| Lee | Fitz | | Private | Tayabacoa |
| Mills | Albert | L. | Capt./Asst. Adj. Gen. | Near Santiago |
| Nash | James | J. | Private | Santiago |
| Nee | George | H. | Private | Santiago |
| Pfisterer | Herman | | Musician | Santiago |
| Poland | Alfred | | Private | Santiago |
| Quinn | Alexander | M. | Sergeant | Santiago |
| Ressler | Norman | W. | Corporal | El Caney |
| Roberts | Charles | D. | Second Lieutenant | El Caney |
| * Roosevelt | Theodore | | Lieutenant Colonel | San Juan Hill |
| Shepherd | Warren | J. | Corporal | El Caney |
| Thompkins | William | H. | Private | Tayabacoa |
| Wanton | George | H. | Private | Tayabacoa |
| Welborn | Ira | C. | Second Lieutenant | Santiago |
| Wende | Bruno | | Private | El Caney |

#### Marines

| Campbell | Daniel | J. | Private | Cienfuegos |
|---|---|---|---|---|
| Field | Oscar | W. | Private | Cienfuegos |
| Fitzgerald | John | | Private | Cuzco |
| Franklin | Joseph | J. | Private | Cienfuegos |
| Gaughan | Philip | | Sergeant | Cienfuegos |
| Hill | Frank | | Private | Cienfuegos |
| Kearney | Michael | | Private | Cienfuegos |
| Kuchneister | Hermann | W. | Private | Cienfuegos |
| MacNeal | Harry | L. | Private | Santiago de Cuba |
| Meredith | James | | Private | Cienfuegos |
| Parker | Pomeroy | | Private | Cienfuegos |
| Quick | John | H. | Sergeant | Cuzco |
| Scott | Joseph | F. | Private | Cienfuegos |
| Sullivan | Edward | | Private | Cienfuegos |
| West | Walter | S. | Private | Cienfuegos |

| Name | | | Rank at Time of Action | Place of Action |
|---|---|---|---|---|
| **Navy** | | | | |
| Baker | Benjamin | F. | Coxswain | Cienfuegos |
| Barrow | David | D. | Seaman | Cienfuegos |
| Bennett | James | H. | Chief Boatswain's Mate | Cienfuegos |
| Beyer | Albert | | Coxswain | Cienfuegos |
| Blume | Robert | | Seaman | Cienfuegos |
| Brady | George | F. | Chief Gunner's Mate | Cardenas |
| Bright | George | W. | Coal Passer | Cienfuegos |
| Carter | Joseph | E. | Blacksmith | Cienfuegos |
| Chadwick | Leonard | B. | Apprentice First Class | Cienfuegos |
| Charette | George | | Gunner's Mate First Class | Harbor entrance, Santiago de Cuba |
| Clausen | Claus | K. R. | Coxswain | Harbor entrance, Santiago de Cuba |
| Cooney | Thomas | C. | Chief Machinist | Cardenas |
| Crouse | William | A. | Watertender | Off Cavite, Manila Bay, Philippines |
| Davis | John | | Gunner's Mate Third Class | Cienfuegos |
| Deignan | Osborn | W. | Coxswain | Harbor entrance, Santiago de Cuba |
| Doran | John | J. | Boatswain's Mate Second Class | Cienfuegos |
| Durney | Austin | J. | Blacksmith | Cienfuegos |
| Eglit | John | | Seaman | Cienfuegos |
| Ehle | John | W. | Fireman First Class | Off Cavite, Manila Bay, Philippines |
| Erickson | Nicholas | | Coxswain | Cienfuegos |
| Foss | Herbert | L. | Seaman | Cienfuegos |
| Gibbons | Michael | | Oiler | Cienfuegos |
| Gill | Freeman | | Gunner's Mate First Class | Cienfuegos |
| Hart | William | | Machinist First Class | Cienfuegos |
| Hendrickson | Henry | | Seaman | Cienfuegos |
| Hoban | Thomas | | Coxswain | Cienfuegos |
| Hobson | Richmond | P. | Lieutenant | Harbor entrance, Santiago de Cuba |
| Hull | James | L. | Fireman First Class | Off Cavite, Manila Bay, Philippines |
| Itrich | Franz | A. | Chief Carpenter's Mate | Manila, Philippines |
| Johanson | John | P. | Seaman | Cienfuegos |
| Johansson | Johan | J. | Ordinary Seaman | Cienfuegos |
| Johnsen | Hans | | Chief Machinist | Cardenas |
| Johnson | Peter | | Fireman First Class | Off Santiago de Cuba |
| Keefer | Philip | B. | Coppersmith | Santiago de Cuba |
| Kelly | Francis | | Watertender | Harbor entrance, Santiago de Cuba |
| Kramer | Franz | | Seaman | Cienfuegos |
| Krause | Ernest | | Coxswain | Cienfuegos |
| Levery | William | | Apprentice First Class | Cienfuegos |
| Mager | George | F. | Apprentice First Class | Cienfuegos |
| Mahoney | George | | Fireman First Class | Off Santiago de Cuba |
| Maxwell | John | | Fireman Second Class | Cienfuegos |
| Meyer | William | | Carpenter's Mate Third Class | Cienfuegos |
| Miller | Harry | H. | Seaman | Cienfuegos |
| Miller | Willard | D. | Seaman | Cienfuegos |
| Montague | Daniel | | Chief Master-at-Arms | Harbor entrance, Santiago de Cuba |
| Morin | William | H. | Boatswain's Mate Second Class | Approaches to Caimanera, Guantanamo Bay |
| Muller | Frederick | | Mate | Manzanillo |
| Murphy | John | E. | Coxswain | Harbor entrance, Santiago de Cuba |
| Nelson | Lauritz | | Sailmaker's Mate | Cienfuegos |
| Oakley | William | | Gunner's Mate Second Class | Cienfuegos |
| Olsen | Anton | | Ordinary Seaman | Cienfuegos |
| Penn | Robert | | Fireman First Class | Santiago de Cuba |
| Phillips | George | F. | Machinist First Class | Harbor entrance, Santiago de Cuba |
| Rilley | John | P. | Landsman | Cienfuegos |
| Russell | Henry | P. | Landsman | Cienfuegos |
| Spicer | William | | Gunner's Mate First Class | Approaches to Caimanera, Guantanamo Bay |
| Sundquist | Axel | L. | Chief Carpenter's Mate | Approaches to Caimanera, Guantanamo Bay |
| Sundquist | Gustav | A. | Ordinary Seaman | Cienfuegos |
| Triplett | Samuel | S. | Ordinary Seaman | Approaches to Caimanera, Guantanamo Bay |
| Vadas | Albert | | Seaman | Cienfuegos |
| Van Etten | Hudson | | Seaman | Cienfuegos |

| Name | | | Rank at Time of Action | Place of Action |
|---|---|---|---|---|
| Volz | Robert | | Seaman | Cienfuegos |
| Wilke | Julius | A. R. | Boatswain's Mate First Class | Cienfuegos |
| Williams | Frank | | Seaman | Cienfuegos |

## Phillippines/Samoa, 1899–1913
**Army**

| | | | | |
|---|---|---|---|---|
| Anders | Frank | L. | Corporal | San Miguel de Mayumo, Philippines |
| Batson | Matthew | A. | First Lieutenant | Calamba, Philippines |
| Bell | Harry | | Captain | Near Porac, Philippines |
| Bell | James | F. | Colonel | Near Porac, Philippines |
| Bickham | Charles | G. | First Lieutenant | Bayong, Philippines |
| Biegler | George | W. | Captain | Near Loac, Philippines |
| Birkhimer | William | E. | Captain | San Miguel de Mayumo, Philippines |
| Boehler | Otto | A. | Private | Near San Isidro, Philippines |
| Byrne | Bernard | A. | Captain | Bobong, Philippines |
| Carson | Anthony | J. | Corporal | Catubig, Philippines |
| Cawetzka | Charles | | Private | Near Sariaya, Philippines |
| Cecil | Joseph | S. | First Lieutenant | Bud-Dajo, Philippines |
| Condon | Clarence | M. | Sergeant | Near Calulut, Philippines |
| Davis | Charles | P. | Private | Near San Isidro, Philippines |
| Downs | Willis | H. | Private | San Miguel de Mayumo, Philippines |
| Epps | Joseph | L. | Private | Vigan, Philippines |
| Ferguson | Arthur | M. | First Lieutenant | Near Porac, Philippines |
| Funston Sr. | Frederick | | Colonel | Rio Grande de la Pampanga, Philippines |
| Galt | Sterling | A. | Artificer | Bamban, Philippines |
| Gaujot | Antoine | A. | Corporal | San Mateo, Philippines |
| Gedeon | Louis | | Private | Mount Amia, Philippines |
| Gibson | Edward | H. | Sergeant | San Mateo, Philippines |
| Gillenwater | James | R. L. | Corporal | Near Porac, Philippines |
| Greer | Allen | J. | Second Lieutenant | Near Majada, Philippines |
| Grove | William | R. | Lieutenant Colonel | Near Porac, Philippines |
| Hayes | Webb | C. | Lieutenant Colonel | Vigan, Philippines |
| Henderson | Joseph | | Sergeant | Patian Island, Philippines |
| High | Frank | C. | Private | Near San Isidro, Philippines |
| Huntsman | John | A. | Sergeant | Bamban, Philippines |
| Jensen | Gotfred | | Private | San Miguel de Mayumo, Philippines |
| Johnston | Gordon | | First Lieutenant | Mount Bud Dajo, Philippines |
| Kennedy | John | T. | Second Lieutenant | Patian Island, Philippines |
| Kilbourne Jr. | Charles | E. | First Lieutenant | Paco Bridge, Philippines |
| Kinne | John | B. | Private | Near San Isidro, Philippines |
| * Leahy | Cornelius | J. | Private | Near Porac, Philippines |
| * Logan Jr. | John | A. | Major | San Jacinto, Philippines |
| Longfellow | Richard | M. | Private | Near San Isidro, Philippines |
| Lyon | Edward | E. | Private | San Miguel de Mayumo, Philippines |
| Maclay | William | P. | Private | Hilongas, Philippines |
| Mathews | George | W. | Captain/Assistant Surgeon | Near Labo, Philippines |
| McConnell | James | | Private | Vigan, Philippines |
| * McGrath | Hugh | J. | Captain | Calamba, Philippines |
| Miller | Archie | | First Lieutenant | Patian Island, Philippines |
| Moran | John | E. | Captain | Near Mabitac, Philippines |
| Mosher | Louis | C. | Second Lieutenant | Gagsak Mountain, Philippines |
| Nisperos | Jose | B. | Private | Lapurap, Philippines |
| Nolan | Joseph | A. | Artificer | Labo, Philippines |
| Parker | James | | Lieutenant Colonel | Vigan, Philippines |
| Pierce | Charles | H. | Private | San Isidro, Philippines |
| Quinn | Peter | H. | Private | San Miguel de Mayumo, Philippines |
| Ray | Charles | W. | Sergeant | Near San Isidro, Philippines |
| Robertson | Marcus | W. | Private | Near San Isidro, Philippines |
| Ross | Frank | F. | Private | Near San Isidro, Philippines |
| Sage | William | H. | Captain | Near Zapote River, Philippines |
| Schroeder | Henry | F. | Sergeant | Carig, Philippines |
| Shaw | George | C. | First Lieutenant | Fort Pitacus, Philippines |
| Shelton | George | M. | Private | La Paz, Philippines |
| Shiels | George | F. | Major Surgeon | Tuliahan River, Philippines |

| Name | | | Rank at Time of Action | Place of Action |
|---|---|---|---|---|
| Sletteland | Thomas | | Private | Near Paete, Philippines |
| Stewart | George | E. | Second Lieutenant | Passi, Philippines |
| Straub | Paul | F. | Major Surgeon | Alos Zambales, Philippines |
| Trembley | William | B. | Private | Calumpit, Philippines |
| Van Schaick | Louis | J. | First Lieutenant | Near Nasugbu, Philippines |
| Walker | Frank | T. O. | Private | Near Taal, Philippines |
| Wallace | George | W. | Second Lieutenant | Tinuba, Philippines |
| Weaver | Amos | | Sergeant | Between Calubud and Malalong, Philippines |
| Weld | Seth | L. | Corporal | La Paz, Philippines |
| * Wetherby | John | C. | Private | Near Imus, Philippines |
| White | Edward | | Private | Calumpit, Philippines |
| Wilson | Arthur | H. | Second Lieutenant | Patian Island, Philippines |

**Marines**

| Name | | | Rank at Time of Action | Place of Action |
|---|---|---|---|---|
| Bearss | Hiram | I. | Colonel | Cadaean and Sohoton Rivers Junction, Philippines |
| Buckley | Howard | M. | Private | With the Eighth Army Corps |
| Forsterer | Bruno | A. | Sergeant | Near Tagalli, Samoa |
| Harvey | Harry | | Sergeant | Benefictican, Philippines |
| Hulbert | Henry | L. | Private | Samoa |
| Leonard | Joseph | H. | Private | With the Eighth Army Corps |
| McNally | Michael | J. | Sergeant | Samoa |
| Porter | David | D. | Colonel | Cadacan and Sohoton Rivers Junction, Philippines |
| Prendergast | Thomas | F. | Corporal | With the Eighth Army Corps |

**Navy**

| Name | | | Rank at Time of Action | Place of Action |
|---|---|---|---|---|
| Catherwood | John | H. | Ordinary Seaman | Near Mundang, Philippines |
| Fisher | Frederick | T. | Gunner's Mate First Class | Samoa |
| Fitz | Joseph | | Ordinary Seaman | Mount Dajo Jolo, Philippines |
| Forbeck | Andrew | P. | Seaman | Katbalogan, Philippines |
| Galbraith | Robert | | Gunner's Mate Third Class | El Pardo, Philippines |
| Harrison | Bolden | R. | Seaman | Near Mundang, Philippines |
| Henrechon | George | F. | Machinist's Mate Second Class | Near Mundang, Philippines |
| McGuire | Fred | H. | Hospital Apprentice | Near Mundang, Philippines |
| Stoltenberg | Andrew | V. | Gunner's Mate Second Class | Katbalogan, Philippines |
| Thordsen | William | G. | Coxswain | Hilongas, Philippines |
| Volz | Jacob | | Carpenter's Mate Third Class | Near Mundang, Philippines |

## The Boxer Rebellion, 1900

*All actions took place in China.*

**Army**

| Name | | | Rank at Time of Action | Place of Action |
|---|---|---|---|---|
| Brewster | Andre | W. | Captain | Tientsin |
| Lawton | Louis | B. | First Lieutenant | Tientsin |
| Titus | Calvin | P. | Musician | Peking |
| Von Schlick | Robert | H. | Private | Tientsin |

**Marines**

| Name | | | Rank at Time of Action | Place of Action |
|---|---|---|---|---|
| Adams | John | M. | Sergeant | Tientsin |
| Adriance | Harry | C. | Corporal | Tientsin |
| Appleton | Edwin | N. | Corporal | Tientsin |
| Boydston | Erwin | J. | Private | Peking |
| Burnes | James | | Private | Tientsin |
| Campbell | Albert | R. | Private | Tientsin |
| Carr | William | L. | Private | Peking |
| Cooney | James | | Private | Tientsin |
| Dahlgren | John | O. | Corporal | Peking |
| + Daly | Daniel | J. | Private | Peking |
| * Fisher | Harry | | Private | Peking |
| Foley | Alexander | J. | Sergeant | Near Tientsin |
| Francis | Charles | R. | Private | Tientsin |
| Gaiennie | Louis | R. | Private | Peking |
| Heisch | Henry | W. | Private | Tientsin |

| Name | | | Rank at Time of Action | Place of Action |
|---|---|---|---|---|
| Horton | William | M. C. | Private | Peking |
| Hunt | Martin | | Private | Peking |
| Kates | Thomas | W. | Private | Tientsin |
| Mathias | Clarence | E. | Private | Tientsin |
| Moore | Albert | | Private | Peking |
| Murphy | John | A. | Drummer | Peking |
| Murray | William | H. | Private | Peking |
| Orndoff | Harry | W. | Private | China |
| Phillips | Reuben | J. | Corporal | China |
| Preston | Herbert | I. | Private | Peking |
| Scannell | David | J. | Private | Peking |
| Silva | France | | Private | Peking |
| Stewart | Peter | | Gunnery Sergeant | China |
| Sutton | Clarence | E. | Sergeant | Tientsin |
| Upham | Oscar | J. | Private | Peking |
| Walker | Edward | A. | Sergeant | Peking |
| Young | Frank | A. | Private | Peking |
| Zion | William | F. | Private | Peking |

**Navy**

| Name | | | Rank at Time of Action | Place of Action |
|---|---|---|---|---|
| Allen | Edward | G. | Boatswain's Mate First Class | China |
| Chatham | John | P. | Gunner's Mate Second Class | China |
| Clancy | Joseph | | Chief Boatswain's Mate | China |
| Hamberger | William | F. | Chief Carpenter's Mate | China |
| Hanford | Burke | | Machinist First Class | China |
| Hansen | Hans | A. | Seaman | China |
| Holyoke | William | E. | Boatswain's Mate First Class | China |
| Killackey | Joseph | | Landsman | China |
| McAllister | Samuel | | Ordinary Seaman | Tientsin |
| + McCloy | John | | Coxswain | Wu-Tsing-Hune and near Peh-Tsang |
| Mitchell | Joseph | A. | Gunner's Mate First Class | Peking |
| Petersen | Carl | E. | Chief Machinist | Peking |
| Rose | George | H. | Seaman | Peking |
| Ryan | Francis | T. | Coxswain | China |
| Seach | William | | Ordinary Seaman | China |
| Smith | Frank | E. | Oiler | China |
| Smith | James | A. | Landsman | Near Tientsin |
| Stanley | Robert | H. | Hospital Apprentice | Peking |
| Thomas | Karl | | Coxswain | China |
| Torgerson | Martin | T. | Gunner's Mate Third Class | China |
| Westermark | Axel | | Seaman | Peking |
| Williams | Jay | P. | Coxswain | China |

## Mexican Campaign—Veracruz, 1914

*All actions took place in Mexico.*

**Army**

| Name | | | Rank at Time of Action | Place of Action |
|---|---|---|---|---|
| Gaujot | Julien | E. | Captain | Aqua Prieta |

**Marines**

| Name | | | Rank at Time of Action | Place of Action |
|---|---|---|---|---|
| Berkeley | Randolph | C. | Major | Veracruz |
| + Butler | Smedley | D. | Major | Veracruz |
| Catlin | Albertus | W. | Major | Veracruz |
| Dyer | Jesse | F. | Captain | Veracruz |
| Fryer | Eli | T. | Captain | Veracruz |
| Hill | Walter | N. | Captain | Veracruz |
| Hughes | John | A. | Captain | Veracruz |
| Neville | Wendell | C. | Lieutenant Colonel | Veracruz |
| Reid | George | C. | Major | Veracruz |

**Navy**

| Name | | | Rank at Time of Action | Place of Action |
|---|---|---|---|---|
| Anderson | Edwin | A. | Captain | Veracruz |
| Badger | Oscar | C. | Ensign | Veracruz |
| Beasley | Harry | C. | Seaman | Veracruz |
| Bishop | Charles | F. | Quartermaster Second Class | Veracruz |

| Name | | | Rank at Time of Action | Place of Action |
|---|---|---|---|---|
| Bradley | George | | Chief Gunner's Mate | Veracruz |
| Buchanan | Allen | | Lieutenant Commander | Veracruz |
| Castle | Guy | W. S. | Lieutenant | Veracruz |
| Courts | George | M. | Lieutenant (j.g.) | Veracruz |
| Cregan | George | | Coxswain | Veracruz |
| Decker | Percy | A. | Boatswain's Mate Second Class | Veracruz |
| Desomer | Abraham | | Lieutenant | USS *Utah* off the coast of Veracruz |
| Drustrup | Niels | | Lieutenant | Veracruz |
| Elliott | Middleton | S. | Surgeon | Veracruz |
| Fletcher | Frank | F. | Rear Admiral | Veracruz |
| Fletcher | Frank | J. | Lieutenant | Veracruz |
| Foster | Paul | F. | Ensign | Veracruz |
| Frazer | Hugh | C. | Ensign | Veracruz |
| Gisburne | Edward | A. | Electrician Third Class | Veracruz |
| Grady | John | | Lieutenant | Veracruz |
| Harner | Joseph | G. | Boatswain's Mate Second Class | Veracruz |
| Harrison | William | K. | Commander | Veracruz |
| Hartigan | Charles | C. | Lieutenant | Veracruz |
| Huse | Henry | M. P. | Captain | Veracruz |
| Ingram | Jonas | H. | Lieutenant (j.g.) | Veracruz |
| Jarrett | Berrie | H. | Seaman | Veracruz |
| Johnston Jr. | Rufus | Z. | Lieutenant Commander | Veracruz |
| Langhorne | Cary | D. | Surgeon | Veracruz |
| Lannon | James | P. | Lieutenant | Veracruz |
| Lowry | George | M. | Ensign | Veracruz |
| + McCloy | John | | Chief Boatswain | Veracruz |
| McDonnell | Edward | O. | Ensign | Veracruz |
| McNair Jr. | Frederick | V. | Lieutenant | Veracruz |
| Moffett | William | A. | Commander | Veracruz |
| Nickerson | Henry | N. | Boatswain's Mate Second Class | Veracruz |
| Nordsiek | Charles | L. | Ordinary Seaman | Veracruz |
| Rush | William | R. | Captain | Veracruz |
| Schnepel | Fred | J. | Ordinary Seaman | Veracruz |
| Semple | Robert | | Chief Gunner | Veracruz |
| Sinnett | Lawrence | C. | Seaman | Veracruz |
| Staton | Adolphus | | Lieutenant | Veracruz |
| Stickney | Herman | O. | Commander | Veracruz |
| Townsend | Julius | C. | Lieutenant | Veracruz |
| Wainwright Jr. | Richard | | Lieutenant | Veracruz |
| Walsh | James | A. | Seaman | Veracruz |
| Wilkinson Jr. | Theodore | S. | Ensign | Veracruz |
| Zuiderveld | William | | Hospital Apprentice First Class | Veracruz |

## Haiti, 1915
### Marines
| | | | | |
|---|---|---|---|---|
| + Butler | Smedley | D. | Major | Fort Rivière |
| + Daly | Daniel | J. | Gunnery Sergeant | Fort Dipitie |
| Gross | Samuel | | Private | Fort Rivière |
| Iams | Ross | L. | Sergeant | Fort Rivière |
| Ostermann | Edward | A. | First Lieutenant | Fort Dipitie |
| Upshur | William | P. | Captain | Fort Dipitie |

## Dominican Republic, 1916–1924
### Marines
| | | | | |
|---|---|---|---|---|
| Glowin | Joseph | A. | Corporal | Guayacanas |
| Williams | Ernest | C. | First Lieutenant | San Francisco de Macoris |
| Winans | Roswell | | First Sergeant | Guayacanas |

| Name | | | Rank at Time of Action | Place of Action |
|---|---|---|---|---|

## Haiti, 1919–1920
### Marines
| | | | | |
|---|---|---|---|---|
| Button | William | R. | Corporal | Near Grande Rivière |
| Hanneken | Herman | H. | Second Lieutenant | Near Grande Rivière |

## Nicaragua, 1927–1933
### Marines
| | | | | |
|---|---|---|---|---|
| Schilt | Christian | F. | First Lieutenant | Quilali |
| Truesdell | Donald | L. | Corporal | Vicinity of Constancia, near Coco River |

## The Medal in Peacetime, 1865–1940
### 1865–1870
#### Army
| | | | | |
|---|---|---|---|---|
| Gerber | Frederick | W. | Sergeant Major | 1839 to 1871 |

### 1839–1871
#### Navy
| | | | | |
|---|---|---|---|---|
| Bates | Richard | | Seaman | Off Eastport, Maine |
| Brown | John | | Captain of the Afterguard | Off Eastport, Maine |
| Burke | Thomas | | Seaman | Off Eastport, Maine |
| Carey | James | | Seaman | Near Rio de Janeiro, Brazil |
| + Cooper | John | | Quartermaster | Mobile, Alabama |
| Du Moulin | Frank | | Apprentice | New London Harbor, Connecticut |
| Halford | William | | Coxswain | Sandwich Islands |
| + Mullen | Patrick | | Boatswain's Mate | Off the coast of Virginia |
| Robinson | John | | Captain of the Hold | Pensacola Bay, Florida |
| Robinson | Thomas | | Captain of the Afterguard | Off New Orleans, Louisiana |
| Stacy | William | B. | Seaman | In the harbor of Cape Haiten, Haiti |
| Taylor | John | | Seaman | New York Navy Yard |

### 1871–1898
#### Marines
| | | | | |
|---|---|---|---|---|
| Morris | John | | Corporal | Villefranche, France |
| Stewart | James | A. | Corporal | Villefranche Harbor, France |

#### Navy
| | | | | |
|---|---|---|---|---|
| Ahern | William | | Watertender | USS *Puritan* |
| Anderson | William | | Coxswain | USS *Powhatan* |
| Atkins | Daniel | | Ship's Cook First Class | USS *Cushing* |
| Auer | John | F. | Ordinary Seaman Apprentice | Marseille, France |
| Barrett | Edward | | Second Class Fireman | Callao Bay, Peru |
| Belpitt | William | H. | Captain of the Afterguard | Foochow, China |
| Benson | James | | Seaman | At sea |
| Bradley | Alexander | | Landsman | Off Cowes, Isle of Wight, England |
| Buchanan | David | M. | Apprentice | Off the Battery, New York Harbor, New York |
| Cavanaugh | Thomas | | Fireman First Class | At sea between Cat Island and Nassau |
| Chandron | August | | Seaman Apprentice Second Class | Alexandria, Egypt |
| Connolly | Michael | | Ordinary Seaman | Halifax Harbor, Nova Scotia, Canada |
| Corey | William | | Landsman | Navy Yard, New York |
| Costello | John | | Ordinary Seaman | Philadelphia, Pennsylvania |
| Courtney | Henry | C. | Seaman | Navy Yard, Washington, D.C. |
| Cramen | Thomas | | Boatswain's Mate | Navy Yard, Washington, D.C. |
| Creelman | William | J. | Landsman | At sea |
| Cutter | George | W. | Landsman | Norfolk, Virginia |
| Davis | John | | Ordinary Seaman | Toulon, France |
| Davis | Joseph | H. | Landsman | Off the wharf, Norfolk, Virginia |
| Dempsey | John | | Seaman | Shanghai, China |
| Deneef | Michael | | Captain of the Top | Para, Brazil |
| Denham | Austin | | Seaman | Near Greytown, Nicaragua |
| Eilers | Henry | A. | Gunner's Mate | Fort McHenry, Baltimore, Maryland |
| Elmore | Walter | | Landsman | Mediterranean Sea |
| Enright | John | | Landsman | Off Ensenada, Mexico |
| Everetts | John | | Gunner's Mate Third Class | At sea |

| Name | | | Rank at Time of Action | Place of Action |
|---|---|---|---|---|
| Fasseur | Isaac | L. | Ordinary Seaman | Callao, Peru |
| Flannagan | John | | Boatswain's Mate | Le Havre, France |
| Fowler | Christopher | | Quartermaster | Off Point Zapotitlan, Mexico |
| Gidding | Charles | | Seaman | Navy Yard, New York |
| Gillick | Matthew | | Boatswain's Mate | Marseille, France |
| Handran | John | | Seaman | Lisbon, Portugal |
| Harrington | David | | First Class Fireman | Off Vineyard Haven, Massachusetts |
| Hayden | John | | Apprentice | Off the Battery, New York Harbor, New York |
| Hill | George | | Chief Quarter Gunner | Near Greytown, Nicaragua |
| Hill | William | L. | Captain of the Top | Newport, Rhode Island |
| Holt | George | | Quarter Gunner | Hamburg Harbor, Germany |
| Horton | James | | Captain of the Top | At sea, Northeast Atlantic, west of the English Channel |
| Jardine | Alexander | | Fireman First Class | At sea between Cat Island and Nassau |
| Johnson | John | | Seaman | Near Greytown, Nicaragua |
| Johnson | William | | Cooper | Navy Yard, Mare Island, California |
| Kersey | Thomas | J. | Ordinary Seaman | Navy Yard, New York |
| King | Hugh | | Ordinary Seaman | Delaware River |
| Kyle | Patrick | J. | Landsman | Port Mahon, Menorca, Spain |
| Lakin | Thomas | | Seaman | Navy Yard, Mare Island, California |
| [4]+Laverty | John | | First Class Fireman | Callao Bay, Peru |
| Lejeune | Emile | | Seaman | Port Royal, South Carolina |
| Low | George | | Seaman | New Orleans, Louisiana |
| Lucy | John | | Second Class Boy | Castle Garden, New York City, New York |
| Maddin | Edward | | Ordinary Seaman | Lisbon, Portugal |
| Magee | John | W. | Second Class Fireman | Off Vineyard Haven, Massachusetts |
| Manning | Henry | J. | Quartermaster | Off Coasters Harbor Island, Newport, Rhode Island |
| Matthews | Joseph | | Captain of the Top | At sea, Northeast Atlantic, west of the English Channel |
| McCarton | John | | Ship's Printer | Off Coasters Harbor Island, Newport, Rhode Island |
| Miller | Hugh | | Boatswain's Mate | Alexandria, Egypt |
| Millmore | John | | Ordinary Seaman | Monrovia, Liberia |
| Mitchell | Thomas | | Landsman | Shanghai, China |
| Moore | Francis | | Boatswain's Mate | Navy Yard, Washington, D.C. |
| Moore | Philip | | Seaman | Genoa, Italy |
| Morse | William | | Seaman | Rio de Janeiro, Brazil |
| Noil | Joseph | B. | Seaman | Norfolk, Virginia |
| Norris | J. | W. | Landsman | Navy Yard, New York |
| O'Conner | James | F. | Landsman Engineer's Force | Opposite the Navy Yard, Norfolk, Virginia |
| O'Neal | John | | Boatswain's Mate | Greytown, Nicaragua |
| Ohmsen | August | | Master-at-Arms | Off Woods Hole, Massachusetts |
| Osborne | John | | Seaman | Philadelphia, Pennsylvania |
| Osepins | Christian | | Seaman | Hampton Roads, Virginia |
| Parker | Alexander | | Boatswain's Mate | Mare Island Navy Yard, California |
| Pile | Richard | | Ordinary Seaman | Greytown, Nicaragua |
| Regan | Patrick | | Ordinary Seaman | In the harbor of Coquimbo, Chile |
| Rouning | Johannes | | Ordinary Seaman | Hampton Roads, Virginia |
| Russell | John | | Seaman | Genoa, Italy |
| Ryan | Richard | | Ordinary Seaman | Norfolk, Virginia |
| Sadler | William | | Captain of the Top | Off Coasters Harbor Island, Newport, Rhode Island |
| Sapp | Isaac | | Seaman Engineer's Force | Villefranche, France |
| Simpson | D. | Henry L. | Fireman First Class | Monrovia, Liberia |
| Smith | James | | Seaman | Greytown, Nicaragua |
| Smith | John | | Seaman | Rio de Janeiro, Brazil |
| Smith | Thomas | | Seaman | Off Para, Brazil |
| Sullivan | James | F. | Boatswain's Mate | Newport, Rhode Island |
| # Sweeney | Robert | A. | Ordinary Seaman | Hampton Roads, Virginia, and Navy Yard, New York |
| Sweeney | William | | Landsman Engineer's Force | Opposite the Navy Yard, Norfolk, Virginia |
| Taylor | Richard | H. | Quartermaster | Apia, Samoa |
| Thayer | James | | Ship's Corporal | Navy Yard, Norfolk, Virginia |
| Thompson | Henry | | Seaman | Mare Island, California |
| Thornton | Michael | | Seaman | Near Boston, Massachusetts |
| Tobin | Paul | | Landsman | Hamburg Harbor, Germany |
| Trout | James | M. | Fireman Second Class | Montevideo, Uruguay |
| Troy | Jeremiah | | Chief Boatswain's Mate | Newport, Rhode Island |
| Turvelin | Alexander | H. | Seaman | Toulon, France |

| Name | | | Rank at Time of Action | Place of Action |
|---|---|---|---|---|
| # Weisbogel | Albert | | Captain of the Mizzen Top | At sea |
| Weissel | Adam | | Ship's Cook | Newport, Rhode Island |
| Williams | Antonio | | Seaman | Off Nags Head, North Carolina |
| Williams | Henry | | Carpenter's Mate | At sea, Northeast Atlantic, west of the English Channel |
| # Williams | Louis | | Captain of the Hold | Honolulu, Territory of Hawaii, and Callao, Peru |
| Willis | George | | Coxswain | Off the coast of Greenland |
| Wilson | August | | Boilermaker | Brooklyn Navy Yard, Brooklyn, New York |

## 1899–1910
### Marines

| Name | | | Rank at Time of Action | Place of Action |
|---|---|---|---|---|
| Helms | John | H. | Sergeant | Montevideo, Uruguay |
| Pfeifer | Louis | F. | Private | USS *Petrel* |

### Navy

| Name | | | Rank at Time of Action | Place of Action |
|---|---|---|---|---|
| Behne | Frederick | | Fireman First Class | USS *Iowa* |
| Behnke | Heinrich | | Seaman First Class | USS *Iowa* |
| Bjorkman | Ernest | H. | Ordinary Seaman | On the rocks of Block Island, Rhode Island |
| Boers | Edward | W. | Seaman | USS *Bennington* |
| Bonney | Robert | E. | Chief Watertender | USS *Hopkins* |
| Breeman | George | | Seaman | USS *Kearsarge* |
| Bresnahan | Patrick | F. | Watertender | USS *Iowa* |
| Brock | George | F. | Carpenter's Mate Second Class | USS *Bennington* |
| Cahey | Thomas | | Seaman | USS *Petrel* |
| Clary | Edward | A. | Watertender | USS *Hopkins* |
| Clausey | John | J. | Chief Gunner's Mate | USS *Bennington* |
| Corahorgi | Demetri | | Fireman First Class | USS *Iowa* |
| Cox | Robert | E. | Chief Gunner | USS *Missouri* |
| Cronan | William | S. | Boatswain's Mate | USS *Bennington* |
| Davis | Raymond | E. | Quartermaster Third Class | USS *Bennington* |
| Fadden | Harry | D. | Coxswain | Off the California coast |
| Floyd | Edward | | Boilermaker | USS *Iowa* |
| Fredericksen | Emil | | Watertender | USS *Bennington* |
| Girandy | Alphonse | | Seaman | USS *Petrel* |
| Gowan | William | H. | Boatswain's Mate | Coquimbo, Chile |
| Grbitch | Rade | | Seaman | USS *Bennington* |
| Halling | Luovi | | Boatswain's Mate First Class | Off Martha's Vineyard, Massachusetts |
| Hill | Frank | E. | Ship's Cook First Class | San Diego, California |
| Holtz | August | | Chief Watertender | USS *North Dakota* |
| Johannessen | Johannes | J. | Chief Watertender | USS *Iowa* |
| # King | John | | Watertender | USS *Vicksburg* and USS *Salem* |
| Klein | Robert | | Chief Carpenter's Mate | Olongapo, Philippines |
| Lipscomb | Harry | | Watertender | USS *North Dakota* |
| Monssen | Mons | | Chief Gunner's Mate | USS *Missouri* |
| Mullin | Hugh | P. | Seaman | Hampton Roads, Virginia |
| Nelson | Oscar | F. | Machinist's Mate First Class | USS *Bennington* |
| Nordstrom | Isador | A. | Chief Boatswain | USS *Kearsarge* |
| Peters | Alexander | | Boatswain's Mate First Class | Off Martha's Vineyard, Massachusetts |
| Quick | Joseph | | Coxswain | Yokohama, Japan |
| Reid | Patrick | | Chief Watertender | USS *North Dakota* |
| Roberts | Charles | C. | Machinist's Mate First Class | USS *North Dakota* |
| Schepke | Charles | S. | Gunner's Mate First Class | USS *Missouri* |
| Schmidt | Otto | D. | Seaman | USS *Bennington* |
| Shacklette | William | S. | Hospital Steward | USS *Bennington* |
| Shanahan | Patrick | | Chief Boatswain's Mate | Off Annapolis, Maryland |
| Snyder | William | E. | Chief Electrician | USS *Birmingham* |
| Stanton | Thomas | | Chief Machinist's Mate | USS *North Dakota* |
| Stokes | John | S. | Chief Master-at-Arms | Off the coast of Jamaica |
| Stupka | Laddie | | Fireman First Class | On the rocks of Block Island, Rhode Island |
| Teytand | August | P. | Quartermaster Third Class | On the rocks of Block Island, Rhode Island |
| Walsh | Michael | | Chief Machinist | On the rocks of Block Island, Rhode Island |
| Westa | Karl | | Chief Machinist's Mate | USS *North Dakota* |
| Wheeler | George | H. | Shipfitter First Class | Coquimbo, Chile |

| Name | | | Rank at Time of Action | Place of Action |
|---|---|---|---|---|
| **1915–1916** | | | | |
| **Navy** | | | | |
| Cary | Robert | W. | Ensign | USS *San Diego* |
| Crilley | Frank | W. | Chief Gunner's Mate | Off Honolulu, Territory of Hawaii |
| Jones | Claud | A. | Lieutenant | Off Santo Domingo City, Santo Domingo |
| * Rud | George | W. | Chief Machinist's Mate | Off Santo Domingo City, Santo Domingo |
| Smith | Eugene | P. | Chief Watertender | USS *Decatur* |
| Smith | Wilhelm | | Gunner's Mate First Class | USS *New York* |
| Trinidad | Telesforo | D. | Fireman Second Class | USS *San Diego* |
| Willey | Charles | H. | Machinist | Off Santo Domingo City, Santo Domingo |
| **1920–1940** | | | | |
| **Army** | | | | |
| Greely | Adolphus | W. | Major General | 1861 to 1906 |
| Lindbergh Jr. | Charles | A. | Captain | From New York City to Paris, France |
| **Marines** | | | | |
| Smith | Albert | J. | Private | Marine Barracks, Naval Air Station, Pensacola, Florida |
| **Navy** | | | | |
| Badders | William | | Chief Machinist's Mate | Portsmouth, New Hampshire |
| Bennett | Floyd | | Machinist | Spitsbergen, Norway, to the North Pole |
| Breault | Henry | | Torpedoman Second Class | Limon Bay, Canal Zone, Panama |
| Byrd Jr. | Richard | E. | Commander | Spitsbergen, Norway, to the North Pole |
| * Cholister | George | R. | Boatswain's Mate First Class | USS *Trenton* |
| * Corry Jr. | William | M. | Lieutenant Commander | Near Hartford, Connecticut |
| Crandall | Orson | L. | Chief Boatswain's Mate | Portsmouth, New Hampshire |
| * Drexler | Henry | C. | Ensign | USS *Trenton* |
| Eadie | Thomas | | Chief Gunner's Mate | Off Provincetown, Massachusetts |
| Edwards | Walter | A. | Lieutenant Commander | Sea of Marmora, Turkey |
| Huber | William | R. | Machinist's Mate | Navy Yard, Norfolk, Virginia |
| * Hutchins | Carlton | B. | Lieutenant | Off the California coast |
| McDonald | James | H. | Chief Metalsmith | Portsmouth, New Hampshire |
| Mihalowski | John | | Torpedoman First Class | Portsmouth, New Hampshire |
| Ryan Jr. | Thomas | J. | Ensign | Yokohama, Japan |

## World War I, 1914–1918

*Actions took place in France unless otherwise noted.*

| Name | | | Rank at Time of Action | Place of Action |
|---|---|---|---|---|
| **Unknown** | | | | |
| * Belgium | Unknown Soldier | | | |
| * France | Unknown Soldier | | | |
| * Great Britain | Unknown Soldier | | | |
| * Italy | Unknown Soldier | | | |
| * Romania | Unknown Soldier | | | |
| * United States | Unknown Soldier | | | |
| **Army** | | | | |
| Adkison | Joseph | B. | Sergeant | Near Bellicourt |
| Allex | Jake | | Corporal | Chipilly Ridge |
| Allworth | Edward | C. | Captain | Cléry-le-Petit |
| Anderson | Johannes | S. | First Sergeant | Consenvoye |
| * Baesel | Albert | E. | Second Lieutenant | Near Ivry |
| Barger | Charles | D. | Private First Class | Near Bois de Bantheville |
| * Barkeley | David | B. | Private | Near Pouilly |
| Barkley | John | L. | Private First Class | Near Cunel |
| Bart | Frank | J. | Private | Near Medeah Ferme |
| * Blackwell | Robert | L. | Private | Near St. Souplet |
| * Bleckley | Erwin | R. | Second Lieutenant | Near Binarville |
| Bronson | Deming | | First Lieutenant | Near Eclisfontaine |
| Call | Donald | M. | Corporal | Near Varennes |
| * Chiles | Marcellus | H. | Captain | Near Le Champy-Bas |
| * Colyer | Wilbur | E. | Sergeant | Near Verdun |
| * Costin | Henry | G. | Private | Near Bois de Consenvoye |
| * Dilboy | George | | Private First Class | Near Belleau |
| Donaldson | Michael | A. | Sergeant | Road between Sommerance and Landres-et-Saint-Georges |
| Donovan | William | J. | Lieutenant Colonel | Near Landres-et-Saint-Georges |
| Dozier | James | C. | First Lieutenant | Near Montbrehain |
| * Dunn | Parker | F. | Private First Class | Near Grand-Pré |
| Edwards | Daniel | R. | Private First Class | Near Soissons |
| Eggers | Alan | L. | Sergeant | Near Le Catelet |
| Ellis | Michael | B. | Sergeant | Near Exermont |
| Forrest | Arthur | J. | Sergeant | Near Remonville |
| Foster | Gary | E. | Sergeant | Near Montbrehain |
| Funk | Jesse | N. | Private First Class | Near Bois de Bantheville |
| Furlong | Harold | A. | First Lieutenant | Near Bantheville |
| Gaffney | Frank | J. | Private First Class | Near Ronssoy |
| * Goettler | Harold | E. | First Lieutenant | Near Binarville |
| Gregory | Earl | D. | Sergeant | Bois de Consenvoye |
| Gumpertz | Sydney | G. | First Sergeant | Bois de Forges |
| * Hall | Thomas | L. | Sergeant | Near Montbrehain |
| Hatler | M. | Waldo | Sergeant | Near Pouilly |
| Hays | George | P. | First Lieutenant | Near Greves Farm |
| * Heriot | James | D. | Corporal | Vaux-Andigny |
| Hill | Ralyn | M. | Corporal | Near Donnevoux |
| Hilton | Richmond | H. | Sergeant | Brancourt |
| Holderman | Nelson | M. | Captain | Argonne Forest |
| Johnston | Harold | I. | Private First Class | Near Pouilly |
| Karnes | James | E. | Sergeant | Near Estrées |
| Katz | Phillip | C. | Sergeant | Near Eclisfontaine |
| Kaufman | Benjamin | | First Sergeant | Argonne Forest |
| Latham | John | C. | Sergeant | Near Le Catelet |
| * Lemert | Milo | | First Sergeant | Near Bellicourt |
| Loman | Berger | H. | Private | Near Consenvoye |
| * Luke Jr. | Frank | | Second Lieutenant | Near Murvaux |
| Mallon | George | H. | Captain | Bois de Forges |
| Manning | Sidney | E. | Corporal | Near Breuvannes |
| McMurtry | George | G. | Captain | Argonne Forest |
| * Mestrovitch | James | I. | Sergeant | Fismette |
| Miles | Louis | W. | Captain | Near Revillon |
| * Miller | Oscar | F. | Major | Near Gesnes |
| Morelock | Sterling | L. | Private | Near Exermont |
| Neibaur | Thomas | C. | Private | Near Landres-et-Saint-Georges |
| O'Neill | Richard | W. | Sergeant | Ourcq River |
| * O'Shea | Thomas | E. | Corporal | Near Le Catelet |
| Parker | Samuel | I. | Second Lieutenant | Near Soissons |
| Peck | Archie | A. | Private | Argonne Forest |
| * Perkins | Michael | J. | Private First Class | Belieu Bois |
| * Pike | Emory | J. | Lieutenant Colonel | Near Vandières |
| Pope | Thomas | A. | Corporal | Hamel |
| Regan | Patrick | J. | Second Lieutenant | Bois de Consenvoye |
| Rickenbacker | Edward | V. | First Lieutenant | Near Billy |
| Robb | George | S. | First Lieutenant | Near Sechault |
| * Roberts | Harold | W. | Corporal | Montrebeau Woods |
| Sampler | Samuel | M. | Corporal | Near St. Etienne |
| Sandlin | Willie | | Sergeant | Bois de Forges |
| * Sawelson | William | | Sergeant | Grand-Pré |
| Schaffner | Dwite | H. | First Lieutenant | Near St. Hubert's Pavillion, Boureuilles |
| Seibert | Lloyd | M. | Sergeant | Near Epinonville |
| * Skinker | Alexander | R. | Captain | Cheppy |
| Slack | Clayton | K. | Private | Near Consenvoye |
| * Smith | Fred | E. | Lieutenant Colonel | Near Binarville |
| * Stowers | Freddie | | Corporal | Hill 188, Champagne-Marne Sector |
| Talley | Edward | R. | Sergeant | Near Ponchaux |
| Thompson | Joseph | H. | Major | Near Apremont |
| Turner | Harold | L. | Corporal | Near St. Etienne |
| * Turner | William | B. | First Lieutenant | Near Ronssoy |
| Valente | Michael | | Private | Hindenburg Line, east of Ronssoy |

| Name | | | Rank at Time of Action | Place of Action |
|------|--|--|------------------------|-----------------|
| Van Iersel | Ludovicus | M. M. | Sergeant | Mouzon |
| Villepigue | John | C. | Corporal | Vaux-Andigny |
| Waaler | Reidar | | Sergeant | Near Ronssoy |
| Ward | Calvin | J. | Private | Near Estrées |
| West | Chester | H. | First Sergeant | Near Bois de Cheppy |
| Whittlesey | Charles | W. | Major | Northeast of Binarville, in the Argonne Forest |
| * Wickersham | John | H. | Second Lieutenant | Near Limey |
| * Wold | Nels | T. | Private | Near Cheppy |
| Woodfill | Samuel | | First Lieutenant | Cunel |
| York | Alvin | C. | Corporal | Near Châtel-Chéhéry |

**Marines**

| Name | | | Rank at Time of Action | Place of Action |
|------|--|--|------------------------|-----------------|
| ^ Cukela | Louis | | Sergeant | Near Villers-Cotterêts |
| 5 ^ Janson | Ernest | A. | Gunnery Sergeant | Near Château-Thierry |
| ^ Kelly | John | J. | Private | Blanc Mont Ridge |
| *^ Kocak | Matej | | Sergeant | Soissons |
| *^ Pruitt | John | H. | Corporal | Blanc Mont Ridge |
| Robinson | Robert | G. | Gunnery Sergeant | Pittham, Belgium |
| 6* Stockham | Fred | W. | Gunnery Sergeant | Bois de Belleau |
| * Talbot | Ralph | | Second Lieutenant | France |

**Navy**

| Name | | | Rank at Time of Action | Place of Action |
|------|--|--|------------------------|-----------------|
| Balch | John | H. | Pharmacist's Mate First Class | Vierzy and Somme-Py |
| Boone | Joel | T. | Lieutenant | Vicinity of Vierzy |
| Bradley Jr. | Willis | W. | Commander | USS Pittsburgh |
| Cann | Tedford | H. | Seaman | Between Bermuda and the Azores |
| Covington | Jesse | W. | Ship's Cook Third Class | At sea |
| Graves | Ora | | Seaman | At sea aboard the USS Pittsburgh |
| Hammann | Charles | H. | Ensign | Off Pola, Austria |
| Hayden | David | E. | Hospital Apprentice First Class | Thiaucourt |
| * Ingram | Osmond | K. | Gunner's Mate First Class | At sea, 20 miles south of Mind Head, Ireland |
| Izac | Edouard | V. M. | Lieutenant | Aboard German submarine U-90 as POW |
| Lyle | Alexander | G. | Lieutenant Commander | French front |
| MacKenzie | John | | Chief Boatswain's Mate | At sea |
| Madison | James | J. | Lieutenant Commander | At sea |
| McGunigal | Patrick | | Shipfitter First Class | At sea |
| Ormsbee Jr. | Francis | E. | Chief Machinist's Mate | Pensacola, Florida |
| * Osborne | Weedon | E. | Lieutenant (j.g.) | Bouresche |
| Petty | Orlando | H. | Lieutenant | Bois de Belleau |
| Schmidt Jr. | Oscar | | Chief Gunner's Mate | At sea |
| Siegel | John | O. | Boatswain's Mate Second Class | Norfolk Navy Yard, Portsmouth, Virginia |
| Sullivan | Daniel | A. J. | Ensign | At sea |
| Upton | Frank | M. | Quartermaster | At sea |

## World War II, 1939–1945

**Unknown**

| Name | | | Rank at Time of Action | Place of Action |
|------|--|--|------------------------|-----------------|
| * United States | Unknown Soldier | | | |

**Army**

| Name | | | Rank at Time of Action | Place of Action |
|------|--|--|------------------------|-----------------|
| Adams | Lucian | | Staff Sergeant | Near Saint-Dié, France |
| Anderson | Beauford | T. | Technical Sergeant | Okinawa |
| * Antolak | Sylvester | | Sergeant | Near Cisterna di Littoria, Italy |
| Atkins | Thomas | E. | Private First Class | Villa Verde Trail, Philippines |
| Baker | Vernon | J. | First Lieutenant | Near Castle Aghinolfi, Germany |
| * Baker | Addison | E. | Lieutenant Colonel | Ploieşti, Romania |
| * Baker Jr. | Thomas | A. | Private | Saipan |
| Barfoot | Van | T. | Technical Sergeant | Near Carano, Italy |
| Barrett | Carlton | W. | Private | Vicinity of St. Laurent-sur-Mer, France |
| * Beaudoin | Raymond | O. | First Lieutenant | Hamelin, Germany |
| Bell | Bernard | P. | Technical Sergeant | Mittelwihr, France |
| Bender | Stanley | | Staff Sergeant | La Lande, France |
| * Benjamin Jr. | George | | Private First Class | Leyte, Philippines |

| Name | | | Rank at Time of Action | Place of Action |
|------|--|--|------------------------|-----------------|
| Bennett | Edward | A. | Corporal | Heckhuscheid, Germany |
| Bertoldo | Vito | R. | Master Sergeant | Hatten, France |
| Beyer | Arthur | O. | Corporal | Near Arloncourt, Belgium |
| * Bianchi | Willibald | C. | First Lieutenant | Near Bagac, Bataan Province, Philippines |
| Biddle | Melvin | E. | Private First Class | Between Soy and Hotton, Belgium |
| Bjorklund | Arnold | L. | First Lieutenant | Altavilla, Italy |
| Bloch | Orville | E. | First Lieutenant | Near Firenzuola, Italy |
| Bolden | Paul | L. | Staff Sergeant | Petit Coo, Belgium |
| Bolton | Cecil | H. | First Lieutenant | Mark River, Holland |
| Bong | Richard | I. | Major | Over Borneo and Leyte, Philippines |
| * Booker | Robert | D. | Private | Near Fondouk, Tunisia |
| * Boyce Jr. | George | W. G. | Second Lieutenant | Near Afua, New Guinea |
| Briles | Herschel | F. | Staff Sergeant | Scherpenseel, Germany |
| Britt | Maurice | L. | Lieutenant | North of Mignano, Italy |
| * Brostrom | Leonard | C. | Private First Class | Near Dagami, Philippines |
| Brown Jr. | Bobbie | E. | Captain | Crucifix Hill, Germany |
| Burke | Francis | X. | First Lieutenant | Nuremberg, Germany |
| * Burr | Elmer | J. | First Sergeant | Buna, New Guinea |
| Burr | Herbert | H. | Private First Class | Dorrmoschel, Germany |
| Burt | James | M. | Captain | Wurselen, Germany |
| * Butts | John | E. | Second Lieutenant | Normandy, France |
| Calugas | Jose | | Sergeant | Culis, Philippines |
| * Cano | Pedro | | Private | Schevenhutte, Germany |
| * Carey | Alvin | P. | Staff Sergeant | Near Plougastel, France |
| * Carey Jr. | Charles | F. | Technical Sergeant | Rimling, France |
| Carr | Chris | | Sergeant | Near Guignola, Italy |
| * Carswell Jr. | Horace | S. | Major | South China Sea |
| * Carter Jr. | Edward | A. | Staff Sergeant | Near Speyer, Germany |
| * Castle | Frederick | W. | Brigadier General | Germany |
| * Cheli | Ralph | | Major | Near Wewak, New Guinea |
| Childers | Ernest | | Second Lieutenant | Oliveto, Italy |
| Choate | Clyde | L. | Staff Sergeant | Bruyeres, France |
| * Christensen | Dale | E. | Second Lieutenant | Driniumor River, New Guinea |
| * Christian | Herbert | F. | Private | Near Valmontone, Italy |
| * Cicchetti | Joseph | J. | Private First Class | South Manila, Philippines |
| Clark | Francis | J. | Technical Sergeant | Kalborn, Luxembourg; Sevenig, Germany |
| Colalillo | Michael | | Private First Class | Near Untergriesheim, Germany |
| * Cole | Robert | G. | Lieutenant Colonel | Near Carentan, France |
| Connor | James | P. | Sergeant | Cape Cavalaire, southern France |
| Cooley | Raymond | H. | Staff Sergeant | Near Lumboy, Philippines |
| Coolidge | Charles | H. | Technical Sergeant | East of Belmont-sur-Buttant, France |
| * Cowan | Richard | E. | Private First Class | Near Krinkelter Wald, Belgium |
| Craft | Clarence | B. | Private First Class | Hen Hill, Okinawa |
| * Craig | Robert | | Second Lieutenant | Near Favoratta, Sicily |
| * Crain | Morris | E. | Technical Sergeant | Haguenau, France |
| * Craw | Demas | T. | Colonel | Near Port Lyautey, French Morocco |
| Crawford | William | J. | Private | Near Altavilla, Italy |
| Crews | John | R. | Staff Sergeant | Lobenbacherhof, Germany |
| Currey | Francis | S. | Private First Class | Malmedy, Belgium |
| Dahlgren | Edward | C. | Second Lieutenant | Oberhoffen, France |
| Dalessondro | Peter | J. | Technical Sergeant | Kalterherberg, Germany |
| Daly | Michael | J. | Lieutenant | Nuremberg, Germany |
| Davila | Rudolph | B. | Second Lieutenant | Artena, Italy |
| Davis | Charles | W. | Captain | Guadalcanal |
| * DeFranzo | Arthur | F. | Staff Sergeant | Near Vaubadon, France |
| * DeGlopper | Charles | N. | Private First Class | Merderet River, France |
| * Deleau Jr. | Emile | | Sergeant | Oberhoffen, France |
| Dervishian | Ernest | H. | Technical Sergeant | Near Cisterna, Italy |
| * Diamond | James | H. | Private First Class | Mintal, Philippines |
| * Dietz | Robert | H. | Staff Sergeant | Kirchain, Germany |
| Doolittle | James | H. | Brigadier General | Over Tokyo, Japan |
| Doss | Desmond | T. | Private First Class | Urasoe-Mura, Okinawa |
| Drowley | Jesse | R. | Staff Sergeant | Bougainville, Solomon Islands |
| Dunham | Russell | | Technical Sergeant | Kaysersberg, France |

| Name | | | Rank at Time of Action | Place of Action |
|---|---|---|---|---|
| * Dutko | John | W. | Private First Class | Near Ponte Rotto, Italy |
| Ehlers | Walter | D. | Staff Sergeant | Near Goville, France |
| * Endl | Gerald | L. | Staff Sergeant | Near Anamo, New Guinea |
| Erwin | Henry | E. | Staff Sergeant | Koriyama, Japan |
| * Eubanks | Ray | E. | Sergeant | Noemfoor Island, Dutch New Guinea |
| Everhart Sr. | Forrest | E. | Technical Sergeant | Near Kerling, France |
| * Femoyer | Robert | E. | Second Lieutenant | Over Merseburg, Germany |
| Fields | James | H. | First Lieutenant | Rechicourt, France |
| Fisher | Almond | E. | Second Lieutenant | Near Grammont, France |
| * Fournier | William | G. | Sergeant | Mount Austen, Guadalcanal |
| * Fowler | Thomas | W. | Second Lieutenant | Near Carano, Italy |
| * Fox | John | R. | First Lieutenant | Serchio River Valley, Italy |
| * Fryar | Elmer | E. | Private | Leyte, Philippines |
| Funk Jr. | Leonard | A. | First Sergeant | Holzheim, Belgium |
| * Galt | William | W. | Captain | Villa Crocetta, Italy |
| * Gammon | Archer | T. | Staff Sergeant | Near Bastogne, Belgium |
| * Gandara | Joe | | Private | Amfreville, France |
| Garcia | Marcario | | Private | Near Grosshau, Germany |
| Garman | Harold | A. | Private | Near Montereau, France |
| Gerstung | Robert | E. | Technical Sergeant | Siegfried Line, Germany |
| * Gibson | Eric | G. | Technician Fifth Grade | Near Isola Bella, Italy |
| * Gonzales | David | M. | Private First Class | Hill 507, Villa Verde Trail, Philippines |
| * Gott | Donald | J. | First Lieutenant | Saarbrücken, Germany |
| * Grabiarz | William | J. | Private First Class | Manila, Philippines |
| Gregg | Stephen | R. | Technical Sergeant | Near Montelimar, France |
| * Gruennert | Kenneth | E. | Sergeant | Near Buna, New Guinea |
| Hajiro | Barney | F. | Private | Vicinity of Bruyeres and Biffontaine, France |
| Hall | George | J. | Staff Sergeant | Near Anzio, Italy |
| * Hall | Lewis | R. | Technician Fifth Grade | Mount Austen, Guadalcanal |
| * Hallman | Sherwood | H. | Staff Sergeant | Brest, France |
| Hamilton | Pierpont | M. | Major | Near Port Lyautey, French Morocco |
| * Harmon | Roy | W. | Sergeant | Near Casaglia, Italy |
| * Harr | Harry | R. | Corporal | Near Maglamin, Philippines |
| * Harris | James | L. | Second Lieutenant | Vagney, France |
| * Hasemoto | Mikio | | Private | Vicinity of Cerasuolo, Italy |
| * Hastings | Joe | R. | Private First Class | Drabenderhohe, Germany |
| Hawk | John | D. | Sergeant | Near Chambois, France |
| Hawks | Lloyd | C. | Private First Class | Near Carano, Italy |
| * Hayashi | Joe | | Private | Near Tendola, Italy |
| Hayashi | Shizuya | | Private | Near Cerasuolo, Italy |
| * Hedrick | Clinton | M. | Technical Sergeant | Near Lembeck, Germany |
| Hendrix | James | R. | Private | Near Assenois, Belgium |
| * Henry | Robert | T. | Private | Luchem, Germany |
| Herrera | Silvestre | S. | Private First Class | Near Merzwiller, France |
| Horner | Freeman | V. | Staff Sergeant | Wurselen, Germany |
| Howard | James | H. | Major | Over Oschersleben, Germany |
| Huff | Paul | B. | Corporal | Near Carano, Italy |
| * Hughes | Lloyd | H. | Second Lieutenant | Ploiești, Romania |
| Inouye | Daniel | K. | First Lieutenant | Vicinity of San Terenzo, Italy |
| * Jachman | Isadore | S. | Staff Sergeant | Flamierge, Belgium |
| * James Jr. | Willy | F. | Private First Class | Weser River Valley, Germany |
| * Jerstad | John | L. | Major | Ploiești, Romania |
| * Johnson | Elden | H. | Private | Near Valmontone, Italy |
| * Johnson | Leroy | | Sergeant | Near Limon, Leyte, Philippines |
| Johnson | Leon | W. | Colonel | Ploiești, Romania |
| Johnson Jr. | Oscar | G. | Private First Class | Near Scarperia, Italy |
| Johnston Sr. | William | J. | Private First Class | Near Padiglione, Italy |
| * Kandle | Victor | L. | First Lieutenant | Near La Forge, France |
| Kane | John | R. | Colonel | Ploiești, Romania |
| Kearby | Neel | E. | Colonel | Near Wewak, New Guinea |
| * Keathley | George | D. | Staff Sergeant | Mount Altuzzo, Italy |
| * Kefurt | Gus | | Staff Sergeant | Near Bennwihr, France |
| * Kelley | Jonah | E. | Staff Sergeant | Kesternich, Germany |
| * Kelley | Ova | A. | Private | Leyte, Philippines |
| Kelly | Charles | E. | Corporal | Near Altavilla, Italy |
| * Kelly | John | D. | Corporal | Fort du Roule, France |
| Kelly | Thomas | J. | Corporal | Alemert, Germany |
| Kerstetter | Dexter | J. | Private First Class | Near Galiano, Philippines |
| * Kessler | Patrick | L. | Private First Class | Near Ponte Rotto, Italy |
| * Kimbro | Truman | | Technician Fourth Grade | Near Rocherath, Belgium |
| * Kiner | Harold | G. | Private | Near Palenberg, Germany |
| * Kingsley | David | R. | Second Lieutenant | Ploiești, Romania |
| Kisters | Gerry | H. | Sergeant | Near Gagliano, Sicily |
| Knappenberger | Alton | W. | Private First Class | Near Cisterna di Littoria, Italy |
| * Knight | Jack | L. | First Lieutenant | Near Loi-Kang, Burma |
| * Knight | Raymond | L. | First Lieutenant | Northern Po Valley, Italy |
| Kobashigawa | Yeiki | | Technical Sergeant | Vicinity of Lanuvio, Italy |
| * Krotiak | Anton | L. | Private First Class | Balete Pass, Philippines |
| * Kuroda | Robert | T. | Staff Sergeant | Near Bruyères, France |
| * Lara | Salvador | J. | Private First Class | Aprilia, Italy |
| Lawley Jr. | William | R. | First Lieutenant | Over Liepzig, Germany |
| Laws | Robert | E. | Staff Sergeant | Luzon, Philippines |
| Lee Sr. | Daniel | W. | Second Lieutenant | Montreval, France |
| * Leonard | Turney | W. | First Lieutenant | Kommerscheidt, Germany |
| * Leonard | William | F. | Private First Class | Saint-Dié, France |
| * Lindsey | Darrell | R. | Captain | L'Isle Adam Railroad Bridge, France |
| Lindsey Sr. | Jake | W. | Technical Sergeant | Near Hamich, Germany |
| * Lindstrom | Floyd | K. | Private First Class | Near Mignano, Italy |
| * Lloyd | Edgar | H. | First Lieutenant | Near Pompey, France |
| * Lobaugh | Donald | R. | Private | Near Afua, New Guinea |
| Logan | James | M. | Sergeant | Near Salerno, Italy |
| Lopez | Jose | M. | Sergeant | Near Krinkelt, Belgium |
| Mabry Jr. | George | L. | Lieutenant Colonel | Schevenhutte, Germany |
| MacArthur | Douglas | | General of the Armies | Bataan Peninsula, Philippines |
| MacGillivary | Charles | A. | Sergeant | Near Woelfling, France |
| * Magrath | John | D. | Private First Class | Near Castel d'Aiano, Italy |
| * Mann | Joe | E. | Private First Class | Best, Holland |
| * Martinez | Joe | P. | Private | Attu, Aleutian Islands |
| * Mathies | Archibald | | Staff Sergeant | Over Europe |
| * Mathis | Jack | W. | First Lieutenant | Over Vegesack, Germany |
| Maxwell | Robert | D. | Technician Fifth Grade | Near Besancon, France |
| * May | Martin | O. | Private First Class | Iegusuku-Yama, Ryukyu Islands |
| Mayfield | Melvin | | Corporal | Cordillera Mountains, Philippines |
| McCall | Thomas | E. | Staff Sergeant | Near San Angelo, Italy |
| McCarter | Lloyd | G. | Private | Corregidor, Philippines |
| McGaha | Charles | L. | Master Sergeant | Near Lupao, Philippines |
| McGarity | Vernon | | Technical Sergeant | Near Krinkelt, Belgium |
| * McGee | William | D. | Private | Near Mulheim, Germany |
| * McGill | Troy | A. | Sergeant | Los Negros Island, Admiralty Group |
| * McGraw | Francis | X. | Private First Class | Near Schevenhutte, Germany |
| * McGuire Jr. | Thomas | B. | Major | Over Luzon, Philippines |
| McKinney | John | R. | Private | Tayabas Province, Philippines |
| * McVeigh | John | J. | Sergeant | Near Brest, France |
| * McWhorter | William | A. | Private First Class | Leyte, Philippines |
| Meagher | John | W. | Technical Sergeant | Near Ozato, Okinawa |
| * Mendoza | Manuel | V. | Master Sergeant | Mt. Battaglia, Italy |
| Merli | Gino | J. | Private First Class | Near Sars-la-Bruyère, Belgium |
| * Merrell | Joseph | F. | Private | Near Lohe, Germany |
| * Messerschmidt | Harold | O. | Sergeant | Near Radden, France |
| * Metzger Jr. | William | E. | Second Lieutenant | Saarbrücken, Germany |
| * Michael | Harry | J. | Second Lieutenant | Near Neiderzerf, Germany |
| Michael | Edward | S. | First Lieutenant | Over Stettin, Germany |
| * Miller | Andrew | | Staff Sergeant | France to Germany |
| Milis | James | H. | Private | Near Cisterna di Littoria, Italy |
| * Minick | John | W. | Staff Sergeant | Near Hürtgen, Germany |
| * Minue | Nicholas | | Private | Near Medjez-el-Bab, Tunisia |
| * Monteith Jr. | Jimmie | W. | First Lieutenant | Near Colleville-sur-Mer, France |
| Montgomery | Jack | C. | First Lieutenant | Near Padiglione, Italy |

| Name | | | Rank at Time of Action | Place of Action |
|---|---|---|---|---|
| * Moon Jr. | Harold | H. | Private | Pawig, Philippines |
| Morgan | John | C. | Flight Officer | Over Kiel, Germany |
| * Moskala | Edward | J. | Private First Class | Kakazu Ridge, Okinawa |
| * Moto | Kaoru | | Private First Class | Near Castellina, Italy |
| * Mower | Charles | E. | Sergeant | Near Capoocan, Philippines |
| * Muller | Joseph | E. | Sergeant | Near Ishimmi, Okinawa |
| * Munemori | Sadao | S. | Private First Class | Near Seravezza, Italy |
| * Muranaga | Kiyoshi | | Private First Class | Near Suvereto, Italy |
| Murphy | Audie | L. | Second Lieutenant | Near Holtzwihr, France |
| * Murphy | Frederick | C. | Private First Class | Siegfried Line at Saarlautern, Germany |
| Murray Jr. | Charles | P. | First Lieutenant | Near Kaysersberg, France |
| * Nakae | Masato | | Private | Near Pisa, Italy |
| * Nakamine | Shinyei | | Private | Near La Torreto, Italy |
| * Nakamura | William | K. | Private First Class | Near Castellina Italy, Hill 140 |
| * Nelson | William | L. | Sergeant | Djebel Dardys, Tunisia |
| Neppel | Ralph | G. | Sergeant | Birgel, Germany |
| Nett | Robert | B. | First Lieutenant | Near Cognon, Philippines |
| Newman | Beryl | R. | First Lieutenant | Near Cisterna, Italy |
| * Nietzel | Alfred | B. | Sergeant | Heistern, Germany |
| * Nininger Jr. | Alexander | R. | Second Lieutenant | Near Abucay, Philippines |
| * Nishimoto | Joe | M. | Private First Class | Near La Houssière, France |
| * O'Brien | William | J. | Lieutenant Colonel | Saipan |
| Ogden Sr. | Carlos | C. | First Lieutenant | Near Fort du Roule, France |
| * Ohata | Allan | M. | Staff Sergeant | Near Cerasuolo, Italy |
| Okubo | James | K. | Technician Fifth Grade | Foret Domaniale de Champ, France |
| Okutsu | Yukio | | Technical Sergeant | Mount Belvedere, Italy |
| * Olson | Arlo | L. | Captain | Crossing of the Volturno River, Italy |
| * Olson | Truman | O. | Sergeant | Near Cisterna di Littoria, Italy |
| * Ono | Frank | H. | Private First Class | Near Castellina, Italy |
| Oresko | Nicholas | | Master Sergeant | Near Tettington, Germany |
| * Otani | Kazuo | | Staff Sergeant | Near Pieve di Santa Luce, Italy |
| * Parrish | Laverne | | Technician Fourth Grade | Binalonan, Philippines |
| * Pease Jr. | Harl | | Captain | Near Rabaul, Bismarck Archipelago |
| * Peden | Forrest | E. | Technician Fifth Grade | Near Biesheim, France |
| * Pendleton | Jack | J. | Staff Sergeant | Bardenberg, Germany |
| * Peregory | Frank | D. | Technical Sergeant | Grandcampe, France |
| * Perez Jr. | Manuel | | Private First Class | Fort William McKinley, Philippines |
| * Peters | George | J. | Private | Near Fluren, Germany |
| * Peterson | George | | Staff Sergeant | Near Eisern, Germany |
| * Petrarca | Frank | J. | Private First Class | Horseshoe Hill, New Georgia, Solomon Islands |
| * Pinder Jr. | John | J. | Technician Fifth Grade | Near Colleville-sur-Mer, France |
| Powers | Leo | J. | Private First Class | Hill 175, Northwest of Casino, Italy |
| * Prussman | Ernest | W. | Private First Class | Near Les Coates, France |
| * Pucket | Donald | D. | First Lieutenant | Ploiești, Romania |
| * Ray | Bernard | J. | First Lieutenant | Hürtgen Forest, Germany |
| * Reese | James | W. | Private | Mount Vassillio, Sicily |
| * Reese Jr. | John | N. | Private First Class | Paco Railroad Station, Manila, Philippines |
| * Riordan | Paul | F. | Second Lieutenant | Near Cassino, Italy |
| * Rivers | Ruben | | Staff Sergeant | Guébling, France |
| * Robinson Jr. | James | E. | First Lieutenant | Near Untergriesheim, Germany |
| Rodriguez | Cleto | L. | Private | Paco Railroad Station, Manila, Philippines |
| * Roeder | Robert | E. | Captain | Mount Battaglia, Italy |
| * Roosevelt Jr. | Theodore | | Brigadier General | Normandy Invasion, France |
| Ross | Wilburn | K. | Private | Near St. Jacques, France |
| Rudolph | Donald | E. | Technical Sergeant | Munoz, Philippines |
| Ruiz | Alejandro | R. | Private First Class | Okinawa |
| * Sadowski | Joseph | J. | Sergeant | Valhey, France |
| Sakato | George | T. | Private | Hill 617, Near Biffontaine, France |
| * Salomon | Benjamin | L. | Captain | Saipan |
| * Sarnoski | Joseph | R. | Second Lieutenant | Over Buka Area, Solomon Islands |
| * Sayers | Foster | J. | Private First Class | Near Thionville, France |
| Schaefer | Joseph | E. | Staff Sergeant | Near Stolberg, Germany |
| Schauer | Henry | | Private First Class | Near Cisterna di Littoria, Italy |
| * Schwab | Donald | K. | First Lieutenant | Near Lure, France |
| Scott | Robert | S. | Second Lieutenant | Near Munda Air Strip, New Georgia, Solomon Islands |
| Shea | Charles | W. | Staff Sergeant | Near Mount Damiano, Italy |
| * Sheridan | Carl | V. | Private First Class | Frenzenberg Castle, Germany |
| * Shockley | William | R. | Private First Class | Villa Verde Trail, Philippines |
| Shomo | William | A. | Major | Over Luzon, Philippines |
| * Shoup | Curtis | F. | Staff Sergeant | Near Tillet, Belgium |
| Silk | Edward | A. | First Lieutenant | Near St. Pravel, France |
| Sjogren | John | C. | Staff Sergeant | Near San Jose Hacienda, Philippines |
| Slaton | James | D. | Corporal | Near Oliveto, Italy |
| * Smith | Furman | L. | Private | Near Lanuvio, Italy |
| Smith Sr. | Maynard | H. | Sergeant | Brest, France |
| Soderman | William | A. | Private First Class | Near Rocherath, Belgium |
| * Specker | Joe | C. | Sergeant | Mount Porchia, Italy |
| Spurrier | Junior | J. | Staff Sergeant | Achain, France |
| * Squires | John | C. | Private First Class | Near Padiglione, Italy |
| * Stryker | Stuart | S. | Private First Class | Near Wesel, Germany |
| * Tanouye | Ted | T. | Technical Sergeant | Near Molino a Ventoabbto, Italy |
| * Terry | Seymour | W. | Captain | Zebra Hill, Okinawa |
| * Thomas | Charles | L. | First Lieutenant | Climbach, France |
| * Thomas | William | H. | Private First Class | Zambales Mountains, Philippines |
| Thompson | Max | | Sergeant | Near Haaren, Germany |
| * Thorne | Horace | M. | Corporal | Near Grufflingen, Belgium |
| * Thorson | John | F. | Private First Class | Dagami, Philippines |
| Tominac | John | J. | First Lieutenant | Saulx de Vesoul, France |
| * Towle | John | R. | Private | Near Oosterhout, Holland |
| Treadwell | Jack | L. | First Lieutenant | Near Niederwürzbach, Germany |
| * Truemper | Walter | E. | Second Lieutenant | Over Leipzig, Germany |
| * Turner | Day | G. | Sergeant | Dahl, Luxembourg |
| Turner | George | B. | Private First Class | Philippsbourg, France |
| Urban | Matt | L. | Captain | France and Belgium |
| * Valdez | Jose | F. | Private First Class | Near Rosenkrantz, France |
| * Van Noy | Junior | | Private | Near Finschafen, New Guinea |
| * Vance Jr. | Leon | R. | Lieutenant Colonel | Over Wimereaux, France |
| * Viale | Robert | M. | Second Lieutenant | Manila, Philippines |
| * Villegas | Ysmael | R. | Staff Sergeant | Villa Verde Trail, Philippines |
| Vlug | Dirk | J. C. | Private First Class | Near Limon, Philippines |
| Vosler | Forrest | L. | Technical Sergeant | Over Bremen, Germany |
| * Wai | Francis | B. | Captain | Red Beach, Philippines |
| Wainwright IV | Jonathan | M. | General | Philippines |
| * Walker | Kenneth | N. | Brigadier General | Over Rabaul, Bismarck Archipelago |
| * Wallace | Herman | C. | Private First Class | Near Prumzurley, Germany |
| Ware | Keith | L. | Lieutenant Colonel | Near Sigolsheim, France |
| * Warner | Henry | F. | Corporal | Near Dom Butgenbach, Belgium |
| * Watson | George | | Private | Near Porlock Harbor, New Guinea |
| * Waugh | Robert | T. | First Lieutenant | Hill 79, near Tremensucli, Italy |
| Waybur | David | C. | First Lieutenant | Near Agrigento, Sicily |
| * Weicht | Ellis | R. | Sergeant | St. Hippolyte, France |
| * Wetzel | Walter | C. | Private First Class | Birken, Germany |
| Whiteley | Eli | L. | First Lieutenant | Sigolsheim, France |
| Whittington | Hulon | B. | Sergeant | Near Grimesnil, France |
| Wiedorfer | Paul | J. | Private | Near Chaumont, Belgium |
| * Wigle | Thomas | W. | Second Lieutenant | Monte Frassino, Italy |
| Wilbur | William | H. | Colonel | Fedala, North Africa |
| * Wilkin | Edward | G. | Corporal | Siegfried Line, Germany |
| * Wilkins | Raymond | H. | Major | Near Rabaul, Bismarck Archipelago |
| * Will | Walter | J. | First Lieutenant | Near Eisern, Germany |
| * Wilson | Alfred | L. | Technician Grade Five | Near Bezange-la-Petite, France |
| Wise | Homer | L. | Staff Sergeant | Magliano, Italy |
| * Woodford | Howard | E. | Staff Sergeant | Near Tabio, Philippines |
| * Young | Rodger | W. | Private | New Georgia, Solomon Islands |
| Zeamer Jr. | Jay | | Captain | Over Buka Area, Solomon Islands |
| * Zussman | Raymond | | Second Lieutenant | Noroy-le-Bourg, France |

| Name | | | Rank at Time of Action | Place of Action |
| --- | --- | --- | --- | --- |
| **Coast Guard** | | | | |
| * Munro | Douglas | A. | Signalman First Class | Point Cruz, Guadalcanal |
| | | | | |
| **Marines** | | | | |
| * Agerholm | Harold | C. | Private First Class | Saipan |
| * Anderson | Richard | B. | Private First Class | Roi Island, Marshall Islands |
| * Bailey | Kenneth | D. | Major | Henderson Field, Guadalcanal |
| Basilone | John | | Sergeant | Lunga Area, Guadalcanal |
| * Bauer | Harold | W. | Lieutenant Colonel | Guadalcanal |
| * Bausell | Lewis | K. | Corporal | Peleliu Island, Palau Group |
| * Berry | Charles | J. | Corporal | Iwo Jima |
| * Bonnyman Jr. | Alexander | | First Lieutenant | Betio Island, Gilbert Islands |
| * Bordelon | William | J. | Staff Sergeant | Tarawa, Gilbert Islands |
| Boyington | Gregory | | Major | Central Solomons Area |
| Bush | Richard | E. | Corporal | Mount Yaetake, Okinawa |
| * Caddy | William | R. | Private First Class | Iwo Jima |
| * Cannon | George | H. | First Lieutenant | Sand Island, Midway Islands |
| Casamento | Anthony | | Corporal | Guadalcanal |
| Chambers | Justice | M. | Lieutenant Colonel | Iwo Jima |
| * Cole | Darrell | S. | Sergeant | Iwo Jima |
| * Courtney Jr. | Henry | A. | Major | Sugar Loaf Hill, Okinawa Shima |
| * Damato | Anthony | P. | Corporal | Engebi Island, Marshall Islands |
| Day | James | L. | Major General | Okinawa |
| DeBlanc | Jefferson | J. | Captain | Kolombangara Island, Solomon Islands |
| Dunlap | Robert | H. | Captain | Iwo Jima |
| * Dyess | Aquilla | J. | Lieutenant Colonel | Namur Island, Marshall Islands |
| Edson | Merritt | A. | Colonel | Guadalcanal |
| * Elrod | Henry | T. | Captain | Wake Island |
| * Epperson | Harold | G. | Private First Class | Saipan |
| * Fardy | John | P. | Corporal | Okinawa Shima |
| * Fleming | Richard | E. | Captain | Midway Island |
| Foss | Joseph | J. | Captain | Over Guadalcanal |
| * Foster | William | A. | Private First Class | Okinawa Shima |
| Galer | Robert | E. | Major | Guadalcanal |
| * Gonsalves | Harold | | Private First Class | Okinawa Shima |
| * Gray | Ross | F. | Sergeant | Iwo Jima |
| * Gurke | Henry | | Private First Class | Near Empress Augusta Bay, Solomon Islands |
| * Hansen | Dale | M. | Private | Okinawa Shima |
| * Hanson | Robert | M. | First Lieutenant | Bougainville and New Britain Islands |
| Harrell | William | G. | Sergeant | Iwo Jima |
| * Hauge Jr. | Louis | J. | Corporal | Okinawa Shima |
| * Hawkins | William | D. | First Lieutenant | Tarawa, Gilbert Islands |
| Jackson | Arthur | J. | Private First Class | Peleliu Island, Palau Islands |
| Jacobson | Douglas | T. | Private First Class | Hill 382, Iwo Jima |
| * Julian | Joseph | R. | Platoon Sergeant | Iwo Jima |
| * Kinser | Elbert | L. | Sergeant | Okinawa Shima |
| * Kraus | Richard | E. | Private First Class | Peleliu Island, Palau Islands |
| * La Belle | James | D. | Private First Class | Iwo Jima |
| Leims | John | H. | Second Lieutenant | Iwo Jima |
| Lucas | Jacklyn | H. | Private First Class | Iwo Jima |
| * Lummus | Jack | | First Lieutenant | Iwo Jima |
| * Martin | Harry | L. | First Lieutenant | Iwo Jima |
| * Mason | Leonard | F. | Private First Class | Asan-Adelup Beachhead, Guam |
| * McCard | Robert | H. | Gunnery Sergeant | Saipan |
| McCarthy | Joseph | J. | Captain | Iwo Jima |
| * McTureous Jr. | Robert | M. | Private | Okinawa |
| * New | John | D. | Private First Class | Peleliu Island, Palau Islands |
| * Owens | Robert | A. | Sergeant | Cape Torokina, Solomon Islands |
| * Ozbourn | Joseph | W. | Private | Tinian Island, Marianas Islands |
| Paige | Mitchell | | Platoon Sergeant | Guadalcanal |
| * Phelps | Wesley | P. | Private | Peleliu Island, Palau Islands |
| * Phillips | George | | Private | Iwo Jima |
| Pope | Everett | P. | Captain | Peleliu Island, Palau Islands |
| * Power | John | V. | First Lieutenant | Namur Island, Marshall Islands |
| * Roan | Charles | H. | Private First Class | Peleliu Island, Palau Islands |
| Rouh | Carlton | R. | First Lieutenant | Peleliu Island, Palau Islands |
| * Ruhl | Donald | J. | Private First Class | Iwo Jima |
| * Schwab | Albert | E. | Private First Class | Okinawa Shima |
| Shoup | David | M. | Colonel | Betio Island, Gilbert Islands |
| Sigler | Franklin | E. | Private | Iwo Jima |
| Skaggs Jr. | Luther | | Private First Class | Asan-Adelup Beachhead, Guam |
| Smith | John | L. | Major | Guadalcanal |
| Sorenson | Richard | K. | Private | Namur Island, Marshall Islands |
| * Stein | Tony | | Corporal | Iwo Jima |
| Swett | James | E. | First Lieutenant | Solomon Islands Area |
| * Thomas | Herbert | J. | Sergeant | Koromokina River, Solomon Islands |
| * Thomason | Clyde | A. | Sergeant | Makin Island, Gilbert Islands |
| * Timmerman | Grant | F. | Sergeant | Saipan |
| Vandegrift | Alexander | A. | Major General | Solomon Islands |
| Walsh | Kenneth | A. | First Lieutenant | Vella Lavella and Kahili, Solomon Islands |
| * Walsh | William | G. | Gunnery Sergeant | Iwo Jima |
| Watson | Wilson | D. | Private | Iwo Jima |
| Williams | Hershel | W. | Corporal | Iwo Jima |
| * Wilson | Robert | L. | Private First Class | Tinian Island, Mariana Islands |
| Wilson Jr. | Louis | H. | Captain | Fonte Hill, Guam |
| * Witek | Frank | P. | Private First Class | Finegayen, Guam |
| | | | | |
| **Navy** | | | | |
| Antrim | Richard | N. | Lieutenant | Macassar, Netherlands East Indies |
| * Bennion | Mervyn | S. | Captain | Pearl Harbor, Territory of Hawaii |
| * Bigelow | Elmer | C. | Watertender First Class | Off Corregidor Island, Philippines |
| Bulkeley | John | D. | Lieutenant | Philippine waters |
| Bush | Robert | E. | Hospital Apprentice First Class | Okinawa Jima |
| * Callaghan | Daniel | J. | Rear Admiral | Ironbottom Sound off Savo Island, Solomon Islands |
| * Cromwell | John | P. | Captain | Off Truk Island |
| * David | Albert | L. | Lieutenant (j.g.) | Off the coast of French West Africa |
| * Davis | George | F. | Commander | Lingayen Gulf, Philippines |
| * Dealey | Samuel | D. | Commander | Off Tawi Tawi, Sulu Archipelago |
| * Evans | Ernest | E. | Commander | Off Samar, Philippines |
| Finn | John | W. | Aviation Chf. Ordnance | Kaneohe Bay, Territory of Hawaii |
| * Flaherty | Francis | C. | Ensign | Pearl Harbor, Territory of Hawaii |
| Fluckey | Eugene | B. | Commander | Namkwan Harbor, China |
| Fuqua | Samuel | G. | Lieutenant Commander | Pearl Harbor, Territory of Hawaii |
| Gary | Donald | A. | Lieutenant (j.g.) | Near Kobe, Japan |
| * Gilmore | Howard | W. | Commander | Southwest Pacific |
| Gordon | Nathan | G. | Lieutenant | Kavieng Harbor, Bismark Sea |
| Hall | William | E. | Lieutenant (j.g.) | Coral Sea |
| * Halyburton Jr. | William | D. | Pharmacist's Mate Second Class | Okinawa Shima |
| * Hammerberg | Owen | F. P. | Boatswain's Mate Second Class | Pearl Harbor, Territory of Hawaii |
| Herring | Rufus | G. | Lieutenant (j.g.) | Iwo Jima |
| * Hill | Edwin | J. | Chief Boatswain | Pearl Harbor, Territory of Hawaii |
| * Hutchins | Johnnie | D. | Seaman First Class | Lae, New Guinea |
| * Jones | Herbert | C. | Ensign | Pearl Harbor, Territory of Hawaii |
| * Keppler | Reinhardt | J. | Boatswain's Mate First Class | Ironbottom Sound, Savo Island, Solomon Islands |
| * Kidd | Isaac | C. | Rear Admiral | Pearl Harbor, Territory of Hawaii |
| * Lester | Fred | F. | Hospital Apprentice First Class | Okinawa Shima |
| McCampbell | David | | Commander | Battle of the Philippine Sea and Battle of Leyte Gulf |
| McCandless | Bruce | | Commander | Ironbottom Sound, Savo Island, Solomon Islands |
| McCool Jr. | Richard | M. | Lieutenant | North of Okinawa |
| O'Callahan | Joseph | T. | Commander (Chaplain Corps) | Near Kobe, Japan |
| O'Hare | Edward | H. | Lieutenant | South Pacific |
| O'Kane | Richard | H. | Commander | Vicinity of Formosa Straits, Philippines |
| * Parle | John | J. | Ensign | Sicily |
| * Peterson | Oscar | V. | Chief Watertender | Coral Sea |

| Name | | | Rank at Time of Action | Place of Action |
|---|---|---|---|---|
| Pharris | Jackson | C. | Gunner | Pearl Harbor, Territory of Hawaii |
| Pierce | Francis | J. | Pharmacist's Mate First Class | Iwo Jima |
| * Powers | John | J. | Lieutenant | Coral Sea |
| Preston | Arthur | M. | Lieutenant | Halmahera Island, Netherlands Indies |
| Ramage | Lawson | P. | Commander | Off Taiwan, South China Sea |
| * Reeves | Thomas | J. | Radio Electrician | Pearl Harbor, Territory of Hawaii |
| * Ricketts | Milton | E. | Lieutenant | Coral Sea |
| * Rooks | Albert | H. | Captain | From Darwin to Koepang, Netherlands East Indies |
| Ross | Donald | K. | Warrant Machinist | Pearl Harbor, Territory of Hawaii |
| Schonland | Herbert | E. | Lieutenant Commander | Ironbottom Sound, Savo Island, Solomon Islands |
| * Scott | Norman | | Rear Admiral | Ironbottom Sound, Savo Island, Solomon Islands |
| * Scott | Robert | R. | Machinist's Mate First Class | Pearl Harbor, Territory of Hawaii |
| Street III | George | L. | Commander | Quelpart Island off the coast of Korea |
| * Tomich | Peter | | Chief Watertender | Pearl Harbor, Territory of Hawaii |
| * Van Valkenburgh | Franklin | | Captain | Pearl Harbor, Territory of Hawaii |
| * Van Voorhis | Bruce | A. | Lieutenant Commander | Greenwich Island, Solomon Islands |
| Wahlen | George | E. | Pharmacist's Mate Second Class | Iwo Jima |
| * Ward | James | R. | Seaman First Class | Pearl Harbor, Territory of Hawaii |
| * Williams | Jack | | Pharmacist's Mate Third Class | Iwo Jima |
| * Willis | John | H. | Pharmacist's Mate First Class | Iwo Jima |
| Young | Cassin | | Commander | Pearl Harbor, Territory of Hawaii |

## The Korean War, 1950–1953

*All actions took place in Korea.*

### Unknown

| | | | | |
|---|---|---|---|---|
| * United States | Unknown Soldier | | | |

### Air Force

| Name | | | Rank at Time of Action | Place of Action |
|---|---|---|---|---|
| * Davis Jr. | George | A. | Major | Sinuiju-Yalu River Area |
| * Loring Jr. | Charles | J. | Major | Near Sniper Ridge, North Korea |
| * Sebille | Louis | J. | Major | Near Hanchang |
| * Walmsley Jr. | John | S. | Captain | Near Yangdok |

### Army

| Name | | | Rank at Time of Action | Place of Action |
|---|---|---|---|---|
| Adams | Stanley | T. | Sergeant First Class | Sesim-Ni |
| * Baldonado | Joe | R. | Corporal | Kangdong |
| * Barker | Chalres | H. | Private First Class | Sokkogae |
| * Bennett | Emory | L. | Private First Class | Sobangsan |
| Bleak | David | B. | Sergeant | Minari-Gol |
| * Brittin | Nelson | V. | Sergeant First Class | Yonggong-Ni |
| * Brown | Melvin | L. | Private First Class | Kasan |
| Burke | Lloyd | L. | First Lieutenant | Chong-Dong |
| * Burris | Tony | K. | Sergeant First Class | Mundung-Ni |
| * Charlton | Cornelius | H. | Sergeant | Chipo-Ri |
| * Collier | Gilbert | G. | Corporal | Tutayon |
| * Collier | John | W. | Corporal | Chindoing-Ni |
| * Coursen | Samuel | S. | First Lieutenant | Kaesong |
| * Craig | Gordon | M. | Corporal | Kasan |
| Crump | Jerry | K. | Corporal | Chorwon |
| Dean Sr. | William | F. | Major General | Taejon |
| * Desiderio | Reginald | B. | Captain | Ipsok |
| Dodd | Carl | H. | Second Lieutenant | Subuk |
| * Duke | Ray | E. | Sergeant First Class | Mugok |
| * Edwards | Junior | D. | Sergeant First Class | Changbong-Ni |
| * Espinoza | Victor | H. | Corporal | Chorwon |
| * Essebagger Jr. | John | | Corporal | Popsu-Dong |
| * Faith Jr. | Don | C. | Lieutenant Colonel | Hagaru-Ri |
| * George | Charles | | Private First Class | Songnae-Dong |
| * Gilliland | Charles | L. | Private First Class | Tongmang-Ni |
| * Gomez | Eduardo | C. | Sergeant First Class | Tabu-Dong |
| * Goodblood | Clair | | Corporal | Popsu-Dong |
| * Hammond Jr. | Lester | | Corporal | Kumwha |
| * Handrich | Melvin | O. | Master Sergeant | Sobuk San Mountain |

| Name | | | Rank at Time of Action | Place of Action |
|---|---|---|---|---|
| * Hanson | Jack | G. | Private First Class | Pachi-Dong |
| * Hartell | Lee | R. | First Lieutenant | Kobangsan-Ni |
| Harvey | Raymond | | Captain | Vicinity of Taemi-Dong |
| * Henry | Frederick | F. | First Lieutenant | Am-Dong |
| Hernandez | Rodolfo | P. | Corporal | Near Wontong-Ni |
| Ingman Jr. | Einar | H. | Corporal | Near Maltari |
| * Jecelin | William | R. | Sergeant | Near Saga |
| * Jordon | Mack | A. | Private First Class | Near Kumsong |
| * Kaho'ohanohano | Anthony | T. | Private First Class | Vicinity of Chupa-Ri |
| * Kanell | Billie | G. | Private | Near Pyongyang |
| * Kapaun | Emil | J. | Chaplain (Captain) | Unsan |
| * Kaufman | Loren | R. | Sergeant First Class | Near Yongsan |
| * Keeble | Woodrow | W. | Master Sergeant | Hill 765, near Sangsan-Ni |
| * Knight | Noah | O. | Private First Class | Near Kowang-San |
| Kouma | Ernest | R. | Sergeant First Class | Vicinity of Agok |
| * Kravitz | Leonard | M. | Private First Class | Yangpyong |
| * Krzyzowski | Edward | C. | Captain | Near Tondul |
| * Kyle | Darwin | K. | Second Lieutenant | Near Kamil-Ni |
| Lee | Hubert | L. | Master Sergeant | Near Ip'o-Ri |
| * Libby | George | D. | Sergeant | Near Taejon |
| * Long | Charles | R. | Sergeant | Near Hoeng-Song |
| * Lyell | William | F. | Corporal | Near Chup'a-Ri |
| * Martinez | Benito | | Corporal | Near Satae-Ri |
| * McGovern | Robert | M. | First Lieutenant | Near Kamyangjan-Ni |
| * Mendonca | Leroy | A. | Sergeant | Near Chich-On |
| Millett | Lewis | L. | Captain | Vicinity of Hill 180, Soam-Ni |
| Miyamura | Hiroshi | | Corporal | Near Taejon-Ni |
| Mize | Ola | L. | Sergeant | Near Surang-Ni |
| * Moyer | Donald | R. | Sergeant First Class | Near Seoul |
| * Negron | Juan | E. | Sergeant | Near Kalma-Eri |
| * Ouellette | Joseph | R. | Private First Class | Near Yongsan |
| * Page | John | U. D. | Lieutenant Colonel | Near Chosin Reservoir |
| * Pena | Mike | C. | Master Sergeant | Near Waegwan |
| * Pendleton | Charles | F. | Corporal | Near Choo Gung-Dong |
| * Pililaau | Herbert | K. | Private First Class | Near Pia-Ri |
| Pittman | John | A. | Sergeant | Near Kujang-Dong |
| * Pomeroy | Ralph | E. | Private First Class | Near Kumhwa |
| * Porter | Donn | F. | Sergeant | Near Mundung-Ni |
| * Red Cloud Jr. | Mitchell | | Corporal | Near Chonghyon |
| * Rivera | Demensio | | Private | Changyongni |
| Rodriguez | Joseph | C. | Private First Class | Near Munye-Ri |
| Rosser | Ronald | E. | Corporal | Near Ponggilli |
| Rubin | Tibor | | Corporal | Korea |
| * Schoonover | Dan | D. | Corporal | Pork Chop Hill, Near Sokkogae |
| Schowalter Jr. | Edward | R. | First Lieutenant | Near Kumhwa |
| * Shea Jr. | Richard | T. | First Lieutenant | Pork Chop Hill, Near Sokkogae |
| * Sitman | William | S. | Sergeant First Class | Near Chipyong-Ni |
| * Smith | David | M. | Private First Class | Near Yongsan |
| * Speicher | Clifton | T. | Corporal | Near Minarigol |
| Stone | James | L. | First Lieutenant | Near Sokkogae |
| * Story | Luther | H. | Private First Class | Near Agok |
| * Sudut | Jerome | A. | Second Lieutenant | Near Kumhwa |
| * Svehla | Henry | | Private First Class | Pyongony |
| * Thompson | William | H. | Private First Class | Near Haman |
| * Turner | Charles | W. | Sergeant First Class | Near Yongsan |
| * Vera | Miguel | A. | Private | Chorwon |
| * Watkins | Travis | E. | Master Sergeant | Near Yongsan |
| * Weinstein | Jack | | Sergeant | Near Kumson |
| West | Ernest | E. | Private First Class | Near Sataeri |
| * Wilson | Benjamin | F. | Master Sergeant | Near Hwach'on-Myon |
| Wilson | Richard | G. | Private First Class | Near Opari |
| * Womack | Bryant | H. | Private | Near Sokso-Ri |
| * Young | Robert | H. | Private First Class | North of Kaesong |

| Name | | | Rank at Time of Action | Place of Action |
|---|---|---|---|---|
| **Marines** | | | | |
| * Abrell | Charles | G. | Corporal | Hangnyong |
| Barber | William | E. | Captain | Chosin Reservoir |
| * Baugh | William | B. | Private First Class | Road From Koto-Ri to Hagaru-Ri |
| Cafferata Jr. | Hector | A. | Private | Toktong Pass |
| * Champagne | David | B. | Corporal | Korea |
| * Christianson | Stanley | R. | Private First Class | Seoul |
| Commiskey Sr. | Henry | A. | Second Lieutenant | Yongdungp'o |
| * Davenport | Jack | A. | Corporal | Songnae-Dong |
| Davis | Raymond | G. | Lieutenant Colonel | Hagaru-Ri |
| Dewey | Duane | E. | Corporal | Near Panmunjom |
| * Garcia | Fernando | L. | Private First Class | Korea |
| * Gomez | Edward | | Private First Class | Hill 749 |
| * Guillen | Ambrosio | | Staff Sergeant | Songuch-On |
| * Johnson | James | E. | Sergeant | Yudam-Ni |
| * Kelly | John | D. | Private First Class | Korea |
| * Kelso | Jack | W. | Private First Class | Korea |
| Kennemore | Robert | S. | Staff Sergeant | North of Yudam-Ni |
| * Littleton | Herbert | A | Private First Class | Chungchon |
| * Lopez | Baldomero | | First Lieutenant | Inchon |
| * Matthews | Daniel | P. | Sergeant | Vegas Hill |
| * Mausert III | Frederick | W. | Sergeant | Songnap-Yong |
| McLaughlin | Alford | L. | Private First Class | Outpost Bruce |
| * Mitchell | Frank | N. | First Lieutenant | Near Hansan-Ni |
| * Monegan Jr. | Walter | C. | Private First Class | Near Sosa-Ri |
| * Moreland | Whitt | L. | Private First Class | Kwagch'i-Dong |
| Murphy | Raymond | G. | Second Lieutenant | Ungok Hill |
| Myers | Reginald | R. | Major | Near Hagaru-Ri |
| O'Brien Jr. | George | H. | Second Lieutenant | The Hook |
| * Obregon | Eugene | A. | Private First Class | Seoul |
| * Phillips | Lee | H. | Corporal | Korea |
| * Poynter | James | I. | Sergeant | Near Sudong |
| * Ramer | George | H. | Second Lieutenant | Korea |
| * Reem | Robert | D. | Second Lieutenant | Vicinity of Chinhung-Ni |
| * Shuck Jr. | William | E. | Staff Sergeant | Korea |
| Simanek | Robert | E. | Private First Class | Outpost Irene |
| Sitter | Carl | L. | Captain | Hagaru-Ri |
| * Skinner Jr. | Sherrod | E. | Second Lieutenant | Korea |
| Van Winkle | Archie | | Staff Sergeant | Near Sudong |
| * Vittori | Joseph | | Corporal | Hill 749 |
| * Watkins | Lewis | G. | Staff Sergeant | Korea |
| Wilson | Harold | E. | Technical Sergeant | Hill 902 near Hwachon Reservoir, North Korea |
| * Windrich | William | G. | Staff Sergeant | Yudam-Ni |

| Name | | | Rank at Time of Action | Place of Action |
|---|---|---|---|---|
| **Navy** | | | | |
| * Benfold | Edward | C. | Hospital Corpsman Third Class | Korea |
| Charette | William | R. | Hospital Corpsman Third Class | Panmunjom Corridor (DMZ) |
| * Dewert | Richard | D. | Hospital Corpsman | Korea |
| * Hammond | Francis | C. | Hospitalman | Near Sanae-Dong |
| Hudner Jr. | Thomas | J. | Lieutenant (j.g.) | Chosin Reservoir |
| * Kilmer | John | E. | Hospital Corpsman | Korea |
| * Koelsch | John | K. | Lieutenant (j.g.) | Near Wonsan, North Korea |

## The Vietnam War, 1954–1975

*Actions took place in the Republic of Vietnam (South Vietnam) unless otherwise noted.*

### Unknown

| | | | | |
|---|---|---|---|---|
| * United States | Unknown Soldier | | | |

### Air Force

| | | | | |
|---|---|---|---|---|
| * Bennett | Steven | L. | Captain | Quang Tri Province |
| Day | George | E. | Major | Over North Vietnam |

| Name | | | Rank at Time of Action | Place of Action |
|---|---|---|---|---|
| Dethlefsen | Merlyn | H. | Captain | Thai Nguyen, North Vietnam |
| * Etchberger | Richard | L. | Chief Master Sergeant | Phou Pha Thi, Laos |
| Fisher | Bernard | F. | Major | Bien Hoa and Pleiku |
| Fleming | James | P. | First Lieutenant | Near Duc Co |
| Jackson | Joe | M. | Lieutenant Colonel | Kham Duc |
| * Jones III | William | A. | Colonel | Near Dong Hoi, North Vietnam |
| Levitow | John | L. | Airman First Class | Long Binh Army Post |
| * Pitsenbarger | William | H. | Airman First Class | Near Cam My |
| * Sijan | Lance | P. | Captain | Laos and Ban Kari Pass, Vietnam |
| Thorsness | Leo | K. | Major | Over North Vietnam |
| * Wilbanks | Hilliard | A. | Captain | Near Dalat |
| Young | Gerald | O. | Captain | Khe Sanh |

| Name | | | Rank at Time of Action | Place of Action |
|---|---|---|---|---|
| **Army** | | | | |
| * Adams | William | E. | Major | Kontum Province |
| * Albanese | Lewis | | Private First Class | Near Phu Huu II |
| * Alvarado | Leonard | L. | Specialist Fourth Class | Phuoc Long Province |
| Anderson | Webster | | Staff Sergeant | Tam Ky |
| * Ashley Jr. | Eugene | | Sergeant First Class | Near Lang Vei |
| Baca | John | P. | Specialist Fourth Class | Near Quan Loi, Phuoc Long Province |
| Bacon | Nicky | D. | Staff Sergeant | West Of Tam Ky |
| Baker Jr. | John | F. | Private First Class | Near Dau Tieng |
| * Barnes III | John | A. | Private First Class | Dak To |
| Beikirch | Gary | B. | Sergeant | Kontum Province |
| * Belcher | Ted | | Sergeant | Plei Djerang |
| * Bellrichard | Leslie | A. | Private First Class | Kontum Province |
| Benavidez | Roy | P. | Staff Sergeant | West of Loc Ninh, Cambodia |
| * Bennett | Thomas | W. | Corporal | Chu Pa Region, Pleiku Province |
| * Blanchfield | Michael | R. | Specialist Fourth Class | Binh Dinh Province |
| Bondsteel | James | L. | Staff Sergeant | Near Lang Sau, An Loc Province |
| * Bowen Jr. | Hammett | L. | Staff Sergeant | Binh Duong Province |
| Brady | Patrick | H. | Major | Near Chu Lai |
| * Bryant | William | M. | Sergeant First Class | Long Khanh Province |
| Bucha | Paul | W. | Captain | Near Phuoc Vinh, Binh Duong Province |
| * Buker | Brian | L. | Sergeant | Chau Doc Province |
| Cavaiani | Jon | R. | Staff Sergeant | Hill 1050, overlooking Khe Sahn Airfield |
| * Conde-Falcon | Felix | M. | Staff Sergeant | Near Ap Tan Hoa |
| * Copas | Ardie | R. | Specialist Fourth Class | Near Ph Romeas Hek, Cambodia |
| Crandall | Bruce | P. | Major | Ia Drang Valley |
| * Crescenz | Michael | J. | Corporal | Hiep Duc Valley Area |
| * Cutinha | Nicholas | J. | Specialist Fourth Class | Near Gia Dinh |
| * Dahl | Larry | G. | Specialist Fourth Class | An Khe, Binh Dinh Province |
| Davis | Sammy | L. | Private First Class | Firebase Cudgil, west of Cai Lay |
| * DeVore Jr. | Edward | A. | Specialist Fourth Class | Near Saigon |
| Dix | Drew | D. | Staff Sergeant | Chau Doc Province |
| * Doane | Stephen | H. | First Lieutenant | Hau Nghia Province |
| Dolby | David | C. | Specialist Fourth Class | Republic of Vietnam |
| Donlon | Roger | H. C. | Captain | Near Nam Dong |
| Dunagan | Kern | W. | Captain | Quang Tin Province |
| * Duran | Jesus | S. | Specialist Fourth Class | Vietnam |
| * Durham Jr. | Harold | B. | Second Lieutenant | Republic of Vietnam |
| * English Jr. | Glenn | H. | Staff Sergeant | Phu My District |
| Erevia | Santiago | J. | Specialist Fourth Class | Near Tam Ky City |
| * Evans | Rodney | J. | Sergeant | Tay Ninh Province |
| * Evans Jr. | Donald | W. | Specialist Fourth Class | Tri Tam |
| Ferguson | Frederick | E. | Chief Warrant Officer | Hue |
| * Fernandez | Daniel | O. | Specialist Fourth Class | Cu Chi, Hau Nghia Province |
| Fitzmaurice | Michael | J. | Specialist Fourth Class | Khe Sanh |
| * Fleek | Charles | C. | Sergeant | Binh Duong Province |
| Foley | Robert | F. | Captain | Near Quan Dau Tieng |
| * Folland | Michael | F. | Corporal | Long Khanh Province |
| * Fournet | Douglas | B. | First Lieutenant | A Shau Valley |
| * Fous | James | W. | Private First Class | Kien Hoa Province |
| * Fratellenico | Frank | R. | Corporal | Near Fire Base Barnett, Quang Tri Province |

| Name | | | Rank at Time of Action | Place of Action |
|---|---|---|---|---|
| Freeman | Ed | W. | Captain | Landing Zone X-Ray, Ia Drang Valley |
| Fritz | Harold | A. | First Lieutenant | Near An Loc, Binh Long Province |
| * Garcia | Candelario | | Sergeant | Near Lai Khe |
| * Gardner | James | A. | First Lieutenant | My Canh |
| * Gertsch | John | G. | Staff Sergeant | A Shau Valley |
| * Grandstaff | Bruce | A. | Platoon Sergeant | Pleiku Province |
| * Grant | Joseph | X. | First Lieutenant | Near Plei Djereng |
| * Guenette | Peter | M. | Specialist Fourth Class | Quan Tan Uyen Province |
| Hagemeister | Charles | C. | Specialist Fourth Class | Binh Dinh Province |
| * Hagen | Loren | D. | First Lieutenant | Republic of Vietnam |
| * Hartsock | Robert | W. | Staff Sergeant | Dau Tieng Base Camp, Hau Nghia Province |
| * Harvey Jr. | Carmel | B. | Specialist Fourth Class | Binh Dinh Province |
| Herda | Frank | A. | Private First Class | Near Dak To, Quang Trang Province |
| * Hibbs | Robert | J. | Second Lieutenant | Don Dien Lo Ke |
| * Holcomb | John | N. | Sergeant | Near Quan Loi |
| Hooper | Joe | R. | Sergeant | Near Hue |
| * Hosking Jr. | Charles | E. | Staff Sergeant | Don Luan District, Phuoc Long Province |
| Howard | Robert | L. | Sergeant First Class | Republic of Vietnam |
| * Ingalls | George | A. | Specialist Fourth Class | Near Duc Pho |
| Jacobs | Jack | H. | First Lieutenant | Kien Phong Province |
| Jenkins | Don | | Private First Class | Kien Phong Province |
| Jennings | Delbert | O. | Staff Sergeant | Kim Song Valley |
| Joel | Lawrence | | Specialist Fifth Class | Republic of Vietnam |
| Johnson | Dwight | H. | Specialist Fifth Class | Near Dak To, Kontum Province |
| * Johnston | Donald | R. | Specialist Fourth Class | Tay Ninh Province |
| * Karopczyc | Stephen | E. | First Lieutenant | Kontum Province |
| * Kawamura | Terry | T. | Corporal | Camp Radcliff |
| Kays | Kenneth | M. | Private | Thua Thien Province |
| * Kedenburg | John | J. | Specialist Fifth Class | Republic of Vietnam |
| Keller | Leonard | B. | Sergeant | Ap Bac Zone |
| Kinsman | Thomas | J. | Private First Class | Near Vinh Long |
| Lambers | Paul | R. | Staff Sergeant | Tay Ninh Province |
| Lang | George | C. | Specialist Fourth Class | Near Ben Tre City, Kien Hoa Province |
| * Langhorn | Garfield | M. | Private First Class | Near Plei Djereng, Pleiku Province |
| * LaPointe Jr. | Joseph | G. | Specialist Fourth Class | Quang Tin Province |
| * Lauffer | Billy | L. | Private First Class | Near Bon Son, Binh Dinh Province |
| * Law | Robert | D. | Specialist Fourth Class | Tinh Phuoc Thanh Province |
| * Lee | Milton | A. | Private First Class | Near Phu Bai, Thua Thien Province |
| * Leisy | Robert | R. | Second Lieutenant | Phuoc Long Province |
| Lemon | Peter | C. | Specialist Fourth Class | Fire Support Base Illingworth, Tay Ninh Province |
| * Leonard | Matthew | | Sergeant First Class | Near Suoi Da |
| Liteky | Charles | J. | Captain | Near Phuoc-Lac, Bien Hoa Province |
| Littrell | Gary | L. | Sergeant First Class | Kontum Province |
| * Long | Donald | R. | Sergeant | Republic of Vietnam |
| * Lozada | Carlos | J. | Private First Class | Hill 875, Near Dak To, Kontum Province |
| * Lucas | Andre | C. | Lieutenant Colonel | Fire Support Base Ripcord |
| Lynch | Allen | J. | Specialist Fourth Class | Near My An, Binh Dinh Province |
| Marm Jr. | Walter | J. | Second Lieutenant | Vicinity of Ia Drang Valley |
| McCleery | Finnis | D. | Sergeant First Class | Quang Tin Province |
| * McDonald | Phill | G. | Private First Class | Near Kontum City |
| * McKibben | Ray | | Sergeant | Near Song Mao |
| * McMahon | Thomas | J. | Specialist Fourth Class | Quang Tin Province |
| McNerney | David | H. | First Sergeant | Polei Doc |
| * McWethy Jr. | Edgar | L. | Specialist Fifth Class | Binh Dinh Province |
| * Michael | Don | L. | Specialist Fourth Class | Republic of Vietnam |
| Miller | Franklin | D. | Staff Sergeant | Kontum Province |
| * Miller | Gary | L. | First Lieutenant | Binh Duong Province |
| * Molnar | Frankie | Z. | Staff Sergeant | Kontum Province |
| * Monroe | James | H. | Private First Class | Bong Son, Hoai Nhon Province |
| Morris | Charles | B. | Sergeant | Near Xuan Loc |
| Morris | Melvin | | Staff Sergeant | Near Chi Lang |
| * Murray | Robert | C. | Staff Sergeant | Near the Village of Hiep Duc |
| * Nash | David | P. | Private First Class | Giao Duc District, Dinh Tuong Province |
| Novosel | Michael | J. | Chief Warrant Officer | Kien Tuong Province |
| * Olive III | Milton | L. | Private First Class | Phu Cuong |
| * Olson | Kenneth | L. | Specialist Fourth Class | Republic of Vietnam |
| Patterson | Robert | M. | Specialist Fourth Class | Near La Chu |
| Penry | Richard | A. | Sergeant | Binh Tuy Province |
| * Petersen | Danny | J. | Specialist Fourth Class | Tay Ninh Province |
| * Pierce | Larry | S. | Sergeant | Near Ben Cat |
| * Pitts | Riley | L. | Captain | Ap Dong |
| * Port | William | D. | Private First Class | Que Son Valley, Heip Duc Province |
| * Poxon | Robert | L. | First Lieutenant | Tay Ninh Province |
| * Pruden | Robert | J. | Staff Sergeant | Quang Ngai Province |
| * Rabel | Laszlo | | Staff Sergeant | Binh Dinh Province |
| Rascon | Alfred | | Special Fourth Class | Long Khanh Province |
| Ray | Ronald | E. | First Lieutenant | Ia Drang Valley |
| * Roark | Anund | C. | Sergeant | Kontum Province |
| Roberts | Gordon | R. | Specialist Fourth Class | Thua Thien Province |
| * Robinson Jr. | James | W. | Sergeant | Republic of Vietnam |
| Rocco | Louis | R. | Sergeant First Class | Northeast of Katum |
| Rodela | Jose | | Sergeant First Class | Phuoc Long Province |
| Rogers | Charles | C. | Lieutenant Colonel | Fishhook near Cambodian Border |
| * Rubio | Euripides | | Captain | Tay Ninh Province |
| * Sabo | Leslie | H. | Specialist Fourth Class | Se San, Cambodia |
| * Santiago-Colon | Hector | | Specialist Fourth Class | Quang Tri Province |
| * Sargent | Ruppert | L. | First Lieutenant | Hau Nghia Province |
| Sasser | Clarence | E. | Private First Class | Ding Tuong Province |
| * Seay | William | W. | Sergeant | Near Ap Nhi |
| * Shea | Daniel | J. | Private First Class | Quang Tri Province |
| * Sims | Clifford | C. | Staff Sergeant | Near Hue |
| * Sisler | George | K. | First Lieutenant | Republic of Vietnam |
| * Skidgel | Donald | S. | Sergeant | Near Song Be |
| * Smith | Elmelindo | R. | Staff Sergeant | Republic of Vietnam |
| Sprayberry | James | M. | First Lieutenant | Republic of Vietnam |
| * Steindam | Russell | A. | First Lieutenant | Tay Ninh Province |
| * Stewart | Jimmy | G. | Staff Sergeant | Republic of Vietnam |
| * Stone Jr. | Lester | R. | Sergeant | West of Landing Zone Liz |
| * Stout | Mitchell | W. | Sergeant | Khe Gio Bridge |
| * Stryker | Robert | F. | Specialist Fourth Class | Near Loc Ninh |
| Stumpf | Kenneth | E. | Specialist Fourth Class | Near Duc Pho |
| * Swanson | Jon | E. | Captain | Cambodia |
| Taylor | James | A. | First Lieutenant | West of Que Son |
| Thacker | Brian | M. | First Lieutenant | Fire Base 6, Kontum Province |
| * Versace | Humbert | R. | Captain | An Xuyen Province |
| * Warren Jr. | John | E. | First Lieutenant | Tay Ninh Province |
| * Watters | Charles | J. | Major | Hill 875, near Dak To, Kontum Province |
| * Wayrynen | Dale | E. | Specialist Fourth Class | Near Duc Pho, Quang Ngai Province |
| Wetzel | Gary | G. | Private First Class | Near Ap Dong An |
| * Wickam | Jerry | W. | Corporal | Near Loc Ninh |
| * Willett | Louis | E. | Private First Class | Kontum Province |
| Williams | Charles | Q. | Second Lieutenant | Dong Xoai |
| * Winder | David | F. | Private First Class | Republic of Vietnam |
| Wright | Raymond | R. | Specialist Fourth Class | Ap Bac Zone |
| * Yabes | Maximo | | First Sergeant | Near Phu Hoa Dong |
| * Yano | Rodney | J. T. | First Sergeant | Near Bien Hao |
| * Yntema | Gordon | D. | Sergeant | Near Thong Binh |
| * Young | Marvin | R. | Staff Sergeant | Near Ben Cui |
| Zabitosky | Fred | W. | Staff Sergeant | Laos |

**Marines**

| Name | | | Rank at Time of Action | Place of Action |
|---|---|---|---|---|
| * Anderson | Richard | A. | Lance Corporal | Quang Tri Province |
| * Anderson Jr. | James | | Private First Class | Northwest of Cam Lo |
| * Austin | Oscar | P. | Private First Class | West of Da Nang |
| * Barker | Jedh | C. | Lance Corporal | Near Con Thien |
| Barnum Jr. | Harvey | C. | First Lieutenant | Outside the Village of Ky Phu, Quang Tin Province |
| * Bobo | John | P. | Second Lieutenant | Quang Tri Province |
| * Bruce | Daniel | D. | Private First Class | Fire Support Base Tomahawk, Quang Nam Province |

| Name | | | Rank at Time of Action | Place of Action |
|---|---|---|---|---|
| * Burke | Robert | C. | Private First Class | Le Nam 1, Go Nai Island, Southern Quang Nam Province |
| * Carter | Bruce | W. | Private First Class | Quang Tri Province |
| Clausen Jr. | Raymond | M. | Private First Class | Republic of Vietnam |
| * Coker | Ronald | L. | Private First Class | Northwest Quang Tri Province |
| * Connor | Peter | S. | Staff Sergeant | Quang Ngai Province |
| * Cook | Donald | G. | Captain | Vicinity of Binh Gia, Phouc Tuy Province |
| * Creek | Thomas | E. | Lance Corporal | Near Cam Lo |
| * Davis | Rodney | M. | Sergeant | Quang Nam Province |
| * De La Garza Jr. | Emilio | A. | Lance Corporal | Near Da Nang |
| * Dias | Ralph | E. | Private First Class | Que Son Mountains |
| * Dickey | Douglas | E. | Private First Class | Near Gio An, Quang Tri Province |
| * Foster | Paul | H. | Sergeant | Near Con Thien, Quang Tri Province |
| Fox | Wesley | L. | First Lieutenant | A Shau Valley, Quang Tri Province |
| * Gonzalez | Alfredo | | Sergeant | Near Thua Thien |
| * Graham | James | A. | Captain | Quang Tin Province |
| * Graves | Terrence | C. | Second Lieutenant | Quang Tri Province |
| Howard | Jimmie | E. | Staff Sergeant | Near Chu Lai |
| * Howe | James | D. | Lance Corporal | Republic of Vietnam |
| * Jenkins Jr. | Robert | H. | Private First Class | Fire Support Base Argonne, DMZ |
| * Jimenez | Jose | F. | Lance Corporal | South of Da Nang, Quang Nam Province |
| * Johnson | Ralph | H. | Private First Class | Hill 146, near Quan Duc Valley |
| * Keith | Miguel | | Lance Corporal | Quang Ngai Province |
| Kellogg Jr. | Allan | J. | Staff Sergeant | Quang Nam Province |
| Lee | Howard | V. | Captain | Near Cam Lo |
| Livingston | James | E. | Captain | Dai Do, Quang Tri Province |
| * Martini | Gary | W. | Private First Class | Binh Son |
| * Maxam | Larry | L. | Corporal | Cam Lo District, Quang Tri Province |
| McGinty III | John | J. | Staff Sergeant | Quang Tri Province |
| Modrzejewski | Robert | J. | Captain | Republic of Vietnam |
| * Morgan | William | D. | Corporal | Southeast of Vandegrift Combat Base, Quang Tri Province |
| * Newlin | Melvin | E. | Private First Class | Quang Nam Province |
| * Noonan Jr. | Thomas | P. | Lance Corporal | Near Vandergrift Combat Base, A Shau Valley |
| O'Malley | Robert | E. | Corporal | Near An Cu'ong 2 |
| * Paul | Joe | C. | Lance Corporal | Near Chu Lai |
| * Perkins Jr. | William | T. | Corporal | Quang Tri Province |
| * Peters | Lawrence | D. | Sergeant | Quang Tin Province |
| * Phipps | Jimmy | W. | Private First Class | Near An Hoa |
| Pittman | Richard | A. | Lance Corporal | Near DMZ |
| Pless | Stephen | W. | Captain | Near Quang Nai |
| * Prom | William | R. | Lance Corporal | Near An Hoa |
| * Reasoner | Frank | S. | First Lieutenant | Near Da Nang |
| * Singleton | Walter | K. | Sergeant | Gio Linh District, Quang Tri Province |
| * Smedley | Larry | E. | Corporal | Mouth of Happy Valley, Quang Nam Province |
| * Taylor Sr. | Karl | G. | Staff Sergeant | Republic of Vietnam |
| Vargas | Jay | R. | Captain | Dai Do, Quang Tri Province |
| * Weber | Lester | W. | Lance Corporal | Bo Ban Area, Hieu Duc District, Quang Nam Province |
| * Wheat | Roy | M. | Lance Corporal | Liberty Road, Dien Ban District, Quang Nam Province |
| * Williams | Dewayne | T. | Private First Class | Quang Nam Province |
| * Wilson | Alfred | M. | Private First Class | Fire Support Base Cunningham, Quang Tri Province |
| * Worley | Kenneth | L. | Lance Corporal | Bo Ban, Quang Nam Province |

**Navy**

| Name | | | Rank at Time of Action | Place of Action |
|---|---|---|---|---|
| Ballard | Donald | E. | Hospital Corpsman Second Class | Quang Tri Province |

| Name | | | Rank at Time of Action | Place of Action |
|---|---|---|---|---|
| * Capodanno | Vincent | R. | Lieutenant | Quang Tin Province |
| * Caron | Wayne | M. | Hospital Corpsman Third Class | Quang Nam Province |
| * Estocin | Michael | J. | Lieutenant Commander | Haiphong, North Vietnam |
| Ingram | Robert | R. | Petty Officer | Quang Ngai Province |
| Kelley | Thomas | G. | Lieutenant | Ong Muong Canal, Kien Hoa Province |
| Kerrey | Joseph | R. | Lieutenant (j.g.) | Near Nha Trang Bay |
| Lassen | Clyde | E. | Lieutenant | Republic of Vietnam |
| [7] McGonagle | William | L. | Commander | USS *Liberty*, Eastern Mediterranean |
| Norris | Thomas | R. | Lieutenant | Quang Tri Province |
| * Ouellet | David | G. | Seaman | Mekong River |
| * Ray | David | R. | Hospital Corpsman Second Class | Phu Loc 6, near An Hoa, Quang Nam Province |
| * Shields | Marvin | G. | Construction Mechanic Third Class | Dong Xoai |
| Stockdale | James | B. | Captain | Hoa Lo Prison, Hanoi |
| Thornton | Michael | E. | Petty Officer | Republic of Vietnam |
| Williams | James | E. | Boatswain's Mate First Class | Mekong River |

## Somalia, 1993

**Army**

| Name | | | Rank at Time of Action | Place of Action |
|---|---|---|---|---|
| * Gordon | Gary | I. | Master Sergeant | Mogadishu |
| * Shughart | Randall | D. | Sergeant First Class | Mogadishu |

## War on Terror, 2001–Present

**Afghanistan**

**Army**

| Name | | | Rank at Time of Action | Place of Action |
|---|---|---|---|---|
| Carter | Ty | M. | Staff Sergeant | Outpost Keating, Kamdesh District, Nuristan Province |
| Giunta | Salvatore | A. | Specialist | Korengal Valley |
| * Miller | Robert | J. | Staff Sergeant | Konar Province |
| * Monti | Jared | C. | Staff Sergeant | Nuristan Province |
| Petry | Leroy | A. | Staff Sergeant | Paktva Province |
| Romesha | Clinton | L. | Staff Sergeant | Outpost Keating, Kamdesh District, Nuristan Province |
| Swenson | William | D. | Captain | Kunar Province |
| White | Kyle | J. | Specialist | Nuristan Province |

**Marines**

| Name | | | Rank at Time of Action | Place of Action |
|---|---|---|---|---|
| Meyer | Dakota | L. | Corporal | Kunar Province |

**Navy**

| Name | | | Rank at Time of Action | Place of Action |
|---|---|---|---|---|
| * Murphy | Michael | P. | Lieutenant | Asadabad, Konar Province |

**Iraq**

**Army**

| Name | | | Rank at Time of Action | Place of Action |
|---|---|---|---|---|
| * McGinnis | Ross | A. | Private First Class | Adhamiya, Northeast Baghdad |
| * Smith | Paul | R. | Sergeant First Class | Near Baghdad Airport, Baghdad |

**Marines**

| Name | | | Rank at Time of Action | Place of Action |
|---|---|---|---|---|
| Carpenter | William | K. | Lance Corporal | Helmand Province |
| * Dunham | Jason | L. | Corporal | Karabilah |

**Navy**

| Name | | | Rank at Time of Action | Place of Action |
|---|---|---|---|---|
| * Monsoor | Michael | A. | Master-at-Arms | Ar Ramadi |

# BIBLIOGRAPHY

## BOOKS AND ARTICLES

### General Works

Belden, Bauman L. *United States War Medals.* The American Numismatic Society, 1916.

Beyer, Walter F., and Oscar F. Keydel. *Deeds of Valor.* 2 vols. Perrien-Keydel Co., 1906.

Dewey, William S. "Epitome of the History of Military Medals." *The Numismatist,* April 1943.

Donovan, Frank. *The Medal.* Dodd, Mead, 1962.

Gleim, Lt. Col. Albert F. *The Certificate of Merit,* 1979.

Jacobs, Bruce. *Heroes of the Army.* Norton, 1956.

Kayser, Hugh. *The Spirit of America.* ETC Publications, 1982.

Kerrigan, Evans E. *American War Medals and Decorations.* Rev. ed. Viking, 1971.

Lee, Irvin. *Negro Medal of Honor Men.* Dodd, Mead, 1967.

McSherry, Richard M. *The National Medals of the United States.* Maryland Historical Society, 1887.

Peterson, Mendel L. "The Navy Medal of Honor." *The Numismatist,* June 1950.

Pullen, John J. *A Shower of Stars.* Lippincott, 1966.

Ross, Donald K., and Helen Ross. *Washington State Men of Valor.* Coffee Break Press, 1980.

Schott, Joseph L. *Above and Beyond.* G. P. Putnam's Sons, 1963.

US Congress. Senate Committee on Veterans Affairs. *Medal of Honor Recipients, 1863–1978.* Government Printing Office, 1979.

US Congress. Senate. *General Staff Corps and Medals of Honor.* 66th Cong., 1st sess., July 23, 1919, Doc. 58.

US Department of the Army, Public Information Division. *The Medal of Honor of the United States Army.* Government Printing Office, 1948.

US Department of the Navy, Bureau of Naval Personnel. *Medal of Honor 1861–1949.* Government Printing Office, 1949.

Willey, W. L., and John C. Fitzpatrick. *The Order of Military Merit/The Story of the Purple Heart.* Society of the Cincinnati in the State of New Hampshire, 1925.

### Chapter One: The Civil War

*The American Heritage Picture History of the Civil War.* American Heritage Publishing Co., 1960.

Blassingame, John W. "The Freedom Fighters." *Negro History Bulletin,* February 1965.

Boatner, Mark M. *Civil War Dictionary.* David McKay Co., 1959.

Buel, C. C., and Robert Johnson. *Battles and Leaders of the Civil War.* Century, 1884.

Chesnut, Mary B. *A Diary From Dixie.* Yale University Press, 1982.

Davis, William C. *The Battle of New Market.* Doubleday, 1975.

———. *Duel Between the First Ironclads.* Doubleday, 1975.

Heitman, Francis B. *Historical Register and Dictionary of the United States Army.* Government Printing office, 1903.

Kurtz, Wilbur G. "The Andrews Railroad Raid." *Civil War Times,* April 1966.

Lockwood, Allison. "Pantsuited Pioneer of Women's Lib, Dr. Mary Walker." *Smithsonian,* March 1977.

Long, E. B. *The Civil War Day by Day.* Doubleday, 1974.

Ott, Lana. "Dr. Mary Walker: Civil War Surgeon." *Soldiers,* November 1979.

Pittenger, William. *In Pursuit of the General.* Sunset Press, 1965.

Rodenbough, Theophilus F. *The Bravest Five Hundred of '61.* Putnam, 1891.

*Southern Historical Society Papers.* Vols. 26 (1898), 36 (1908), 45 (1923–1925), and 46 (1925).

*War of the Rebellion: Official Records of the Union and Confederate Armies.* 70 vols. U.S. War Department, 1880–1901.

Warner, Ezra. *Generals in Blue.* Louisiana State University Press, 1964.

Werlich, Robert. "Mary Walker: From Union Army Surgeon to Sideshow Freak." *Civil War Times,* June 1967.

## Chapter Two: The Indian Campaigns

*The American Heritage Book of Indians.* American Heritage Co., 1961.

*Annual Report of the Secretary of War.* U.S. Department of War, 1846–1991.

Brady, Cyrus T. *Indian Fights and Fighters.* Doubleday, Page & Co., 1913.

———. *Northwest Fights and Fighters.* McClure Co., 1907.

Brandes, Ray, ed. *Troopers West.* Frontier Heritage Press, 1970.

Brown, Dee. *Bury My Heart at Wounded Knee.* Holt, Rinehart & Winston, 1973.

Capps, Benjamin. *The Old West: The Great Chiefs.* Time-Life Books, 1975.

———. *The Old West: The Indians.* Time-Life Books, 1973.

Cruse, Thomas. *Apache Days and After.* Caxton Printer, Ltd., 1941.

Dillon, Richard. *Burnt-Out Fires.* Prentice-Hall, 1973.

Dunlay, Thomas. *Wolves for the Blue Soldiers.* University of Nebraska Press, 1982.

Faulk, Odie B. *Crimson Desert.* Oxford University Press, 1974.

Hagedorn, Hermann. *Leonard Wood: A Biography.* Harper & Bros., 1931.

Ingersoll, L. D. *A History of the War Department of the United States.* Francis B. Mohun Co., 1879.

Johnson, Virginia W. *The Unregimented General.* Houghton Mifflin, 1962.

Josephy, Alvin M., Jr. *The Nez Perce Indians and the Opening of the Northwest.* Yale University Press, 1965.

Krause, Herbert, and Gary D. Olson. *Prelude to Glory.* Brevet Press, 1974.

Lane, Jack C., ed. *Chasing Geronimo.* University of New Mexico Press, 1970.

Leckie, William H. *The Buffalo Soldiers.* University of Oklahoma Press, 1967.

Magnussen, Daniel O., ed. *Peter Thompson's Narrative of the Little Bighorn Campaign.* Arthur H. Clark Co., 1974.

Marshall, S. L. A. *Crimsoned Prairie.* Charles Scribner's Sons, 1972.

Miles, Gen. Nelson A. *Personal Recollections and Observations.* The Werner Co., 1896.

Murray, Keith A. *The Modocs and Their War.* University of Oklahoma Press, 1959.

Nevin, David. *The Old West: The Soldiers.* Time-Life Books, 1974.

Rickey, Don, Jr. *Forty Miles a Day on Beans and Hay.* University of Oklahoma Press, 1963.

Stewart, Edgar I. *Custer's Luck.* University of Oklahoma Press, 1955.

Tebbel, John. *The Compact History of the Indian Wars.* Tower Books, 1966.

Thompson, Neil B. *Crazy Horse Called Them Walk-a-Heaps.* North Star Press, 1979.

Utley, Robert M. *Frontier Regulars.* Macmillan, 1967.

———. *Frontiersmen in Blue.* Macmillan, 1967.

———. *The Indian Frontier of the American West, 1846–1890.* University of New Mexico Press, 1984.

———. *Indian, Soldier and Settler.* Jefferson National Expansion Historical Association, 1979.

———. *The Last Days of the Sioux Nation.* Yale University Press, 1963.

———. and Wilcomb E. Washburn. *The American Heritage History of the Indian Wars.* American Heritage Co., 1977.

Wellman, Paul I. *The Indian Wars of the West.* Doubleday, 1947.

White, Lonnie J. *Hostiles and Horse Soldiers.* Pruett Publishing Co., 1972.

## Chapter Three: The Wars of American Expansion

Butler, Maj. Gen. Smedley D. "Americas Armed Forces, 2. 'In Time of Peace': The Army." *Common Sense,* November 1935.

Craige, John H. *Cannibal Cousins.* Minton, Balch & Co., 1934.

Fleming, Peter. *The Siege at Peking.* Harper & Row, 1959.

Fuller, Stephen M., and Graham Cosmas. *Marines in the Dominican Republic, 1861–1924.* History and Museums Division, USMC, 1975.

Hagan, Kenneth J., ed. *In Peace and War.* Greenwood Press, 1984.

Heinl, Robert D. *Soldiers of the Sea.* U.S. Naval Institute Press, 1962.

———. and Nancy G. Heinl. *Written in Blood.* Houghton Mifflin, 1978.

Hobson, Richmond P. *The Sinking of the Merrimac.* The Century Co., 1899.

Jacobs, Bruce. "Heroes of the National Guard." *The National Guardsman,* November 1960.

Johnson, Robert E. *Rear Admiral John Rodgers, 1812–1883.* US Naval Institute Press, 1967.

Langley, Lester D. *The Banana Wars.* The University Press of Kentucky, 1983.

Lodge, Henry Cabot. *Selections From the Correspondence of Theodore Roosevelt and Henry Cabot Lodge, 1884–1918.* Charles Scribner's Sons, 1925.

McAndrews, Eugene V. "Theodore Roosevelt and the Medal of Honor." *Military Review,* September 1967.

Macauley, Neill. *The Sandino Affair.* Quadrangle Books, 1971.

McCrocklin, James H. *Garde d'Haiti, 1915–1934.* US Naval Institute Press, 1956.

Millett, Allan R. *Semper Fidelis.* Macmillan, 1980.

Morison, Elting E., and John Blum, eds. *The Letters of Theodore Roosevelt.* 8 vols. Harvard University Press, 1951–1954.

Moskin, J. Robert. *The U.S. Marine Corps Story.* McGraw-Hill, 1977.

Mulholland, St. Clair. *Military Orders, Congressional Medal of Honor Legion of the United States.* Town Printing Co., 1905.

Nalty, Bernard C. *The United States Marines in Nicaragua.* Historical Branch, USMC, 1968.

Roosevelt, Theodore. *Theodore Roosevelt: An Autobiography.* Macmillan, 1913.

Roth, Russell. *Muddy Glory.* Christopher Publishing House, 1981.

Schott, Joseph L. *The Ordeal of Samar.* Bobbs-Merrill, 1964.

Schuon, Karl. *U.S. Marine Corps Autobiographical Dictionary.* Franklin Watts, 1963.

——. *U.S. Navy Biographical Dictionary.* Franklin Watts, 1964.

Simmons, Edwin H. *The United States Marines.* Viking, 1976.

Sweetman, Jack. *American Naval History.* US Naval Institute Press, 1984.

——. *The Landing at Veracruz: 1914.* US Naval Institute Press, 1968.

Thomas, Lowell. *Old Gimlet Eye.* Farrar & Rinehart, 1933.

Wise, Frederic M., and Miegs O. Frost. *A Marine Tells It All to You.* J. H. Sears & Co., 1929.

## Chapter Four: World War I

Asprey, Robert B. *At Belleau Wood.* G. P. Putnam's Sons, 1965.

Bamford, Master Sgt. Hal. "Mystery of an Airman." *Airman.* November 1958.

Barrows, Nat A. *Blow All Ballast!* Dodd, Mead, 1940.

Bennet, Tech. Sgt. William. "Medal of Honor." *American Aviation Historical Society Quarterly,* Fall 1975.

Botting, Douglas. *The Epic of Flight: The Giant Airships.* Time-Life Books, 1981.

Bowen, Ezra. *The Epic of Flight: Knights of the Air.* Time-Life Books, 1981.

Byrd, Richard E. *Skyward.* G. P. Putnam's Sons, 1928.

Coffman, Edward M. *The War to End All Wars.* Oxford University Press, 1968.

"Conscience Plus Red Hair Are Bad for Germans." *The Literary Digest,* June 14, 1919.

Cowan, Sam K. *Sergeant York and His People.* Funk & Wagnalls, 1922.

Davis, Burke. *The Billy Mitchell Affair.* Random House, 1967.

De Chambrun, Col., and Capt. De Marenches. *The American Army in the European Conflict.* Macmillan, 1919.

Esposito, Col. Vincent H., ed. *The Concise History of World War I.* Praeger, 1964.

Everett, Susanne, and Brig. Gen. Peter Young. *The Two World Wars.* Bison Books, 1980.

Fredette, Lt. Col. Raymond H. "Luke: Watch for Burning Balloons." *Air Force.* May 9, 1973.

Harbord, James G. *The American Army in France, 1917–19.* Little, Brown & Co., 1936.

Hartney, Lt. Col. Harold. *Wings Over France.* Bailey Bros. & Swinfen, 1971.

Hudson, James H. *Hostile Skies.* Syracuse University Press, 1968.

Hurley, Alfred F. *Billy Mitchell, Crusader for Air Power.* Indiana University Press, 1964.

Isaacs [Izac], Edouard. *Prisoner of the U-90.* Houghton Mifflin, 1919.

Jackson, Donald D. *The Epic of Flight: The Explorers.* Time-Life Books, 1983.

Jablonski, Edward. *The Great War.* Whitman, 1965.

Johnson, Thomas M., and Fletcher Pratt. *The Lost Battalion.* Bobbs-Merrill, 1938.

Lindbergh, Charles A. *The Spirit of St. Louis.* Charles Scribner's Sons, 1953.

Marshall, S. L. A. *The American Heritage History of World War I.* Bonanza Books, 1982.

Mosley, Leonard. *Lindbergh: A Biography.* Doubleday, 1976.

Nevin, David. *The Epic of Flight: The Pathfinders.* Time-Life Books, 1980.

Powell, Theodore. *The Long Rescue.* Doubleday, 1960.

Rickenbacker, Eddie V. *Fighting the Flying Circus.* Avon Books, 1965.

Roosevelt, Theodore. *Rank and File.* Charles Scribner's Sons, 1928.

Ross, Walter S. *The Last Hero.* Harper & Row, 1964.

Stallings, Laurence. *The Doughboys.* Harper & Row, 1963.

Todd, A. L. *Abandoned.* McGraw-Hill, 1961.

Toland, John. *No Man's Land.* Doubleday, 1980.

## Chapter Five: World War II

Allen, Mel. "Only Afraid to Show Fear." *Yankee,* May 1983.

Auden, W. H. *The Collected Poetry of W. H. Auden.* Random House, 1945.

Bailey, Ronald H. *World War II: The Air War in Europe.* Time-Life Books, 1979.

Baudot, Marcel, et al. *The Historical Encyclopedia of World War II.* Greenwich House, 1984.

Blum, John M. *V Was for Victory.* Harcourt Brace Jovanovich, 1976.

Boyington, Gregory. *Baa Baa Black Sheep.* Arno, 1972.

Brereton, Lewis H. *The Brereton Diaries.* Morrow, 1946.

Buchanan, A. Russell. *The U.S. and World War II.* 2 vols. Harper & Row, 1964.

Churchill, Winston. *The Second World War.* 6 vols. Houghton Mifflin, 1949–1960.

Congdon, Don, ed. *Combat: European Theater.* Dell, 1958.

———. *Combat: The War With Germany.* Dell, 1963.

Conroy, Robert. *The Battle of Bataan.* Macmillan, 1969.

Craven, Wesley F., and James L. Cate, eds. *The Army Air Forces in World War II.* 7 vols. University of Chicago Press, 1948–1955.

Divine, Robert. *The Reluctant Belligerent.* Wiley, 1967.

Dugan, James, and Carroll Stewart. *Ploesti.* Random House, 1962.

Elson, Robert. *World War II: Prelude to War.* Time-Life Books, 1977.

Esposito, Col. Vincent H. *The West Point Atlas of American Wars.* Vol. 2. Praeger, 1959.

Fuqua, Samuel. Unpublished speeches.

Glines, Carroll V. *Doolittle's Tokyo Raiders.* D. Van Nostrand, 1964.

Haines, C. Grove, and Ross J. S. Hoffman. *The Origins and Background of the Second World War.* Oxford University Press, 1943.

Henn, Sharon. "Heart of Courage, Body of Steel." Unpublished paper, May 27, 1975.

Hirsch, Phil, ed. *Medal of Honor.* Pyramid, 1967.

*The History of the U.S. Marine Corps Operations in World War II.* 5 vols. Historical Division, USMC, 1958–1971.

Hoyle, Martha B. *A World in Flames.* Atheneum, 1970.

Hubbel, John G. "The Hero We Nearly Forgot." *Reader's Digest,* December 1981.

Jones, James. *World War II.* Ballantine, 1977.

Kelly, Charles, with Pete Martin. *One Man's War.* Knopf, 1944.

Kenney, Gen. George C. *Dick Bong: Ace of Aces.* Popular Library, 1960.

Lawson, Ted W. *Thirty Seconds Over Tokyo.* Random House, 1943.

Liddell-Hart, B. H. *History of the Second World War.* Cassell, 1970.

Lord, Walter. *Incredible Victory.* Harper & Row, 1967.

MacArthur, Gen. Douglas. *Reminiscences.* McGraw-Hill, 1964.

Manchester, William. *American Caesar.* Little, Brown, 1978.

Morelia, Joe, et al. *The Films of World War II.* Citadel Press, 1973.

Morison, Samuel E. *History of U.S. Naval Operations in World War II.* 15 vols. Little, Brown & Co., 1947–1962.

———. *The Two-Ocean War.* Atlantic-Little, Brown & Co., 1963.

Murphy, Audie. *To Hell and Back.* Bantam, 1983.

O'Kane, Richard H. *Clear the Bridge!* Rand McNally, 1977.

Parker, William, ed. *Above and Beyond the Call of Duty.* McFadden, 1963.

Prange, Gordon W. *At Dawn We Slept.* McGraw-Hill, 1981.

Pyle, Ernie. *Brave Men.* Holt, 1944.

———. *Last Chapter.* Holt, 1946.

Reck, Franklin M. *Beyond the Call of Duty.* Thomas Crowell Co., 1944.

Reynolds, Clark G. *The Epic of Flight: The Carrier War.* Time-Life Books, 1982.

Roscoe, Theodore. *U.S. Submarine Operations in World War II.* US Naval Institute Press, 1965.

Ross, Bill D. *Iwo Jima: Legacy of Valor.* The Vanguard Press, 1985.

Salisbury, Harrison E. *The 900 Days.* Harper & Row, 1969.

Scott, Jay. *America's War Heroes.* Monarch, 1961.

Sherrod, Robert. *History of Marine Corps Aviation in World War II.* Combat Forces Press, 1952.

Simpson, Col. Harold B. *Audie Murphy, American Soldier.* Hill Jr. College Press, 1975.

Steiner, George. *In Bluebeard's Castle.* Yale University Press, 1971.

Suid, Lawrence H. *Guts and Glory.* Addison-Wesley, 1978.

Sulzberger, C. L. *The American Heritage Pictorial History of World War II.* American Heritage Co., 1966.

Taylor, A. J. P. *The Origins of the Second World War.* Atheneum, 1966.

Thomas, Lowell. *These Men Shall Never Die.* John C. Winston Co., 1943.

Toland, John. *But Not in Shame.* Random House, 1961.

———. *Infamy.* Berkley, 1982.

*The U.S. Army in World War II.* 80 vols. Government Printing Office, 1947–68.

Wainwright, Jonathan. *General Wainwright's Story.* Greenwood, 1970.

Wheeler, Keith. *World War II: War Under the Pacific.* Time-Life Books, 1980.

Wolff, Leon. *Low Level Mission.* Doubleday, 1957.

## Chapter Six: The Cold War

Appleman, Roy E. *South to Naktong, North to Yalu.* Government Printing Office, 1961.

Bamford, James. *The Puzzle Palace.* Penguin Books, 1983.

Barbee, Fred. "Roy Benavidez . . . Sometimes Patience Wears Thin." *El Campo Leader-News,* February 22, 1978.

Binder, L. James. "Dean of the Dustoffers." *Army,* August 1971.

Canzona, Capt. N. A., and John C. Hubbell. "The Twelve Incredible Days of Col. John Page." *Reader's Digest,* April 1956.

Caputo, Philip. *A Rumor of War.* Ballantine, 1977.

Cooke, Donald E. *For Conspicuous Gallantry.* C. S. Hammond & Co., 1966.

Combat Operations After-Action Report. Battle for Dak To: 173d Airborne Brigade (Separate), November 1–December 1, 1967; Company C, 4th Battalion, 503d Infantry, November 11–12, 1967.

Combat Operations After-Action Report. Operation Dewey Canyon: 2d Battalion, 9th Marines, 3d Marine Division, February 25, 1969.

"Confinement Summary of Captain James Bond Stockdale, USN, Senior US Navy Returnee From Captivity . . . " US Navy, July 1976.

"The Cross and the Flag." Advisory Council of the Military Vicariate, April 1976.

Davis, 1st Lt. Gordon M. "Dewey Canyon: All Weather Classic." *Marine Corps Gazette,* July 1969.

Dean, William F. *General Dean's Story.* Viking, 1954.

Donlon, Capt. Roger H. C., and Warren Rogers. *Outpost of Freedom.* McGraw-Hill, 1965.

Dorland, Peter, and James Nanney. *Dustoff.* U.S. Army Center of Military History, 1982.

Dougan, Clark, et al. *The Vietnam Experience.* Vols. 1–12. Boston Publishing Co., 1981–1984.

Du Pre, Flint. "Rescue at a Place Called Kham Due." *Air Force,* March 1969.

Ennes, James M., Jr. *Assault on the Liberty.* Random House, 1979.

Fallaci, Oriana. *Nothing and So Be It.* Doubleday, 1972.

Fehrenbach, T. R. *This Kind of War.* Macmillan, 1963.

"For Leo K. Thorsness, the Medal of Honor." *Air Force,* December 1973.

Futrell, Frank. *The U.S. Air Force in Korea, 1950–53.* Duell, Sloan & Pearce, 1961.

Goulden, Joseph C. *Korea: The Untold Story of the War.* Times Books, 1982.

Gropman, Lt. Col. Alan L. *Airpower and the Airlift Evacuation of Kham Due.* Government Printing Office, 1979.

Gugeler, Russell A. *Combat Actions in Korea.* Office of the Chief of Military History, 1970.

Guimond, Capt. Gary A. "Hot Flare! Hot Flare!" *Airman,* June 1970.

Hammel, Eric M. *Chosin.* Vanguard Press, 1981.

Hermes, Walter G. *Truce Tent and Fighting Front.* Government Printing Office, 1966.

Herring, George C. *America's Longest War.* Wiley, 1979.

Jackson, Lt. Col. Wilfred A. "Stay Clear of Hue!" *U.S. Army Aviation Digest,* April 1970.

Jacobs, Bruce. *Korea's Heroes.* Berkley, 1961.

Karnow, Stanley. *Vietnam: A History.* Viking, 1983.

Kleinman, Master Sgt. Forrest K. "Truth of Taejon." *Army,* June 1960.

Lowther, William A. "A Medal for Roy Benavidez." *Reader's Digest,* April 1983.

Marshall, S. L. A. *The Military History of the Korean War.* Franklin Watts, 1963.

———. *The River and the Gauntlet.* Morrow, 1953.

"Medals of Honor to Two Air Force Heroes." *Air Force,* July 1970.

Middleton, Harry J. *Compact History of the Korean War.* Hawthorn, 1965.

Miller, Merle. *Plain Speaking.* G. P. Putnam's Sons, 1973.

Ministry of National Defense, Republic of Korea. *History of U.S. Forces in the Korean War.* Vols. 4–5. Government Printing Office, ROK, 1975–1976.

Montross, Lynn, et al. *U.S. Marine Operations in Korea, 1950–53.* Vols. 1–4. Historical Branch, USMC, 1954–1955, 1957, 1962.

Munroe, Lt. Clark C. *The 2nd U.S. Infantry Division in Korea 1950–51.* Toppan Printing Co., n.d.

Neustadt, Richard E. *Presidential Power.* Rev. Ed. Wiley, 1980.

Oberdorfer, Don. *Tet!* Doubleday, 1971.

Pearson, Anthony. *Conspiracy of Silence.* Quartet Books, 1978.

Poats, Rutherford M. *Decision in Korea.* McBride Co., 1954.

Ruhl, Robert K. "All Day's Tomorrows." *Airman,* November 1976.

———. "Rendezvous with the Rattlesnake." *Airman,* December 1974.

Schneider, Maj. Donald K. *Air Force Heroes in Vietnam.* Airpower Research Institute/Government Printing Office, 1979.

Smith, Richard K. "The Violation of the *Liberty.*" *U.S. Naval Institute Proceedings,* June 1978.

Smith, William. "Honor Times 29." *U.S. Army Aviation Digest,* January 1974.

Stockdale, Jim, and Sybil Stockdale. *In Love and War.* Harper & Row, 1984.

Sturm, Ted R. "Flight Check to Glory." *Airman,* September 1969.

Truman, Harry S. *Memoirs,* vol. 2, *Years of Trial and Hope, 1946–1952.* Doubleday, 1956.

"Up From the Ranks. " *Marine Corps Gazette,* November 1970.

White, Cpl. Larry. "Firefight Rages as Co. Claims Hill." *Sea Tiger,* March 28, 1969.

### Chapter Seven: New Enemies, New Conflicts

Filkins, Dexter. *The Forever War.* Knopf, 2008.

# NEWSPAPERS AND PERIODICALS CONSULTED

*Boston Globe, Life, Medal of Honor Historical Notes,* Medal of Honor Historical Society *Annals, New York Times, Newsweek, Time, Washington Post.*

# ARCHIVES

The authors consulted documents held in the archives of the Congressional Medal of Honor Society of the United States of America, New York, New York; the Freedoms Foundation at Valley Forge, Valley Forge, Pennsylvania; and the Medal of Honor Historical Society, Lombard, Illinois.

# INTERVIEWS AND CORRESPONDENCE WITH MEDAL OF HONOR RECIPIENTS

Nicky D. Bacon; William E. Barber; Roy P. Benavidez; Melvin E. Biddle; Patrick H. Brady; John D. Bulkeley; Richard E. Bush; Robert E. Bush; Jose Calugas; Anthony Casamento; William R. Charette; Michael J. Daly; Charles W. Davis; Raymond G. Davis; George E. Day; Merlyn H. Dethlefsen; Drew D. Dix; Roger H. C. Donlon; James H. Doolittle; Walter D. Ehlers; Henry E. Erwin; Frederick E. Ferguson; Joseph Foss; Wesley L. Fox; Leonard A. Funk, Jr.; Samuel G. Fuqua; Harold A. Furlong; Thomas J. Hudner; Edouard V. Izac; Joe M. Jackson; Leon W. Johnson; Phillip C. Katz; Charles E. Kelly; Gerry H. Kisters; Clyde E. Lassen; William R. Lawley, Jr.; John L. Levitow; David McCampbell; Charles A. MacGillivary; John Mihalowski; Hiroshi H. Miyamura; Reginald R. Myers; Ralph G. Neppel; Michael J. Novosel; Richard H. O'Kane; Nicholas Oresko; Francis J. Pierce; Thomas A. Pope; Lawson P. Ramage; Ronald E. Ray; Donald K. Ross; Donald E. Rudolph; Herbert E. Schonland; William A. Shomo; Carl L. Sitter; John C. Sjogren; Richard K. Sorenson; James B. Stockdale; George L. Street III; Leo K. Thorsness; Donald L. Truesdell; Matt Urban; Louis M. Van Iersel; Jay R. Vargas; Forrest L. Vosler; Gerald O. Young.

# WEBSITES

www.army.mil, www.marines.mil, www.navy.mil

# CREDITS

**303rd Bomb Group**: 156; **Air Force Historical Studies Office**: 158; **Air National Guard**: 120 (bottom); **Associated Press**: 190; **Battlefield Historian**: 168; **Boston Publishing Company**: 23, 216, 221(bottom), 252, 263; **Bridgeman Art Library**: 30 (photo © Civil War Archives), 67 (Peter Newark American Pictures), 106–107, 127 (Peter Newark Military Pictures), 131 (Leach Corp., Heritage of the Air Collection); **Buffalo Bill Historical Center**: 65; **Congressional Medal of Honor Society**: 52, 72, 88 (left), 101 (bottom center), 114 (top), 119 (top), 122 (bottom), 146 (bottom), 159 (bottom), 162 (right), 167 (bottom), 170, 182, 183 (top), 205, 219 (top), 234 (top left, top right); **Corbis**: 118; **Corbis/AP**: 138; **Corbis/Bettmann**: 108, 113, 122 (top), 124 (left), 125, 162 (left), 186, 192, 194, 224, 225 (bottom), 226 (bottom), 229 (bottom), 233, 241; **Corbis/Bettman/AP**: 110, 129; **Corbis/George Steinmetz**: 244–245; **Corbis/GS/AP**: 204; **Corbis/Hansi Krauss/AP**: 254 (bottom right); **Corbis/Horst Faas/AP**: 226 (center); **Corbis/Hulton-Deutsch Collection**: 137, 174; **Corbis/Neville Elder**: 246; **Corbis/Peter Turnley**: 251; **Corbis/Reuters**: 249; **Corbis/Thomas Mukoya/Reuters**: 248; **David Douglas Duncan, courtesy Univ. of Texas at Austin, Harry Ransom Center**: 188–189, 200, 201 (bottom); *Deeds of Valor*, W. F. Beyer and O. F. Keydel: 29 (bottom), 31, 32, 34 (all), 42 (bottom); **Edward F. Murphy**: 101 (bottom left); **Frank and Marie Wood Print Collection**: 38; **Franklin D. Roosevelt Presidential Library**: 78–79; **Courtesy Fred Ferguson**: 227; **Getty Images**: 242; **Getty/STR/AFP**: 253; **Getty/the Print Collector**: 119 (bottom); **Getty/Time and Life Pictures**: 240; **HomeOfHeroes.com**: 123, 197 (bottom); **Courtesy Leo Thorsness**: 236 (all), 237; **Library of Congress**: 14, 15, 16-17, 19 (all), 20, 21, 25 (bottom left), 28, 33, 35, 36, 41, 43 (top), 45, 46, 59 (bottom), 60 (left), 60 (top right), 61 (bottom), 62, 64, 66, 68, 69 (all), 70 (top), 73, 74, 76 (top), 77 (bottom), 80 (left), 80 (right), 82 (all), 90 (top), 93 (top), 96 (top), 102 (top), 103, 104, 105 (bottom), 112 (top right), 114 (bottom), 115, 116, 117, 143, 145, 164, 183 (bottom); **Library of Congress/Denver Public Library, Western History Division**: 75; **Lincoln Libraries**: 112 (top left); **Maine State Archives**: 37; **Mariners' Museum**: 177 (bottom); **National Archives**: 25 (bottom right), 25 (top right), 25 (center), 39, 42 (top), 59 (top), 60 (bottom right), 61 (top), 70 (bottom), 71, 86 (center), 87, 91 (right), 92, 99 (all), 102 (bottom), 111 (all), 112 (bottom), 121 (bottom), 126, 132, 140, 148, 167 (top), 171, 172, 178, 195, 214, 232, 247; **National Museum of the US Air Force**: 121 (top), 159 (top), 238; **National Naval Aviation Museum**: 144 (top), 176 (top); **Naval History and Heritage Command**: 49, 85, 86 (top), 86 (bottom), 90 (bottom), 91 (left), 93 (bottom), 96 (bottom), 97 (top), 142, 146 (top), 152 (bottom), 152-153, 154 (all), 155 (all), 175, 176 (bottom), 177 (top), 180, 181 (top), 209, 210, 212; **Navy Memorial Museum**: 101 (top left, bottom right); **New York Historical Society**: 81 (No. 52498); **Courtesy Paul Wright**: 29 (top); **Richard Glass**: 101 (top center); **Robert Capa/Magnum Photos**: frontis, 134–135; **Robert Lindneux, courtesy History Colorado**: 54–55 (scan # 10026419); **Roche Family Collection/www.patrickdelacy.com**: 101 (top right); **Russell Burrows**: 239; *Stars and Stripes*: 199; **State Historical Society of North Dakota**: 105 (top); **Courtesy Thomas Hudner**: 208; **Underwood Archives**: 109; **Universal Images Group**: 124 (right); **Univ. of Oklahoma Libraries, Western History Collections**: 76 (bottom), 77 (top); **Univ. of Texas, Briscoe Center**: 243; **US Air Force**: 149, 157, 181 (bottom), 185, 220, 221 (top), 235; **US Army**: 27, 50, 88 (right), 120 (top), 165, 169, 173 (all), 187, 218, 219 (bottom), 225 (top), 226 (top), 230 (all), 254 (portraits), 255, 256, 258 (bottom), 262 (bottom), 264, 265; **US Army Institute of Heraldry**: 100 (all); **US Army Medical Dept.**: 29 (center), 231, 234 (bottom left); **US Army Military History Institute**: 196, 197 (top), 198; **US Marine Corps**: 84, 98 (bottom), 152 (top left), 179, 201 (top), 203, 222 (all), 223, 229 (top), 257, 262 (top); **US Marine Corps History Division**: 97 (center, bottom), 98 (top left); **US Navy**: 48, 144 (bottom), 151, 206, 258 (top), 261; **Valor Studios**: 207 (all); **West Point Museum**: 43 (bottom), 63

**Map References**: 23, 216, 221 (bottom), 252, and 263 created by Kate Blackmer; 221 (bottom) based on *Air Force* magazine drawing; 252, 263 based on US Army information

**Editorial Credits, Previous Edition**
**Senior Editor**: Gordon Hardy
**Assistant Editor**: Denis Kennedy
**Contributing Writers**: Dr. Melanie Billings-Yun, William C. Davis, Gordon Hardy, Denis Kennedy, Jack Sweetman, Richard Young
**Historical Consultant**: Edward F. Murphy

# INDEX